A FIRST BOOK OF C

Fundamentals of C Programing

AT&T

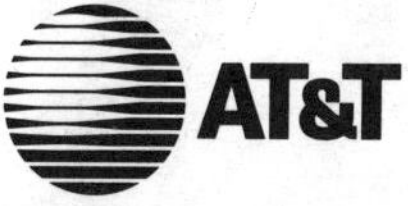

A FIRST BOOK OF C

Fundamentals of C Programing

Gary J. Bronson
Fairleigh Dickinson University

Stephen J. Menconi
AT&T

AT&T Professional Series

PRODUCTION CREDITS

Copy Editors:	Gary Falk Marlene Thich
Data Entry:	Donna Guettler
Composition:	Vincent Mattaliano
Cover:	Nancy Loughlin
Cover Illustration:	AT&T Pixel Machines, Somerset, NJ

The Illustration on the front cover was created using a C language program on the AT&T Pixel Machine.

International Standard Book Number 0-932764-19-3

AT&T Customer Information Center Select Code 320-609

Published by AT&T Document Development Organization

Printed by AT&T Customer Information Center
2855 North Franklin Road
Indianapolis, IN 46219

Printed in United States of America.

dedicated to

Rochelle,
David,
Matthew,
Jeremy Bronson

Maryann,
Annamaria Menconi

Acknowledgments

This professional version of *A First Book of C* is based on the highly acclaimed college edition published by and available from West Publishing Company, St. Paul, Minnesota. We thank West Publishing for allowing us to publish this edition through AT&T.

We acknowledge the contributions of the many people who have assisted in making this book a reality. These include the encouragement and support of Jack Garrett, Ron Hoth, Yolanda Hardin, and the insightful comments and suggestions made by Paul Guettler.

We would like to thank Leroy Woodard, Bruno Jedrezejak, and Dave Roller of the AT&T Customer Information Center. Additionally, we would like to thank the AT&T Document Development Organization (DDO) production staff assigned to this project for their enthusiastic support. They include Gary Falk and Marlene Thich, copy editors; Nancy Loughlin, cover artist; Donna Guettler, line-art illustrator and text compositor; and Vincent Mattaliano (Victory Graphics), head compositor/graphics designer. We give special thanks to Richard Oliveri of AT&T Pixel Machines for creating the illustration used on the front cover.

Finally, we deeply appreciate the patience and understanding provided by our wives, Rochelle and Maryann, throughout this project.

Gary Bronson
Stephen Menconi

Contents

Fundamentals

Part One

Getting Started

Chapter One

To write computer programs successfully in C requires the knowledge of three interrelated topics. First, the programmer must know the basic elements of the language. This is very similar to knowing the words and punctuation marks available in such spoken languages as English, French, or German. Next, the programmer must know what specific result he or she wants. This is like knowing what you want to say in a spoken language. The third element is knowing how to produce the desired result. Everyone has had the experience of wanting to produce a certain effect, but doing or saying something in such a way as to produce an entirely unexpected or even unwanted response. The same is true in programming. Even if you know the elements of the language and the output that you want, there is still the necessity of combining the fundamental program language elements in a specific order to achieve the desired output.

In this chapter, we begin learning the basic elements of C. Since C is a structured language, it is appropriate to start with an understanding of its modular nature. This is followed by a discussion of a working program that illustrates the standard C program structure and introduces the displaying of simple messages.

1.1 Modules and Functions

To make programs easier to develop, correct, and maintain, all C programs are built from smaller, more manageable segments called *modules*. Each module is designed and developed to perform a specific task and is really a small subprogram all by itself. A complete C program is constructed by linking together as many modules as necessary to produce the overall desired result (see Figure 1-1).

FIGURE 1-1 C Programs are Built Using Modules

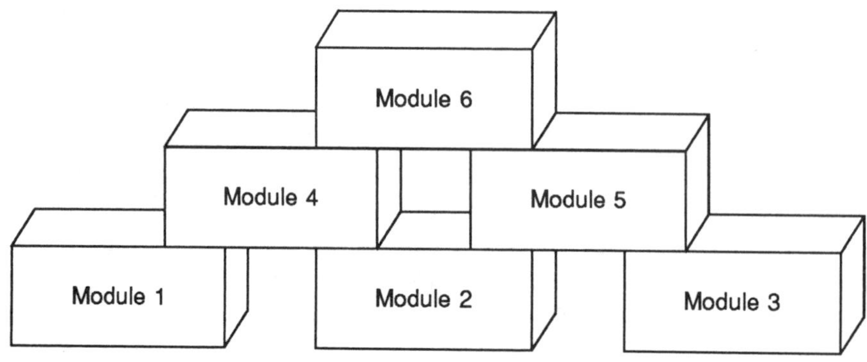

Since a module is really a small subprogram, each module must be able to do what is required of all programs: receive data, operate on the data, and return a result (see Figure 1-2). Unlike a larger program, a module performs operations that are very limited in scope. Modules are meant to handle at most one or two functions required by the complete program. Since each module is designed to perform specific functions, the modules themselves are called *functions.*

It is useful to think of a function as a small machine that transforms the data it receives into a finished product. For example, Figure 1-3 illustrates a function that accepts two numbers as inputs and multiplies the two numbers to produce one output.

One important requirement for designing a good function is to give it a name that conveys to the reader some idea of what the function does. Function names can be made up of any combination of letters, digits, and underscores (_), selected according to the rules listed on the following page.

FIGURE 1-2 A Module Must Accept Data, Operate on the Data, and Return a Result

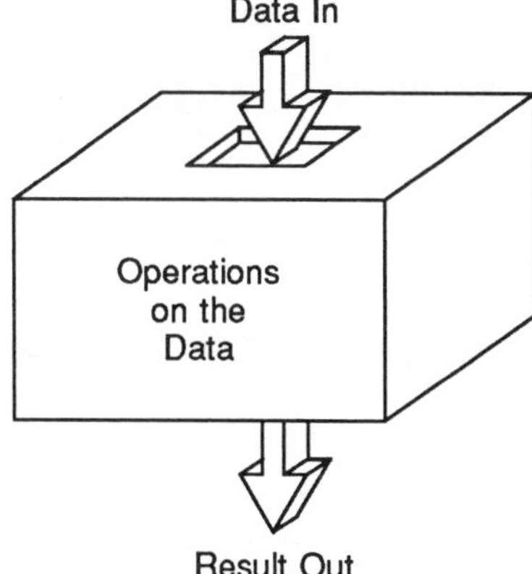

FIGURE 1-3 A Multiplying Function

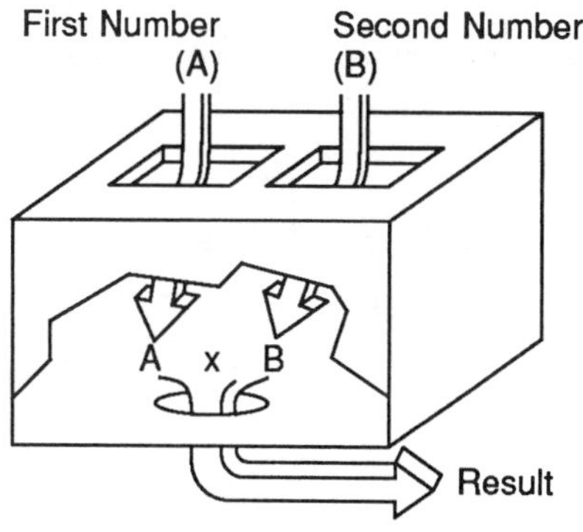

1. The function name must begin with a letter.
2. Only letters, numbers, or underscores can follow the initial letter. Blank spaces are not allowed; the underscore must be used in place of a blank space.
3. A function name cannot be one of the reserved words listed in Table 1-1.
4. Usually only the first eight characters of a function name are actually used and recorded by the computer; however, some systems recognize and use more than the first eight characters.
5. All function names must be followed by parentheses.

Examples of valid C function names, including the required parentheses*, are:

```
grosspay()    tax_calc()    add_nums()    deg2rad()
mult_two()    salestax()    netpay()      bessel1()
```

Examples of invalid function names are:

`1AB3()`	(begins with a number, which violates Rule 1)
`E*6()`	(contains a special character, which violates Rule 2)
`while()`	(uses a reserved word, which violates Rule 3)

Besides conforming to the rules for naming functions, a good function name should also be a mnemonic. A *mnemonic* is a word or name designed as a memory aid. For example, the function name `deg2rad()` is a mnemonic if it is the name of a function that converts degrees to radians. Here, the name itself helps to identify what the function does.

Examples of valid function names that are not mnemonics are:

```
easy()    c3po()    r2d2()    theforce()    mike()
```

Nonmnemonic function names should not be used because they convey no information about what the function does.

Notice that all function names have been typed in lowercase letters. This is traditional in C, although it is not absolutely necessary. Uppercase letters are usually reserved for *named constants,* a topic covered in Chapter 3.

*No space is required between the function name and the parenthesis. Any space that appears is a result of the type font used.

TABLE 1-1 Reserved Words

auto	do	for	return	typedef
break	double	goto	short	union
case	else	if	sizeof	unsigned
char	enum	int	static	void
continue	extern	long	struct	while
default	float	register	switch	

1.2 The main() Function

Once functions have been named, we need a way to combine them into a complete program (see Figure 1-4). Notice that we have not yet described the actual writing of the functions. One of the nice features of C is that we can plan a program by first deciding what functions are needed and how they are to be linked together. Then, we can write each function to perform the task it is required to do.

To provide for the orderly placement and execution of functions, each C program must have one function called `main()`. The `main()` function is sometimes referred to as a *driver* function, because it tells the other functions the sequence in which they are to operate (see Figure 1-5).

Figure 1-6 illustrates a completed `main()` function. The word `main` identifies the start of each C program. The braces, `{` and `}`, determine the beginning and end of the function body and enclose the statements making up the function. The statements inside the braces determine what the function does. Each statement inside the function must end with a semicolon (;).

The `main()` function illustrated in Figure 1-6 consists of four statements. In this case, each statement is a command to execute another function. First the `gross_pay()` function is called for execution. When `gross_pay()` is finished, the `taxes()` function is called. After the `taxes()` function is completed, the `net_pay()` function is called. Finally, the `output()` function is executed. Although the functions `gross_pay()`, `taxes()`, `net_pay()`, and `output()` must still be written, the `main()` function is complete. After the four other functions are written, the program, consisting of `main()`, `gross_pay()`, `taxes()`, `net_pay()`, and `output()`, is complete.

You will be naming and writing many of your own C functions. In fact, the rest of this book is primarily about the statements required to construct useful functions and about how to combine the functions to form useful programs.

FIGURE 1-4 We Need Some Order Here!

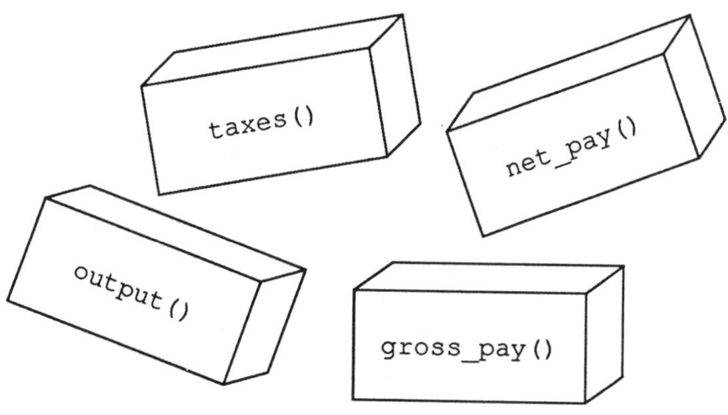

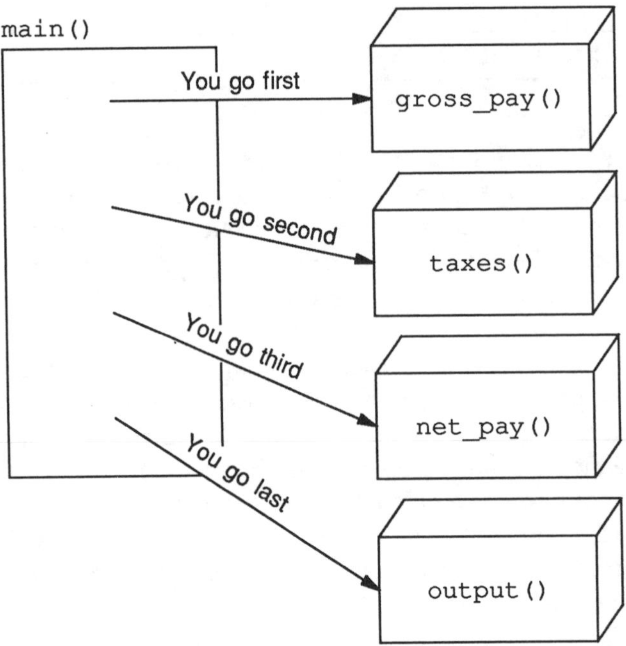

FIGURE 1-5 The `main()` Function Controls All Other Functions

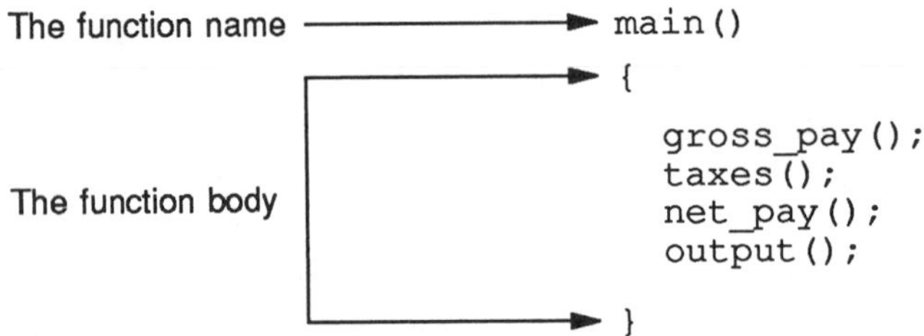

FIGURE 1-6 A Sample `main()` Function

Fortunately many useful functions have already been written for us. In the next section we will use one of these functions to create our first working C program.

1.3 The `printf()` Function

One of the most popular and useful prewritten functions in C is named `printf()`. This function, as its name suggests, is a print function that sends data given to it to the standard system display device. For most systems this display device is a video screen. This function prints out whatever is given to it.

For example, if the message `Hello there world!` is given to `printf()`, this message is printed (or displayed) on your terminal by the `printf()` function. Inputting data or messages to a function is called passing data to the function. The message `Hello there world!` is passed to the `printf()` function by simply putting the message inside the parentheses in the function's name (see Figure 1-7).

The purpose of the parentheses in all function names is to provide a funnel through which information can be passed to the function (see Figure 1-8). The items that are passed to the function through the parentheses are called *arguments* of the function.

Now let us put all of this together into a working C program that can be run on your computer. Consider Program 1-1.

Program 1-1

```
main()
{
  printf("Hello there world!");
}
```

As required, Program 1-1 has one `main()` function. The `main()` function itself has one statement. Remember that statements end with a semicolon (;).

FIGURE 1-7 Passing a Message to `printf()`

```
printf ("Hello there world!");
```

FIGURE 1-8 Passing Data to a Function

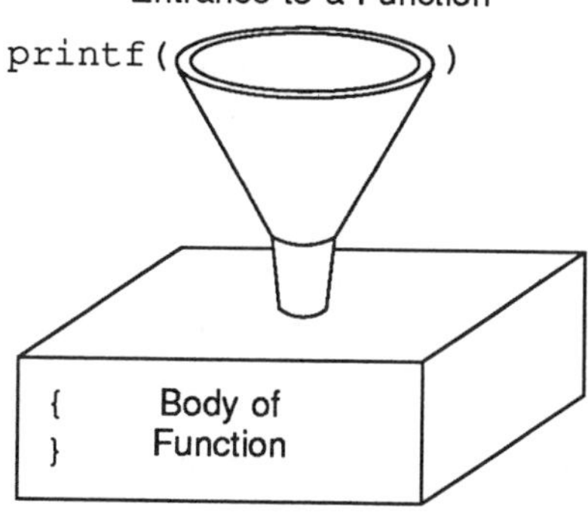

The statement in `main()` calls the function `printf()`, and passes one argument to it. The argument is the message `Hello there world!`

Since `printf()` is a prewritten function, we do not have to write it; it is available for use just by calling it correctly. Like all C functions, `printf()` was written to do a specific task, which is to print results. It is a very versatile function that can print results in many different forms. When a message is passed to `printf()`, the function sees to it that the message is correctly printed on your terminal. The output from Program 1-1 is:

```
Hello there world!
```

Messages are called *strings* because they consist of a string of characters made up of letters, numbers, and special characters. The beginning and end of a string of characters is marked by using double quotation marks ("*message in here*") around the string. Thus, to pass a message to `printf()`, the string of characters making up the message must be enclosed in double quotation marks, as we have done in Program 1-1.

Let us write another program to illustrate `printf()`'s versatility. Read Program 1-2 to determine what it does.

Program 1-2

```
main()
{
  printf("Computers, computers, everywhere");
  printf("\n   as far as I can C");
}
```

When Program 1-2 is run, the following is displayed:

```
Computers, computers, everywhere
   as far as I can C
```

You might be wondering why the `\n` did not appear in the output. The two characters \ and `n`, when used together, are called a *newline escape sequence*. They tell `printf()` to start on a new line. In C, the backslash (\) character provides an "escape" from the normal interpretation of the character following it by altering the meaning of the next character. If the backslash were omitted from the second `printf()` call in Program 1-2, the `n` would be printed as the letter *n* and the program would print out:

```
Computers, computers, everywheren   as far as I can C
```

Newline escape sequences can be placed anywhere within the message passed to `printf()`. See if you can determine what the following program prints:

```
main()
{
  printf("Computers everywhere\n as far as\n\nI can C");
}
```

The output for this program is:

```
Computers everywhere
 as far as

I can C
```

1.4 Programming Style

The word `main` in a C program tells the computer where the program starts. Since a program can have only one starting point, every C language program must contain one, and only one, `main()` function. As we have seen, all of the statements that make up the `main()` function are then included within the braces `{ }` following the function name. Although the `main()` function must be present in every C program, C does not require that the word `main`, the parentheses `()`, or the braces `{ }` be placed in any particular form. The form used in the last section

```
main()
{
  program statements in here;
}
```

was chosen strictly for clarity and ease in reading the program. For example, the following general form of a `main()` function would also work:

```
main
(
){ first statement;second statement;
third statement;fourth
statement;}
```

Notice that more than one statement can be put on a line, or one statement can be written across lines. Except for messages contained within double quotes, function names, and reserved words, C ignores all *white space* (white space refers to any combination of one or more blank spaces, tabs, or new lines). For example, changing the white space in Program 1-1, and making sure not to split the message `Hello there world!` or the function names `printf` and `main` across two lines results in the following valid program:

```
main
(
){printf
("Hello there world!"
);}
```

Although this version of `main()` works, it is an example of extremely poor programming style. It is difficult to read and understand. For readability, the `main()` function should always be written in standard form, for example:

```
main()
{
  program statements in here;
}
```

In this standard form, the function name starts in column 1 and is placed with the required parentheses on a line by itself. The opening brace of the function body follows on the next line and is placed under the first letter of the function name. Similarly, the closing function brace is placed by itself in column 1 as the last line of the function. This structure serves to highlight the function as a single unit.

Within the function itself, all program statements are indented two spaces. *Indentation* is another sign of good programming practice, especially if the same indentation is used for similar groups of statements. Review Program 1-2 to see that the same indentation was used for both `printf()` function calls.

As you progress in your understanding and mastery of C, you will develop your own indentation standards. Just keep in mind that the final form of your programs should be consistent and should always serve as an aid in the reading and understanding of your programs.

Comments

Comments are explanatory remarks made within a program. When used carefully, comments can be very helpful in clarifying what the complete program is about, what a specific group of statements is meant to accomplish, or what one line is intended to do.

Any line of text bounded by asterisks and enclosed within slashes (/) is a comment. For example,

```
/* this is a comment                    */
/* this program prints out a message    */
/* this program calculates a square root */
```

are all comment lines. The symbols `/*`, with no white space between them, designate the start of a comment. Similarly, the symbols `*/`, as a single unit with no intervening white space, designate the end of a comment.

Comments can be placed anywhere within a program and have no effect on program execution. The computer ignores all comments — they are there strictly for the convenience of anyone reading the program.

A comment can be written either on a line by itself or on the same line as a program statement. Program 1-3 illustrates the use of comments within a program.

Program 1-3

```
main()                  /* this program prints a message */
{
  printf("Hello there world!");  /* call to printf() */
}
```

The first comment appears on the same line as the function name and describes what the program does. This is generally a good location to include a short comment describing the program's purpose. If more comments are required, they can be placed, one per line, between the function name and the opening brace that encloses the function's statements. If a comment is too long to be contained on one line, it can be separated into two or more comments, with each separate comment enclosed within the comment symbol set /* */.

The comment

```
/* this comment may be invalid because it
extends over two lines */
```

may result in a C error message on your computer (however, some computers accept comments written across lines). This comment is always correct when written as:

```
/* this comment is used to illustrate a  */
/* comment that extends across two lines */
```

When using nonstructured programming languages, many comments are often required. These comments are necessary to clarify either the purpose of the program itself or individual sections and lines of code within the program. In C, the program's structure is intended to make the program readable, making the use of extensive comments unnecessary. This is reinforced if both function names and the variable names, described in the next chapter, are carefully selected to convey their meaning to anyone reading the program. However, if the purpose of a either a function or any of its statements is still not clear from its structure, name, or context, include comments where clarification is needed.

1.5 Common Programming Errors

Part of learning any programming language is making the elementary mistakes commonly encountered as you use the language. These mistakes tend to be frustrating, since each language has its own set of common programming errors waiting for the unwary. The more common errors made when initially programming in C are:

1. Omitting the parentheses after `main`.
2. Omitting or incorrectly typing the opening brace, `{`, that signifies the start of a function body.
3. Omitting or incorrectly typing the closing brace, `}`, that signifies the end of a function.
4. Misspelling the name of a function; for example, typing `pint()` instead of `printf()`.
5. Forgetting to close the message to `printf()` with a double quotation mark.
6. Omitting the semicolon at the end of each statement.

Our experience is that the third, fifth, and sixth errors in this list tend to be the most common. We suggest that you write a program and intentionally introduce each of these errors, one at a time, to see what error messages are produced by your compiler. The knowledge you gain interpreting these error messages and the actions you take to correct the errors provide the experience you need when these mistakes occur in the future.

1.6 Chapter Summary

1. C programs consist of one or more modules called functions. One of these functions must be `main()`. The `main()` function identifies the starting point of a C program.
2. Many functions, such as `printf()`, are supplied in a standard library of functions provided with each C compiler.
3. The simplest C program consists of a single function: `main()`.
4. Following the function name, the body of a function has the general form:

```
{
  All program statements in here;
}
```

5. All C statements must be terminated by a semicolon.
6. The `printf()` function is used to display text or numerical results. The first argument to `printf()` can be a message, which is enclosed in double quotes. The text in the message is displayed directly on the screen and may include newline escape sequences for format control.

Sample Program

The following program displays a series of messages.

```
main()
{
  printf("Every C program");
  printf("\nmust have one and only one ");
  printf("main function");
  printf("\n the escape sequence for a newline");
   printf(" can be placed \nanywhere\n");
  printf("within the message passed to printf()");
}
```

The output produced by this program is:

```
Every C program
must have one and only one main function
 the escape sequence for a newline can be placed
anywhere
within the message passed to printf()
```

As illustrated, a new line only occurs when the escape sequence, \n, is encountered in a `printf()` function call. The first line of the output is the result of the first call to `printf()`. The second line is produced by the second and third calls to `printf()`. The newline escape sequence contained within the second `printf()` call causes this message to start on a new line. Since no additional newline escape sequence is located in either the second or third `printf()` function calls, no new line is generated in the display. Notice that in the next to last `printf()` function call, the word anywhere is surrounded by newline escape sequences. This indicates that this word is to begin on a new line and that a new line will be generated after the word is displayed.

Data Types, Declarations, and Displays

Chapter Two

2.1 Data Types
2.2 Arithmetic Operators
2.3 Displaying Numerical Results
2.4 Variables and Declarations
2.5 Integer Qualifiers
2.6 Common Programming Errors
2.7 Chapter Summary
2.8 Chapter Supplement: Bits, Bytes, Addresses, and Number Codes

We continue our introduction to the fundamentals of C in this chapter by presenting C's elementary data types, variables, and declarations, and additional information on using the `printf()` function. These new concepts and tools enable us to both expand our programming abilities and gain useful insight into how data is stored in a computer.

Before reading this chapter, you should have an understanding of basic computer storage concepts and terms. If you are unfamiliar with the terms *bit, byte,* and *memory address,* read Section 2.8 at the end of this chapter for an introduction to these terms.

2.1 Data Types

There are four basic *data types* used in C: integer, floating point, double precision, and character data. Each of these data types is described below.

Integer Values

An *integer* value, which is called an integer constant in C, is any positive or negative number without a decimal point. Examples of valid integer constants are:

```
5     -10     +25     1000     253     -586251     +36
```

As seen in these examples, integers can be signed (have a leading + or – sign) or unsigned (no leading + or – sign). No commas, decimal points, or special symbols, such as the dollar sign, are allowed. Examples of invalid integer constants are:

```
$255.62     2,52     3.     6,243,892     1,492.89     +6.0
```

Each computer has its own internal limit on the most positive and most negative integer values that can be used in a program. These limits depend on the amount of storage each computer sets aside for an integer. The more commonly used storage allocations are listed in Table 2-1. By referring to your computer's reference manual or using the `sizeof` operator introduced in Section 2.5, you can determine the actual number of bytes allocated by your computer for each integer value. (Review Section 2.8 if you are unfamiliar with the concept of a byte.)

TABLE 2-1 **Integer Values and Byte Storage**

Storage Area Reserved	Maximum Integer Value	Minimum Integer Value
1 byte	127	−128
2 bytes	32767	−32768
4 bytes	2147483647	−2147483648

Floating Point and Double Precision Numbers

Floating point and *double precision* numbers are any signed or unsigned numbers having a decimal point. Examples of floating point and double precision numbers are:

```
+10.625   5.   -6.2   3251.92   0.0   0.33   -6.67   +2.
```

As with integers, special symbols, such as the dollar sign and the comma, are not permitted in floating point or double precision numbers. Examples of invalid floating point and double precision constants are:

```
5,326.25     24     123     6,459     $10.29
```

The difference between floating point and double precision numbers is the amount of storage that a computer uses for each type. Most computers use twice the amount of storage for double precision numbers as for floating point numbers, which allows a double precision number to have approximately twice the precision of a floating point number (for this reason, floating point numbers are sometimes referred to as *single precision* numbers). The actual storage allocation for each data type, however, depends on the particular computer. In computers that use the same amount of storage for double precision and floating point numbers, these two data types are identical. The `sizeof` operator introduced in Section 2.5 allows you to determine the amount of storage reserved by your computer for each of these data types.

Exponential Notation

Floating point and double precision numbers can be written in exponential notation, which is commonly used to express either very large or very small numbers in a compact form. The following examples illustrate how numbers with decimal points can be expressed in exponential notation.

Decimal Notation	Exponential Notation
1625.	1.625*e*3
63421.	6.3421*e*4
.00731	7.31*e*–3
.000625	6.25*e*–4

In exponential notation the letter *e* stands for *exponent.* The number following the *e* represents a power of 10 and indicates the number of places the decimal point should be moved to obtain the standard decimal value. The decimal point is moved to the right if the number after the *e* is positive and is moved to the left if the number after the *e* is negative. For example, the *e*3 in the number 1.625*e*3 means "move the decimal place three places to the right," so that the number becomes 1625. The *e*–3 in the number 7.31*e*–3 means "move the decimal point three places to the left," so that 7.31*e*–3 becomes .00731.

Character Type

The fourth basic data type recognized by C is the *character type.* Characters are the letters of the alphabet, the ten digits 0 through 9, and such special symbols as + $. , – !. A *single character constant* is any one letter, digit, or special symbol enclosed by single quotes. Examples of valid character constants are:

```
'A'   '$ '   'b'   '7'   'y'   '!'   'M'   'q'
```

Character constants are typically stored in a computer in either the ASCII or EBCDIC codes. ASCII, pronounced AS-KEY, is an acronym for American Standard Code for Information Interchange. EBCDIC, pronounced EBB-SAH-DICK, is an acronym for Extended Binary Coded Decimal Interchange Code. Each of these codes assigns individual characters to a specific pattern of 0s and 1s. Table 2-2 lists the correspondence between byte patterns and the letters of the alphabet used by the ASCII code.

Using Table 2-2, we can determine how the character constants 'J', 'O', 'N', 'E', and 'S', for example, are stored inside a computer that uses the ASCII character code. Using the ASCII code, this sequence of characters requires five bytes of storage (one byte for each letter) and is stored as illustrated in Figure 2-1.

FIGURE 2-1 The Letters JONES Stored Inside a Computer

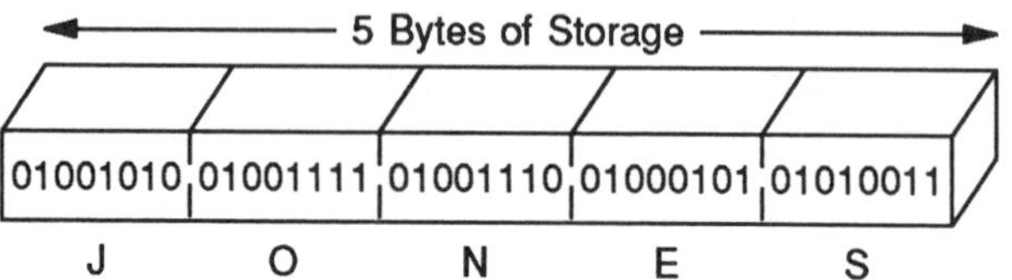

TABLE 2-2 The ASCII Uppercase Letter Codes

Letter	Computer Code	Letter	Computer Code
A	01000001	N	01001110
B	01000010	O	01001111
C	01000011	P	01010000
D	01000100	Q	01010001
E	01000101	R	01010010
F	01000110	S	01010011
G	01000111	T	01010100
H	01001000	U	01010101
I	01001001	V	01010110
J	01001010	W	01010111
K	01001011	X	01011000
L	01001100	Y	01011001
M	01001101	Z	01011010

Escape Sequences

When a backslash (\) is used directly in front of a selected group of characters, the backslash tells the computer to "escape" from the way these characters would normally be interpreted. For this reason, the combination of a backslash and these specific characters are called *escape sequences.* We have already encountered an example of this in the newline escape sequence, `\n`. Table 2-3 lists other common escape sequences.

TABLE 2-3 Escape Sequences

Escape Sequence	Meaning
`\b`	move back one space
`\f`	move to next page
`\n`	move to next line
`\r`	carriage return
`\\`	backslash character
`\'`	single quote

Although each escape sequence listed in Table 2-3 is made up of two distinct characters, the combination of the two characters, with no intervening white space, causes the computer to store a one-character code. Table 2-4 lists the ASCII code byte patterns for the escape sequences listed in Table 2-3.

TABLE 2-4 The ASCII Escape Sequence Codes

C Escape Sequence	Meaning	Computer Code
`\b`	backspace	00001000
`\f`	form feed	00001100
`\n`	newline	00001010
`\r`	carriage return	00001101
`\\`	backslash	01011100
`\'`	single quote	00100111

2.2 Arithmetic Operators

Integers, floating point numbers, and double precision numbers can be added, subtracted, divided, and multiplied. Although it is better not to mix integers with the other two numerical data types when performing arithmetic operations, predictable results are obtained when different data types are used in the same arithmetic expression. Somewhat surprising is the fact that character data can also be added to and subtracted from both character and integer data to produce useful results.

The operators used for these arithmetic operations are called *arithmetic operators*. These are:

Operation	Operator
Addition	+
Subtraction	-
Multiplication	*
Division	/

Each of these arithmetic operators is a binary operator that requires two operands. A simple arithmetic expression consists of an arithmetic operator connecting two arithmetic operands. Examples of simple arithmetic expressions are:

```
3 + 7
18 - 3
```

```
12.62 + 9.8
.08 * 12.2
12.6 / 2.
```

The spaces around the arithmetic operators in these examples are inserted strictly for clarity and can be omitted without affecting the value of the expression. When evaluating simple arithmetic expressions, the data type of the result is determined by the following rules:

1. If all operands are integers, the result is an integer.
2. If any operand is a floating point or double precision number, the result is a double precision number.

Notice that the result of an arithmetic expression is never a floating point number because the computer temporarily converts all floating point numbers to double precision when arithmetic is being done.

Integer Division

The division of two integers can produce unexpected results for the unwary. For example, dividing the integer 15 by the integer 2 yields an integer result. Since integers cannot contain a fractional part, the correct result, 7.5, is not obtained. In C, the fractional part of the result obtained when dividing two integers is dropped or *truncated*. Thus, the value of 15/2 is 7, the value of 9/4 is 2, and the value of 17/5 is 3.

There are times when we would like to retain the remainder of an integer division. To do this, C provides an arithmetic operator that captures the remainder when two integers are divided. This operator, called the *modulus operator*, has the symbol % . The modulus operator can be used only with integers. For example,

```
 9 % 4 is 1
17 % 3 is 2
```

A Unary Operator (Negation)

Besides the binary operators for addition, subtraction, multiplication, and division, C also provides *unary operators*. One of these unary operators uses the same symbol used for binary subtraction (–). The minus sign used in front of a single integer operand negates (reverses the sign of) the number.

Table 2-5 summarizes the six arithmetic operations we have described so far and lists the data type of the result produced by each operator according to the data type of the operands involved.

TABLE 2-5 **Summary of Arithmetic Operators**

Operation	Operator	Type	Operand	Result
Addition	+	Binary	Both integers	Integer
			One operand not an integer	Double precision
Subtraction	−	Binary	Both integers	Integer
			One operand not an integer	Double precision
Multiplication	*	Binary	Both integers	Integer
			One operand not an integer	Double precision
Division	/	Binary	Both integers	Integer
			One operand not an integer	Double precision
Remainder	%	Binary	Both integers	Integer
Negation	−	Unary	One integer	Integer
			One floating point or double precision operand	Double precision

Operator Precedence and Associativity

Besides such simple expressions as 5 + 12 and .08 * 26.2, we frequently need to create more complex arithmetic expressions. C, like most other programming languages, requires that certain rules be followed when writing expressions containing more than one arithmetic operator. These rules are:

1. Never place two binary arithmetic operator symbols side by side. For example, 5 * %6 is invalid because the two operators * and % are placed next to each other.
2. Parentheses can be used to form groupings, and all expressions enclosed within parentheses are evaluated first.

   For example, in the expression (6 + 4) / (2 + 3), the 6 + 4 and 2 + 3 are evaluated first to yield 10 / 5. The 10 / 5 is then evaluated to yield 2.

   Sets of parentheses can also be enclosed by other parentheses. For example, the expression (2 * (3 + 7)) / 5 is valid. When parentheses are used within parentheses, the expressions in the innermost parentheses are always evaluated first. The evaluation continues from innermost to outermost parentheses until the expressions of all parentheses have been evaluated. The number of right-facing parentheses must always equal the number of left-facing parentheses so that there are no unpaired parentheses.

3. Parentheses cannot be used to indicate multiplication. The multiplication operator, *, must be used.

   For example, the expression (3 + 4) (5 + 1) is invalid. The correct expression is (3 + 4) * (5 + 1).

As a general rule, parentheses should be used to specify logical groupings of operands and to clearly indicate to both the computer and programmers the intended order of arithmetic operations. In the absence of parentheses, expressions containing multiple operators are evaluated by the priority, or *precedence,* of each operator. Table 2-6 lists both the precedence and associativity of the operators considered in this section.

TABLE 2-6 Operator Precedence and Associativity

Operator	Associativity
unary –	right to left
* / %	left to right
+ –	left to right

The precedence of an operator establishes its priority relative to all other operators. Operators at the top of Table 2-6 have a higher priority than operators at the bottom of the table. In expressions with multiple operators, the operator with the higher precedence is used before an operator with a lower precedence. For example, in the expression 6 + 4 / 2 + 3, the division is done before the addition, yielding an intermediate result of 6 + 2 + 3. The additions are then performed to yield a final result of 11.

Expressions containing operators with the same precedence are evaluated according to their *associativity.* This means that evaluation is either from left to right or from right to left as each operator is encountered. For example, in the expression 8 + 5 * 7 % 2 * 4, the multiplication and modulus operator are of higher precedence than the addition operator and are evaluated first. Both of these operators, however, are of equal priority. Therefore, these operators are evaluated according to their left-to-right associativity, yielding

```
8 + 5 * 7 % 2 * 4 =
    8 + 35 % 2 * 4 =
         8 + 1 * 4 =
             8 + 4 =   12
```

2.3 Displaying Numerical Results

In addition to displaying messages, the `printf()` function allows us to both evaluate arithmetic expressions and display their results. Doing this requires that we pass at least two items to `printf()`: a control string that tells the function where and in what form the result is to be displayed, and the value that we wish to be displayed. Recall that items passed to a function are always placed within the function name parentheses and are called arguments. Arguments must be separated from one another with commas, so that the function knows where one argument ends and the next begins. For example, in the statement

```
printf("The total of 6 and 15 is %d", 6 + 15);
```

the first argument is the message `The total of 6 and 15 is %d`, and the second argument is the expression `6 + 15`.

The first argument passed to `printf()` must always be a *message*. A message that also includes a *control sequence*, such as the `%d`, is termed a *control string*. Control sequences have a special meaning to the `printf()` function. They tell the function what type of value is to be displayed and where to display it.

The percent sign, `%`, in a control sequence tells `printf()` that we wish to print a number at the place in the message where the `%` is located. The `d`, placed immediately after the `%`, tells `printf()` to print the number as an integer.

When `printf()` sees the control sequence in its control string, it substitutes the value of the next argument in place of the control sequence. Since this next argument is the expression `6 + 15`, which has a value of `21`, it is this value that is displayed. Thus, the statement

```
printf("The total of 6 and 15 is %d.", 6 + 15);
```

causes the printout

```
The total of 6 and 15 is 21.
```

Just as the `%d` control sequence alerts `printf()` that an integer value is to be displayed, the control sequence `%f` (the `f` stands for floating point) indicates that a number with a decimal point is to be displayed. For example, the statement

```
printf("Sum of %f and %f is %f.", 12.2, 1.5, 12.2 + 1.5);
```

causes the display

```
Sum of 12.200000 + 1.500000 is 13.700000.
```

As this display shows, the `%f` control sequence causes `printf()` to display six digits to the right of the decimal place. If the number does not have six decimal digits, zeros are added to the number to fill the fractional part. If the number has more than six decimal digits, the fractional part is rounded to six decimal digits.

One caution should be mentioned here. The `printf()` function does not check the values it is given. If an integer control sequence is used (`%d`, for example) and the value given the function is either a floating point or double precision number, the value that will be displayed cannot be predicted. Similarly, if a floating point control sequence is used and the corresponding number is an integer, an unanticipated result will occur.

Character data is displayed using the `%c` control sequence. For example, the statement

```
printf("The first letter of the alphabet is an %c.", 'a');
```

causes the display

```
The first letter of the alphabet is an a.
```

Program 2-1 illustrates using `printf()` to display the results of an expression within the statements of a complete program.

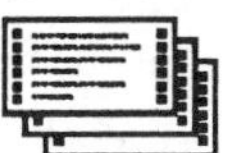

Program 2-1

```
main()
{

  printf("%f plus %f equals %f\n\n", 15.0, 2.0, 15.0 + 2.0);
  printf("%f minus %f equals %f\n\n", 15.0, 2.0, 15.0 - 2.0);
  printf("%f times %f equals %f\n\n", 15.0, 2.0, 15.0 * 2.0);
  printf("%f divided by %f equals %f", 15.0, 2.0, 15.0 / 2.0);

}
```

The output of Program 2-1 is:

```
15.000000 plus 2.000000 equals 17.000000

15.000000 minus 2.000000 equals 13.000000

15.000000 times 2.000000 equals 30.000000

15.000000 divided by 2.000000 equals 7.500000
```

Formatted Output

Besides displaying correct results, it is extremely important for a program to present its results attractively. Most programs are judged, in fact, on the perceived ease of data entry and the style and presentation of their output. For example, displaying a monetary result as 1.897000 is not in keeping with accepted report conventions. The display should be either $1.90 or $1.89, depending on whether rounding, or truncation, is used.

The format of numbers displayed by `printf()` can be controlled by including *field width specifiers* as part of each control sequence. For example, the statement

```
printf("The sum of%3d and%4d is%5d.", 6, 15, 21);
```

causes the printout

```
The sum of  6 and  15 is   21.
```

The numbers 3, 4, and 5 in the control string are the field width specifiers. The 3 causes the first number to be printed in a total field width of three spaces, in this case two blank spaces followed by the number 6. The field width specifier for the second control sequence, `%4d`, causes two blank spaces and the number 15 to be printed for a total field width of four spaces. The last field width specifier causes the 21 to be printed in a field of five spaces, which includes three blanks and the number 21. As illustrated, each integer is right-justified within the specified field.

Field width specifiers are useful in printing columns of numbers so that the numbers in each column align correctly. For example, Program 2-2 illustrates how a column of integers would align in the absence of field width specifiers.

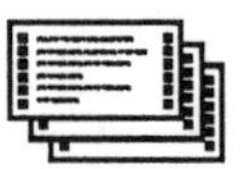

Program 2-2

```
main()
{
  printf("\n%d", 6);
  printf("\n%d", 18);
  printf("\n%d", 124);
  printf("\n---");
  printf("\n%d", 6+18+124);
}
```

The output of Program 2-2 is

```
6
18
124
---
148
```

Since no field widths are given, the `printf()` function allocates enough space for each number as it is received. To force the numbers to align on the units digit requires a field width wide enough for the largest displayed number. For Program 2-2, a field width of three is enough. The use of this field width is illustrated in Program 2-3.

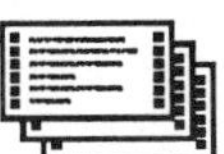

Program 2-3

```
main()
{
  printf("\n%3d", 6);
  printf("\n%3d", 18);
  printf("\n%3d", 124);
  printf("\n---");
  printf("\n%3d", 6+18+124);
}
```

The output of Program 2-3 is

```
  6
 18
124
---
148
```

Formatted floating point numbers require the use of two field width specifiers. The first specifier determines the total width of the display, including the decimal point; the second determines how many digits are printed to the right of the decimal point. For example, the statement

```
printf("|%10.3f|", 25.67);
```

causes the printout

```
|    25.670|
```

The bar symbol, `|`, is used to clearly mark the beginning and end of the display field. The field width specifier 10.3 tells `printf()` to display the number in a total field of `10`, which includes the decimal point with three digits to the right of the decimal point. Since the number contains only two digits to the right of the decimal point, the decimal part of the number is padded with a trailing zero.

For all numbers (integers, floating point, and double precision), `printf()` ignores the specified field width if the total field width is too small and allocates enough space for the integer part of the number to be printed. The fractional part of both floating point and double precision numbers is always displayed with the number of specified digits. If the fractional part contains fewer digits than specified, the number is padded with trailing zeros; if the fractional part contains more digits than called for in the specifier, the number is rounded to the indicated number of decimal places. Table 2-7 illustrates the effect of various field width specifiers.

TABLE 2-7 Effect of Field Width Specifiers

Specifier	Number	Display	Comments
`|%2d|`	3	`| 3|`	Number fits in field
`|%2d|`	43	`|43|`	Number fits in field
`|%2d|`	143	`|143|`	Field width ignored
`|%2d|`	2.3	Unpredictable	Floating point in an integer field
`|%5.2f|`	2.366	`| 2.37|`	Field of 5 with 2 decimal digits
`|%5.2f|`	42.3	`|42.30|`	Number fits in field
`|%5.2f|`	142.364	`|142.36|`	Field width ignored but fractional specifier used
`|%5.2f|`	142	Unpredictable	Integer in a floating point field

Other Number Bases

When outputting integers, several display conversions are possible. As we have seen, the control sequence `%d`, with or without a field width specifier, causes integers to be displayed in decimal (base 10) form. To have the value of an integer displayed as either a base 8 (octal) or base 16 (hexadecimal) number requires the use of the control sequences `%o` and `%x`, respectively. Program 2-4 illustrates each of these control sequences.

Program 2-4

```
main()   /* a program to illustrate output conversions */
{
  printf("The decimal (base 10) value of 15 is %d.", 15);
  printf("\nThe octal (base 8) value of 15 is %o.", 15);
  printf("\nThe hexadecimal (base 16) value of 15 is %x.", 15);
}
```

The output produced by Program 2-4 is:

```
The decimal (base 10) value of 15 is 15.
The octal (base 8) value of 15 is 17.
The hexadecimal (base 16) value of 15 is F.
```

The display of integer values in one of the three possible number systems (decimal, octal, and hexadecimal) does not affect how the number is actually stored inside a computer. All numbers are stored in the computer's own internal codes. The control sequences used in `printf()` simply tell the function how to convert the internal code for output display purposes.

Besides displaying integers in octal or hexadecimal form, integer constants can also be written in a program in these forms. To designate an octal integer, the number must have a leading zero. The number 023, for example, is an octal number in C. Hexadecimal (hex) numbers are denoted with a leading 0x. The use of octal and hexadecimal number input to `printf()` is illustrated in Program 2-5.

Program 2-5

```
main()
{
  printf("The decimal value of 025 is %d.\n",025);
  printf("The decimal value of 0x37 is %d.\n",0x37);
}
```

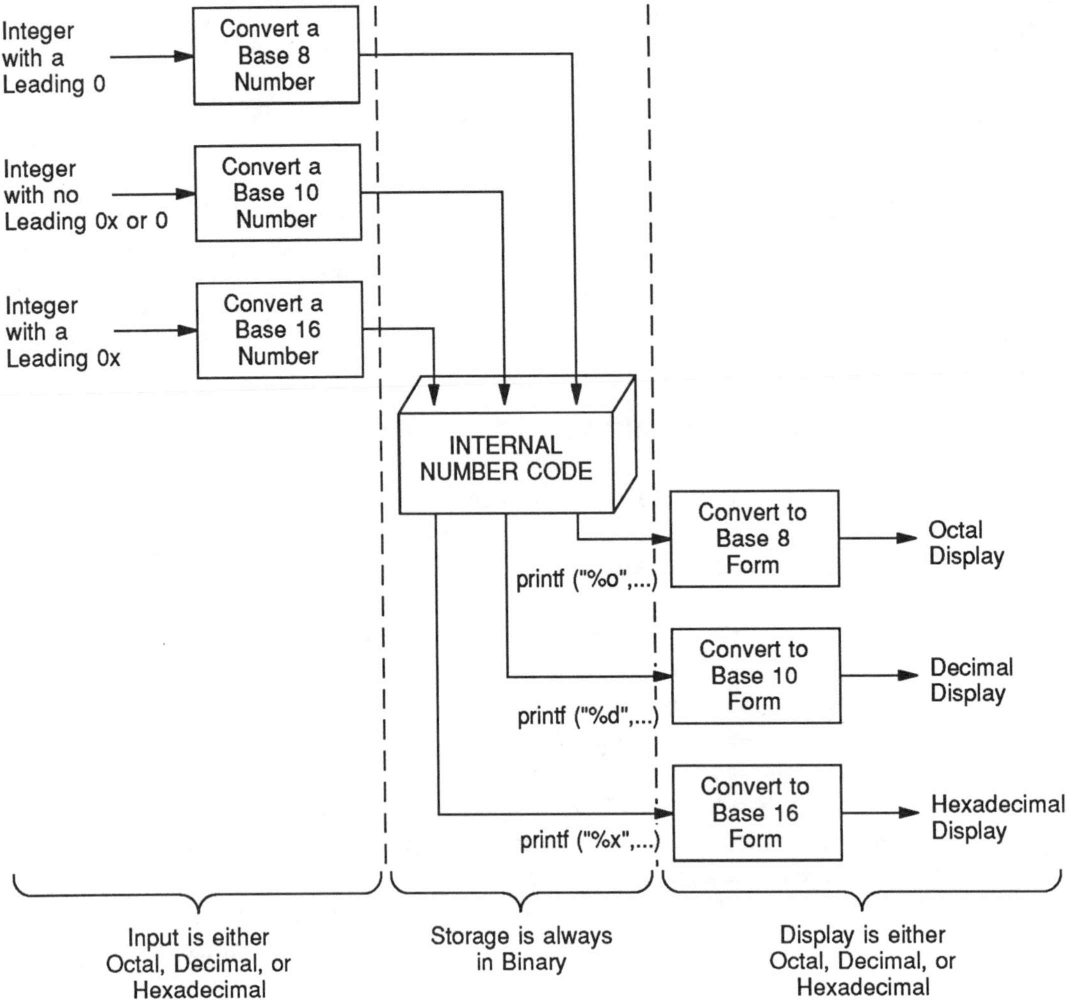

FIGURE 2-2 Input, Storage, and Display of Integers

When Program 2-5 is run, the following output is obtained:

```
The decimal value of 025 is 21.
The decimal value of 0x37 is 55.
```

The relationship between the input, storage, and display of integers is illustrated in Figure 2-2.

The same display conversions available for integers can also be used to display characters. In addition to the `%c` control sequence, the `%d` control sequence displays the value of the internal character code as a decimal number and the %o and %x control sequences cause the character code to be displayed in octal and hexadecimal form, respectively. These display conversions are illustrated in Program 2-6.

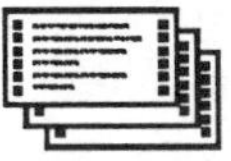

Program 2-6

```
main()
{
  printf("The decimal value of the letter %c is %d.", 'a', 'a');
  printf("\nThe octal value of the letter %c is %o.", 'a', 'a');
  printf("\nThe hex value of the letter %c is %x.", 'a', 'a');
}
```

When Program 2-6 is run, the output produced is:

```
The decimal value of the letter a is 97.
The octal value of the letter a is 141.
The hex value of the letter a is 61.
```

The display conversions for character data are illustrated in Figure 2-3.

FIGURE 2-3 Character Display Options

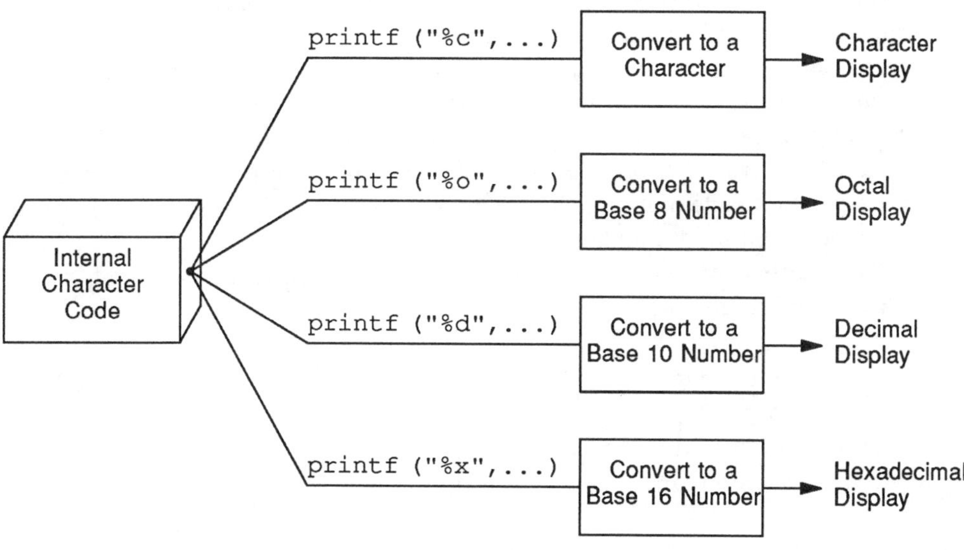

2.4 Variables and Declarations

All data used in a computer program must be stored and retrieved from the computer's memory. Consider the four bytes of memory storage illustrated in Figure 2-4. For purposes of illustration, assume that the two bytes with addresses 1321 and 1322 are used to store one integer number and that the bytes with addresses 2649 and 2450 are used to store a second integer.

Before such high-level languages as C existed, actual memory addresses were used to store and retrieve data. For example, storing the number 62 in the first set of bytes illustrated in Figure 2-4 and the number 17 in the next set of bytes required instructions equivalent to

```
put a 62 in location 1321
put a 17 in location 2649
```

Notice that only the address of the first byte in each set of locations is given. The computer needs only this first address to correctly locate the starting point for storage or retrieval. Adding the two numbers just stored and saving the result in another set of memory locations, for example at location 45, required a statement comparable to

```
add the contents of location 1321
to the contents of location 2649
and store the result into location 45
```

Clearly this method of storage and retrieval was a cumbersome process. In C, symbolic names are used in place of actual memory addresses. These symbolic names are called *variables*. A variable is simply a name, given by the programmer, to computer storage locations. The term *variable* is used because the value stored in the variable can change, or vary. For each name that the programmer uses, the computer keeps track of the actual addresses. Naming a variable is equivalent to putting a name on the door of a hotel room and referring to the room (or suite of rooms) by this name, such as the Blue Room, rather than using the actual room number.

The selection of variable names is left to the programmer, as long as the following rules are observed:

1. The variable name must begin with a letter or underscore (_) and can contain only letters, underscores, or digits. It cannot contain any blanks, commas, or special symbols, such as () & , $ # . !
2. A variable name cannot be a reserved word (see Table 1-1).

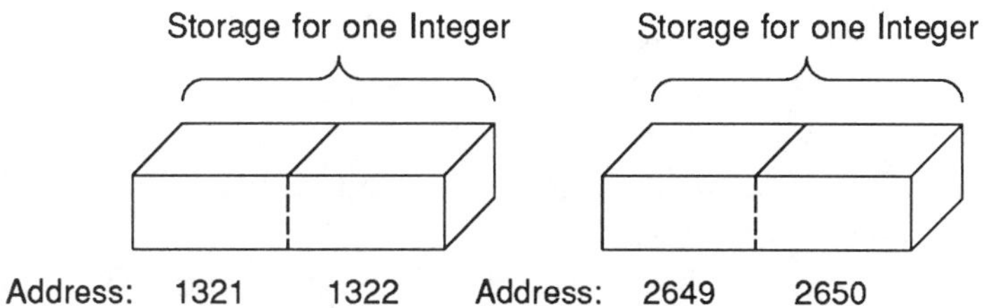

FIGURE 2-4 Enough Storage for Two Integers

3. Only the first eight characters of a variable name are used by most computers that run C programs.

These rules are very similar to those used to name functions. As with function names, variable names should be mnemonics that give some indication of the variable's use. For example, a variable named `total` indicates that this variable will probably be used to store a value that is the total of some other values. As with function names, all variable names are typed in lowercase letters. This, again, is traditional in C, although not required.

Now, assume that the two bytes previously illustrated in Figure 2-4 starting at address 1321 are given the variable name `num1`. Also assume that the two bytes starting at address 2649 are given the variable name `num2` and that the two bytes starting at address 45 are given the name `result`, as illustrated in Figure 2-5.

Using these variable names, storing a 62 in location 1321, a 17 in location 2649, and adding the contents of these two locations is accomplished by the C statements

```
num1 = 62;
num2 = 17;
result = num1 + num2;
```

These statements are called *assignment statements* because they tell the computer to assign (store) a value into a variable. Assignment statements always have an equal sign (=) and one variable name immediately to the left of this sign.

FIGURE 2-5 Giving Storage Locations Names

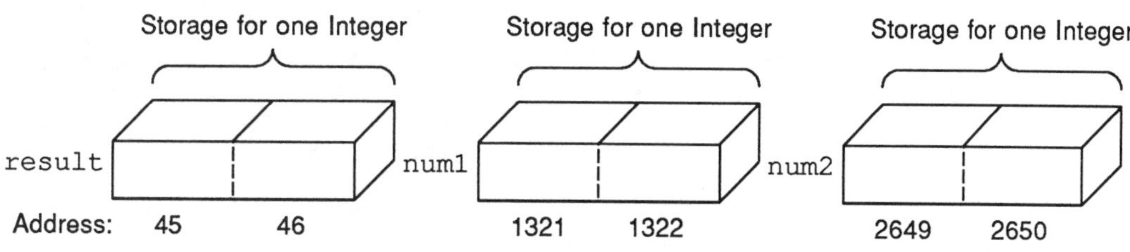

The value on the right of the equal sign is determined first and this value is assigned to the variable on the left of the equal sign. The blank spaces in the assignment statements are inserted for readability. We will have much more to say about assignment statements in the next chapter but, for now, we can use them to store values in variables.

A variable name is useful because it frees the programmer from concern over where data is physically stored inside the computer. We simply use the variable names and let the computer worry about where in memory the data is actually stored. Before storing values into variables, however, C requires that we clearly define the type of data that will be stored in each variable. We must tell the computer, in advance, the names of the variables that will be used for characters, the names that will be used for integers, and the names that will be used for the other data types supported by C. Then, when the variable name is used, the computer will know how many bytes of storage to access.

Naming and defining the data type that can be stored in each variable is accomplished with *declaration statements.* Declaration statements within a function appear immediately after the opening brace of a function and, like all C statements, must end with a semicolon. C functions containing declaration statements have the general form

```
function name()
{
  declaration statements;

  other statements;
}
```

Declaration statements, in their simplest form, provide a data type and variable name. For example, the declaration statement

```
int total;
```

declares `total` to be the name of a variable capable of storing an integer value.

Variables used to hold floating point values are declared by using the reserved word `float`, while variables that are used to hold double precision values are declared by using the reserved word `double`. For example, the statement

```
float firstnum;
```

declares `firstnum` to be a variable that can be used to store a floating point number. Similarly, the statement

```
double secnum;
```

declares that the variable will be used to store a double precision number.

Program 2-7 illustrates the declaration and use of four floating point variables. The `printf()` function is then used to display the contents of one of these variables.

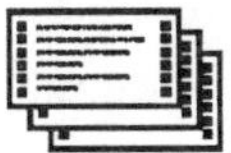

Program 2-7

```
main()
{
  float grade1;    /* declare grade1 as a float variable  */
  float grade2;    /* declare grade2 as a float variable  */
  float total;     /* declare total as a float variable   */
  float average;   /* declare average as a float variable */

  grade1 = 85.5;
  grade2 = 97.0;
  total = grade1 + grade2;
  average = total/2.0;          /* divide the total by 2.0 */

  printf("The average grade is %f\n",average);
}
```

The placement of the declaration statements in Program 2-7 is straightforward, although we will shortly see that the four individual declarations can be combined into a single declaration. When Program 2-7 is run, the following output is displayed:

```
The average grade is 91.250000
```

Two comments with respect to the `printf()` function call made in Program 2-7 should be made here. If a variable name is one of the arguments passed to a function, as it is to `printf()` in Program 2-7, the function receives only a copy of the value stored in the variable. It does not receive the variable's name. When the program sees a variable name in the function parentheses, it first goes to the variable and retrieves the value stored. It is this value that is passed to the function. Thus, when a variable is included in the `printf()` argument list, `printf()` receives the value stored in the variable and then displays this value. Internally, `printf()` has no knowledge of where the value it receives came from or the variable name under which the value was stored.

Although this procedure for passing data into a function may seem surprising, it really is a safety procedure for ensuring that a called function does not have access to the original variable. This guarantees that the called function cannot inadvertently change data in a variable declared outside itself. We will have more to say about this in Chapter 7 when we examine and begin writing our own called functions.

The second comment concerns the use of the `%f` control sequence in Program 2-7. Although this control sequence works for both floating point and double precision numbers, the control sequence `%lf` can also be used for displaying the values of double precision variables. The `l` indicates that the number is a long floating point number, which is what a double precision number really is. Omitting the `l` control character has no effect on the `printf()` function when double precision values are displayed. As we will see, however, it is essential in entering double precision values when the input function `scanf()` is used. This function is presented in the next chapter.

Just as integers, floating point, and double precision variables must be declared before they can be used, a variable used to store a character must also be declared. Character variables are declared by using the reserved word char. For example, the declaration

```
char ch;
```

declares `ch` to be a character variable. Program 2-8 illustrates this declaration and the use of `printf()` to display the value stored in a character variable.

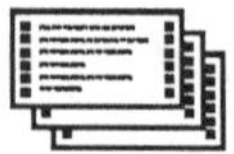

Program 2-8

```
main()
{
  char ch;          /* this declares a character variable */

  ch = 'a';         /* store the letter a into ch          */
  printf("\nThe character stored in ch is %c.", ch);
  ch = 'm';         /* now store the letter m into ch      */
  printf("\nThe character now stored in ch is %c.", ch);
}
```

When Program 2-8 is run, the output produced is:

```
The character stored in ch is a.
The character now stored in ch is m.
```

Notice in Program 2-8 that the first letter stored in the variable `ch` is `a` and the second letter stored is `m`. Since a variable can be used to store only one value at a time, the assignment of the `m` to the variable automatically causes the `a` to be erased.

Variables having the same data type can always be grouped together and declared in a single declaration statement. For example, the four separate declarations

```
float grade1;
float grade2;
float total;
float average;
```

can be replaced by the single declaration statement

```
float grade1, grade2, total, average;
```

Similarly, the two character declarations

```
char ch;
char key;
```

can be replaced by the single declaration statement

```
char ch, key;
```

Notice that declaring multiple variables in a single declaration requires that the data type of the variables be given only once, that all of the variables be separated by commas, and that only one semicolon be used to terminate the declaration. The space after each comma is inserted for readability and is not required.

Declaration statements can also be used to store an initial value in declared variables. For example, the declaration statement

```
int num1 = 15;
```

both declares the variable `num1` as an integer variable and sets the value of 15 in the variable. Similarly, the declaration statement

```
float grade1 = 87.0, grade2 = 93.5, total;
```

declares three floating point variables and initializes two of them. Constants, expressions using only constants (such as 87.0 + 93.5), and expressions using constants and previously initialized variables can all be used as initializers within a function. For example, Program 2-8 with initialization included would appear as:

```
main()
{
  char ch = 'a';     /* declaration and initialization */

  printf("\nThe character stored in ch is %c.", ch);
  ch = 'm';          /* now store the letter m into ch */
  printf("\nThe character now stored in ch is %c.", ch);
}
```

Declaration Statements as Definition Statements

The declaration statements we have introduced have performed both software and hardware tasks. From a software perspective, declaration statements always provide a convenient, up-front list of all variables and their data types. In this software role, variable declarations also eliminate an otherwise common and troublesome error caused by the misspelling of a variable's name within a program. For example, assume that a variable named `distance` is declared and initialized using the statement

```
int distance = 26;
```

Now, assume that this variable is inadvertently misspelled in the statement

```
mpg = distnce / gallons;
```

In languages that do not require variable declarations, the program would treat `distnce` as a new variable and either assign an initial value of zero to the variable or use whatever value happened to be in the variable's storage area. In either case, a value would be calculated and assigned to `mpg`, and finding the error or even knowing that an error occurred could be extremely troublesome. Such errors are impossible in C, because the compiler will flag `distnce` as an undeclared variable. The compiler cannot, of course, detect when one declared variable is typed in place of another declared variable.

In addition to their software role, declaration statements can also perform a distinct hardware task. Since each data type has its own storage requirements, the computer can allocate sufficient storage for a variable only after it knows the variable's data type. Because variable declarations provide this information, they can be used to force the computer to physically reserve sufficient memory storage for each variable. Declaration statements used for this hardware purpose are also called *definition statements*, because they define, or tell, the computer how much memory is needed for data storage.

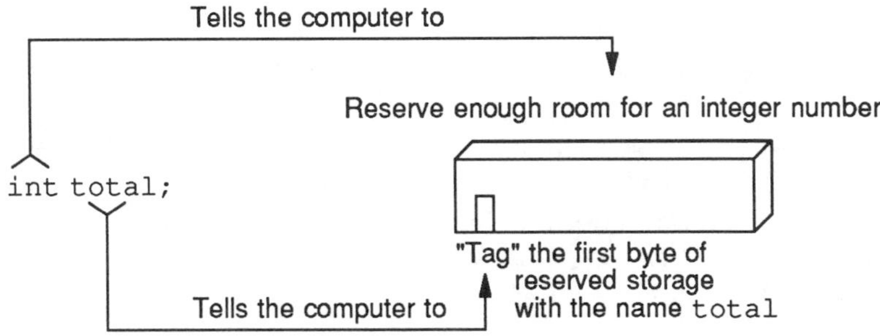

FIGURE 2-6a Defining the Integer Variable Named `total`

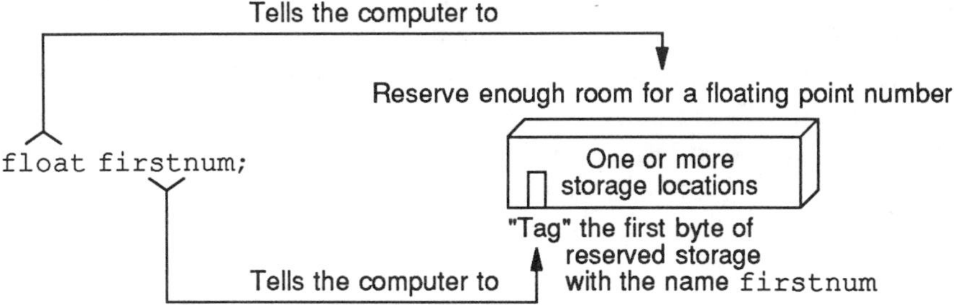

FIGURE 2-6b Defining the Floating Point Variable Named `firstnum`

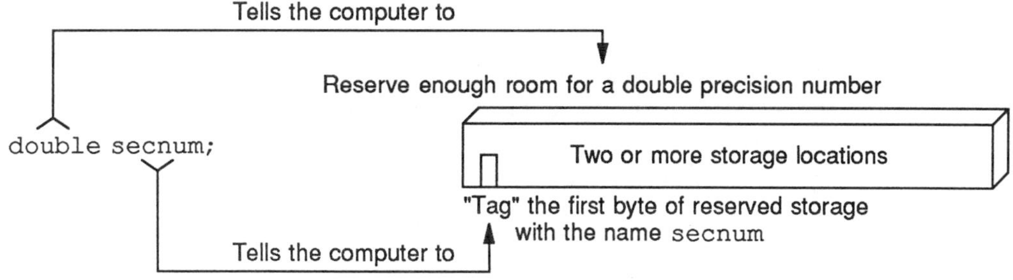

FIGURE 2-6c Defining the Double Precision Variable Named `secnum`

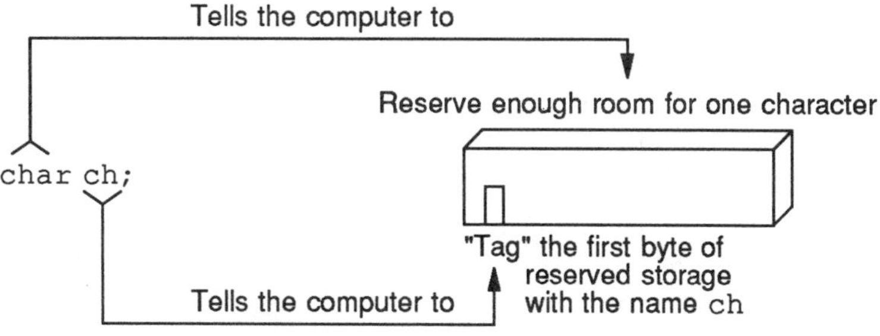

FIGURE 2-6d Defining the character Variable Named `ch`

All of the declaration statements we have encountered so far have also been definition statements. Later, we will see cases of declaration statements that do not cause any new storage to be allocated and are used simply to declare or alert the program to the data types of previously created and existing variables.

Figure 2-6 illustrates the series of operations set in motion by declaration statements that also perform a definition role. The figure shows that definition statements (or, if you prefer, declaration statements that also cause memory to be allocated) "tag" the first byte of each set of reserved bytes with a name. This name is the variable's name and is used by the computer to correctly locate the starting byte of each variable's reserved memory area.

Within a program, after a variable has been declared, it is typically used by a programmer to refer to the contents of the variable (the variable's value). Where in memory this value is stored is generally of little concern to the programmer. The computer, however, must be concerned with where each value is stored and with correctly locating each variable. In this task, the computer uses the variable name to locate the first byte of storage previously allocated to the variable. Knowing the variable's data type then allows the computer to store or retrieve the correct number of bytes.

2.5 Integer Qualifiers

Integer numbers are generally used in programs as counters to keep track of the number of times that something has occurred. For most applications, the counts needed are less than 32,767, which is the maximum integer value that can be stored in two bytes. Since most computers allocate at least two bytes for integers, there is usually no problem.

Cases do arise, however, where larger integer numbers are needed. In financial applications, for example, dates such as 7/12/89 are typically converted to the number of days from the turn of the century. This conversion makes it possible to store and sort dates by using a single number for each date. Unfortunately, for dates after 1987, the number of days from the turn of the century is larger than the maximum value of 32,767 allowed when only two bytes are allocated for each integer variable. For financial programs dealing with mortgages and bonds maturing after 1987 that are run on computers allocating only two bytes per integer (PCs, for example), the limitation on the maximum integer value must be overcome.

To accommodate real application requirements such as this, C provides a *long integer, short integer,* and *unsigned integer* data types. These three additional integer data types are obtained by adding the *qualifiers* long, short, or unsigned, respectively, to the normal integer declaration statements. For example, the declaration statement

```
long int days;
```

declares the variable `days` to be a long integer. The word `int` in a long integer declaration statement is optional, so the previous declaration statement can also be written as `long days;` . The amount of storage allocated for a long integer depends on the computer being used. Although you would expect that a long integer variable would be allocated more space than a standard integer, this may not be the case, especially for computers that reserve more than two bytes for normal integer variables. About all that can be said is that long integers will provide no less space than regular integers. The actual amount of storage allocated by your computer should be checked by using the `sizeof` operator.

Once a variable is declared as a long integer, integer values can be assigned as usual for standard integers, or an optional letter `L` (either uppercase or lowercase, with no space between the number and letter) can be appended to the integer. For example, the declaration statement

```
long days = 38276L;
```

declares `days` to be of type long integer, and assigns the long integer constant 38276 to the variable days.

Printing long integers values by using the `printf()` function requires the use of a lowercase `l`. Thus, to display a long integer, the control sequence `%ld` must be used.

In addition to the `long` qualifier, C also provides a `short` qualifier. Although you would expect a short integer to conserve computer storage by reserving fewer bytes than for an integer, this is not always the case. Some computers use the same amount of storage for both integers and short integers. Again, the amount of memory space allocated for a short integer data type depends on your computer and can be checked by using the `sizeof` operator (described at the end of this section). As with long integers, short integers can be declared by using the term `short` or `short int` in a declaration statement.

Once a variable is declared to be a short integer, values are assigned as they normally are with integers. Printing short integers by using the `printf()` function also requires no modifications to any of the control sequences used for integers.

The final integer data type is the unsigned integer. This data type is obtained by prefixing the reserved word `int` to the qualifier `unsigned`. For example, the declaration statement

```
unsigned int days;
```

declares the variable `days` to be of type `unsigned`.

The unsigned integer data type is used to store positive integers only and effectively doubles the positive value that can be stored without increasing the

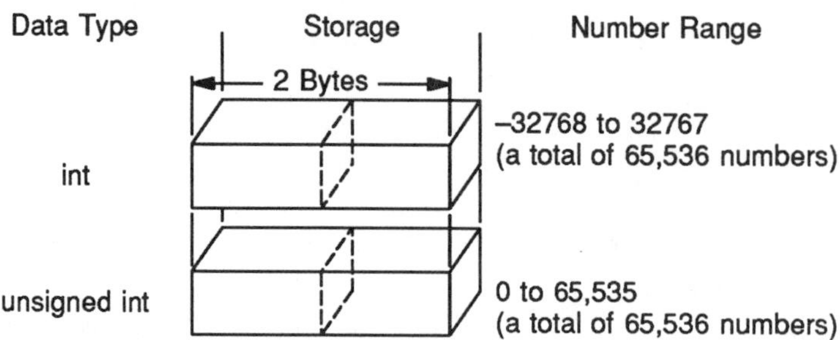

FIGURE 2-8 Unsigned Integers Can Only Be Positive Numbers

number of bytes allocated to an integer. This is accomplished by treating all unsigned integers as positive numbers, as illustrated in Figure 2-8.

Printing unsigned integers using the `printf()` function requires the use of the `%u` control sequence in place of the `%d` normally used for integers. The `%u` control sequence is especially convenient for displaying memory addresses, which is the topic of Section 3.2.

Determining Storage Size

C provides an operator for determining the amount of storage your computer allocates for each data type. This operator is called the `sizeof` operator, and it returns the number of bytes of the object or data type following it. Unlike a function, which itself is made up of C statements, the `sizeof` operator is an integral part of the C language itself.

If the item following the reserved word `sizeof` is a variable, `sizeof` returns the number of bytes of storage that the computer reserved for the variable. If the item following the word `sizeof` is a data type, such as `int` or `char`, `sizeof` will return the number of bytes of storage that the computer uses for the given data type. Using either approach, we can use `sizeof` to determine the amount of storage used by different data types. Consider Program 2-9:

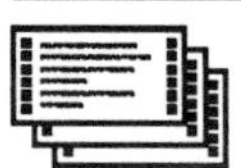

Program 2-9

```
main()
{
  char ch;
  int num1;

  printf("Bytes of storage used by a character: %d ", sizeof(ch));
  printf("\nBytes of storage used by an integer: %d", sizeof(num1));
}
```

Program 2-9 declares that the variable `ch` is used to store a character and that the variable `num1` is used to store an integer. From our discussion in the last section, we know that each of these declaration statements is also a definition statement. As such, the first declaration statement instructs the computer to reserve enough storage for a character, and the second declaration instructs the computer to reserve enough storage for an integer. The `sizeof` operator is then used to tell us how much room the computer set aside for these two variables. The `sizeof` operator itself is used as an argument to the `printf()` function. When Program 2-9 is run on an IBM personal computer, the following output is obtained:

```
Bytes of storage used by a character: 1
Bytes of storage used by an integer: 2
```

One caution should be noted. The number of bytes given by the `sizeof` operator is in terms of the storage reserved for one character. Since almost all computers store one character in one byte, the value given by `sizeof` is normally a true byte count. If, however, a computer uses two bytes to store one character (possible, but not very likely), the number given by the `sizeof` operator represents the number of double bytes reserved for each data type. The true byte count is obtained by multiplying the number given by `sizeof` by two.

2.6 Common Programming Errors

The common programming errors associated with the material presented in this chapter are:

1. Forgetting to declare all of the variables used in a program. This error is detected by the compiler and an error message is generated for all undeclared variables.
2. Storing an incorrect data type in a declared variable. This error is not detected by the compiler. Here, the assigned value is converted to the data type of the variable it is assigned to.
3. Using a variable in an expression before a value has been assigned to the variable. Here, whatever value happens to be in the variable will be used when the expression is evaluated, and the result will be meaningless.
4. Dividing integer values incorrectly. This error is usually disguised within a larger expression and can be a very troublesome error to detect. For example, the expression

```
3.425 + 2/3 + 7.9
```

yields the same result as the expression

```
3.425 + 7.9
```

because the integer division of 2/3 is 0.

5. Mixing data types in the same expression without clearly understanding the effect produced. Since C allows expressions with "mixed" data types, it is important to be clear about the order of evaluation and the data type of all intermediate calculations. As a general rule, it is better to never mix data types in an expression unless a specific effect is desired.
6. Not including the correct control sequence in `printf()` function calls for the data types of the remaining arguments.
7. Not closing the control string in `printf()` with a double quotation mark followed by a comma when additional arguments are passed to `printf()`.
8. Forgetting to separate all arguments passed to printf() with commas.

2.7 Chapter Summary

1. The four basic types of data recognized by C are integers, floating point, double precision, and character data. A computer uses different amounts of memory to store each of these data types.
2. The `printf()` function can be used to display all of C's data types. The control sequences for displaying integers, floating point, double precision, and character values are `%d`, `%f`, `%lf`, and `%c`, respectively. The `%f` control sequence can be used in place of the `%lf` sequence for double precision values. Additionally, field control specifiers can be used to format displays.
3. Every variable in a C program must be declared as to the type of value it can store. Declarations must be placed as the first statements after a left brace. Variables can also be initialized when they are declared. Additionally, variables of the same type can be declared in a single declaration statement.
4. A simple C program containing declaration statements has the form:

```
main()
{
  declaration statements;

  other statements;
}
```

5. Declaration statements always play the software role of informing the compiler of a function's valid variable names. When a variable declaration also

causes the computer to physically set aside memory locations for the variable, the declaration statement is also called a *definition statement.* (All of the declarations we have encountered have also been definition statements.)

6. The `sizeof` operator can be used to determine the amount of storage reserved for variables.

Sample Problem

To visualize how variables are stored in a computer's memory, assume that a character requires one byte of storage, an integer two bytes, a floating point number four bytes, and a double precision number eight bytes. For example, consider the following variable declarations:

```
int num1, num2;
char cc1 = 's', cc2 = 'n', cc3 = 'a', cc4 = 'p';
float volts, current;
double power;
```

Suppose that the variables are assigned to storage in the order they are declared and that the first variable declared is assigned to start at memory byte address 159. The starting memory addresses of the variables declared in these statements then become:

	159	160	161	162	163	164	165	166
Address:					s	n	a	p
	num1		num1		cc1	cc2	cc3	cc4

	167	168	169	170	171	172	173	174
Address:								
	volts				current			

	175	176	177	178	179	180	181	182
Address:								
	power							

Values have been specifically assigned to the variables `cc1, cc2, cc3,` and `cc4;` the contents of the other variables are worthless values left over from some previously run program and these variables must be initialized before being used.

2.8 Chapter Supplement: Bits, Bytes, Addresses, and Number Codes

It would have been very convenient if computers stored numbers and letters the way that people do. The number 126, for example, would then be stored as 126, and the letter A stored as the letter A. Unfortunately, due to the physical components used in building a computer, this is not the case.

The smallest and most basic storage unit in a computer is called a *bit*. Physically, a bit is really a switch that can either be open or closed. By convention, the open and closed positions of each switch are represented as a 0 and a 1, respectively.

A single bit that can represent the values 0 and 1, by itself, has limited usefulness. All computers, therefore, group a set number of bits together. The grouping of eight bits to form a larger unit is almost a universal computer standard, and such groups are commonly referred to as *bytes*. A single byte consisting of eight bits, where each bit can be a 0 or 1, can represent any one of 256 different bit patterns. These consist of the pattern 00000000 (all eight switches open) to the pattern 11111111 (all eight switches closed), and all possible combinations of 0s and 1s in between. Each of these patterns can be used to represent either a character (single letter, digit, or other punctuation mark) or a value (quantity). The pattern of 0s and 1s used to represent characters are called *character codes* (one such code, called the ASCII code, is presented in Section 2.1). The patterns used to store values are called *number codes* (one such code, called two's complement, is presented at the end of this section).

Words and Addresses

One or more bytes can themselves be grouped into larger units called *words*. The advantage of combining bytes into words is that multiple bytes are stored or retrieved by the computer for each word access. For example, retrieving a word consisting of four bytes results in more information than that obtained by retrieving a word consisting of a single byte. Such a retrieval is also considerably faster than individual retrievals of four single bytes. The increase in speed, however, is achieved by an increase in cost and complexity of the computer.

Personal computers, such as the Apple and Commodore machines, have words consisting of single bytes. AT&T and IBM personal computers, as well as Digital Equipment, Data General, and Prime minicomputers, have words consisting of two bytes each. Main frame computers and advanced microprocessors have four-byte words.

The arrangement of words in a computer's memory can be compared to the arrangement of suites in a very large hotel, where each suite is made up of rooms of the same size. Just as each suite has a unique room number to locate and identify it, each word has a unique numeric address. For computers that allow each byte to be individually accessed, each byte has its own address. Like room

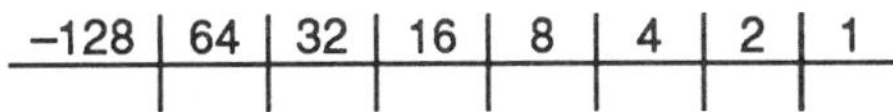

FIGURE 2-9 An Eight-Bit Value Box

numbers, word and byte addresses are always positive, whole numbers that are used for location and identification purposes. Also, like hotel rooms with connecting doors for forming larger suites, words can be combined to form larger units for the accommodation of different size data types.

Two's Complement Numbers

The most common integer code using bit patterns is called the *two's complement* representation. Using this code, the integer equivalent of any bit pattern, such as 10001101, is easy to determine and can be found for either positive or negative numbers with no change in the conversion method. For convenience we will assume words consisting of a single byte, although the procedure carries directly over to larger size words.

The easiest way to determine what integer each bit pattern represents is to first construct a simple device called a *value box*. Figure 2-9 illustrates such a box for a single byte.

Mathematically, each value in the box illustrated in Figure 2- 9 represents an increasing power of two. Since two's complement numbers must be capable of representing both positive and negative integers, the leftmost position, in addition to having the largest absolute magnitude, also has a negative sign.

Conversion of any binary number, for example, 10001101, simply requires inserting the bit pattern in the value box and adding the values having 1s under them. Thus, as illustrated in Figure 2-10, the bit pattern 10001101 represents the integer number –115.

In reviewing the value box, it is evident that any binary number with a leading 1 represents a negative number, and any bit pattern with a leading 0 represents a positive number. The value box can also be used in reverse, to convert a base 10 integer number into its equivalent binary bit pattern. Some conversions, in fact, can be made by inspection. For example, the base 10 number –125 is obtained by adding 3 to –128. Thus, the binary representation of –125 is 10000011, which equals –128 + 2 + 1. Similarly, the representation of the number +40 is 00101000, which is a 32 plus 8.

FIGURE 2-10 Converting 10001101 to a Base Number

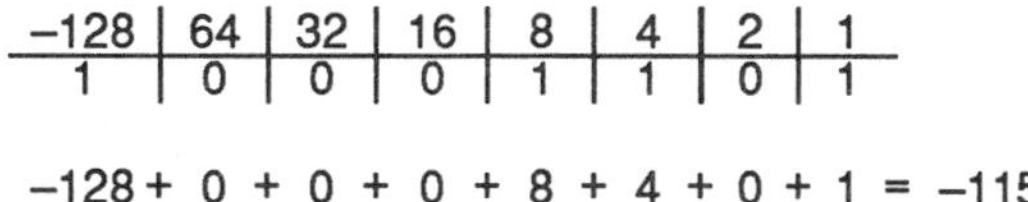

Although the value box conversion method is deceptively simple, the method is directly related to the mathematical basis of two's complement binary numbers. The original name of the two's complement binary code was the weighted-sign binary code, which correlates directly to the value box. As the name *weighted-sign* implies, each bit position has a weight, or value, of two raised to a power and a sign. The signs of all bits except the leftmost bit are positive and the sign of the leftmost or most significant bit is negative.

Assignments, Addresses, and Interactive Input

Chapter Three

In Chapter 2, we explored how data is stored, introduced variables and their associated declaration statements, and became more comfortable using the `printf()` function. This chapter completes our introduction to C by discussing the proper use of both constants and variables in constructing expressions, presenting assignment expressions, and introducing addresses and the `scanf()` function for entering data interactively while a program is running.

Almost all of the processing statements in C, except for function calls, use expressions, so it is important to have a clear understanding of what an expression is before proceeding. In its most general form, an *expression* is any combination of variables and constants that can be evaluated to yield a result. The simplest expressions consist of a single constant or variable, such as:

```
12.62      'a'      5      -10      rate      total
```

Here, each constant or variable yields a result; for individual constants, the result is the constant itself, while for individual variables the result is the value stored in the variable.

Slightly more complex expressions involve combining both constants and variables, using the arithmetic operators introduced in the last chapter. Examples of such expressions are:

1. `10 + amount`
2. `count + 1`
3. `16.3 + total`
4. `.08 * purchase`
5. `rate * total`
6. `grade1 + grade2 + grade3 + grade4`

If an expression used in a program contains one or more variables, as in these examples, the variables must first be declared and have values stored in them before the expression can be evaluated to yield a useful result. For example, if you are asked to multiply `rate` times `total` (Example 5), you cannot do it unless you first know the values of `rate` and `total`. However, if you are told that `rate` is `5` and total is `10`, you can multiply the two variables to yield `50`. Expressions using both constants and variables are evaluated according to the rules presented in Chapter 2.

3.1 Assignment

We have already encountered simple assignment statements in Chapter 2. An *assignment statement* is simply an assignment expression that is terminated by a semicolon. In C, the equals sign, `=`, used in assignment statements is itself a binary operator. This differs from the way most other high-level languages process this symbol. The = symbol is called the *assignment operator* and is used in assignment expressions having the general form

```
variable = operand
```

The operand to the right of the assignment operator can be a constant, a variable, or another valid C expression. The assignment operator causes the value of the operand to the right of the equal sign to be stored in the variable to the left of the equal sign. Examples of valid assignment expressions are:

```
    year = 1990
   value = 3000
     sum = 90.2 + 80.3 + 65.0
    rate = prime
  inches = 12 * feet
   total = total + newvalue
     tax = salestax * amount
interest = principal * interest
     sum = (grade1 + grade2 + grade3) * factor
```

The assignment operator has the lowest precedence of all binary and unary arithmetic operators (see Table A-1 in Appendix A). Thus, any other operators contained in an expression using an assignment operator are always evaluated first. For example, in the expression `tax = salestax * amount`, the expression `salestax * amount` is first evaluated to yield a value. This value is then stored in the variable `tax`.

Like all expressions, assignment expressions themselves have a value. The value of the complete assignment expression is the value assigned to the variable on the left of the assignment operator. For example, the expression `x = 5` both assigns a value of `5` to the variable `x` and results in the expression itself having a value of `5`. The value of the expression can always be verified by using a statement such as

```
printf("The value of the expression is %d", x = 5);
```

Here, the value of the expression itself is displayed and not the contents of the variable `x`. Although both the contents of the variable and the expression have the same value, it is worthwhile noting that we are dealing with two distinct entities.

From a programming perspective, it is the actual assignment of a value to a variable that is significant in an assignment expression; the final value of the assignment expression itself is of little consequence. However, the fact that assignment expressions have a value has implications that must be considered when relational operators are presented in C.

When writing assignment expressions, you must be aware of two aspects of C. Since the assignment operator has a lower precedence than any other arithmetic operator, the value of the operand to the right of the equal sign is always obtained first. For this value to have any meaning, all variables used in an expression to the right of the equal sign must have known values. For example, the expression `interest = principal * rate` causes a valid number to be stored in `interest` if the programmer first takes care to put valid numbers in `principal` and `rate`.

The second thing to keep in mind is that, since the value of an expression is stored in the variable to the left of the equal sign, there must be one variable listed immediately to the left of the equal sign. For example, the expression

```
amount + 1892 = 1000 + 10 * 5
```

is invalid. The right-side of the expression evaluates to the integer `1050`, which can be stored only in a variable. Since `amount + 1892` is not a valid variable name, the computer does not know where to store the calculated value.

Any expression that is terminated by a semicolon becomes a C statement. The most common example of this is the assignment statement, which is simply an assignment expression terminated with a semicolon. For example, terminating the assignment expression `x = 33` with a semicolon results in the assignment statement `x = 33;`, which can be used in a program on a line by itself.

Since the equal sign is an operator in C, multiple assignments are possible in the same expression or its equivalent statement. For example, in the expression `x = y = z = 25`, all the assignment operators have the same precedence. Since the assignment operator has a right-to-left associativity, the final evaluation proceeds in the sequence

```
z = 25
y = z
x = y
```

This has the effect of assigning the number `25` to each of the variables individually, and can be represented as

```
x = (y = (z = 25))
```

Appending a semicolon to the original expression results in the multiple assignment statement

```
x = y = z = 25;
```

This latter statement is equivalent to the three individual statements

```
z = 25;
y = 25;
x = 25;
```

Program 3-1 illustrates the use of assignment statements in calculating the area of a rectangle.

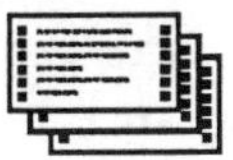

Program 3-1

```
main()
{
  float length, width, area;

  length = 27.2;
  width = 13.6;
  area = length * width;
  printf("The length of the rectangle is %f",length);
  printf("\nThe width of the rectangle is %f",width);
  printf("\nThe area of the rectangle is %f",area);
}
```

When Program 3-1 is run, the output obtained is:

```
The length of the rectangle is 27.200000
The width of the rectangle is 13.600000
The area of the rectangle is 369.920000
```

Notice the flow of control that the computer uses in executing Program 3-1. The program begins with the reserved word `main` and continues sequentially, statement by statement, until the closing brace is encountered. This flow of control is true for all programs. The computer works on one statement at a time, executing that statement with no knowledge of what the next statement will be. This explains why all operands used in an expression must have values assigned to them before the expression is evaluated.

When the computer executes the statement `area = length * width;` in Program 3-1, it uses whatever value is stored in the variables `length` and `width` at the time the assignment is executed. If values have not been assigned to these variables before being used in the expression `length * width`, the computer uses whatever values happen to occupy these variables when they are referenced. The computer does not "look ahead" to see if you have assigned values to these variables later in the program.

Assignment Variations

Although only one variable is allowed immediately to the left of the equal sign in an assignment expression, the variable on the left of the equal sign can also be used on the right of the equal sign. For example, the assignment expression `sum = sum + 10` is valid. Clearly, as an algebraic equation `sum` could never be equal to itself plus 10. But in C, the expression `sum = sum + 10` is not an equation — it is an expression that is evaluated in two major steps. The first step is to calculate the value of `sum + 10`. The second step is to store the computed value in sum. See if you can determine the output of Program 3-2.

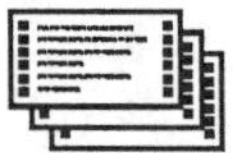

Program 3-2

```
main()
{
  int sum;

  sum = 25;
  printf("\nThe number stored in sum is %d.",sum);
  sum = sum + 10;
  printf("\nThe number now stored in sum is %d.",sum);
}
```

The assignment statement `sum = 25;` tells the computer to store the number `25` in `sum`, as shown in Figure 3-1. The first call to `printf()` causes the value stored in `sum` to be displayed by the message `The number stored in sum is 25.` The second assignment statement in Program 3-2, `sum = sum + 10;`, causes the computer to retrieve the `25` stored in sum and add `10` to this number, yielding the number `35.` The number `35` is then stored in the variable on the left side of the equal sign, which is the variable `sum.` The `25` that was in `sum` is overwritten and replaced with the new value of `35,` as shown in Figure 3-2.

FIGURE 3-1 The Integer `25` Is Stored in `sum`

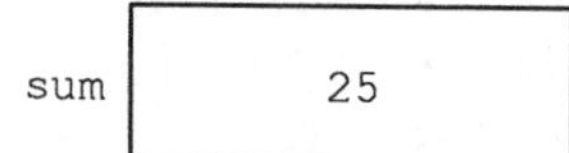

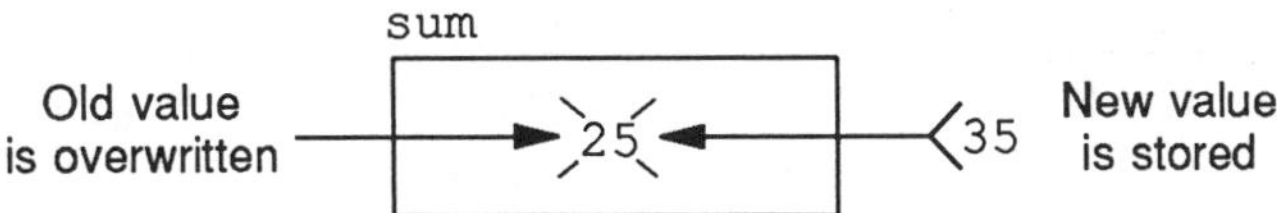

FIGURE 3-2 `sum = sum + 10;` Causes a New Value to be Stored in `sum`

Assignment expressions like `sum = sum + 25`, which use the same variable on both sides of the assignment operator, can be written by using the following assignment operators:

`+=` `-=` `*=` `/=` `%=`

For example, the expression `sum = sum + 10` can be written as `sum += 10`. Similarly, the expression `price *= rate` is equivalent to the expression `price = price * rate`.

In using these new assignment operators, it is important to consider that the variable to the left of the assignment operator is applied to the complete expression on the right. For example, the expression `price *= rate + 1` is equivalent to the expression `price = price * (rate + 1)`, not `price = price * rate + 1`.

Accumulating

Assignment expressions like `sum += 10` or its equivalent, `sum = sum + 10`, are very common in programming. These expressions are required in accumulating subtotals when data is entered one number at a time. For example, if we want to add the numbers 96, 70, 85, and 60 in calculator fashion, the following statements could be used:

Statement	Value in sum
`sum = 0;`	0
`sum = sum + 96;`	96
`sum = sum + 70;`	166
`sum = sum + 85;`	251
`sum = sum + 60;`	311

The first statement clears `sum` by storing a 0 in the variable. This removes any number ("garbage" value) in `sum` that would invalidate the final total. As each number is added, the value stored in `sum` is increased accordingly. After completion of the last statement, `sum` contains the total of all of the added numbers.

Program 3-3 illustrates the effect of these statements by displaying `sum`'s contents after each addition is made.

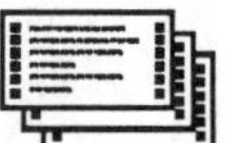

Program 3-3

```
main()
{
  int sum;

  sum = 0;
  printf("\nThe value of sum is initially set to %d.", sum);
  sum = sum + 96;
  printf("\n  sum is now %d.", sum);
  sum = sum + 70;
  printf("\n  sum is now %d.", sum);
  sum = sum + 85;
  printf("\n  sum is now %d.", sum);
  sum = sum + 60;
  printf("\n  The final sum is %d.", sum);
}
```

The output displayed by Program 3-3 is:

```
The value of sum is initially set to 0.
  sum is now 96.
  sum is now 166.
  sum is now 251.
  The final sum is 311
```

Although Program 3-3 is not a practical program (it is easier to add the numbers by hand), it does illustrate the subtotaling effect of repeated use of statements having the form

```
variable = variable + new_value;
```

We will find many uses for this type of statement when we become more familiar with the repetition statements introduced in Chapter 5.

Counting

An assignment statement that is very similar to the accumulating statement is the *counting statement*. Counting statements have the form

```
variable = variable + fixed_number;
```

Examples of counting statements are:

```
i = i + 1;
n = n + 1;
count = count + 1;
j = j + 2;
m = m + 2;
kk = kk + 3;
```

In each of these examples, the same variable is used on both sides of the equal sign. After the statement is executed, the value of the respective variable is increased by a fixed amount. In the first three examples, the variables `i`, `n`, and `count` have all been increased by one; in the next two examples, the respective variables have been increased by two; and, in the final example, the variable `kk` has been increased by three.

For the special case in which a variable is either increased or decreased by one, C provides two unary operators. Using the *increment operator*, `++`, the expression *variable* = *variable* `+ 1` can be replaced by the expression `++`*variable*. Examples of the increment operator are:

Expression	**Alternative**
`i = i + 1`	`++i`
`n = n + 1`	`++n`
`count = count + 1`	`++count`

Program 3-4 illustrates the use of the increment operator.

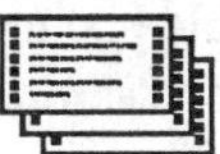

Program 3-4

```
main()
{
  int count;

  count = 0;
  printf("\nThe initial value of count is %d.", count);
  ++count;
  printf("\n   count is now %d.", count);
  ++count;
  printf("\n   count is now %d.", count);
  ++count;
```

continued

```
  printf("\n   count is now %d.", count);
  ++count;
  printf("\n   count is now %d.", count);
}
```

The output displayed by Program 3-4 is:

```
The initial value of count is 0.
   count is now 1.
   count is now 2.
   count is now 3.
   count is now 4.
```

In addition to the increment operator, C also provides a *decrement operator*, `--`. As you might expect, the expression *--variable* is equivalent to the expression *variable* = *variable* `- 1`. Examples of the decrement operator are:

Expression	**Alternative**
`i = i - 1`	`--i`
`n = n - 1`	`--n`
`count = count - 1`	`--count`

When the ++ appears before a variable, it is called a *prefix increment operator*. Besides appearing before (pre) a variable, the increment operator can also appear after a variable; for example, the expression `n++`. When the increment appears after a variable, it is called a *postfix increment*. Both of these expressions, `++n` and `n++`, correspond to the longer expression `n = n + 1`. The distinction between a prefix and postfix increment operator occurs when the variable being incremented is used in an assignment expression. For example, the expression `k = ++n` does two things in one expression. Initially, the value of `n` is incremented by one, and then the new value of `n` is assigned to the variable `k`. Thus, the statement `k = ++n;` is equivalent to the two statements

```
n = n + 1;    /* increment n first     */
k = n;        /* assign n's value to k */
```

The assignment expression `k = n++`, which uses a postfix increment operator, reverses this procedure. A postfix increment operates after the assignment is completed. Thus, the statement `k = n++;` first assigns the current value of `n` to `k` and then increments the value of `n` by one. This is equivalent to the two statements

```
k = n;        /* assign n's value to k */
n = n + 1;    /* and then increment n  */
```

Just as there are prefix and postfix increment operators, C also provides *prefix* and *postfix decrement operators*. For example, both of the expressions `--n` and `n--` reduce the value of `n` by one. These expressions are equivalent to the longer expression `n = n - 1`. As with the increment operator, however, the prefix and postfix decrement operators produce different results when used in assignment expressions. For example, the expression `k = --n` first decrements the value of `n` by one before assigning the value of `n` to `k`. On the other hand, the expression `k = n--` first assigns the current value of `n` to `k`, and then reduces the value of `n` by one.

The increment and decrement operators can often be used to significantly reduce program storage requirements and increase execution speed. For example, consider the following three statements:

```
count = count + 1;
count += 1;
++count;
```

All perform the same function; however, when these instructions are compiled for execution on an IBM personal computer, the storage requirements for the instructions are 9, 4, and 3 bytes, respectively. Using the assignment operator, `=`, instead of the increment operator results in using three times the storage space for the instruction, with an accompanying decrease in execution speed.

3.2 Addresses

Every variable has two major items associated with it: the value stored in the variable and the address of the variable. In C, the value stored in a variable is formally referred to as the variable's *rvalue* and the address of the variable is called the variable's *lvalue.* These two terms make more sense when a typical variable is considered, as illustrated in Figure 3-3. As shown in this figure, the address of the variable is typically written on the left of the figure and the variable's contents (the value in the box) on the right.

FIGURE 3-3 A Typical Variable

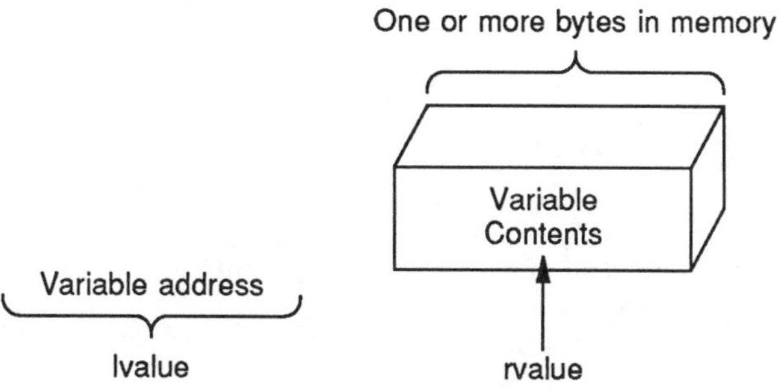

Programmers are usually concerned only with the value assigned to a variable (its contents, or rvalue) and give little attention to where the value is stored (its address, or lvalue). For example, consider Program 3-5.

Program 3-5

```
main()
{
  int num;

  num = 22;
  printf("The value stored in num is %d.",num);
  printf("\n%d bytes are used to store this value.",sizeof(num));
}
```

The output displayed by Program 3-5 is

```
The value stored in num is 22.
2 bytes are used to store this value.
```

Program 3-5 displays both the number 22, which is the value stored in the integer variable `num` (its rvalue), and the amount of storage used for this number. The information provided by Program 3-5 is illustrated in Figure 3-4.

We can go further and obtain the address, or lvalue, of the variable `num`. The address that is displayed corresponds to the address of the first byte set aside in the computer's memory for the variable.

To determine the address of num, we must use the address operator, `&`, which means *the address of,* directly in front of the variable name (no space

FIGURE 3-4 Somewhere in Memory

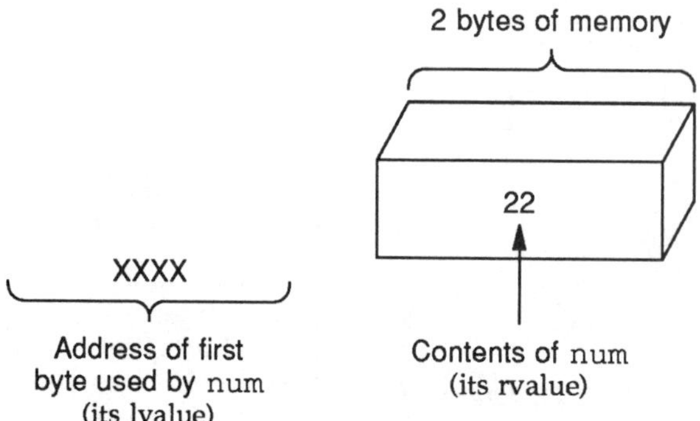

between the `&` and the variable). For example, `&num` means "the address of `num`", `&total` means "the address of `total`", and `&price` means "the address of `price`." Program 3-6 uses the address operator to display the address of the variable `num`.

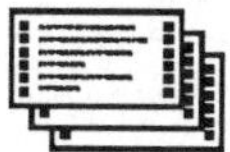

Program 3-6

```
main()
{
  int num;

  num = 22;
  printf("num = %d  The address of num = %u.", num, &num);
}
```

The output of Program 3-6 is

```
num = 22  The address of num = 65460.
```

Figure 3-5 illustrates the additional address information provided by the output of Program 3-5.

Clearly, the address output by Program 3-6 depends on the computer used to run the program. Every time Program 3-6 is executed, however, it displays a representation of the address of the first byte used to store the variable `num`. Note also that the address is printed using the unsigned conversion sequence `%u`. The use of the control sequence `%u` in the call to `printf()` forces the address to be treated as an unsigned integer data type, and what is displayed is the `printf()` representation of the address in this format. An address is

FIGURE 3-5 A More Complete Picture of the Variable num

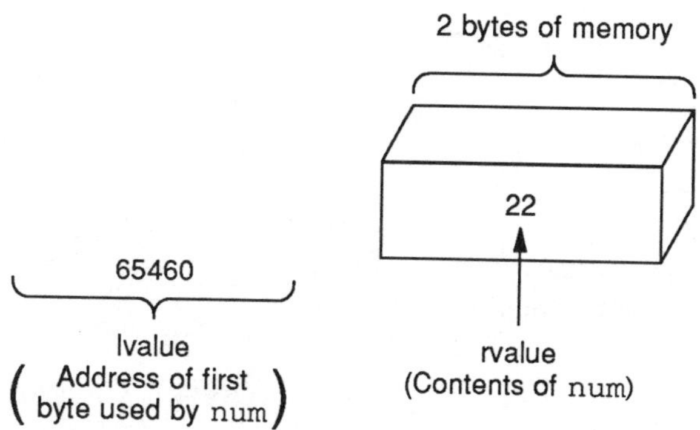

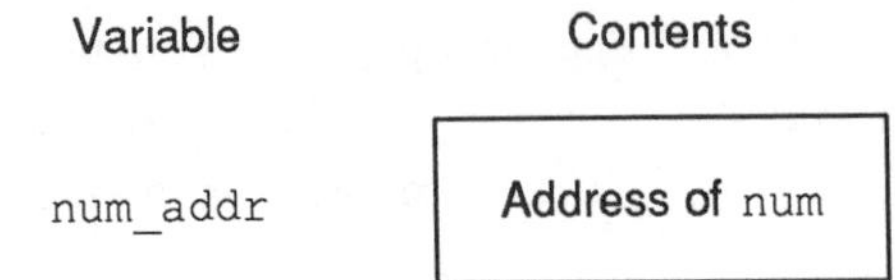

FIGURE 3-6 Storing `num`'s Address into `num_addr`

not an unsigned integer data type; it is a unique data type that may or may not require the same amount of storage as an unsigned integer. The use of the `%u` control sequence simply provides us with a convenient way of displaying an address (some C compilers also provide a `%p` to do this), since no specific control sequence exists for its display. The display has no impact on how addresses are used inside the program and merely provides us with a representation that is helpful in understanding what addresses are.

As we shall see, using addresses as opposed to only displaying them provides the C programmer with an extremely powerful programming tool. They provide the ability to penetrate directly into the inner workings of the computer and access the computer's basic storage structure. This ability gives the C programmer capabilities and programming power that are just not available in most other computer languages.

Storing Addresses

Besides displaying the address of a variable, as was done in Program 3-6, we can also store addresses in suitably declared variables. For example, the statement

```
num_addr = &num;
```

stores the address corresponding to the variable `num` in the variable `num_addr`, as illustrated in Figure 3-6. Similarly, the statements

```
d = &m;
tab_point = &list;
chr_point = &ch;
```

store the addresses of the variables `m`, `list`, and `ch` in the variables `d`, `tab_point`, and `chr_point`, respectively, as illustrated in Figure 3-7.

The variables `num_addr`, `d`, `tab_point`, and `chr_point` are all called *pointer variables*, or *pointers*. Pointers are simply variables that are used to store the addresses of other variables.

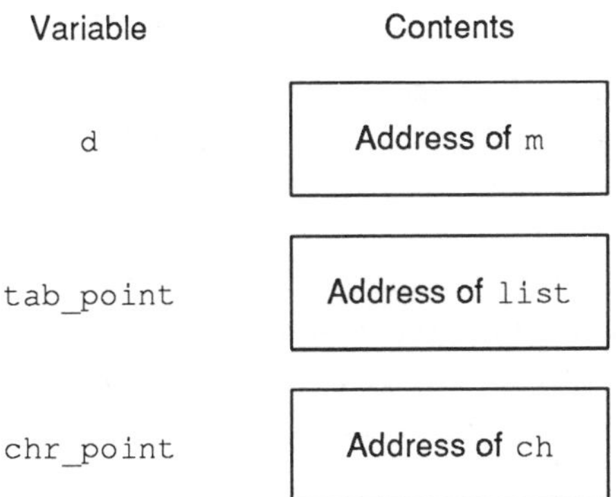

FIGURE 3-7 Storing More Addresses

Using Addresses

To use a stored address, C provides us with an *indirection operator,* `*`. The `*` symbol, when followed immediately by a pointer (no space allowed between the `*` and the pointer) means "the variable whose address is stored in." Thus, if `num_addr` is a pointer (remember that a pointer is a variable that contains an address), `*num_addr` means "the variable whose address is stored in `num_addr`." Similarly, `*tab_point` means "the variable whose address is stored in `tab_point`," and `*chr_point` means "the variable whose address is stored in `chr_point`." Figure 3-8 shows the relationship between the address contained in a pointer variable and the variable ultimately addressed.

Although `*d` literally means "the variable whose address is stored in `d`," this is commonly shortened to "the variable pointed to by `d`." Similarly, referring to Figure 3-8, `*y` can be read as "the variable pointed to by `y`." The value ultimately obtained, as shown in Figure 3-8, is `qqqq`.

When using a pointer variable, the value that is finally obtained is always found by first going to the pointer variable (or pointer, for short) for an address. The address contained in the pointer is then used to get the desired contents.

FIGURE 3-8 Using a Pointer Variable

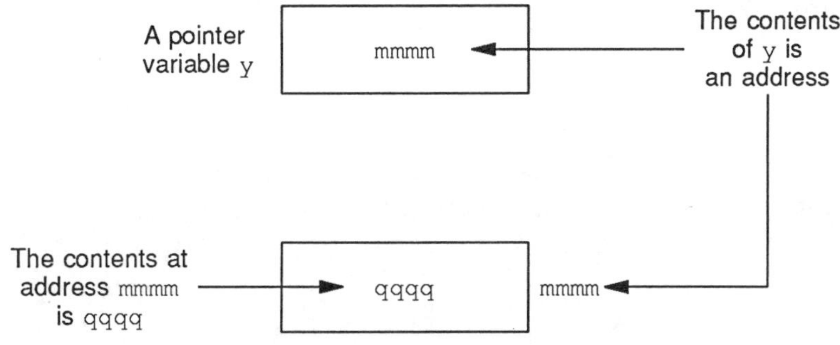

Certainly, this is a rather indirect way of getting to the final value and, not unexpectedly, the term *indirect addressing* is used to describe this procedure.

Since using a pointer requires the computer to do a double look-up (first the address is retrieved, and then the address is used to retrieve the actual data), a worthwhile question is, Why would you want to store an address in the first place? The answer to this question must be deferred until we get to real applications, when the use of pointers becomes invaluable. However, given what was previously presented for a variable's storage locations, the idea of storing an address should not seem overly strange.

Declaring Pointers

Like all variables, pointers must be declared before they can be used. In declaring a pointer variable, C requires that we also specify the type of variable that is pointed to. For example, if the address in the pointer `num_addr` is the address of an integer, the correct declaration for the pointer is

```
int *num_addr;
```

This declaration is read as "the variable pointed to by `num_addr` (from the `*num_addr` in the declaration) is an integer."

Notice that the declaration `int *num_addr;` specifies two things: first, that the variable pointed to by `num_addr` is an integer; second, that `num_addr` must be a pointer (because it is used with the indirection operator `*`). Similarly, if the pointer `tab_point` points to (contains the address of) a floating point number and `chr_point` points to a character variable, the required declarations for these pointers are

```
float *tab_point;
char *chr_point;
```

These last two declarations can be read as "the variable pointed to by `tab_point` is a float," and "the variable pointed to by `chr_point` is a char." Consider Program 3-7.

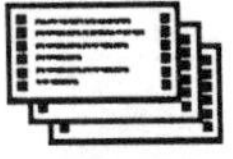

Program 3-7

```
main()
{
  int *num_addr;          /* declare a pointer to an int          */
  int miles,dist;         /* declare two integer variables        */
  dist = 158;             /* store the number 158 into dist       */
```

continued

```
    miles = 22;              /* store the number 22 into miles            */
    num_addr = &miles;       /* store 'address of miles' in num_addr      */

    printf("Address stored in num_addr is %u\n",num_addr);
    printf("Value pointed to by num_addr is %d\n\n",*num_addr);

    num_addr = &dist;        /* now store address of dist in num_addr */
    printf("Address now stored in num_addr is %u\n",num_addr);
    printf("Value now pointed to by num_addr is %d\n",*num_addr);
}
```

The output of Program 3-7 is:

```
The address stored in num_addr is 65460
The value pointed to by num_addr is 22

The address now stored in num_addr is 65462
The value now pointed to by num_addr is 158
```

The only value of Program 3-7 is in helping us understand what gets stored where. Let's review the program to see how the output was produced.

The declaration statement `int *num_addr;` declares `num_addr` to be a pointer variable used to store the address of an integer variable. The statement `num_addr = &miles;` stores the address of the variable `miles` into the pointer `num_addr`. The first call to `printf()` causes this address to be displayed. Notice that we have again used the control sequence `%u` to print out the address. The second call to `printf()` in Program 3-7 uses the indirection operator to retrieve and print out the "value pointed to by `num_addr`," which is, of course, the value stored in `miles`.

Since `num_addr` has been declared to be a pointer to an integer variable, we can use this pointer to store the address of any integer variable. The statement `num_addr = &dist` illustrates this by storing the address of the variable `dist` in `num_addr`. The last two `printf()` calls verify the change in `num_addr`'s value and that the new stored address points to the variable `dist`. As illustrated in Program 3-7, only addresses should be stored in pointers.

It certainly would have been much simpler if the pointer used in Program 3-7 could have been declared as `point num_addr;`. Such a declaration, however, conveys no information as to the storage used by the variable whose address is stored in `num_addr`. This information is essential when the pointer is used with the indirection operator, as it is in the second `printf()` call in Program 3-7. For example, if the address of an integer is stored in `num_addr`, only two bytes of storage are typically retrieved when the address is used; if the address

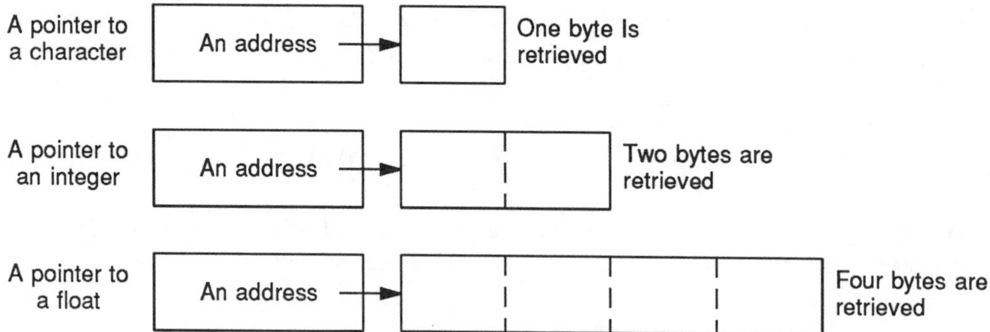

FIGURE 3-9 Addressing Different Data Types Using Pointers

of a character is stored in `num_addr`, only one byte of storage is retrieved; and a floating point number typically requires the retrieval of four bytes of storage. The declaration of a pointer must, therefore, include the type of variable being pointed to. Figure 3-9 illustrates this concept.

3.3 The `scanf()` Function

Data for programs that are going to be executed only once can be included directly in the program. For example, if we wanted to multiply the numbers 300.0 and .05, we could use Program 3-8.

Program 3-8

```
main()
{
  float num1,num2,product;

  num1 = 300.0;
  num2 = .05;
  product = num1 * num2;
  printf("%f times %f is %f", num1, num2, product);
}
```

The output displayed by Program 3-8 is:

```
300.000000 times .050000 is 15.000000
```

Program 3-8 can be shortened, as illustrated in Program 3-9. Both programs, however, suffer from the same basic problem in that they must be rewritten in order to multiply different numbers. Neither program can accept data values other than those originally entered.

Except for the practice provided to the programmer in writing, entering, and running the program, programs that do the same calculation only once, on the same set of numbers, are clearly not very useful. After all, it is simpler to use a calculator to multiply two numbers than enter and run either Programs 3-8 or 3-9.

Program 3-9

```
main()
{
  printf("%f times %f is %f", 300.0, .05, 300.0*.05);
}
```

This section presents the `scanf()` function, which is used to enter data into a program while it is executing. Just as the `printf()` function displays a copy of the value stored inside a variable, the `scanf()` function allows the user to enter a value at the terminal. The value is then stored directly in a variable.

Like the `printf()` function, the `scanf()` function requires a control string as the first argument inside the function name parentheses. The control string tells the function the type of data being input and uses the same control sequences as the `printf()` function. Unlike the control string used in a `printf()` function, however, the control string passed to `scanf()` cannot contain a message. Also, unlike `printf()`, where a list of variable names can follow the control string, `scanf()` requires that a list of variable addresses follow the control string. For example, the statement `scanf("%d", &num1);` is a call to the `scanf()` function. The control sequence `%d` is identical to the control sequence used in `printf()` in that it tells the `scanf()` function that it will be dealing with an integer number. The address operator, `&`, in front of the variable `num1` is required for `scanf()`. Recall from Section 3.2 that `&num1` is read as "the address of `num1`."

When a statement such as `scanf("%d",&num1);` is encountered, the computer stops program execution and continuously scans the keyboard for data (`scanf` is short for scan function). When a data item is typed, the `scanf()` function stores the item, using the address it was given. The program then continues execution with the next statement after the call to `scanf()`. To see this, consider Program 3-10.

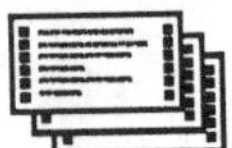

Program 3-10

```
main()
{
  float num1, num2, product;

  printf("Please type in a number: ");
  scanf("%f",&num1);
  printf("Please type in another number: ");
  scanf("%f",&num2);
  product = num1 * num2;
  printf("\n%f times %f is %f",num1,num2,product);
}
```

The first call to `printf()` in Program 3-10 prints a message that tells the person at the terminal what should be typed. In this case, the user is told to type a number. The computer then executes the next statement, which is a call to `scanf()`. The `scanf()` function puts the computer into a temporary pause (or wait) state. The user then types a value and signals the `scanf()` function that a value is available by pressing the return key. The entered value is stored in the variable whose address was passed to `scanf()`, and the computer is taken out of its paused state. Program execution then proceeds with the next statement, which in Program 3-10 is another call to `printf()`. This call causes the next message to be displayed. The second call to `scanf()` again puts the computer into a temporary wait state while the user types a second value. This second number is stored in the variable `num2`.

The following sample run was made by using Program 3-10.

```
Please type in a number: 300.
Please type in another number: .05

300.000000 times .050000 is 15.000000
```

In Program 3-10, each call to `scanf()` is used to store one value in a variable. The `scanf()` function, however, can be used to enter and store as many values as there are control sequences in the control string. For example, the statement

```
scanf("%f %f",&num1,&num2);
```

results in two values being read from the terminal and assigned to the variables `num1` and `num2`. If the data entered at the terminal were

```
0.052 245.79
```

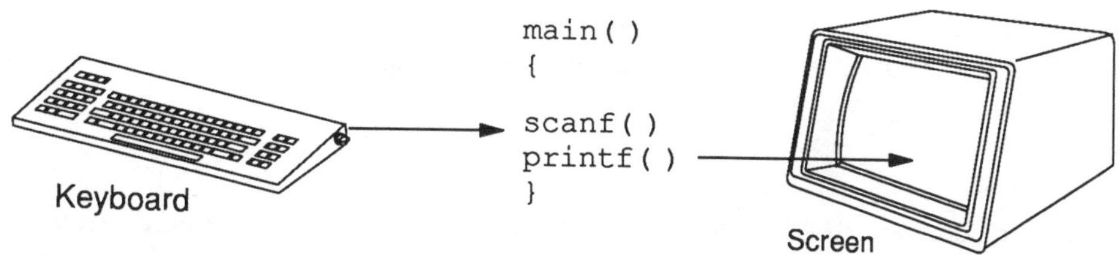

FIGURE 3-12 scanf() Is Used to Enter Data; printf() Is Used to Display Data

the variables num1 and num2 would contain the values 0.052 and 245.79, respectively. The space in the control string between the two conversion sequences, "%f %f", is strictly for readability. The control string"%f%f" would work equally well. When actually entering numbers such as 0.052 and 245.79, however, you must leave at least one space between the numbers, regardless of which control string,"%f %f" or "%f%f", is used. The space between the entered numbers clearly indicates where one number ends and the next begins. Inserting more than one space between numbers has no effect on scanf().

The only time that a space can affect the value being entered is when scanf() is expecting a character data type. For example, the statement scanf("%c%c%c",&ch1,&ch2,&ch3); causes scanf() to store the next three characters typed in the variables ch1, ch2 and ch3, respectively. If you type x y z, the x is stored in ch1, a blank is stored in ch2, and y is stored in ch3. If, however, the statement scanf("%c %c %c",&ch1,&ch2,&ch3); was used, scanf() looks for three characters separated by exactly one space.

Any number of scanf() function calls can be made in a program, and any number of values can be input with a single scanf() function. Just be sure that a control sequence is used for each value to be entered and that the address operator is used in front of the variable name in which the value is to be stored. The control sequences used in a scanf() control string are the same as used in printf() calls, with one exception. When using printf() to print a double precision number, the control sequence for a floating point variable, %f, can be used. This is not true when using scanf(): If a double precision number is to be entered, the conversion sequence %lf must be used.

The scanf() function, again like the printf() function, does not test the data type of the values being entered. It is up to the user to ensure that all variables are declared correctly and that any numbers entered are of the correct type. However, scanf() is intelligent enough to make a few data type conversions. For example, if an integer is entered in place of a floating point or double precision number, the scanf() function automatically adds a decimal point at the end of the integer before storing the number. Similarly, if a floating point or double precision number is entered when an integer is expected, the scanf() function uses only the integer part of the number. For example, assume that the following numbers are typed in response to the function call `scanf("%f %d %f",&num1,&num2,&num3);` where `num1` and `num3` are floating point variables and `num2` is an integer variable:

```
56   22.879   33.923
```

`scanf()` converts the `56` to `56.0` and stores this value in the variable num1. The function continues scanning the input, expecting an integer value. As far as `scanf()` is concerned, the decimal point after the `22` in the number `22.879` indicates the end of an integer and the start of a decimal number. Thus, the number `22` is stored in `num2`. Continuing to scan the typed input, `scanf()` takes the `.879` as the next floating point number and stores this value in `num3`. As far as `scanf()` is concerned, the `33.923` is extra input and is ignored. If, however, you do not initially type enough data, the `scanf()` function will continue to make the computer pause until sufficient data has been entered.

3.4 scanf() with Buffered Input

Seemingly strange results are sometimes obtained when the `scanf()` function is used to accept characters. To see how this can occur, consider Program 3-11, which uses `scanf()` to accept the next character entered at the keyboard and to store the character in the variable `fkey`.

Program 3-11

```
main()
{
  char fkey;

  printf("Type in a character: ");
  scanf("%c", &fkey);
  printf("The key just accepted is %d", fkey);
}
```

When Program 3-11 is run, the character entered in response to the prompt `Type in a character:` is stored in the character variable `fkey` and the decimal code for the character is displayed by the last `printf()` function call. The following sample run illustrates this:

```
Type in a character: m
The key just accepted is 109
```

At this point, everything seems to be working just fine, although you might be wondering why we displayed the decimal value of m rather than the character itself. The reason for this will soon become apparent.

In typing the m, two keys are usually pressed — the m key and the ENTER key. On most computer systems, these two characters are stored in a temporary holding area called a *buffer* immediately after they are pressed, as illustrated on Figure 3-13.

The first key pressed, m in this case, is taken from the buffer and stored in fkey. This, however, still leaves the code for the ENTER key in the buffer. Any subsequent call to scanf() for a character input will automatically pick up the code for the ENTER key as the next character. For example, consider Program 3-12.

Program 3-12

```
main()
{
  char fkey, skey;

  printf("Type in a character: ");
  scanf("%c", &fkey);
  printf("The key just accepted is %d", fkey);
  printf("\nType in another character: ");
  scanf("%c", &skey);
  printf("The key just accepted is %d", skey);
}
```

The following is a sample run for Program 3-12.

```
Type in a character: m
The key just accepted is 109
Type in another character: The key just accepted is 10
```

FIGURE 3-13 Typed Keyboard Characters Are First Stored in a Buffer

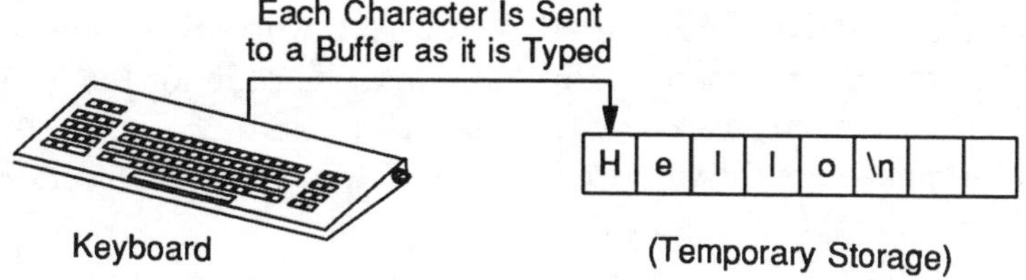

Let us review what has happened. In entering m in response to the first prompt, the ENTER key is also pressed. From a character standpoint, this represents the entry of two distinct characters. The first character is m, which is stored as a 109. The second character also gets stored in the buffer with the numerical code for the ENTER key. The second call to scanf() picks up this code immediately, without waiting for any additional key to be pressed. The last call to printf() displays the code for this key. The reason for displaying the numerical code rather than the character itself is because the ENTER key has no printable character associated with it that can be displayed.

Remember that every key has a numerical code, including the ENTER, SPACE, ESCAPE, and CONTROL keys. These keys generally have no effect when entering numbers, because scanf() ignores them as leading or trailing input with numerical data. Nor do these keys affect the entry of a single character requested as the first user data to be input, as is the case in Program 3-11. Only when a character is requested after the user has already input some other data, as Program 3-12, does the usually invisible ENTER key become noticeable.

There is a quick way to avoid having the ENTER key accepted as a legitimate character input. All we have to do is accept the ENTER key, store it as a character variable, and then just not use it. Program 3-13 illustrates this technique. The ENTER key is accepted along with the first character typed. This clears the computer's buffer and prepares the way for the character input.

Program 3-13

```
main()
{
  char fkey, skey;

  printf("Type in a character: ");
  scanf("%c%c", &fkey, &skey);     /* the enter code goes to skey */
  printf("The key just accepted is %d", fkey);
  printf("\nType in another character: ");
  scanf("%c", &skey);              /* accept another code          */
  printf("The key just accepted is %d", skey);
}
```

In reviewing Program 3-13, observe that the first scanf() function call accepts two back-to-back characters. Now, when the user types an m and presses the ENTER key, the m is assigned to fkey and the code for the ENTER key is automatically assigned to skey. The next call to scanf() stores the code for the next key pressed in the variable skey also. This automatically erases the code for the ENTER key that was previously stored there. From the user's standpoint, the ENTER key has no effect except to signal the end of each character input. The following is a sample run for Program 3-13.

```
Type in a character: m
The key just accepted is 109
Type in another character: b
The key just accepted is 98
```

The solution to the phantom ENTER key used in Program 3-13 is not the only solution possible (there is never just one way of doing something in C). All solutions, however, center on the fact that the ENTER key is a legitimate character input and must be treated as such when using a buffered system.

3.5 Named Constants

Literal data is any data within a program that explicitly identifies itself. For example, the constants 2 and 3.1416 in the assignment statement

```
circum = 2 * 3.1416 * radius;
```

are also called *literals* because they are included literally in the statement. Additional examples of literals are contained in the following C assignment statements. See if you can identify them.

```
perimeter = 2 * length * width;
y = (5 * p) / 7.2;
salestax = 0.05 * purchase;
```

The literals are the numbers `2`, `5` and `7.2`, and `0.05` in the first, second, and third statements, respectively.

Quite frequently, the same literal appears many times in the same program. For example, in a program used to determine bank interest charges, the interest rate would typically appear in a number of different places throughout the program. Similarly, in a program used to calculate taxes, the tax rate might appear in many individual instructions. If either the interest rate or sales tax rate changes, as rates are prone to do, the programmer would have the cumbersome task of changing the literal value everywhere it appears in the program. Multiple changes, however, are subject to error — if just one rate value were overlooked and not changed, the result obtained when the program is run would be incorrect. Literal values that appear many times in the same program are referred to by programmers as *magic numbers.* By themselves, the numbers are quite ordinary, but in the context of a particular application they have a special ("magical") meaning.

To avoid the problem of having a magic number spread throughout a program in many places, C provides the programmer with the capability of defining the value once, by equating the number to a *symbolic name.* Then, instead of using the number throughout the program, the symbolic name is used instead. If the number ever has to be changed, the change need be made only once at the point where the symbolic name is equated to the actual number value. Equating numbers to symbolic names is done by using a `#define` statement. Two such statements are:

```
define SALESTAX 0.05 <——— no semicolon
define PI 3.1416 <———— no semicolon
```

These two statements are called either `#define` or *equivalence* statements. The first `#define` statement equates the value `0.05` to the symbolic name `SALESTAX`, while the second `#define` statement equates the number `3.1416` to the symbolic name `PI`. Other terms for symbolic names are *named constants* or *symbolic constants.* We shall use these terms interchangeably.

Although we have typed the named constants in uppercase letters, lowercase letters could have been used. It is common in C, however, to use uppercase letters for named constants. Then, whenever a programmer sees uppercase letters in a program, he or she will know the name is a named constant defined in a `#define` statement, not a variable name declared in a declaration statement.

The named constants defined above can be used in any C statement in place of the numbers they represent. For example, the assignment statements

```
circum = 2 * PI * radius;
amount = SALESTAX * purchase;
```

are both valid. These statements must, of course, appear after the definitions of the named constants. Usually, all `#define` statements are placed at the top of a file, before any functions, including `main()`, are typed. Program 3-14 illustrates the use of such a `#define` statement.

The following sample run was made using Program 3-14.

```
Enter the amount purchased: 36.00
The sales tax is $1.80
The total bill is $37.80
```

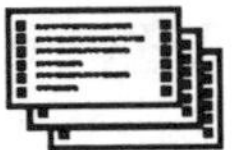

Program 3-14

```
#define SALESTAX 0.05
main()
{
  float amount, taxes, total;

  printf("Enter the amount purchased: ");
  scanf("%f",&amount);
  taxes = SALESTAX * amount;
  total = amount + taxes;
  printf("The sales tax is $%4.2f",taxes);
  printf("\nThe total bill is $%5.2f",total);
}
```

Whenever a named constant appears in an instruction, it has the same effect as if the literal value it represents were used. Thus, `SALESTAX` is simply another way of representing the value `0.05`. Since `SALESTAX` and the number `0.05` are equivalent, the value of `SALESTAX` cannot be subsequently changed by the program. An instruction such as `SALESTAX = 0.06;` is meaningless, because `SALESTAX` is not a variable. Since `SALESTAX` is only a stand-in for the value `0.05`, this statement is equivalent to writing the invalid statement `0.05 = 0.06;`.

Notice also that `#define` statements do not end with a semicolon. The reason for this is that `#define` statements are not processed by the regular C compiler used to translate C statements into machine language. The # sign is a signal to a C *preprocessor*. This preprocessor screens all program statements when a C program is compiled. When the preprocessor encounters a # sign, it recognizes an instruction to itself. The word `define` tells the preprocessor to equate the symbolic constant in the statement with the information or data following it. In the case of a statement like `#define SALESTAX 0.05`, the word `SALESTAX` is equated to the value `0.05`. The preprocessor then replaces each subsequent occurrence of the word `SALESTAX` in the C program with the value `0.05`.

This explains why a `#define` statement does not end with a semicolon. If a semicolon followed the literal value `0.05`, the preprocessor would equate the word `SALESTAX` with `0.05;`. Then, when it replaced `SALESTAX` in the assignment statement `taxes = SALESTAX * amount;`, the statement would become `taxes = 0.05; * amount;`, which is the valid statement `taxes = 0.05;` followed by the invalid statement `* amount;`.

Realizing that #define statements simply relate two items allows us to use them to create individualized programming languages. For example, the #define statements

```
#define BEGIN {
#define END }
```

equates the first brace { to the word BEGIN and the closing brace } to the word END. Once these symbols are equated, the words BEGIN and END can be used in place of the respective braces. This is illustrated in Program 3-15.

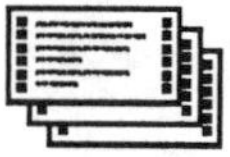

Program 3-15

```
#define SALESTAX 0.05
#define BEGIN {
#define END }
main()
BEGIN
  float amount, taxes, total;

  printf("\nEnter in the amount purchased: ");
  scanf("%f",&amount);
  taxes = SALESTAX * amount;
  total = amount + taxes;
  printf("The sales tax is $%4.2f",taxes);
  printf("\nThe total bill is $%5.2f",total);
END
```

When Program 3-15 is compiled, the preprocessor faithfully replaces all occurrences of the word BEGIN and END with their equivalent symbols. Although using #define statements to create a new set of symbols equivalent to the standard C symbol set is usually not a good idea, Program 3-15 should give you an idea of the richness and diversity that C provides. Generally, the constructions that can be created in C are limited only by the imagination and good sense of the programmer.

3.6 Common Programming Errors

In using the material presented in this chapter, be aware of the following possible errors:

1. Forgetting to assign initial values to all variables before the variables are used in an expression. Initial values can be assigned when the variables are declared either by explicit assignment statements or by interactively entering values with the `scanf()` function.
2. Applying either the increment or decrement operator to an expression. For example, the expression

   ```
   (count + n)++
   ```

   is incorrect. The increment and decrement operators can be applied only to individual variables.
3. Attempting to store an address in a variable that has not been declared as a pointer.
4. Forgetting to pass addresses to `scanf()`. Since `scanf()` treats all arguments following the control string as addresses, it is up to the programmer to ensure that addresses are passed correctly.
5. Including a message within the control string passed to `scanf()`. Unlike `printf()`, `scanf()`'s control string must contain only control sequences.
6. Not including the correct control sequences in `scanf()` function calls for the data values that must be entered.
7. Not closing off the control string passed to `scanf()` with a double quotation mark followed by a comma, and forgetting to separate all arguments passed to `scanf()` with commas.
8. Terminating a `#define` command to the preprocessor with a semicolon. By now, you probably end every line in your C programs with a semicolon, almost automatically. But there are cases, for example preprocessor commands, where a semicolon should not end a line.

A more exotic and less common error occurs when the increment and decrement operators are used with variables that appear more than once in the same expression. Although the cause of this error is explained in more detail later, in Chapter 14, this error basically occurs because C does not specify the order in which operands are accessed within an expression. For example, the value assigned to `result` in the statement

```
result = i + i++;
```

is computer-dependent. If your computer accesses the first operand, `i`, first, the above statement is equivalent to

```
result = 2 * i;
i++;
```

However, if your computer accesses the second operand, `i++`, first, the value of the first operand is altered before it is used and a different value is assigned to `result`. As a general rule, therefore, do not use either the increment or decrement operator in an expression when the variable it operates on appears more than once in the expression.

3.7 Chapter Summary

1. An expression is a sequence of one or more operands separated by operators. An operand is a constant, a variable, or another expression. A value is associated with an expression.
2. Expressions are evaluated according to the precedence and associativity of the operators used in the expression.
3. The assignment symbol, `=`, is an operator. Expressions using this operator assign a value to a variable; additionally, the expression itself takes on a value. Since assignment is an operation in C, multiple uses of the assignment operator are possible in the same expression.
4. The increment operator, `++`, adds one to a variable, while the decrement operator, `--`, subtracts one from a variable. Both of these operators can be used as prefixes or postfixes. In prefix operation, the variable is incremented (or decremented) before its value is used. In postfix operation, the variable is incremented (or decremented) after its value is used.
5. All variables have an `lvalue` and an `rvalue`. The `lvalue` is the address of the variable and the `rvalue` is the contents of the variable. Programmers typically use variable names to reference the variable's contents (its `rvalue`) while computers typically use a variable's name to reference its address (`lvalue`). The address operator, `&`, can be used to obtain a variable's `lvalue`.
6. A pointer is a variable that is used to store the address of another variable. Pointers, like all C variables, must be declared. The indirection operator, `*`, is used both to declare a pointer variable and to access the variable whose address is stored in a pointer.

7. The `scanf()` function is a standard library function used for data input. `scanf()` requires a control string and a list of addresses. The general form of this function call is

```
scanf("control string", &arg1, &arg2, ... , &argn);
```

The control string can contain only control sequences, such as `%d`, and must contain the same number of control sequences as argument addresses.
8. Each complied C program is automatically passed through a preprocessor. Lines beginning with a # in the first column are recognized as commands to this preprocessor. Preprocessor commands are not terminated with a semicolon.
9. Expressions can be made equivalent to a single identifier by using the preprocessor define command. This command has the form

`#define` *identifier expression*

and allows the identifier to be used instead of the expression anywhere in the program after the command. Generally, a `define` command is placed at the top of a C program.

Sample Problem

For this sample problem, we will write a program that displays the prompt:

```
Enter the temperature in degrees Celsius:
```

and then accepts the value entered by the user. The program converts the entered value to an equivalent Fahrenheit value and displays the two temperatures. The program is:

```
main()
{
  float fahren, celsus;
  printf("Enter the temperature in degree Celsius: ");
  scanf("%f", &celsus);
  fahren = (9.0/5.0)*celsus + 32.0;
  printf("\n%5.2f degrees Celsius is %5.2f degrees
           Fahrenheit", celsius, fahren);
}
```

The body of the `main()` function begins by declaring the two variables `fahren` and `celsus`. The required prompt is displayed by using the first call to the `printf()` function, and the value typed by the user is accepted by the `scanf()` function. Notice that the `scanf()` function requires that the address operator be used in front of the variable's name. The entered value is then used in the assignment statement to calculate the value of the variable `fahren`. Finally, both Celsius and Fahrenheit values are displayed by using the last `printf()` function call. A trial run of this program with a response of `100` produces the following output:

```
Enter the temperature in degree Celsius: 100

100.00 degrees Celsius is 212.00 degrees Fahrenheit
```

Flow of Control

Part Two

Selection

Chapter Four

The term *flow of control* refers to the order in which a program's statements are executed. Unless directed otherwise, the normal flow of control for all programs is *sequential*. This means that each statement is executed in sequence, one after another, in the order in which they are placed within the program.

Both selection and repetition statements allow the programmer to alter the normal sequential flow of control. As their names imply, *selection statements* provide the ability to select which statement will be executed next, while *repetition statements* provide the ability to go back and repeat a set of statements. In this chapter, we present C's selection statements. Since selection requires choosing between alternatives, we begin this chapter with a description of C's selection criteria.

4.1 Relational Expressions

Besides providing addition, subtraction, multiplication, and division capabilities, all computers have the ability to compare numbers. Because many intelligent decision-making situations can be reduced to the level of choosing between two values, a computer's comparison capability remarkably mimicks human intelligence.

The expressions used to compare operands are called *relational expressions*. A *simple* relational expression consists of a relational operator connecting two variable and/or constant operands, as shown in Figure 4-1. The relational operators available in C are given in Table 4-1. These relational operators can be used with integer, floating point, double precision, or character data, but must be typed exactly as given in Table 4-1. Thus, while the following examples are all valid:

```
age > 40        length <= 50      temp > 98.6
3 < 4           flag == done      id_num == 682
day != 5        2.0 > 3.3         hours > 40
```

the following are invalid:

```
length =< 50        /* operator out of order  */
2.0 >> 3.3          /* invalid operator       */
flag = = done       /* spaces are not allowed */
```

FIGURE 4-1 Anatomy of a Simple Relational Expression

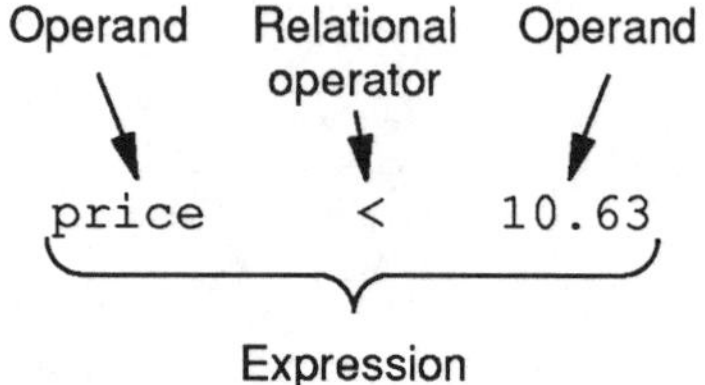

TABLE 4-1 Relational Operators in C

Relational operator	Meaning	Example
<	less than	`age < 30`
>	greater than	`height > 6.2`
<=	less than or equal to	`taxable <= 20000`
>=	greater than or equal to	`temp >= 98.6`
==	equal to	`grade == 100`
!=	not equal to	`number != 250`

Relational expressions are sometimes called *conditions,* and we will use both terms to refer to these expressions. Like all C expressions, relational expressions are evaluated to yield a numerical result. In the case of relational expressions, the value of the expression can only be an integer value of 1 or 0. A condition that we would interpret as *true* evaluates to an integer value of 1, and a *false* condition results in an integer value of 0. For example, because the relationship 3 < 4 is always true, this expression has a value of 1, and because the relationship 2.0 > 3.3 is always false, the value of the expression itself is 0. This can be verified by using the statements

```
printf("The value of 3 < 4 is %d", 3 < 4);
printf("\nThe value of 2.0 > 3.0 is %d, 2.0 > 3.3);
```

which result in the display

```
The value of 3 < 4 is 1
The value of 2.0 > 3.0 is 0
```

The value of a relational expression such as `hours > 0` depends on the value stored in the variable `hours`.

In a C program, a relational expression's value is not as important as the interpretation C places on the value when the expression is used as part of a selection statement. In these statements, which are presented in the next section, we will see that a zero value is used by C to represent a false condition and any nonzero value is used to represent a true condition. The selection of which statement to execute next is then based on the value obtained.

In addition to numerical operands, character data can also be compared by using relational operators. Comparing letters is essential in alphabetizing names or using characters to select a particular option in decision-making situations. For example, in the ASCII code the letter `A` is stored by using a code having a lower numerical value than the letter `B`, the code for a `B` is lower in value than the code for a `C`, and so on. For character sets coded in this manner, the following conditions are evaluated as listed on the following page.

Expression	Value	Interpretation
'A' > 'C'	0	False
'D' <= 'Z'	1	True
'E' == 'F'	0	False
'G' >= 'M'	0	False
'B' != 'C'	1	True

Logical Operators

In addition to using simple relational expressions as conditions, more complex conditions can be created by using the *logical operators* `AND`, `OR`, and `NOT`. These operators are represented by the symbols `&&`, `||`, and `!`, respectively.

When the `AND` operator, `&&`, is used with two simple expressions, the condition is true only if both single expressions are true by themselves. Thus, the compound condition

```
age > 40 && term < 10
```

is true (has a value of 1) only if `age` is greater than `40` and `term` is less than `10`.

The logical `OR` operator, `||`, is also applied between two expressions. When using the `OR` operator, the condition is satisfied if either one or both of the two expressions is true. Thus, the compound condition

```
age > 40 || term < 10
```

is true if either `age` is greater than `40`, `term` is less than `10`, or both conditions are true.

For the declarations

```
int i,j;
float a,b,complete;
```

the following represent valid conditions:

```
a > b
i == j || a < b || complete
a/b > 5 && i <= 20
```

Before these conditions can be evaluated, the values of `a`, `b`, `i`, `j`, and `complete` must be known. Assuming

`a = 12.0,`   `b = 2.0,`   `i= 15,`   `j = 30,`   and   `complete = 0.0`

the previous expressions yield the following results:

Expression	Value	Interpretation
`a > b`	1	True
`i == j || a < b || complete`	0	False
`a/b > 5 && i <= 20`	1	True

The NOT operator is used to change an expression to its opposite state; that is, if the expression has any nonzero value (true), !*expression* produces a zero value (false). If an expression is false to begin with (has a 0 value), !*expression* is true and evaluates to a 1. For example, assuming that the number 26 is stored in the variable age, the expression age > 40 has a value of 0 (it is false), while the expression !(age > 40) has a value of 1. Since the NOT operator is used with only one expression, it is a unary operator.

The relational and logical operators have a hierarchy of execution similar to the arithmetic operators. Table 4-2 lists the precedence of these operators in relation to the other operators we have used.

TABLE 4-2 Operator Precedence

Operator	Associativity
`! unary - ++ --`	right to left
`* / %`	left to right
`+ -`	left to right
`< <= > >=`	left to right
`== !=`	left to right
`&&`	left to right
`||`	left to right
`+= -= *= /=`	right to left

The following examples illustrate the use of an operator's precedence and associativity to evaluate relational expressions if we assume the following declarations:

```
char key = 'm';
int i = 5, j = 7, k = 12;
double x = 22.5;
```

The expressions are evaluated as:

Expression	Equivalent Expression	Value	Interpretation
`i + 2 == k - 1`	`(i + 2) == (k - 1)`	0	False
`3 * i - j < 22`	`((3 * i) - j) < 22`	1	True

continued

Expression	Equivalent Expression	Value	Interpretation
`i + 2 * j > k`	`(i + (2 * j)) > k`	1	True
`k + 3 <= -j + 3 * i`	`(k + 3) <= ((-j) + (3 * i))`	0	False
`'a' + 1 == 'b'`	`('a' + 1) == 'b'`	1	True
`key - 1 > 'p'`	`(key - 1) > 'p'`	0	False
`key + 1 == 'n'`	`(key + 1) == 'n'`	1	True
`25 >= x + 4.0`	`25 >= (x + 4.0)`	0	False

As with all expressions, parentheses can be used to alter the assigned operator priority and improve the readability of relational expressions. By evaluating the expressions within parentheses first, the following compound condition is evaluated as:

```
(6 * 3 == 36 / 2) || (13 < 3 * 3 + 4) && !(6 - 2 < 5)
        (18 == 18) ||    (13 < 9 + 4)    && !(4 < 5)
                 1 ||     (13 < 13)      && !1
                 1 ||         0          && 0
                 1 ||         0
                 1
```

4.2 The `if-else` Statement

The `if-else` statement directs the computer to select a sequence of one or more instructions on the basis of the results of a comparison. For example, let us assume that if a person's income is less than 20,000, the applicable state tax rate is 2 percent, and that if the person's income is greater than $20,000, a different rate is applied to the amount over $20,000. The `if-else` statement can be used in this situation to determine the actual tax, according to whether the gross income is less than or equal to $20,000. The general form of the `if-else` statement is

```
if (expression) statement1;
else statement2;
```

The expression is evaluated first. If the value of the expression is nonzero, *`statement1`* is executed. If the value is zero, the statement after the reserved word `else` is executed. Thus, one of the two statements (either *`statement1`* or *`statement2`*) is always executed, depending on the value of the expression. Notice that the tested expression must be put in parentheses and a semicolon placed after each statement.

For clarity, the if-else statement can also be written on four lines, using the form

```
if (expression) ←——— no semicolon here
  statement1;
else ←———————————— no semicolon here
  statement2;
```

The form of the if-else statement that is selected generally depends on the length of *statement 1* and *2*. However, when using the second form, do not put a semicolon after the parentheses or the reserved word else. The semicolons go only at the ends of the statements.

As an example, let us write an income tax computation program containing an if-else statement. As previously described, a state income tax is assessed at 2 percent of taxable income for incomes less than or equal to $20,000. For taxable income greater than $20,000, state taxes are 2.5 percent of the income that exceeds $20,000 plus a fixed amount of $400. The expression to be tested is whether taxable income is less than or equal to $20,000. An appropriate if-else statement for this situation is:

```
if (taxable <= 20000.0)
  taxes = .02 * taxable;
else
  taxes = .025 * (taxable - 20000.0) + 400.0;
```

Here, we have used the relational operator <= to represent the relation "less than or equal to." If the value of taxable is less than or equal to 20000, the

Program 4-1

```
main()
{
  float taxable, taxes;

  printf("Please type in the taxable income: ");
  scanf("%f",&taxable);

  if (taxable <= 20000.0)
    taxes = .02 * taxable;
  else
  taxes = .025 * (taxable - 20000.0) + 400.0;

  printf("&nTaxes are $%7.2f",taxes);
}
```

condition is true (has a value of 1) and the statement `taxes = .02 * taxable;` is executed. If the condition is not true, the value of the expression is 0, and the statement after the reserved word `else` is executed. Program 4-1 illustrates the use of this statement in a complete program.

A blank line was inserted before and after the `if-else` statement to highlight it in the complete program. We will continue to do this throughout the text to emphasize the statement being presented.

To illustrate selection in action, Program 4-1 was run twice with different input data. The results are:

```
Please type in the taxable income: 10000.
Taxes are $ 200.00
```

and

```
Please type in the taxable income: 30000.
Taxes are $ 650.00
```

Observe that the taxable income input in the first run of the program was less than $20,000, and the tax was correctly calculated as 2 percent of the number entered. In the second run, the taxable income was more than $20,000, and the `else` part of the `if-else` statement was used to yield a correct tax computation of

```
.025 * (30000. - 20000.) + 400. = 650.
```

Although any expression can be tested by an `if-else` statement, generally only relational expressions are used. However, statements such as

```
if (num)
  printf("Bingo!");
else
  printf("You lose!");
```

are valid. Since `num`, by itself, is a valid expression, the message `Bingo!` is displayed if `num` has any nonzero value and the message `You lose!` is displayed if `num` has a value of zero.

Compound Statements

Although only a single statement is permitted in both the `if` and `else` parts of the `if-else` statement, this statement can be a single compound statement. A *compound statement* is any number of single statements contained between braces, as shown in Figure 4-2. The use of braces to enclose a set of individual statements creates a single block of statements, which can be used anywhere in a C program in place of a single statement.

```
{
  statement1;
  statement2;
  statement3;
      •
      •
      •
  last statement;
}
```

FIGURE 4-2 A Compound Statement Consists of Individual Statements Enclosed Within Braces

The next example illustrates the use of two compound statements within the general form of an `if-else` statement.

```
if (expression)
{
 statement1;      /* as many statements as necessary  */
 statement2;      /*  can be put within the braces    */
 statement3;      /* each statement must end with a ; */
}
else
{
 statement4;
 statement5;
      .
      .
 statementn;
}
```

Program 4-2 illustrates the use of a compound statements in an actual program.

Program 4-2

```
main()
{
  char temp_type;
  float temp, fahren, celsius;

  printf("Enter the temperature to be converted: ");
  scanf("%f",&temp);
```

continued

```
    printf("Enter an f if the temperature is in Fahrenheit");
    printf("\n or a c if the temperature is in Celsius: ");
    scanf("%c",&temp_type);

    if (temp_type == 'f')
    {
    celsius = (5.0 / 9.0) * (temp - 32.0);
    printf("\nThe equivalent Celsius temperature is %6.2f",  celsius);
    }
    else
    {
    fahren =  (9.0 / 5.0) * temp + 32.0;
    printf("\nThe equivalent Fahrenheit temperature is %6.2f", fahren);
    }
}
```

Program 4-2 checks whether the value in `temp_type` is an `f`. If the value is `f`, the compound statement corresponding to the `if` part of the `if-else` statement is executed. Any other letter results in execution of the compound statement corresponding to the `else` part. Following is a sample run of Program 4-2:

```
Enter the temperature to be converted: 212
Enter an f if the temperature is in Fahrenheit
 or a c if the temperature is in Celsius: f

The equivalent Celsius temperature is 100.00
```

One-Way Selection

A useful modification of the `if-else` statement involves omitting the `else` part of the statement altogether. In this case, the `if` statement takes the shortened and frequently useful form:

```
if (expression)
  statement;
```

The statement following the `if` (*expression*) is only executed if the expression has a nonzero value (a true condition). As before, the statement may be a compound statement.

This modified form of the `if` statement is called a *one-way* `if` *statement*. It is illustrated in Program 4-3, which checks a car's mileage and prints a message if the car has been driven more than 3000.0 miles.

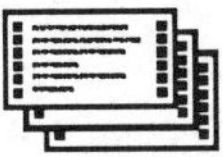

Program 4-3

```
#define LIMIT 3000.0
main()
{
  int id_num;
  float miles;

  printf("Please type in car number and mileage: ");
  scanf("%d %f", &id_num, &miles);

  if(miles > LIMIT)
    printf("  Car %d is over the limit.\n",id_num);

  printf("End of program output.");
}
```

To illustrate the one-way selection criteria in action, Program 4-3 was run twice, each time with different input data. Notice that only the input data for the first run causes the message `Car 256 is over the limit` to be displayed.

The first run displays:

```
Please type in car number and mileage: 256 3562.8
  Car 256 is over the limit.
End of program output.
```

and the second run displays:

```
Please type in car number and mileage: 23 2562.3
End of program output.
```

4.3 Nested `if` Statements

As we have seen, an `if-else` statement can contain simple or compound statements. Any valid C statement can be used, including another `if-else` statement. Thus, one or more `if-else` statements can be included within either part of an `if-else` statement. For example, substituting the one-way `if` statement

```
if (hours > 6)
printf("snap");
```

for *statement1* in the following if statement

```
if (hours < 9)
    statement1;
else
printf("pop");
```

results in the nested `if` statement

```
if (hours < 9)
{
  if (hours > 6)
   printf("snap");
}
else
  printf("pop");
```

The braces around the inner one-way `if` are essential because, in their absence, C associates an `else` with the closest unpaired `if`. Thus, without the braces, the above statement is equivalent to

```
if (hours < 9)
   if (hours > 6)
     printf("snap");
  else
     printf("pop");
```

Here, the `else` is paired with the inner `if`, which destroys the meaning of the original `if-else` statement. Notice also that the indentation is irrelevant as far as the compiler is concerned. Whether the indentation exists or not, the statement is compiled by associating the last `else` with the closest unpaired `if`, unless braces are used to alter the default pairing.

The process of *nesting* `if` statements can be extended indefinitely, so that the `printf("snap");` statement could itself be replaced by either a complete `if-else` statement or another one-way `if` statement.

The `if-else` Chain

Generally, using an `if` statement in the `if` part of an `if-else` statement is confusing and is best avoided. However, an extremely useful construction occurs when the `else` part of an `if` statement contains another `if-else` statement. This takes the form:

```
 if (expression_1)
   statement1;
else
    if (expression_2)
   satement2;
  else
   statement3;
```

As with all C programs, the indentation we have used is not required. In fact, the above construction is so common that it is typically written in the following arrangement:

```
if (expression_1)
  statement1;
else if (expression_2)
  statement2;
else
  statement3;
```

This construction is called an `if-else` *chain*. It is used extensively in applications programs. Each condition is evaluated in order and, if any condition is true the corresponding statement is executed and the remainder of the chain is terminated. The final `else` statement is executed only if none of the previous conditions are satisfied. This serves as a default or catch-all case that is useful for detecting an impossible or error condition.

The chain can be continued indefinitely by repeatedly making the last statement another `if-else` statement. Thus, the general form of an `if-else` chain is:

```
if (expression_1)
  statement1;
else if (expression_2)
  statement2;
else if (expression_3)
  statement3;
        .
        .
        .
else if (expression_n)
  statement_n;
else
  last_statement;
```

As with all C statements, each individual statement can be a compound statement bounded by braces. To illustrate the `if-else` chain, Program 4-4 displays a person's marital status, corresponding to a letter input. The following letter codes are used:

```
Married – M,   Single – S,   Divorced – D,   Widowed – W
```

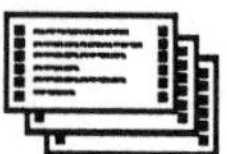

Program 4-4

```
main()
{
 char marcode;

   printf("Enter a marital code: ");
   scanf("%c", &marcode);

   if (marcode == 'M')
    printf("\nIndividual is married.");
   else if (marcode == 'S')
    printf("\nIndividual is single.");
   else if (marcode == 'D')
    printf("\nIndividual is divorced.");
   else if (marcode == 'W')
    printf("\nIndividual is widowed.");
   else
    printf("\nAn invalid code was entered.");
}
```

As a final example of the `if-else` chain, let us calculate the monthly income of a salesperson, using the following commission schedule.

Monthly Sales	Income
greater than or equal to $50,000	$375 plus 16% of sales
less than $50,000 but greater than or equal to $40,000	$350 plus 14% of sales
less than $40,000 but greater than or equal to $30,000	$325 plus 12% of sales
less than $30,000 but greater than or equal to $20,000	$300 plus 9% of sales
less than $20,000 but greater than or equal to $10,000	$250 plus 5% of sales
less than $10,000	$200 plus 3% of sales

The following `if-else` chain can be used to determine the correct monthly income, where the variable `mon_sales` is used to store the salesperson's current monthly sales:

```
if (mon_sales >= 50000.00)
  income = 375.00 + .16 * mon_sales;
```

continued

```
else if (mon_sales >= 40000.00)
  income = 350.00 + .14 * mon_sales;
else if (mon_sales >= 30000.00)
  income = 325.00 + .12 * mon_sales;
else if (mon_sales >= 20000.00)
  income = 300.00 + .09 * mon_sales;
else if (mon_sales >= 10000.00)
  income = 250.00 + .05 * mon_sales;
else
  income = 200.000 + .03 * mon_sales;
```

Notice that this example makes use of the fact that the chain is stopped once a true condition is found. This is accomplished by checking for the highest monthly sales first. If the salesperson's monthly sales is less than $50,000, the `if- else` chain continues checking for the next highest sales amount until the correct category is obtained.

Program 4-5 uses this `if-else` chain to calculate and display the income corresponding to the value of monthly sales input in the `scanf()` function.

Program 4-5

```
main()
{
  float mon_sales, income;

  printf("Enter the value of monthly sales: ");
  scanf("%f", &mon_sales);

  if (mon_sales >= 50000.00)
    income = 375.00 + .16 * mon_sales;
  else if (mon_sales >= 40000.00)
    income = 350.00 + .14 * mon_sales;
  else if (mon_sales >= 30000.00)
    income = 325.00 + .12 * mon_sales;
  else if (mon_sales >= 20000.00)
    income = 300.00 + .09 * mon_sales;
  else if (mon_sales >= 10000.00)
    income = 250.00 + .05 * mon_sales;
  else
    income = 200.000 + .03 * mon_sales;
  printf("\nThe income is $%7.2f",income);
}
```

A sample run using Program 4-5 is illustrated below.

```
Enter the value of monthly sales: 36243.89

The income is $4674.27
```

4.4 The switch Statement

The if-else chain is used in programming applications where one set of instructions must be selected from many possible alternatives. The switch statement provides an alternative to the if-else chain for cases that compare the value of an integer expression to a specific value. The general form of a switch statement is:

```
switch (expression)
{                            /* start of compound statement */
  case value_1:       <----      terminated with a colon
    statement1;
    statement2;
        .
        .
        .
    break;
  case value_2:       <----      terminated with a colon
    statementn;
    statement;
        .
        .
        .
    break;
        .
        .
        .
  case value_n:       <----      terminated with a colon
    statement_w;
    statement_x;
        .
        .
        .
  default:            <----      terminated with a colon
    statement_aa;
    statement_bb;
}                            /* start of compound statement */
```

The switch statement uses four new reserved words: switch, case, default, and break. Let us see what each of these words does.

The reserved word switch identifies the start of the switch statement. The expression in parentheses following this word is evaluated and the result of the expression compared to various alternative values contained within the compound statement. The expression in the switch statement must evaluate to an integer value or a compilation error results.

Inside the switch statement, the reserved word case is used to identify or label individual values that are compared to the value of the switch expression. The switch expression's value is compared to each of these case values in the order that they are listed until a match is found. When a match occurs, execution begins with the statement immediately following the match. As illustrated on Figure 4-3, the value of the expression determines where in the switch statement execution actually begins.

Any number of case labels can be contained within a switch statement, in any order. If the value of the expression does not match any of the case values, however, no statement is executed unless the reserved word default is encountered. The word default is optional and operates the same as the last else in an if-else chain. If the value of the expression does not match any of the case values, program execution begins with the statement following the word default.

Once an entry point has been located by the switch statement, no further case evaluations are done; all statements that follow within the braces are executed unless a break statement is encountered. This is the reason for the break statement, which identifies the end of a particular case and causes an immediate exit from the switch statement. Thus, just as the word case identifies possible starting points in the compound statement, the break statement determines terminating points. If the break statements are omitted, all cases following the matching case value, including the default case, are executed.

When we write a switch statement, we can use multiple case values to refer to the same set of statements; the default label is optional. For example, consider the following:

```
switch (number)
{
  case 1:
    printf("Have a Good Morning");
    break;
  case 2:
    printf("Have a Happy Day");
    break;
  case 3: case 4: case 5:
    printf("Have a Nice Evening");
}
```

If the value stored in the variable number is 1, the message Have a Good Morning is displayed. Similarly, if the value of number is 2, the second message is displayed. Finally, if the value of number is 3 or 4 or 5, the last message is displayed. Since the statement to be executed for these last three `cases` is the same, the `cases` for these values can be stacked together, as shown in the example. Also, since there is no `default`, no message is printed if the value of `number` is not one of the listed `case` values. Although it is good programming practice to list `case` values in increasing order, this is not required by the `switch` statement. A `switch` statement can have any number of `case` values, in any order; only the values being tested for need to be listed.

Program 4-6 uses a `switch` statement to select the arithmetic operation (addition, multiplication, or division) to be performed on two numbers according to the value of the variable `opselect`.

FIGURE 4-3 The Expression Determines an Entry Point

```
                                switch (expression)
                                {
Start here if                 → case value_1:
expression equals value_1           .
                                    .
                                    .
                                  break;
Start here if                 → case value_2:
expression equals value_2           .
                                    .
                                    .
                                  break;
Start here if                 → case value_3:
expression equals value_3           .
                                    .
                                    .
                                  break;
                                    .
                                    .
                                    .
Start here if                 → case value_n:
expression equals value_n           .
                                    .
                                    .
                                  break;
Start here if no              → default:
previous match                      .
                                    .
                                    .
                                }        /* end of switch statement */
```

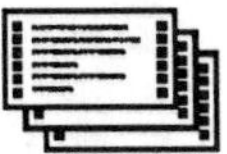

Program 4-6

```
main()
{
  int opselect;
  double fnum, snum;

  printf("Please type in two numbers: ");
  scanf("%lf %lf", &fnum, &snum);
  printf("Enter a select code: ");
  printf("\n          1 for addition");
  printf("\n          2 for multiplication");
  printf("\n          3 for division : ");
  scanf("%d", &opselect);

  switch (opselect)
  {
    case 1:
      printf("Sum of numbers entered is %6.3lf", fnum+snum);
      break;
    case 2:
      printf("Product of numbers entered is %6.3lf",fnum*snum);
      break;
    case 3:
      printf("First number divided by second is %6.3lf",fnum/snum);
      break;
  }     /* end of switch */

}       /* end of main() */
```

Program 4-6 was run twice. The resulting display clearly identifies the case selected. The results are:

```
Please type in two numbers: 12 3
Enter a select code:
          1 for addition
          2 for multiplication
          3 for division : 2
Product of numbers entered is  36.000
```

and

```
Please type in two numbers: 12 3
Enter a select code:
        1 for addition
        2 for multiplication
        3 for division : 3
First number divided by second is   4.000
```

In reviewing Program 4-6, notice the `break` statement in the last `case`. Although this `break` is not necessary, it is a good practice to terminate the last `case` in a `switch` statement with a `break`. This prevents a possible program error later, if a `case` is subsequently added to the `switch` statement. With the addition of a new `case`, the `break` between `case`s becomes necessary; having the `break` in place ensures that you will not forget to include it at the time of the modification.

Since character data types are always converted to integers in an expression, a `switch` statement can also be used to "switch" based on the value of a character expression. For example, assuming that `choice` is a character variable, the following `switch` statement is valid:

```
switch(choice)
{
  case 'a': case 'e': case 'i': case 'o': case 'u':
    printf("\nThe character in choice is a vowel");
    break;
default:
    printf("\nThe character in choice is not a vowel");
    break;
}                        /* end of switch statement */
```

4.5 Common Programming Errors

There are four programming errors common to C's selection statements. The most common of these errors results from the fact that any expression in C can be tested by an `if` statement. Thus, if a relational expression is typed incorrectly but is still a legitimate C expression, the tested expression is valid even though unintended. A common example of this is the inadvertent substitution of the assignment operator, =, for the relational operator, ==. For example, the `if` statement

```
if (age = 40)
  printf("Happy Birthday!");
```

always causes the `Happy Birthday!` message to be displayed. Can you see why? The tested condition does not compare the value in `age` to the number `40`, but assigns the number `40` to the variable `age`. The expression `age = 40` is not a relational expression at all, but an assignment expression. At the completion of the assignment, the expression itself has a value of `40`. Since C treats any nonzero value as true, the call to `printf()` is made. Another way of looking at this is to realize that this `if` statement is equivalent to the following two statements:

```
age = 40;           /* assign 40 to age        */
if (age)            /* test the value of age */
  printf("Happy Birthday!");
```

Since the C compiler has no means of knowing if the expression being tested is not the desired one, you must be especially careful when writing conditions.

A second common error is a typical debugging problem that can surface whenever an expression is evaluated and yields an unexpected result. Here, the problem resides in the values assigned to the variables used in the expression rather than in the expression itself. With selection statements, this takes the form of not executing the expected statement and the programmer concentrates on the selection statement as the source of the problem instead of the values assigned to the tested variables. For example, assume that the following one-way `if` statement is part of your program:

```
if (key == 'a') printf(" Got an a! ");
```

This statement will always display `Got an a!` when the variable key contains an `a`. Therefore, if the message is not displayed when you think it should be, investigation of `key`'s value is called for. As a general rule, whenever a selection statement does not act as you think it should, make sure to test your assumptions about the values assigned to the tested variables. A useful method of doing this is to use `printf()` to display the values of all relevant variables. If an unanticipated value is displayed, you have at least isolated the source of the problem to the variables themselves, rather than the structure of the if statement. From there you will have to determine where and how the incorrect value was assigned.

A third error occurs when nested `if` statements are used and braces are not included to clearly indicate the desired structure. Without braces, the compiler defaults to pairing `elses` with the closest unpaired `ifs`, which sometimes destroys the original intent of the selection statement. To avoid this problem and to create code that is readily adaptable to change it is useful to write all `if-else` statements as compound statements in the form

```
if (expression)
{
  one or more statements in here
```

```
}
else
{
  one or more statements in here
}
```

By using this form, no matter how many statements are added later, the original integrity and intent of the `if` statement is maintained.

The last error common to selection statements is a subtle one and is really a numerical accuracy problem relating to floating point and double precision numbers. Due to the way computers store these values, an expression such as `value == .1` should be avoided. Since decimal numbers like .1 cannot be represented perfectly in binary using a finite number of bits, testing for exact equality of such numbers can fail. To avoid the problem, the equality operator should not be used with floating point or double precision operands; an equivalent test requiring that the absolute value of the difference between operands be less than some small value should be used. This ensures that slight inaccuracies in representing floating point or double precision numbers in binary do not affect the evaluation of the tested expression.

4.6 Chapter Summary

1. Relational expressions are used to compare operands. If a relational expression is true, the value of the expression is the integer 1. If the relational expression is false, it has an integer value of 0.
2. `if-else` statements are used to select between two statements on the basis of the value of an expression. Although relational expressions are usually used for the tested expression, any valid expression can be used. In testing an expression, `if-else` statements interpret a nonzero value as true and a zero value as false.
3. `if-else` statements can contain other `if- else` statements. In the absence of braces, each `else` is associated with the closest unpaired `if`.
4. A compound statement consists of any number of individual statements enclosed within a brace pair. Compound statements are treated as a single unit and can be used anywhere that a single statement is called for.
5. The `switch` statement provides a multidirectional decision branch equivalent to an `if-else` chain. For this statement, the value of an integer expression is compared to a number of integer or character constants or constant expressions. Program execution is transferred to the first matching `case` and continues through the end of the `switch` statement unless an optional `break` statement is encountered. `cases` in a `switch` statement can appear in any

order and an optional `default case` can be included. The `default case` is executed if none of the other `cases` is matched.

Sample Problem

Program 4-4 uses an `if-else` chain to display a person's marital status on the basis of a letter code. In this sample problem, Program 4-4 has been expanded to display messages according to the following set of more complete codes:

Codes	Message to be Displayed
m or M	The individual is married.
s or S	The individual is single.
d or D	The individual is divorced.
w or W	The individual is widowed.
any other letter	An incorrect code was entered.

In addition, the program uses a `switch` statement to select the message to be displayed. The program that accomplishes this task is:

```
main()
{
  char marcode;

  printf("Enter a marital code: ");
  scanf("%c", &marcode);
  switch(marcode)
  {
    case 'm': case 'M':
      printf("The individual is married.");
      break;
    case 's': case 'S':
      printf("The individual is single.");
      break;
    case 'd': case 'D':
      printf("The individual is divorced.");
      break;
    case 'w': case 'W':
      printf("The individual is widowed.");
      break;
    default:
      printf("An incorrect code was entered.");
  }
}
```

A sample run using this program produced the following results:

```
Enter a marital code: s
The individual is single.
```

Repetition

Chapter Five

The programs examined so far have been useful in illustrating the correct structure of C programs and in introducing fundamental C input, output, assignment, and selection capabilities. By this time, you should have gained enough experience to be comfortable with the concepts and mechanics of the C programming process. It is now time to move up a level in our knowledge and abilities.

The real power of most computer programs resides in their ability to repeat the same calculation or sequence of instructions many times over, each time using different data, without the necessity of rerunning the program for each new set of data values. In this chapter, we explore the C statements that permit this. These statements are the `while`, `for`, and `do-while` statements.

5.1 The `while` Statement

The `while` statement is a general repetition statement that can be used in a variety of programming situations. The general form of the `while` statement is:

```
while (expression) statement;
```

The expression contained within the parentheses is evaluated in exactly the same manner as an expression contained in an `if-else` statement; the difference is how the expression is used. As we have seen, when the expression is true (has a nonzero value) in an `if-else` statement, the statement following the expression is executed once. In a `while` statement, the statement following the expression is executed repeatedly as long as the expression retains a nonzero value. This naturally means that somewhere in the `while` statement there must be a statement that alters the value of the tested expression. As we will see, this is indeed the case. For now, however, considering just the expression and the statement following the parentheses, the process used by the computer in evaluating a `while` statement is:

1. test the expression
2. if the expression has a nonzero (true) value
   a. execute the statement following the parentheses
   b. go back to step 1
   `else`
   exit the `while` statement

Notice that step 2b forces program control to be transferred back to step 1. The transfer of control back to the start of a `while` statement in order to re-evaluate the expression is called a *program loop.* The `while` statement literally loops back on itself to recheck the expression until it evaluates to zero (becomes false).

This looping process is illustrated in Figure 5-1. A diamond shape is used to show the two entry and two exit points required in the decision part of the `while` statement.

To make this a little more tangible, consider the relational expression `count <= 10` and the statement `printf("%d  ",count);`. Using these, we can write the valid `while` statement:

```
while (count <= 10)  printf("%d  ",count);
```

Although the above statement is valid, the alert reader will realize that we have created a situation in which the `printf()` function is called forever (or until we stop the program) or is not called at all. Let us see why this happens.

If `count` has a value less than or equal to 10 when the expression is first evaluated, a call to `printf()` is made. The `while` statement then automatically loops back on itself and retests the expression. Since we have not changed the value stored in `count`, the expression is still true and another call to `printf()`

FIGURE 5-1 Anatomy of a `while` Loop

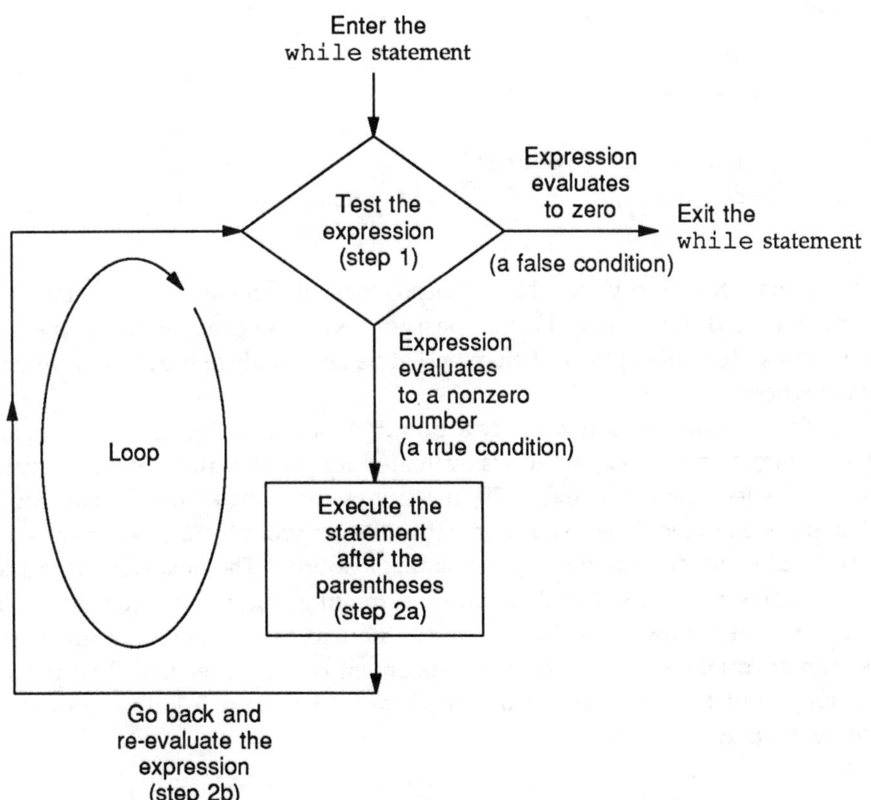

is made. This process continues forever, or until the program containing this statement is stopped by the user. However, if count starts with a value greater than 10, the expression is false to begin with and the printf() function call is never made.

How do we set an initial value in count to control what the while statement does the first time the expression is evaluated? The answer, of course, is to assign values to each variable in the tested expression before the while statement is encountered. For example, the following sequence of instructions is valid:

```
count = 1;
while (count <= 10)  printf("%d  ",count);
```

Using this sequence of instructions, we have ensured that count starts with a value of 1. We could assign any value to count in the assignment statement — the important thing is to assign *some* value. In practice, the assigned value depends on the application.

We must still change the value of count so that we can finally exit the while statement. To do this requires an expression such as ++count to increment the value of count each time the while statement is executed. The fact that a while statement provides for the repetition of a single statement does not prevent us from including an additional statement to change the value of count. All we have to do is replace the single statement with a compound statement. For example:

```
count = 1;                    /* initialize count */
while (count <= 10)
{
 printf("%d  ",count);
 ++count;                     /* increment count  */
}
```

Note that, for clarity, we have placed each statement in the compound statement on a different line. This is consistent with the convention adopted for compound statements in the last chapter. Let us now analyze the above sequence of instructions.

The first assignment statement sets count equal to 1. The while statement is then entered and the expression is evaluated for the first time. Since the value of count is less than or equal to 10, the expression is true and the compound statement is executed. The first statement in the compound statement is a call to the printf() function to display the value of count. The next statement adds 1 to the value currently stored in count, making this value equal to 2. The while statement now loops back to retest the expression. Since count is still less than or equal to 10, the compound statement is again executed. This process continues until the value of count reaches 11. Program 5-1 illustrates these statements in an actual program.

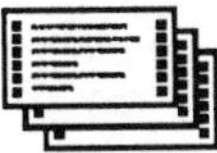

Program 5-1

```
main()
{
  int count;

  count = 1;                    /* initialize count */
  while (count <= 10)
  {
    printf("%d  ",count);
    ++count;                    /* add 1 to count   */
  }
}
```

The output for Program 5-1 is:

```
1  2  3  4  5  6  7  8  9  10
```

There is nothing special about the name count used in Program 5-1. Any valid integer variable could have been used.

Before we consider other examples of the while statement, two comments concerning Program 5-1 must be made. First, the statement ++count can be replaced with any statement that changes the value of count. A statement such as count = count + 2, for example, would cause every second integer to be displayed. Second, it is the programmer's responsibility to ensure that count is changed in a way that ultimately leads to a normal exit from the while. For example, if we replace the expression ++count with the expression --count, the value of count will never reach 11 and an infinite loop will be created. An *infinite loop* is a loop that never ends. The computer will not reach out, touch you, and say, "Excuse me, you have created an infinite loop." It just keeps displaying numbers until you realize that the program is not working as you expected.

Now that you have some familiarity with the while statement, read Program 5-2 and see if you can determine its output.

The assignment statement in Program 5-2 initially sets the integer variable i to 10. The while statement then checks if the value of i is greater than or equal to 1. While the expression is true, the value of i is displayed by the call to printf() and the value of i is decremented by 1. When i finally reaches zero, the expression becomes false and the program exits the while statement.

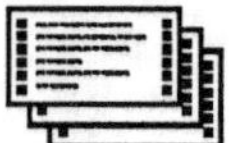

Program 5-2

```
main()
{
  int i;

  i = 10;
  while (i >= 1)
  {
    printf("%d ",i);
    --i;              /* subtract one from i */
  }
}
```

The following display is obtained when Program 5-2 is run:

```
10  9  8  7  6  5  4  3  2  1
```

To illustrate the power of the `while` statement, consider the task of printing a table of numbers from 1 to 10 with their squares and cubes. This can be done with a simple `while` statement as illustrated by Program 5-3.

Program 5-3

```
main()
{
  int num;
  printf("NUMBER    SQUARE    CUBE\n");
  printf("------    ------    ----\n");

  num = 1;
  while (num < 11)
  {
    printf("%3d      %3d      %4d\n", num, num*num, num*num*num);
    ++num;        /* add 1 to num */
  }
}
```

When Program 5-3 is run, the following display is produced:

```
NUMBER      SQUARE      CUBE
------      ------      ----
     1           1         1
     2           4         8
     3           9        27
     4          16        64
     5          25       125
     6          36       216
     7          49       343
     8          64       512
     9          81       729
    10         100      1000
```

Note that the expression used in Program 5-3 is `num < 11`. For the integer variable `num`, this expression is exactly equivalent to the expression `num <= 10`. The choice of which to use is entirely up to you.

If we want to use Program 5-3 to produce a table of 1000 numbers, all we do is change the expression in the `while` statement from `i < 11` to `i < 1001`. Changing the `11` to `1001` produces a table of 1000 lines — not bad for a simple five-line `while` statement.

All the program examples of the `while` statement presented so far check for a fixed-count condition. Since any valid expression can be evaluated by a `while`statement, we are not restricted to constructing such loops. For example, consider the task of producing a Celsius to Fahrenheit temperature conversion table. Assume that Fahrenheit temperatures corresponding to Celsius temperatures ranging from 5 to 50 degrees are to be displayed in increments of five degrees. The desired display can be obtained with the series of statements:

```
celsius = 5;        /* starting Celsius value */
while (celsius <= 50)
{
  fahren = (9.0/5.0) * celsius + 32.0;
  printf("%5d%12.2f",celsius, fahren);
  celsius = celsius + 5;
}
```

As before, the `while` statement consists of everything from the word `while` through the closing brace of the compound statement. Prior to the program entering the `while` loop, a value must be assigned to the operand being evaluated. To ensure an exit from the `while` loop, there is a statement to alter the value of `celsius`. Program 5-4 illustrates the use of this code in a complete program.

Program 5-4

```
main()  /* program to convert Celsius to Fahrenheit */
{
  int celsius;
  float fahren;
  printf("DEGREES   DEGREES\n");
  printf("CELSIUS  FAHRENHEIT\n");
  printf("-------  ----------\n");

  celsius = 5;      /* starting Celsius value */
  while (celsius <= 50)
  {
    fahren = (9.0/5.0) * celsius + 32.0;
    printf("%5d%12.2f",celsius, fahren);
    celsius = celsius + 5;
  }
}
```

The display obtained when Program 5-4 is executed is:

```
DEGREES    DEGREES
CELSIUS  FAHRENHEIT
-------  ----------
    5       41.00
   10       50.00
   15       59.00
   20       68.00
   25       77.00
   30       86.00
   35       95.00
   40      104.00
   45      113.00
   50      122.00
```

5.2 `scanf()` Within a `while` Loop

Combining the `scanf()` function with the repetition capabilities of the `while` statement produces very adaptable and powerful programs. To understand the concept involved, consider Program 5-5, where a while statement is used to accept and then display four user- entered numbers, one at a time. Although it uses a very simple idea, the program highlights the flow of control concepts needed to produce more useful programs.

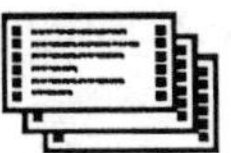

Program 5-5

```
main()
{
  int count;
  float num;

  printf("\nThis program will ask you to enter some numbers.\n");
  count = 1;

  while (count <= 4)
  {
    printf("\nEnter a number: ");
    scanf("%f", &num);
    printf("The number entered is %f", num);
    ++count;
  }
}
```

Following is a sample run of Program 5-5. The underlined items were input in response to the appropriate prompts.

```
This program will ask you to enter some numbers.

Enter a number: 26.2
The number entered is 26.200000
Enter a number: 5
The number entered is 5.000000
Enter a number: 103.456
The number entered is 103.456000
Enter a number: 1267.89
The number entered is 1267.890000
```

Let us review the program to clearly understand how the output was produced. The first message displayed is caused by execution of the first `printf()` function call. This call is outside and before the `while` statement, so it is executed only once, before any statement in the `while` loop.

Once the `while` loop is entered, the statements within the compound statement are executed while the tested condition is true. The first time through the compound statement, the message `Enter a number:` is displayed. The program then calls `scanf()`, which forces the computer to wait for a number to be entered at the keyboard. Once a number is typed and the RETURN key is pressed, the call to `printf()` that displays the number is executed. The variable `count` is then incremented by one. This process continues until four passes through the loop have been made and the value of `count` is 5. Each pass causes the message `Enter a number:` to be displayed, causes one call to `scanf()` to be made, causes the message `The number entered is` to be displayed, and adds `1` to `count`. Figure 5-2 illustrates this flow of control.

Rather than simply displaying the entered numbers, Program 5-5 can be modified to use the entered data. For example, let us add the numbers entered and display the total. To do this, we must be very careful in how we add the numbers, since the same variable, `num`, is used for each number entered. Because of this, the entry of a new number in Program 5-5 automatically causes the previous number stored in `num` to be lost. Thus, each number entered must be added to the total before another number is entered. The required sequence is:

```
Enter a number
Add the number to the total
```

How do we add a single number to a total? A statement such as `total = total + num` does the job perfectly. This is the accumulating statement introduced in Section 3.1. After each number is entered, the accumulating statement adds the number into the total, as illustrated in Figure 5-3. The complete flow of control required for adding the numbers is illustrated in Figure 5-4.

In reviewing Figure 5-4, observe that we have made a provision for initially setting the total to zero before the `while` loop is entered. If we were to clear the total inside the `while` loop, it would be set to zero each time the loop was executed and any value previously stored would be erased.

Program 5-6 incorporates the necessary modifications to Program 5-5 to total the numbers entered. As indicated in the flow diagram shown in Figure 5-4, the statement `total = total + num;` is placed immediately after the `scanf()` function call. Putting the accumulating statement at this point in the program ensures that the entered number is immediately added to `total`.

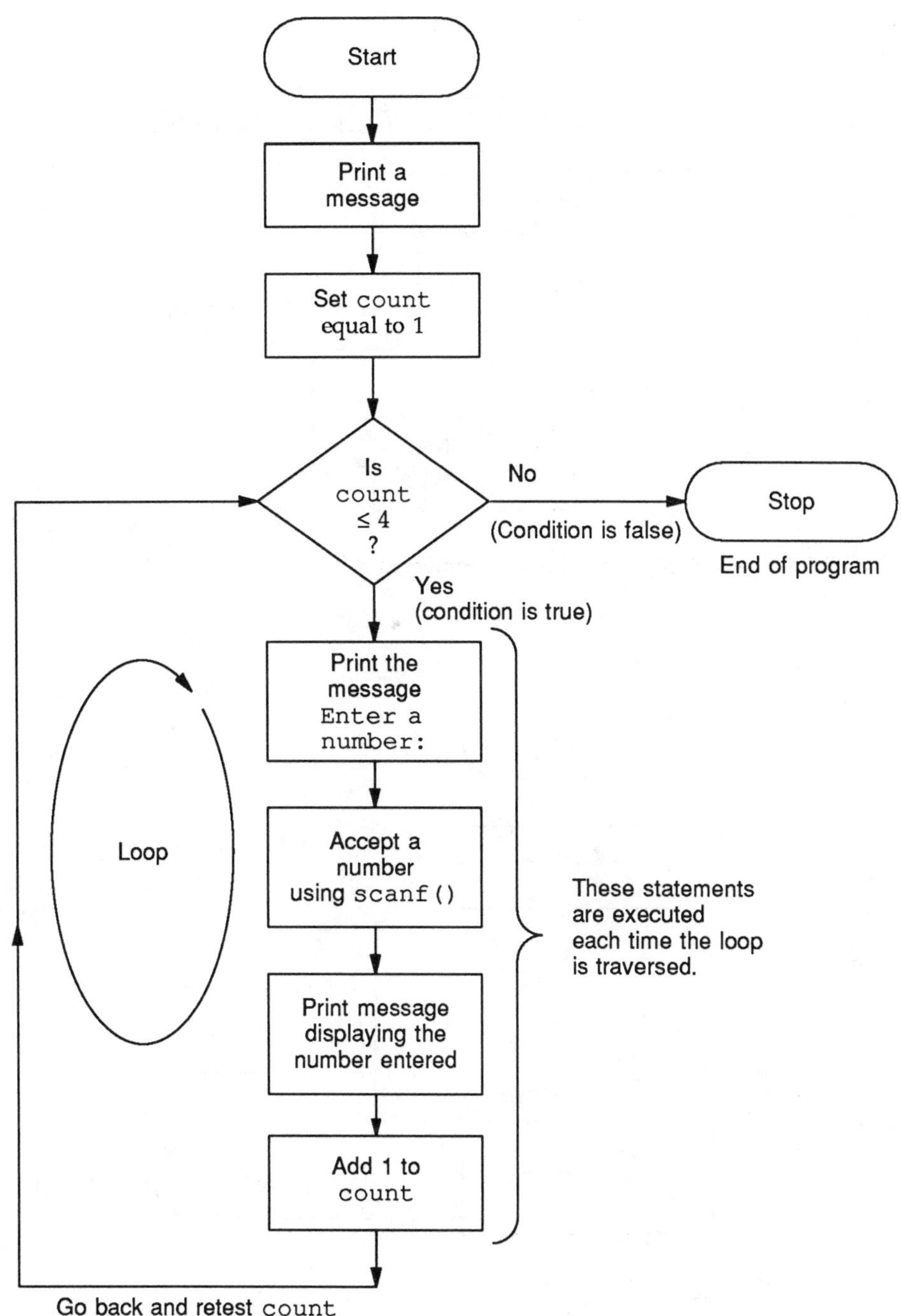

FIGURE 5-2 Flow of Control Diagram for Program 5-5

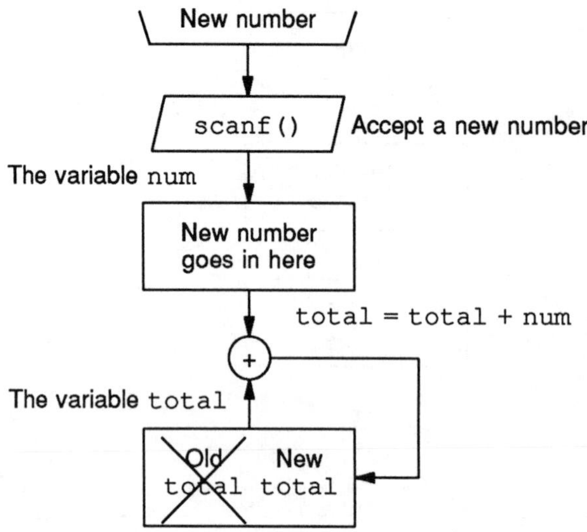

FIGURE 5-3 Accepting and Adding a Number to a Total

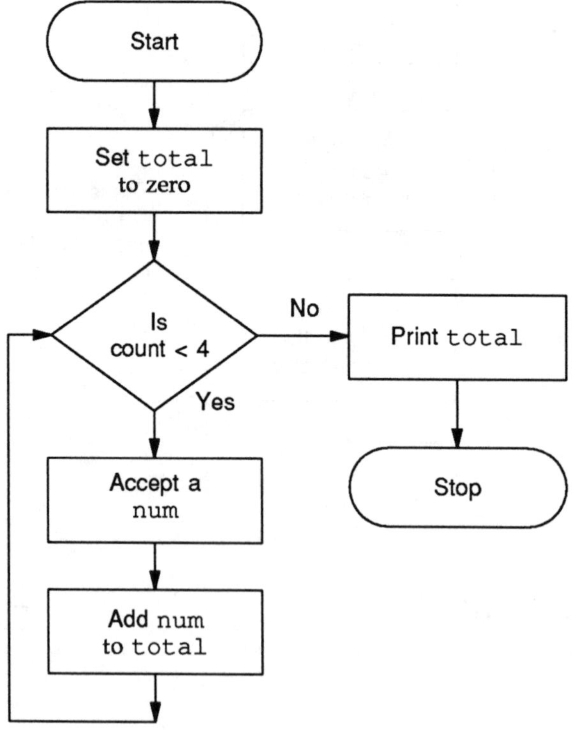

FIGURE 5-4 Accumulation Flow of Control

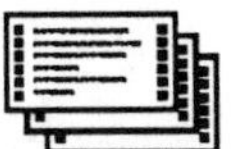

Program 5-6

```
main()
{
  int count;
  float num, total;

  printf("\nThis program will ask you to enter some numbers.\n");
  count = 1;
  total = 0;

  while (count <= 4)
  {
    printf("\nEnter a number: ");
    scanf("%f", &num);
    total = total + num;
    printf("The total is now %f", total);
    ++count;
  }
  printf("\n\nThe final total is %f",total);
}
```

Let us review Program 5-6. The variable `total` was created to store the total of the numbers entered. Prior to entering the `while` statement, the value of `total` is made zero. This ensures that any previous value present in the storage location(s) assigned to the variable `total` is erased. When the `while` loop is entered, the statement `total = total + num;` is used to add the value of the entered number into `total`. As each value is entered, it is added into the existing total to create a new total. Thus, `total` becomes a running subtotal of all the values entered. Only when all numbers are entered does `total` contain the final sum of all of the numbers. After the `while` loop is finished, the last `printf()` function call is used to display this sum.

Using the same data that was entered in the sample run for Program 5-5, the following sample run of Program 5-6 was made:

```
This program will ask you to enter some numbers.

Enter a number: 26.2
The total is now 26.200000
Enter a number: 5
The total is now 31.200000
```

```
Enter a number: 103.456
The total is now 134.656000
Enter a number: 1267.89
The total is now 1402.546000

The final total is 1402.546000
```

Having used an accumulating assignment statement to add the numbers entered, we can now go further and calculate the average of the numbers. Where do we calculate the average — within the `while` loop or outside it?

In this case, calculating an average requires that both a final sum and the number of items in that sum be available. The average is then computed by dividing the final sum by the number of items. At this point, we must ask, "At what point in the program is the correct sum available, and at what point is the number of items available? " In reviewing Program 5-6, we see that the correct sum needed for calculating the average is available after the `while` loop is finished. In fact, the whole purpose of the `while` loop is to ensure that the numbers are entered and added correctly to produce a correct sum. After the loop is finished, we also have a count of the number of items used in the sum. However, due to the way the `while` loop was constructed, the number in `count` (5) when the loop is finished is one more than the number of items (4) used to obtain the total. Knowing this, we simply subtract one from `count` before using it to determine the average. With this as background, see if you can read and understand Program 5-7.

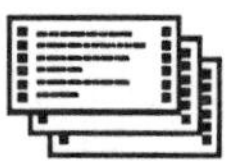

Program 5-7

```
main()
{
  int count;
  float num, total,average;

  printf("\nThis program will ask you to enter some numbers.\n");
  count = 1;
  total = 0;

  while (count <= 4)
  {
    printf("\nEnter a number: ");
    scanf("%f", &num);
    total = total + num;
    ++count;
  }
```

continued

```
  --count;
  average = total / count;
  printf("\n\nThe average of the numbers is %f",average);
}
```

Program 5-7 is almost identical to Program 5-6, the major exception being the way the average is calculated. We have also removed the constant display of the total within and after the `while` loop. The loop in Program 5-7 is used to enter and add four numbers. Immediately after the loop is exited, the average is computed and displayed. When Program 5-7 is run, the output displayed is:

```
This program will ask you to enter some numbers.

Enter a number: 26.2
Enter a number: 5
Enter a number: 103.456
Enter a number: 1267.89

The average of the numbers is 350.636500
```

Sentinels

In many situations the exact number of items to be entered is either not known in advance or the items are too numerous to count beforehand. For example, when entering a large amount of market research data we might not want to take the time to count the number of actual data items that are to be entered. In cases like this, we want to be able to enter data continuously and, at the end, type in a special data value to signal the end of data input.

In computer programming, data values used to signal either the start or end of a data series are called *sentinels*. The sentinel values must, of course, be selected so as not to conflict with legitimate data values. For example, if we were constructing a program that accepts a student's grades, and assuming that no extra credit is given that could produce a grade higher than 100, we could use any grade higher than 100 as a sentinel value. Program 5-8 illustrates this concept. In Program 5-8, data is continuously requested and accepted until a number larger than 100 is entered. Entry of a number higher than 100 alerts the program to exit the `while` loop and display the sum of the numbers entered.

The following output was obtained from a sample run of Program 5-8. As long as grades less than or equal to 100 are entered (underlined items in the output), the program continues to request and accept additional data. When a number greater than 100 is entered, the program adds this number to the total and exits the `while` loop. Outside of the loop and within the `printf()` function call, the value of the sentinel that was added to the total is subtracted and the sum of the legitimate grades that were entered is displayed.

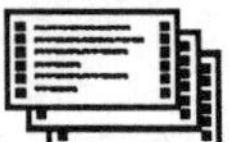

Program 5-8

```
main()
{
  float grade, total;
  grade = 0;
  total = 0;
  printf("\nTo stop entering grades, type in any number");
  printf("\n greater than 100."\n\n);
  while (grade <= 100)
  {
    printf("Enter a grade: ");
    scanf("%f", &grade);
    total = total + grade;
  }
  printf("\n\nThe total of the grades is %f",total-grade);
}
```

```
To stop entering grades, type in any number
  greater than 100.

Enter a grade: 95
Enter a grade: 100
Enter a grade: 82
Enter a grade: 101

The total of the grades is 277.000000
```

`break` and `continue` Statements

Two useful statements in connection with repetition statements are the `break` and `continue` statements. We have previously encountered the `break` statement in relation to the `switch` statement. The general form of this statement is:

```
break;
```

A `break` statement, as its name implies, forces an immediate break, or exit, from `switch`, `while`, `for`, and `do-while` statements only.

For example, execution of the following `while` loop is terminated if a number greater than 76 is entered.

```
while(count <= 10)
{
  printf("Enter a number: ");
  scanf("%f", &num);
  if (num > 76)
  {
    printf("You lose!");
    break;        /* break out of the loop */
  }
  else
  printf("Keep on truckin!");
}
/* break jumps to here */
```

The `break` statement violates pure structured programming principles because it provides a second, nonstandard exit from a loop. Nevertheless, the `break` statement is extremely useful and valuable for breaking out of loops when an unusual condition is detected. The `break` statement is also used to exit from a `switch` statement when the desired case has been detected and processed.

The `continue` statement is similar to the `break` statement but applies only to loops created with `while`, `do-while`, and `for` statements. The general format of a `continue` statement is:

```
continue;
```

When `continue` is encountered in a loop, the next iteration of the loop is immediately begun. For `while` loops this means that execution is automatically transferred to the top of the loop and re-evaluation of the tested expression is initiated. Although the `continue` statement has no direct effect on a `switch` statement, it can be included within a `switch` statement that itself is contained in a loop. Here the effect of the `continue` is the same: the next loop iteration is begun.

As a general rule, the `continue` statement is less useful than the `break` statement, but it is convenient for skipping over data that should not be processed while remaining in a loop. For example, invalid grades are simply ignored in the following section of code and only valid grades are added into the total.

```
while (count < 30)
{
  printf("Enter a grade: ");
  scanf("%f", &grade);
  if(grade < 0 || grade > 100) continue;
  total = total + grade;
}
```

The Null Statement

Statements are always terminated by a semicolon. A semicolon with nothing preceding it is also a valid statement, called the *null statement.* Thus, the statement

```
;
```

is a null statement. This is a do-nothing statement that is used where a statement is syntactically required, but no action is called for. Null statements typically are used with either `while` or `for` statements. An example of a `for` statement using a null statement is found in Program 5-9c in the next section.

5.3 The `for` Statement

The `for` statement performs the same functions as the `while` statement, but uses a different form. In many situations, especially those that use a fixed count condition, the `for` statement format is easier to use than its `while` statement equivalent.

The general form of the `for` statement is:

```
for (initializing list; expression; altering list) statement;
```

Although the `for` statement looks a little complicated, it is really quite simple if we consider each of its parts separately.

Within the parentheses of the `for` statement are three expressions, separated by semicolons. Each of these items is optional and can be described individually, but both semicolons must always be present. As we shall see, the items in parentheses correspond to the initialization, expression evaluation, and alteration of expression values that we have already used with the `while` statement.

The middle item in the parentheses, the expression, is any valid C expression, and there is no difference in the way `for` and `while` statements use this expression. In both statements, as long as the expression has a nonzero (true) value, the statement following the parentheses is executed. This means that prior to the first check of the expression, initial values for the tested expression's variables must be assigned. It also means that before the expression is re-evaluated, there must be one or more statements that alter these values. Recall that the general placement of these statements when using a `while` statement follow the pattern:

```
initializing statements;
while (expression)
{
  loop statements;
       .
       .
  expression altering statements;
}
```

The need to initialize variables or make some other evaluations prior to entering a repetition loop is so common that the `for` statement allows all the initializing statements to be grouped together as the first list within the `for`'s parentheses. The items in this initializing list are executed only once, before the expression is evaluated for the first time.

The `for` statement also provides a single place for all expression-altering statements. These items can be placed in the altering list, which is the last list within the parentheses. All items in the altering list are executed by the `for` statement at the end of the loop, just before the expression is re-evaluated. Figure 5-5 illustrates the `for` statement's flow of control diagram.

FIGURE 5-5 The `for` Statement's Flow of Control

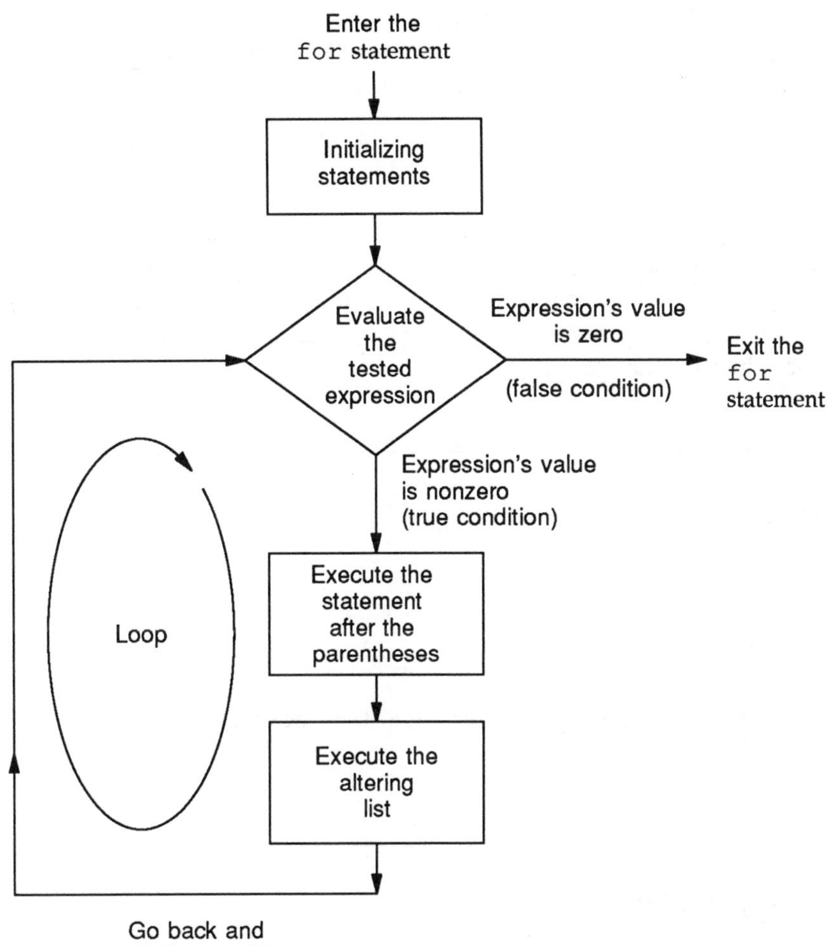

The following section of code illustrates the correspondence between the `for` and `while` statements:

```
count = 1;
while (count <= 10)
{
  printf("%d",  count);
  ++count;
}
```

The `for` statement corresponding to this section of code is:

```
for (count = 1; count <= 10; ++count) printf("%d", count);
```

As seen in this example, the only difference between the `for` statement and the `while` statement is the placement of equivalent expressions. The grouping together of the initialization, expression test, and altering list in the `for` statement is very convenient, especially when they are used to create fixed-count loops. Consider the following `for` statement:

```
for (count = 2; count <= 20; count = count + 2)
  printf("%d  ",count);
```

For clarity, we have placed the statement following the parentheses on a line by itself. All of the loop control information is contained within the parentheses. The loop starts with a count of 2, stops when the count exceeds 20, and increments the loop counter in steps of 2. Program 5-9 illustrates this `for` statement in an actual program.

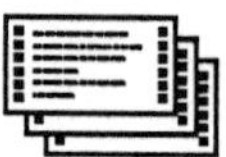

Program 5-9

```
main()
{
  int count;

  for (count = 2; count <= 20; count = count + 2)
    printf("%d  ",count);
}
```

The output of Program 5-9 is:

```
2  4  6  8  10  12  14  16  18  20
```

The `for` statement does not require that any of the items in parentheses be present or that they be used for initializing or altering the values in the expression statements. However, the two semicolons must be present within the `for`'s parentheses. For example, the construction `for ( ; count <= 20 ;)` is valid.

If the initializing list is missing, the initialization step is omitted when the `for` statement is executed. This, of course, means that the programmer must provide the required initializations before the `for` statement is encountered. Similarly, if the altering list is missing, any expressions needed to alter the evaluation of the tested expression must be included directly within the statement part of the loop. The `for` statement ensures only that all expressions in the initializing list are executed once before evaluation of the tested expression and that all expressions in the altering list are executed at the end of the loop before the tested expression is rechecked. Thus, Program 5-9 can be rewritten in any of the three ways shown in Programs 5-9a, 5-9b, and 5-9c.

Program 5-9a

```
main()
{
  int count;

  count = 2;     /* initializer outside for statement */
  for ( ; count <= 20; count = count + 2)
    printf("%d  ",count);
}
```

Program 5-9b

```
main()
{
  int count;

   count = 2;        /* initializer outside for statement */
   for( ; count <= 20; )
   {
     printf("%d  ",count);
     count = count + 2;      /* alteration statement */
   }
}
```

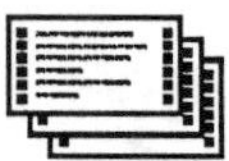

Program 5-9c

```
main()           /* all expressions within the for's parentheses */
{
  int count;

  for (count=2; count<=20; printf("%d ",count), count=count+2);
}
```

In Program 5-9a, `count` is initialized outside the `for` statement and the first list inside the parentheses is left blank. In Program 5-9b, both the initializing list and the altering list are removed from within the parentheses. Program 5-9b also uses a compound statement within the `for` loop, with the expression-altering statement included in the compound statement. Finally, in Program 5-9c, all items are included within the parentheses, so there is no need for any executable statement to follow the parentheses. Here, the null statement satisfies the requirement that a statement follow the `for` statement's parentheses. Observe also in Program 5-9c that the altering list (last set of items in parentheses) consists of two items, and that a comma has been used to separate these items. The use of commas to separate items in both the initializing and altering lists is required if either of these two lists contain more than one item. Last, note that Programs 5-9a, 5-9b, and 5-9c are inferior to Program 5-9. The `for` statement in Program 5-9 is much clearer because all the expressions pertaining to the tested expression are grouped together within the parentheses.

Although the initializing and altering lists can be omitted from a `for` statement, omitting the tested expression results in an infinite loop. For example, such a loop is created by the statement

```
for (count = 2; ; ++count) printf("%d",count);
```

As with the `while` statement, both `break` and `continue` statements can be used within a `for` loop. The `break` forces an immediate exit from the `for` loop, as it does from the `while` loop. The `continue`, however, forces control to be passed to the altering list in a `for` statement, after which the tested expression is re-evaluated. This differs from the action of `continue` in a `while` statement, where control is passed directly to the re-evaluation of the tested expression.

To understand the enormous power of the `for` statement, let us investigate using the `for` statement to print a table of squares and cubes for numbers from 1 to 10. Such a table was previously produced by using a `while` statement (Program 5-3). Program 5-10 prints the table using a `for` statement. You may wish to review Program 5-3 and compare it to Program 5-10 to better understand the equivalence between the `for` and `while` statements.

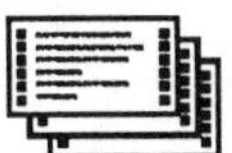

Program 5-10

```
main()
{
  int num;
  printf("NUMBER     SQUARE     CUBE\n");
  printf("------     ------     ----\n");

  for (num = 1; num <= 10; ++num)
    printf("%3d       %3d       %4d\n", num, num*num, num*num*num);
}
```

The following display is obtained when Program 5-10 is run. Changing the number 10 in the `for` statement of Program 5-10 to 1000 creates a loop that is executed 1000 times. This produces a table of numbers from 1 to 1000. (The `printf` statement's field width specifies have to be changed to accommodate the increased number of digits). As with the `while` statement, this small change produces an immense increase in the processing and output provided by the program.

```
NUMBER     SQUARE     CUBE
------     ------     ----
   1          1          1
   2          4          8
   3          9         27
   4         16         64
   5         25        125
   6         36        216
   7         49        343
   8         64        512
   9         81        729
  10        100       1000
```

`for` Loop Containing a `scanf()`

Using a `scanf()` function call inside a `for` loop produces the same effect as when this function is called inside of a `while` loop. For example, in Program 5-11 a `scanf()` function call is used to input a set of numbers. As each number is input, it is added to a total. When the `for` loop is exited, the average is calculated and displayed.

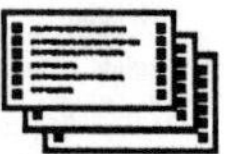

Program 5-11

```
main()
/* This program calculates the average */
/* of five user-entered numbers.       */
{
  int count;
  float num, total, average;

  total = 0.0;

  for (count = 0; count < 5; ++count)
  {
    printf("Enter a number: ");
    scanf("%f", &num);
    total = total + num;
  }
  average = total / count;
  printf("\nThe average of the data entered is %f", average);
}
```

The `for` statement in Program 5-11 creates a loop that is executed five times. The user is prompted to enter a number each time through the loop. After each number is entered, it is immediately added to the total. Although, for clarity, `total` was initialized to 0 before the `for` statement, this initialization could have been included with the initialization of `count` as:

```
for (total = 0.0, count = 0; count < 5; ++count)
```

Nested Loops

There are many situations in which it is very convenient to have a loop contained within another loop. Such loops are called *nested loops*. A simple example of a nested loop is:

```
for(i = 1; i <= 5; ++i)           /* start of outer loop  <-+ */
{                                 /*                        | */
  printf("\ni is now %d\n",i);    /*                        | */
  for(j = 1; j <= 4; ++j)         /* start of inner loop    | */
    printf("  j = %d",  j);       /* end of inner loop      | */
}                                 /* end of outer loop    <-+ */
```

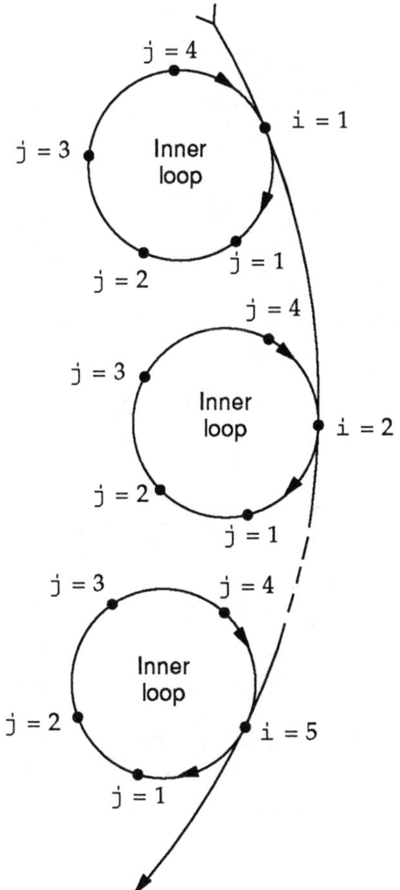

FIGURE 5-6 For Each `i, j` Loops

The first loop, controlled by the value of `i`, is called the *outer loop.* The second loop, controlled by the value of `j`, is called the *inner loop.* Notice that all statements in the inner loop are contained within the boundaries of the outer loop and that we have used a different variable to control each loop. For each single pass through the outer loop, the inner loop runs through its entire sequence. Thus, each time the `i` counter increases by 1, the inner `for` loop executes completely. This situation is illustrated in Figure 5-6.

Program 5-12 includes the sample nested loop code in a working program.

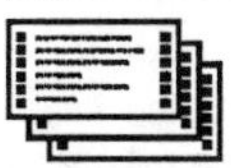

Program 5-12

```
main()
{
  int i,j;
```

continued

```
    for(i = 1; i <= 5; ++i)               /* start of outer loop  <-+ */
    {                                     /*                        | */
      printf("\ni is now %d\n",i);        /*                        | */
      for(j = 1; j <= 4; ++j)             /* start of inner loop    | */
        printf("  j = %d",  j);           /* end of inner loop      | */
    }                                     /* end of outer loop    <-+ */
}
```

The following is a sample output for Program 5-12:

```
i is now 1
 j = 1  j = 2  j = 3  j = 4
i is now 2
 j = 1  j = 2  j = 3  j = 4
i is now 3
 j = 1  j = 2  j = 3  j = 4
i is now 4
 j = 1  j = 2  j = 3  j = 4
i is now 5
 j = 1  j = 2  j = 3  j = 4
```

Let us use a nested loop to compute the average grade for each student in a class of 20 students. Each student has taken four exams during the course of the semester. The final grade is calculated as the average of these examination grades.

The outer loop in our program consists of 20 passes. Each pass through the outer loop is used to compute the average for one student. The inner loop will consist of 4 passes. One examination grade is entered in each inner loop pass. As each grade is entered, it is added to the total for the student and, at the end of the loop, the average is calculated and displayed. Program 5-13 uses a nested loop to make the required calculations.

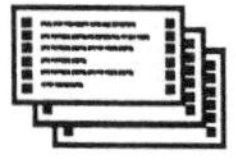

Program 5-13

```
main()
{
  int i,j;
  float grade, total, average;

  for (i = 1; i <= 20; ++i)     /* start of outer loop                  */
```

continued

```
  {
    total = 0;                  /* clear the total for this student */
    for ( j = 1; j <= 4; ++j)   /* start of inner loop              */
    {
      printf("Enter an examination grade for this student: ");
      scanf("%f", &grade);
      total = total + grade;    /* add the grade into the total     */
    }                           /* end of the inner loop            */
    average = total / 4;        /* calculate the average            */
    printf("\n\nThe average for student %d is %f",i,average);
  }                             /* end of the outer loop            */
}
```

In reviewing Program 5-13, pay particular attention to the initialization of `total` within the outer loop, before the inner loop is entered. `total` is initialized 20 times, once for each student. Also notice that the average is calculated and displayed immediately after the inner loop is finished. Since the statements that compute and print the average are also contained within the outer loop, 20 averages are calculated and displayed. The entry and addition of each grade within the inner loop use techniques we have seen before, which should now be familiar to you.

5.4 The do Statement

Both the `while` and `for` statements evaluate an expression at the start of a repetition loop. There are cases, however, where it is more convenient to test the expression at the end of the loop. For example, suppose we have constructed the following `while` loop to calculate sales taxes:

```
printf("Enter a price: ");
scanf("%f", &price);
while (price != SENTINEL)
{
  salestax = RATE * price;
  printf("The sales tax is $%5.2f",salestax);
  printf("\nEnter a price: ");
  scanf("%f", &price);
}
```

Using this `while` statement requires either duplicating the prompt and `scanf()` function calls before the loop and then within the loop, as we have done, or resorting to some other artifice to force initial execution of the statements within the `while` loop.

The `do` statement, as its name implies, allows us to *do* some statements before an expression is evaluated. In many situations, this can be used to eliminate the duplication illustrated in the previous example. The general form of the `do` statement is:

```
do
  statement;
while (expression);      <---(Do not forget the final ;)
```

As with all C programs, the single statement in `do` may be replaced by a compound statement. A flow-control diagram illustrating the operation of the `do` statement is shown in Figure 5-7.

As illustrated in Figure 5-7, all statements within the `do` statement are executed at least once before the expression is evaluated. Then, if the expression has a nonzero value, the statements are executed again. This process continues until the expression evaluates to zero. For example, consider the following `do` statement:

```
do
{
  printf("\nEnter a price: ");
  scanf("%f", &price);
  salestax = RATE * price;
  printf("The sales tax is $%5.2f", salestax);
}
while (price != SENTINEL);
```

Observe that only one prompt and `scanf()` statement are required because the tested expression is evaluated at the end of the loop.

As with all repetition statements, the `do` statement can always replace or be replaced by an equivalent `while` or `for` statement. The choice of which statement to use depends on the application and the style preferred by the programmer. In general, the `while` and `for` statements are preferred because they clearly let anyone reading the program know what is being tested "right up front" at the top of the program loop.

Validity Checks

The `do` statement is particularly useful in filtering user-entered input and providing data validity checks. For example, assume that an operator is required to enter a valid customer identification number between the numbers 1000 and 1999. A number outside this range is to be rejected and a new request for a valid number made. The following section of code provides the necessary data filter to verify the entry of a valid identification number:

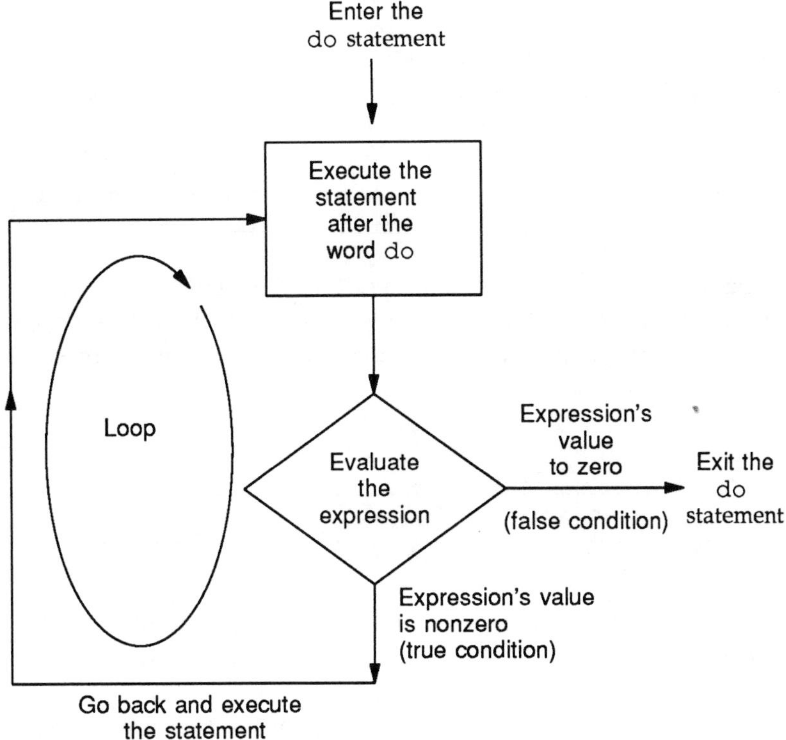

FIGURE 5-7 The do Statement's Flow of Control

```
do
{
  printf("\nEnter an identification number: ");
  scanf("%f", &id_num);
}
while (id_num < 1000 || id_num > 1999);
```

Here, a request for an identification number is repeated until a valid number is entered. This section of code is "bare bones" in that it neither alerts the operator to the cause of the new request for data nor allows premature exit from the loop if a valid identification number cannot be found. An alternative that removes the first drawback is:

```
do
{
  printf("\nEnter an identification number: ");
  scanf("%f", &id_num);
  if (id_num < 1000 || id_num > 1999)
```

continued

```
   {
     printf("\n An invalid number was just entered");
     printf("\nPlease check the ID number and re-enter");
   }
   else
    break;       /* break if a valid id num was entered  */
  } while(1);    /* this expression is always true       */
```

Here we have used a `break` statement to exit from the loop. Since the expression being evaluated by the `do` statement is always 1 (true), an infinite loop has been created that is only exited when the `break` statement is encountered.

5.5 Common Programming Errors

Five errors are commonly made by beginning programmers when using repetition statements. Two of these pertain to the tested expression and have already been encountered with the `if` and `switch` statements. The first is the inadvertent use of the assignment operator, =, for the equality operator, ==, in the tested expression. An example of this error is typing the assignment expression `a = 5` instead of the desired relational expression `a == 5`. Since the tested expression can be any valid C expression, including arithmetic and assignment expressions, this error is not detected by the compiler.

As with the `if` statement, repetition statements should not use the equality operator, ==, when testing floating point or double precision operands. For example, the expression `fnum == .01` should be replaced by an equivalent test requiring that the absolute value of `fnum - .01` be less than an acceptable amount. The reason for this is that all numbers are stored in binary form. Using a finite number of bits, decimal numbers such as `.01` have no exact binary equivalent, so tests that require equality with such numbers can fail.

The next two errors are particular to the `for` statement. The most common is to place a semicolon at the end of the `for`'s parentheses, which frequently produces a do-nothing loop. For example, consider the statements

```
for(count = 0; count < 10; ++ count);
  total = total + num;
```

Here the semicolon at the end of the first line of code is a null statement. This has the effect of creating a loop that is traversed 10 times with nothing done except the incrementing and testing of `count`. This error tends to occur because C programmers end most lines with a semicolon.

The next error occurs when commas are used to separate the items in a `for` statement instead of the required semicolons. An example of this is the statement

```
for (count = 1, count < 10, ++count)
```

Commas are used to separate items *within* the initializing and altering lists, and semicolons are used to separate these lists *from* the tested expression.

The last error occurs when the final semicolon is omitted from the do statement. This error is usually made by programmers who have learned to omit the semicolon after the parentheses of a while statement and carry over this habit when the reserved word while is encountered at the end of a do statement.

5.6 Chapter Summary

1. The while, for, and do repetition statements create program loops. These statements evaluate an expression and, based on the resulting expression value, either terminate the loop or continue it.
2. The while statement checks its expression before any other statement in the loop. This means that any variables in the tested expression must have values assigned before while is encountered. In addition, within a while loop, there must be a statement that alters the tested expression's value.
3. The for statement is extremely useful in creating loops that must be executed a fixed number of times. Initializing expressions, the tested expression, and expressions affecting the tested expression can all be included in parentheses at the top of a for loop. Additionally, any other loop statement can be included within the for's parentheses as part of its altering list.
4. The do statement checks its expression at the end of the loop. This ensures that the body of a do loop is executed at least once. Within a do loop there must be at least one statement that alters the tested expression's value.

Sample Problem

Three experiments were performed, with the following results:

```
Experiment 1 results:   232.46   315.89   169.27   525.42
Experiment 2 results:   348.45   227.93   683.34   394.19
Experiment 3 results:   416.81   220.89   189.13   134.36
```

The following program uses a nested for loop to determine and display the average value of each experiment's results:

```
main()
{
  int i,j;
  float total, avg, data;

  for (i = 1; i <= 3; ++i)
  {
    printf("Enter 4 results for experiment #%d:\n      ",i);
    for (j = 1, total = 0.0; j <= 4; ++j)
    {
      scanf("%f", &data);
      total += data;
    }
    avg = total/4.0;
    printf("The average for experiment #%d is %6.2f\n\n", i, avg);
  }
}
```

The following output is produced by this program:

```
Enter 4 results for experiment #1:
     232.46  315.89  169.27  525.42
The average for experiment #1 is 310.76

Enter 4 results for experiment #2:
     348.45  227.93  683.34  394.19
The average for experiment #2 is 413.48

Enter 4 results for experiment #3:
     416.81  220.89  189.13  134.36
The average for experiment #3 is 240.30
```

Modularity

Part Three

Program Development

Chapter Six

Just as people and products have a life cycle, so do programs. A program's life cycle is divided into three main stages as illustrated in Figure 6-1. These stages consist of program development, program documentation, and program maintenance.

The development stage is where a program is initially developed. It is at this stage that requirements must be understood and the structure of the program planned. The documentation stage, as its name implies, consists of creating, both within the program and in separate documents, sufficient user and programmer support references and explanations. In the maintenance stage, the program is modified or enhanced as new demands and requirements are obtained or program errors are detected. Complete courses and textbooks are devoted to each of these three program stages. Our purpose in listing them is to put the actual writing of a program in the perspective of the total effort needed to produce professional software.

The writing of a program in a computer language is formally called coding (informally, of course, it is called *programming*). And that, after all, is what we have been doing — writing programs in a language, or code, that can be decoded and used by the computer. The coding of a program is but one component in the program's development stage. Examining just the development stage in more detail, we find that it is composed of four distinct phases, as illustrated on Figure 6-2.

Listed below is the relative amount of effort typically expended on each development phase for large commercial programming projects. As can be seen from this listing, the coding phase is not the major effort in overall program development.

Phase	Effort
Analysis	10%
Design	20%
Coding	20%
Testing	50%

FIGURE 6-1 A Program's Life Cycle

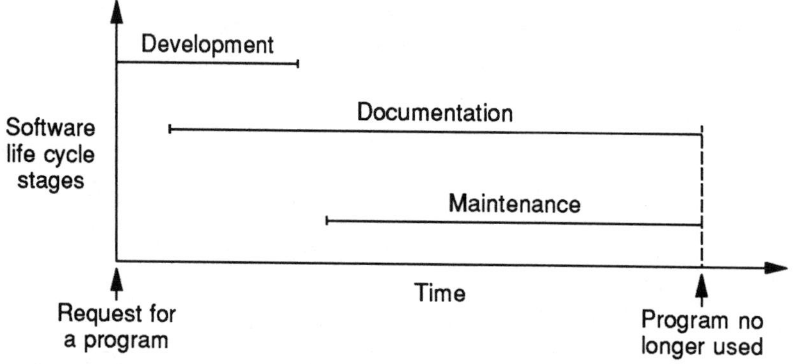

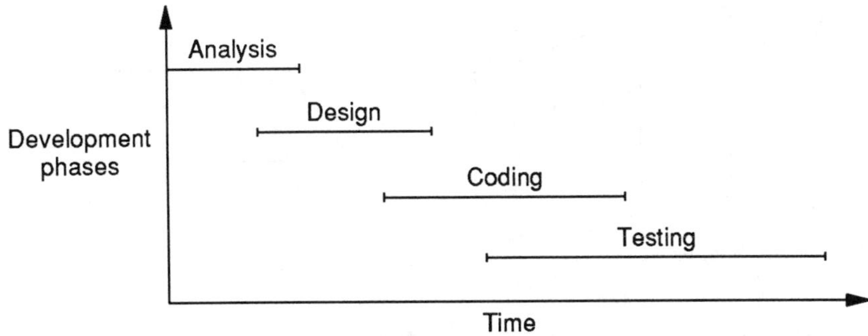

FIGURE 6-2 The Phases of Program Development

Many new programmers have trouble because they spend the majority of their time coding the program, without spending sufficient time understanding and designing the program. In this regard, it is worthwhile to remember the programming proverb, "It is impossible to write a successful program for a problem or application that is not fully understood."

6.1 Analysis, Design, and Testing Phases

The purpose of the analysis phase is to ensure that the program's requirements are understood. This phase is one of the most important, because in it the specifications for the final program or system are determined. If the requirements are not completely and clearly understood before programming begins, the results are almost always disastrous. Once a program structure is created and the program is written, new or reinterpreted requirements often cause havoc. An analogy with house construction is useful to illustrate this point.

Imagine designing and building a house without fully understanding the architect's specifications. After the house is completed, the architect tells you that a bathroom is required on the first floor where you have built a wall between the kitchen and the dining room. In addition, that particular wall is one of the main support walls for the house and contains numerous pipes and electrical cables. Adding one bathroom requires a rather major modification to the basic structure of the house.

Experienced programmers understand the importance of analyzing and understanding a program's requirements before coding, if for no other reason than that they too have constructed programs that later had to be entirely dismantled and redone. The following exercise should give you a sense of this experience.

Figure 6-3 illustrates the outlines of six individual shapes from a classic children's puzzle. As one or more shapes are given, starting with shapes A and B, an easy-to-describe figure must be constructed.

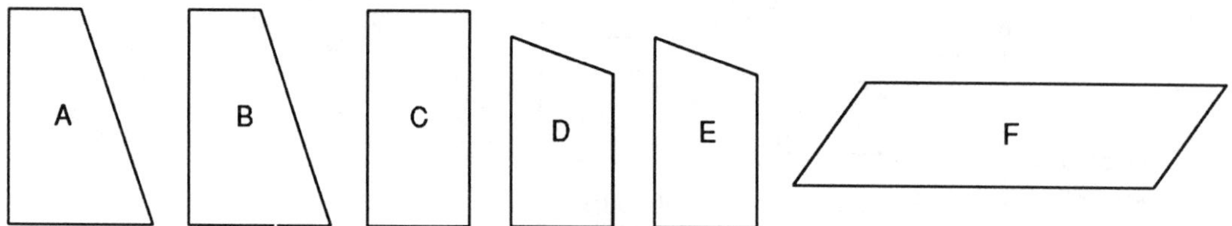

FIGURE 6-3 Six Individual Shapes

Typically, shapes A and B are initially arranged to obtain a square, as illustrated in Figure 6-4. Next, when shape C is considered, it is usually combined with the existing square to form a rectangle, as illustrated in Figure 6-5. Then, when pieces D and E are added, they are usually arranged to form another rectangle, which is placed alongside the existing rectangle to form a square, as shown in Figure 6-6.

The process of adding new pieces onto the existing structure is identical to constructing a program and then adding to it as each subsequent requirement is understood. The problem arises when the program is almost finished and a requirement is added that does not fit easily into the established pattern. For example, assume that the last shape (shape F) is now to be added (see Figure 6-7). This last piece does not fit into the existing pattern that has been

FIGURE 6-4 Typical First Figure

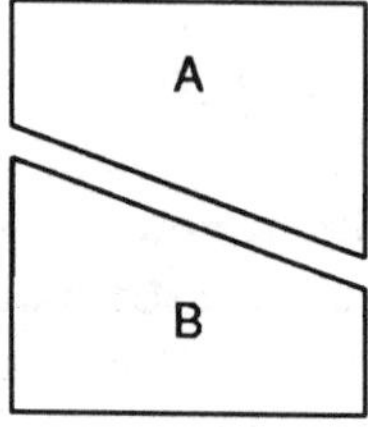

FIGURE 6-5 Typical Second Figure

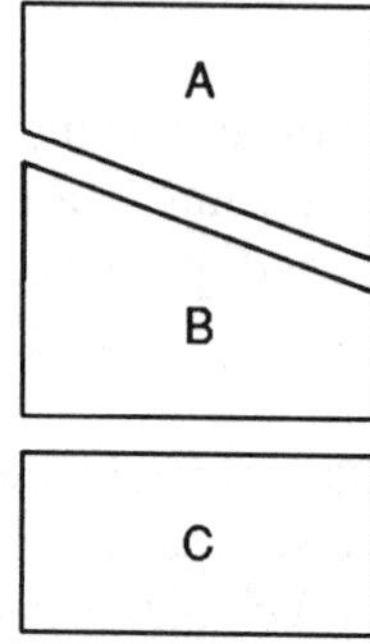

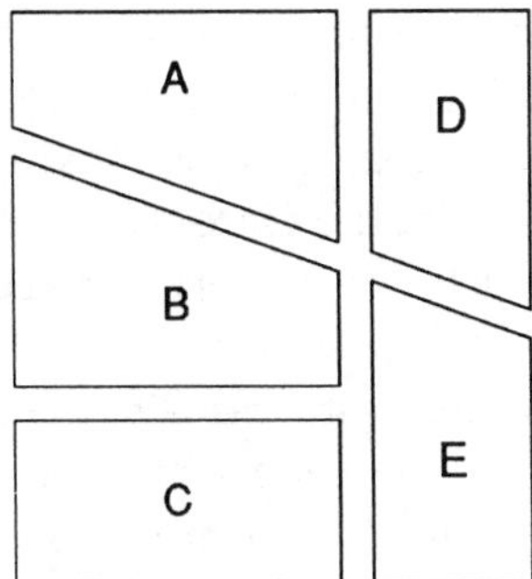

FIGURE 6-6 Typical Third Figure

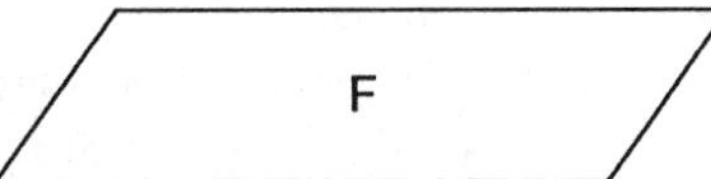

FIGURE 6-7 The Last Piece

constructed. In order to include this piece with the others, the pattern must be completely dismantled and restructured.

Unfortunately, many programmers structure their programs in the same sequential manner used to construct Figure 6-6. Rather than taking the time to understand the complete set of requirements, new programmers frequently start coding when they understand only a small subset of the total requirements. Then, when a subsequent requirement does not fit the existing program structure, the programmer is forced to dismantle and restructure either parts or all of the program.

FIGURE 6-8 Including All the Pieces

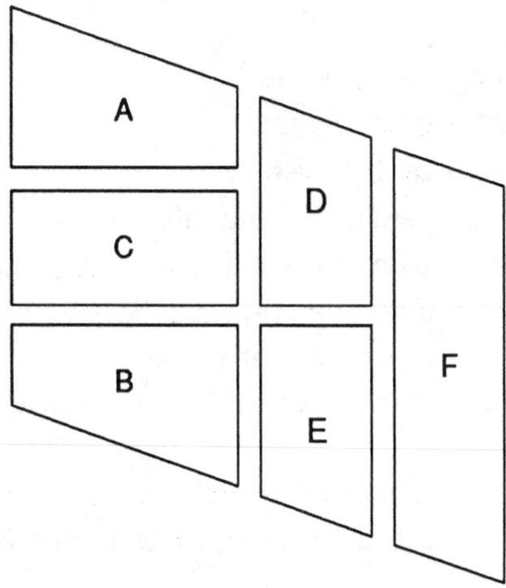

Now, let us approach the problem of creating a figure from another view. If we started by arranging the first set of pieces as a parallelogram, all the pieces could be included in the final figure, as illustrated in Figure 6-8.

It is worthwhile observing that the piece that caused us to dismantle the first figure (Figure 6-6) actually sets the pattern for the final figure illustrated in Figure 6-8. This is often the case with programming requirements. The requirement that seems to be the least clear is frequently the one that determines the main interrelationships of the program. It is worthwhile to include and understand *all* the known requirements before beginning coding.

Analysis

The task of understanding and documenting the requirements of a program or system is part of the analysis phase. In this phase, the person doing the analysis must initially take a broad perspective, see the "big picture," and understand the main purpose of what the program or system is meant to achieve. Using a mixture of interviews, questionnaires, a review of existing procedures and documents, and intuition, the analyst must determine the main purpose of the system as seen by the person making the request. For large systems, the analysis is usually conducted by a systems analyst. For smaller systems or individual programs, the analysis is typically performed directly by the programmer.

Very often, the initial request for a computer program comes from someone who is not totally clear as to what is required and the ramifications of the request. The person may have a problem or an immediate need for certain types of reports and sees the computer as a means of rapidly solving the problem. The analysis phase is used to clearly define the existing problem or need.

An intermediate result of the analysis phase is a determination of whether a computer system or program is necessary at all. Frequently, a change in existing operating procedures or organizational reporting can solve a problem or satisfy the request for a specific type of report. If the initial analysis concludes that a computer program should be installed, the analysis phase continues and results in a final requirements document. This document must clearly specify:

- what the system or program must do
- what outputs the system must produce
- what inputs are required by the system
- the number of users the system will initially handle
- the maximum number of users to which the system can expand
- the average number of transactions that can be processed in a given time period (usually per hour or per day)
- the maximum number of transactions that can be processed in a given time period
- the type and maximum number of records that must be stored by the system before storage capacity must be increased

- backup procedures in case the system goes down
- security procedures for gaining access to the system
- interface requirements with other systems.

The first questions that need to be asked in the analysis phase always involve finding out the motivation of the persons making the request and their expectations for the program. For example, such questions as "What is the main problem you are having with your present system ?" and "What is the main purpose you see the new system fulfilling?" are ways of eliciting very useful information from the requester. Additional questions include, "If you could make a wish list for everything you want from the system, what would it be?" Later, the wish list can be ranked by those items that are essential, those that are very useful but not essential, and those that would be nice to have but could be omitted, if necessary, due to cost, equipment, or time constraints.

These questions are always asked so that the analyst can see the request from the requester's perspective. Frequently, a simple initial request for a program conceals a raft of expectations that are not initially verbalized. It is the job of the analyst to uncover these expectations before the system is assembled. This is equivalent to obtaining all the pieces of the figure illustrated in Figure 6-8 before it is constructed. The analyst's task is completed when the broad objective of the system or program have been understood and further subdivided into a specific set of detailed objectives, which are described in the requirements document.

For example, consider a request from the head of a Wall Street bond trading department for a program to keep track of all bonds traded by the department. The analyst must first find out what "keep track of" means to the department head and why "keeping track" is important. As it turns out, this particular request was made rather late in December, when people are traditionally more concerned with the holiday season and the new year than with pressing business problems. The department head explained that she had to know the total value of all trades made by each individual in her department to determine the end-of-year bonus earned by each trader. Each trade made in the department was recorded daily by hand in a notebook to which only the department head had full access. For reasons of security and because bonuses and raises were based on a trader's activity, the total and type of trades made by each individual were not released to anyone else in the department. The department head was stuck with the job.

As all trades made in the department were sent to the accounting department for processing, the analyst initially thought that the required information could be extracted from the accounting department's computer files. This was impossible because the accounting department did not include in its files either the department or the individual that initiated a particular trade. The trading department produced about 10 percent of the total number of trades cleared by the accounting department for the entire firm, and the accounting department had no intention of entering and storing the additional data in its data base.

Once the head of the trading department started constructing a wish list, however, it was discovered that if the department's own records were kept on a computer, the department head could obtain all kinds of useful reports. These included reports that specified how much trading was done each month, how much trading was done in each of ten regional offices, how much trading was done with each of the other firms the department did business with, who the department's biggest clients were, and, of course, the required end-of-year summary by trader. At that point, the department head made the decision to purchase a small personal computer and to budget funds for programming expenses.

Based on the interviews conducted and an understanding of the type of data that needed to be stored, a requirements document for the tracking system was prepared for the department head. The document listed a sample of each type of report that would be produced by the system, the inputs that had to be entered into the computer, and the data formats of the files kept in the computer for possible transmission to the accounting department. After approval, the document was given to a programmer to consider ways of implementing the required programs.

Design

In the program design phase, potential approaches to achieving the requirements specified in the requirements document are considered, issues of reliability, backup, and ease of use are resolved, and provisions for testing, maintenance, and further enhancements are addressed.

The program designer is in the position of a person receiving the pieces of a puzzle and given the job of constructing the completed structure. Unlike a jigsaw puzzle, however, the pieces of a program design puzzle can be arranged in many different ways. In this regard, the program designer is very similar to an architect who must draw up the plans for a house.

For large systems, the systems designer must organize the system into smaller subsystems, with specifications for how the subsystems will interface with each other. This approach is always top-down, starting from the whole and

FIGURE 6-9 First-Level Refinement Structure Diagram

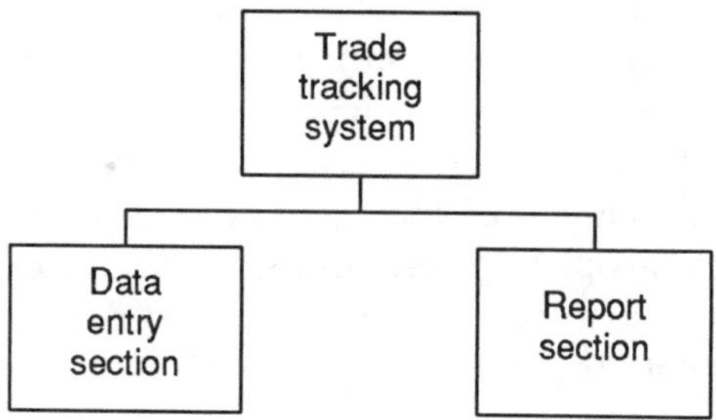

proceeding to the parts. For example, in our trade tracking system, the systems designer may initially divide the system into the two subsystems illustrated in Figure 6-9. This is called a *first-level refinement* because it constitutes the first refinement to the overall system structure.

The designer continues the process of refinement and subdivision until the individual segments are small enough to be programmed as complete tasks in themselves. Both the data entry and report subsections shown in Figure 6-9 would be further refined into suitable segments. The data entry section certainly must include provisions for entering the data. Since it is the system designer's responsibility to plan for contingencies and human error, provisions must also be made for changing incorrect data after it has been entered and for deleting previously entered data altogether. Similar subdivisions for the report section must also be made. Additionally, the format of the data produced in the data entry section must be specified to ensure proper retrieval by the programs that will be coded for the report section. Figure 6-10 illustrates a second-level refinement of the bond tracking system that includes these further subdivisions.

The process of refinement continues until the last level of tasks can be assigned to a programmer to code. The programmer must be given the inputs that will be received, the outputs that are to be produced, and a description of the method for transforming the data inputs into the desired outputs. The methods used for transforming inputs to outputs are formally called *algorithms*. They are discussed in Section 6.2.

Testing

The purpose of testing is to verify that a program works correctly and actually fulfills its requirements. In theory, testing would reveal all existing program errors (in computer terminology, a program error is called a *bug*). In practice, this would require checking all possible combinations of statement execution.

FIGURE 6-10 Second-Level Refinement Structure Diagram

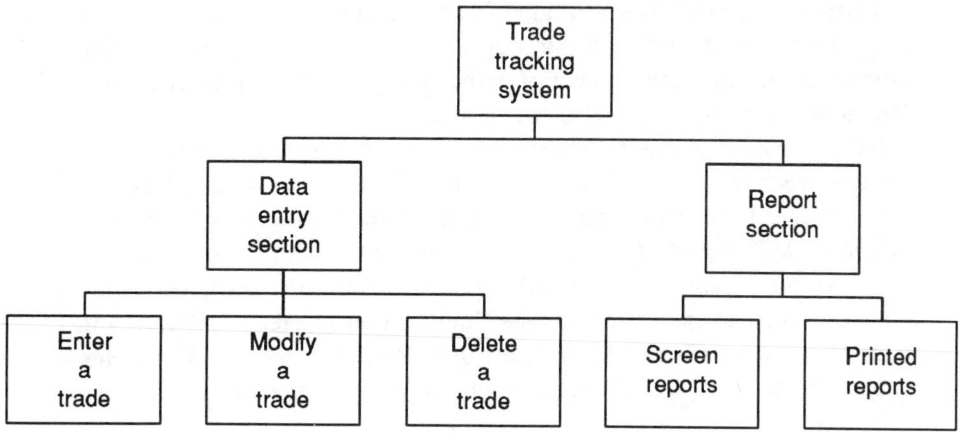

Due to the time and effort required, this is an impossible goal except for extremely simple programs. To see why this is so, consider Program 6-1:

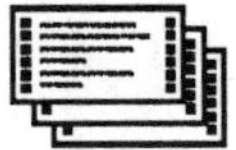

Program 6-1

```
main()
{
  int num;

  printf("Enter a number: ");
  scanf("%d", &num);
  if (num == 5) printf("Bingo!");
  else printf("Bongo!");
}
```

Program 6-1 has two paths that can be traversed when the program is run. The first path includes the execution sequence

```
printf("Enter a number: ");
scanf("%d", &num);
printf("Bingo!");
```

and the second path includes the sequence of instructions

```
printf("Enter a number: ");
scanf("%d", &num);
printf("Bongo!");
```

To test each possible path through Program 6-1 requires two runs of the program, with a careful selection of test input data for each run to ensure that each path is exercised. The addition of one `if` statement in Program 6-1 increases the number of paths through the program by two. Similarly, two additional `if` statements increases the number of paths by a factor of four, three additional `if` statements by a factor or eight, and so on.

Now consider a modest-sized application program consisting of only ten modules, each module containing five `if` statements. Assuming the modules are always called in the same sequence, there are thirty-two possible paths through each module (2 raised to the fifth power) and more than 1,000,000,000,000,000 (2 raised to the fiftieth power) possible paths through the complete program (all modules executed in sequence). The time needed to create individual test data to exercise each path and the actual computer run time required to check each path make the complete testing of such a program impossible.

The inability to fully check all combinations, or paths, in most programs has led to the programming proverb, "There is no error-free program." More importantly, programmers need to realize that testing may reveal the presence of an error, but not the absence of one. Thus, the fact that a test revealed one bug does not indicate that another one is not lurking somewhere else in the program.

Since exhaustive testing is not feasible for most programs, different philosophies and methods of testing have evolved. Two of the more common are bottom-up and top-down approaches.

The *bottom-up test method* includes testing each module of a system individually, then testing groups of modules operating together, and finally testing the complete system. This method is fine for smaller systems, but inappropriate for larger systems because errors are detected in inverse order to the cost and complexity of correcting them. Errors within a module, which are the most easily detected and corrected, are encountered at the start of the testing phase, and the more troublesome and costly module interaction errors are detected at the end of the testing phase when the system is near completion.

In the *top-down test method,* the interaction between modules is tested first. For example, consider the following program:

```
main()
{
  data_ent();
  taxes();
  report();
}
```

Here `main()` is used as a driver program to call the functions `data_ent()`, `taxes()`, and `report()`. In top-down testing, each of these functions is written in an abbreviated form called a *stub*. For example, the body of the `data_ent()` function might initially consist of the single statement:

```
printf("Successfully entered data_ent");
```

Writing such stubs for all the functions called by `main()` allows `main()` to be tested by itself for proper operation. Later, statements can be added to each stub function to display any values passed to the function (writing functions is the topic of the next chapter). Once the proper operation of `main()` is established and it is verified that correct values have been passed to a function, writing and testing of the individual function, in this case `dat_ent()`, `taxes()`, and `report()`, begins.

Notice that top-down testing proceeds from the highest level of program function (the first function executed) down to the lowest level of function execution (the last function called) and mirrors the effort involved in top-down program design.

In either testing approach, considerable thought must be given to the data that will be used in the test and the part of each module to be tested. Once a bug is revealed, the process of *debugging*, which includes locating, correcting, and verifying the correction, can be initiated.

6.2 Algorithms

Before a programmer can begin coding, he or she must clearly understand:

- the function the program is meant to perform
- the output the program must produce
- the inputs the program must accept
- the method for processing the inputs to achieve the correct outputs.

The processing method consists of one or more specific procedures that, collectively, successfully create the desired outputs from the given data inputs. In computer terminology, these procedures are called *algorithms*. An algorithm is simply a step-by-step procedure, or set of rules, used to solve a particular problem or produce a specific result. You must learn to be comfortable with algorithms in order to become a competent programmer.

Let us illustrate an algorithm by considering the rather simple requirement that a particular program must calculate the sum of the numbers from 1 to 100. Figure 6-11 illustrates three methods for finding the required sum. Each method constitutes an algorithm.

Before coding, the algorithm to be used in solving the particular problem must be understood (the specific steps that are required to produce the desired result or output must be known). Only after the algorithm is selected can coding really begin. Coding then becomes the translation of the algorithm (series of steps) into a machine-readable form.

Let us explore this a little further. Suppose you are asked to paint the flower shown in Figure 6-12, with the restriction that each color must be completed before a new color can be started.

Since there are three colors needed to complete the painting, there are six possible algorithms, or procedures, for painting the figure. These are:

```
Use yellow first, green second, black last.
Use yellow first, black second, green last.
Use green first, yellow second, black last.
Use green first, black second, yellow last.
Use black first, yellow second, green last.
Use black first, green second, yellow last.
```

Method 1. *Columns:* Arrange the numbers from 1 to 100 in a column and add them:

```
    1
    2
    3
    4
    .
    .
   98
   99
 +100
 ------
 5050
```

Method 2. *Groups:* Arrange the numbers in convenient groups that sum to 100. Multiply the number of groups by 100 and add in any unused numbers.

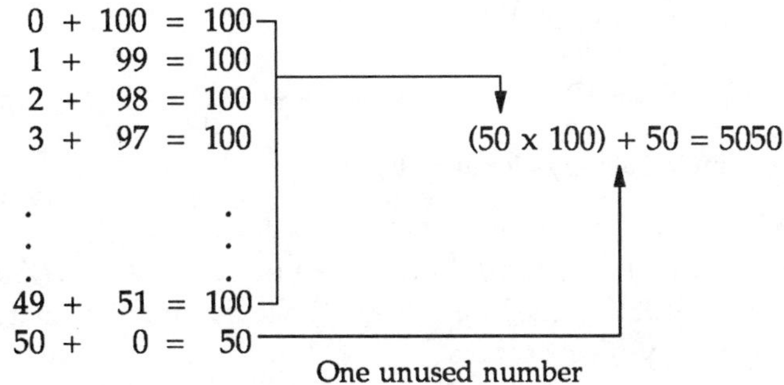

Method 3. *Formula:* Use the formula

$$\text{Sum} = n/2 * (a+l)$$

where

n = number of terms to be added (100)
a = first number to be added (1)
l = last number to be added (100)

$$\text{Sum} = 100/2 * (1 + 100) = 5050$$

FIGURE 6-11 Summing the Numbers 1 through 100

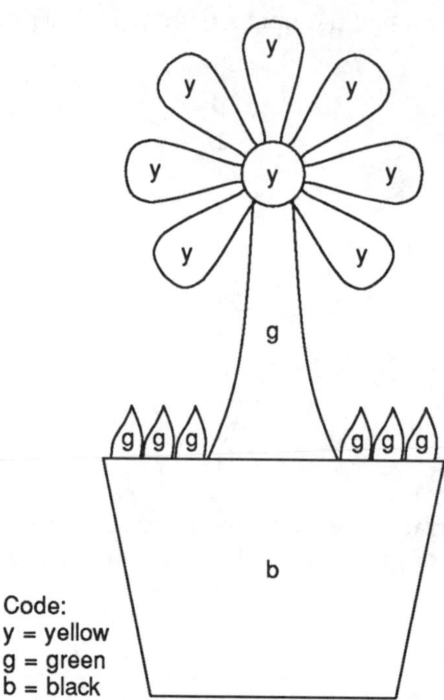

FIGURE 6-12 A Simple Paint-by-Number Figure

Which of the six painting algorithms (series of steps) is best? Since they all produce the same result and they all contain the same number of steps, none of them is superior to any of the others.

Now let us add one constraint. Assume we are limited to using one paintbrush and that there is no turpentine to clean the brush. In this case, which algorithm is best?

Clearly it would now be advisable to choose the algorithm "Use yellow first, green second, black last." This is because yellow is a light color. Green masks the yellow on the brush when green is used, and finally black hides the green when the flowerpot is painted.

Most people would not bother to spend much time writing out the possible alternatives in a detailed step-by-step manner and then selecting the algorithm that does the task in some "best" manner. But then most people do not think algorithmically. They tend to think heuristically or intuitively. For example, if you had to change a flat tire on your car, you would not think of all the steps required — you would simply change the tire or call someone else to do the job. This is an example of heuristic thinking.

Unfortunately, computers do not respond to heuristic commands. A general statement such as "add the numbers from 1 to 100" means nothing to a computer, which responds algorithmically. To program a computer successfully, you must clearly understand the difference between algorithmic thinking and intuitive thinking. A computer is an "algorithm-responding" machine; it is not an

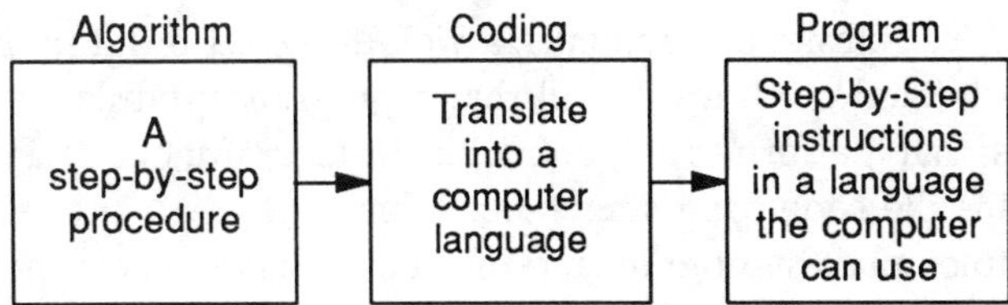

FIGURE 6-13 Coding an Algorithm

"intuitive-thinking" machine. You cannot tell a computer to change a tire or to add the numbers from 1 to 100. Instead, you must give the computer a detailed step-by-step set of instructions that, collectively, forms an algorithm. For example, the set of instructions

```
Set n equal to 100.
Set a equal to 1.
Set l equal to n.
Calculate sum = n/2 * (a + l).
Print the sum.
```

form a detailed method, or algorithm, for adding the numbers from 1 to 100. Once the programmer understands these steps, they can be translated into a computer language. The translation of an algorithm into a computer language is called, as you might expect, *coding the algorithm* (see Figure 6-13).

6.3 Other Program Considerations

Although it is impossible to quantitatively determine the quality of a program, it is possible to list features that a good program should have. A good program features:

- modular, structured functions
- meaningful variable names
- self-documenting instructions
- limited comment lines
- intelligent indentation.

These guidelines will help the programmer create programs that are easily modified and read by any programmer who must work with them.

We have already discussed modules and the importance that C language places on them (in C, each function is considered a module). Just as a well-designed building is based on a firm structure and a well-designed system is composed of well-designed segments, a well-designed program is constructed by using well-defined modules. Recall that a program module consists of a set of instructions that perform an identifiable task, or function. Typically, each module contains the code for a single algorithm.

Using modules makes program modifications easier when changes need to be made or bugs are detected. The necessary changes can usually be isolated and confined to appropriate modules, without radically affecting other modules. Only if the module needs different input data or produces different outputs are its surrounding modules affected. Even then, the changes to the surrounding modules are clear: they must either be modified to output the data needed by the changed module or changed to accept the new output data. Modules help the programmer determine where the changes must be made, while the structure of the module itself determines how easy it will be to make the change.

Although there are no hard and fast rules for well-written modules, specific guidelines do exist. The total number of instructions in a module generally should not exceed fifty lines. This allows the complete module to fit on a standard 8 1/2- by 11-inch sheet of paper for ease of reading. Each module should have one entrance point and one exit point. Internally, each substructure should also contain a single entry and exit. This makes it easy to trace the flow of data when errors are detected. All the C statements that alter the normal sequential program flow, including the `if-else`, `switch`, `while`, and `do-while` statements, conform to this single entry and exit model.

The instructions contained within a module should use variable names that describe the data and are self-documenting. This means that they tell what is happening without a lot of extra comments. For example, the instructions

```
a = 75.30;
b = .05;
c = a *(1 + b);
```

do not contain intelligent variable names that give an indication of what is being calculated. A more useful set of instructions is:

```
price = 75.30;
tax_rate = .05;
total = price + price * tax_rate;
```

Here, the instructions themselves "tell" what the data represents, what is being calculated, and how the calculation is being performed. Always keep in mind that the goal is to produce programs that make sense to any programmer reading them, at any time. The use of mnemonic data names makes excessive comments unnecessary. The program should, however, contain a sufficient number of comments to explain what a module does and any other pertinent information that would be helpful to other programmers; but excessive comments are usually a sign of insufficient program design or poorly constructed coding.

```
if it is below 60 degrees
if it is snowing
wear your lined raincoat
else
wear a topcoat
if it is below 40 degrees
wear a sweater also
if it is below 30 degrees
wear a jacket also
else if it is raining
wear an unlined raincoat
```

FIGURE 6-14 Version 1—What to Wear

```
if it is below 60 degrees
  if it is snowing
    wear your lined raincoat
  else
    wear a topcoat
  if it is below 40 degrees
    wear a sweater also
    if it is below 30 degrees
      wear a jacket also
else if it is raining
  wear an unlined raincoat
```

FIGURE 6-15 Version 2—What to Wear

Another sign of a good program is the use of indentation to signify nested statements and to indicate where one statement ends and another begins. Consider the module "What to Wear" shown in Figure 6-14. Because the `if` and `else` statement matchings are not clearly indicated, the instructions in the module are open to multiple interpretations. For example, using Figure 6-14, try to determine what to wear if the temperature is 35 degrees and it is raining. Now consider Version 2 of "What to Wear" in Figure 6-15.

Version 2 is indented, making it clear that we are dealing with one main `if-else` statement. If it is below 60 degrees the set of instructions indented underneath the first `if` will be executed, else the condition `if it is raining` will be checked.

6.4 Common Programming Errors

A major programming error is the rush to code and run a program before the programmer fully understands what is required and the algorithms that will be used to produce the desired result. A symptom of this haste to get a program entered into the computer is the lack of either an outline of the proposed program or a written program itself. Many problems can be caught just by checking a copy of the program, either handwritten or listed from the computer, before it is ever compiled.

Another error is unwillingness to test a program in depth. After all, since you wrote the program, you assume it is correct or you would have changed it before it was compiled. It is extremely difficult to back away and honestly test your own software. As a programmer, you must constantly remind yourself that just because you *think* your program is correct does not make it so. Finding errors in your own program is a sobering experience, but one that will help you become a master programmer.

6.5 Chapter Summary

1. All programs have a life cycle. This cycle consists of a development stage, a documentation stage, and a maintenance stage.
2. The development stage consists of analysis, design, coding, and testing phases. The purpose of the analysis phase is to ensure that the requirements of the program are understood. In the design phase, a specific program structure is selected and provisions for testing and maintenance are resolved. Coding involves translating the selected procedures into a computer language, and testing is used to verify proper program operation.
3. An algorithm is a set of rules or procedures that produce a specific result. Looked at in this light, coding becomes the translation of algorithms into computer-readable form.
4. As yet, there exists no exact quantitative measure for determining how good a program is. It is possible, however, to list features of good programs. These features include modular structure, meaningful variable names, self-documenting instructions, limited comment lines, and intelligent indentation.

Sample Problem

This sample problem illustrates an algorithm that is used to interchange the contents of two cups of liquid. A third cup must be available to temporarily hold the contents of either cup.

The algorithm that performs the interchange is:

1. Pour the contents of the first cup into the third (empty) cup.
2. Pour the contents of the second cup into the first cup.

3. Pour the contents of the third cup into the second cup.

The main element in this algorithm is that a third cup is used to temporarily hold the contents of one of the cups involved in the interchange. In a similar manner, this algorithm can be adapted to interchange the values contained in two variables. When the values in two variables are to be interchanged, a third variable must be used to temporarily store the contents of one of the variables. For example, to interchange the values in the variables `num1` and `num2` requires that a third variable be available to temporarily store the contents of one of these variables. Calling this third variable `temp`, the algorithm for performing this interchange is:

1. Store the contents of variable `num1` into variable `temp`.
2. Store the contents of variable `num2` into variable `num1`.
3. Store the contents of variable `temp` into variable `num2`.

In C, this algorithm is described by the assignment statements:

```
temp = num1;
num1 = num2;
num2 = temp;
```

The important point in this example is that the value in `num1` is saved in `temp` before `num1` is assigned a new value.

Writing Your Own Functions

Chapter Seven

In the programs we have written so far, the only two functions we have called have been `printf()` and `scanf()`. Although these two functions have been enormously helpful to us, it is now time to create our own useful functions, in addition to the `main()` function that is required in all programs.

In this chapter we learn how to write these functions, pass data to them, process the passed data, and return a result to the calling function.

7.1 Function and Argument Declarations

In creating our own functions we must be concerned with the function itself and how it interfaces with other functions. This is true both in calling a function and in returning a value back from a function. In this section we describe the first part of the interface, passing data to a function and having the data correctly received and stored by the called function.

As we have already seen with the `printf()` and `scanf()` functions, a function is called, or used, by giving the function's name and passing any data to it in the parentheses following the function name (see Figure 7-1).

The called function must be able to accept the data passed to it by the function doing the calling. Only after the called function successfully receives the data can the data be manipulated to produce a useful result.

To clarify the process of sending and receiving data, consider Program 7-1, which calls a function named `find_max()`. The program, as shown, is not yet complete. Once the function `find_max()` is written and included in Program 7-1, the completed program, consisting of the functions `main()` and `find_max()`, can be run.

Program 7-1

```
main()
{
  int firstnum, secnum;

  printf("Enter a number: ");
  scanf("%d", &firstnum);
  printf("Great! Please enter a second number: ");
  scanf("%f", &secnum);

  find_max(firstnum,secnum);
}
```

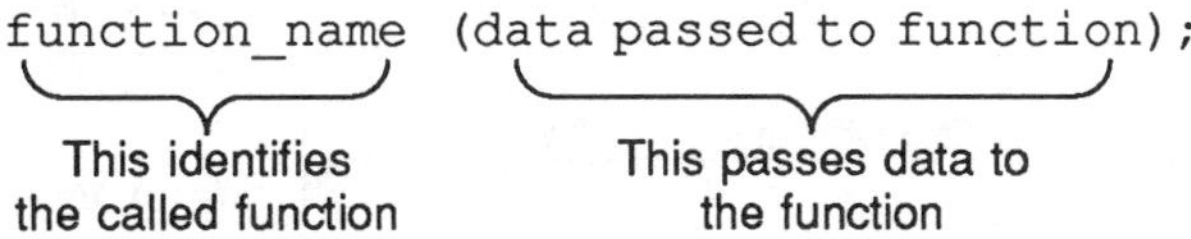

FIGURE 7-1 Calling and Passing Data to a Function

Let us review calling the function `find_max()` from the `main()` function. We will then write `find_max()` to accept the data passed to it and determine and display the largest or maximum value of the two passed values.

The function `find_max()` is referred to as the *called function*, since it is called, or summoned, into action by its reference in the `main()` function. The function that does the calling, in this case `main()`, is referred to as the *calling function*. The terms *called* and *calling* come from standard telephone usage, where one party calls the other on a telephone. The party initiating the call is referred to as the *calling party*, and the party receiving the call is referred to as the *called party*. The same terms describe function calls.

Calling a function is rather trivial. All that is required is that the name of the function be used and that any data passed to the function be enclosed within the parentheses following the function name. The items enclosed within the parentheses are called *actual arguments* of the called function (see Figure 7-2).

If a variable is one of the arguments in a function call, the called function receives a copy of the value stored in the variable. For example, the calling statement `find_max(firstnum,secnum);` causes the values or numbers currently residing in the variables `firstnum` and `secnum` to be passed to `find_max()`. The variable names in the calling statement are there to tell the calling function where to get the values that will be passed. After the values are passed, control is transferred to the called function.

As illustrated in Figure 7-3, the function `find_max()` does not receive the variable names `firstnum` and `secnum` and has no knowledge of these variable names. The function simply receives two values and must itself determine where to store these values before it does anything else. Although this procedure for passing data to a function may seem surprising, it is really a safety procedure for ensuring that a called function does not inadvertently change data stored in a variable. The function gets a copy of the data to use. It may change its copy and, of course, change any variables or arguments declared inside itself.

FIGURE 7-2 Calling and Passing Two Values to `find_max()`

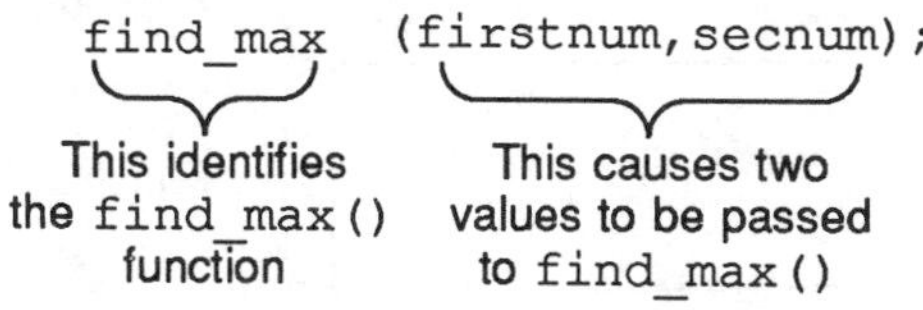

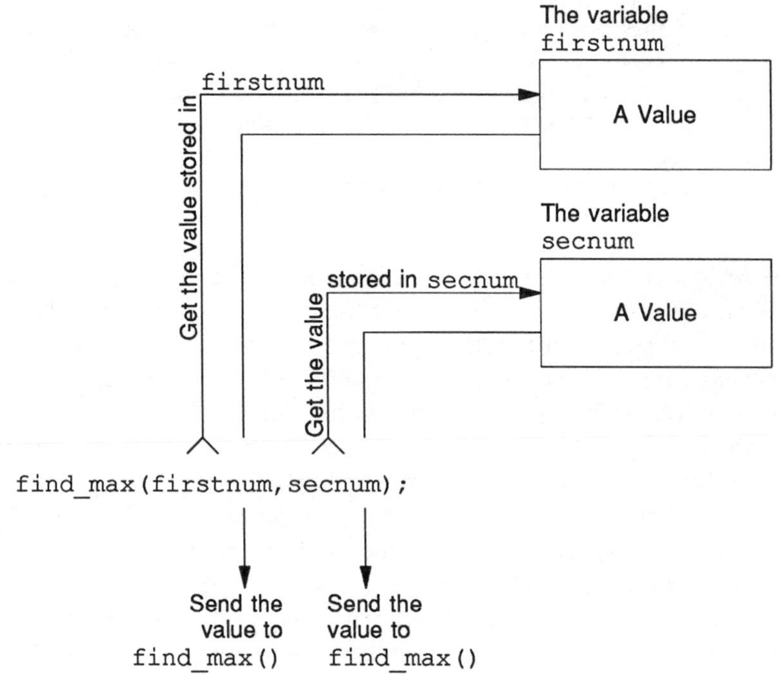

FIGURE 7-3 `find_max()` Receives Actual Values

However, unless specific steps are taken to do so, a function is not allowed to change the contents of variables declared in other functions.

Let us now begin writing the function `find_max()` to process the values passed to it.

Every function consists of two parts, a *function header* and a *function body,* as illustrated in Figure 7-4. One of the purposes of the function header is to ensure correct receipt and storage of any data passed to the function. The purpose of the function body is to operate on the passed data and return, at most, one value to the calling function.

The function header itself consists of two parts, a *function declaration* and *argument declarations.* The function declaration is always the first line of a function and must include the name of the function and the names of the arguments that will be used by it. If the function returns a value, the function

FIGURE 7-4 General Format of a Function

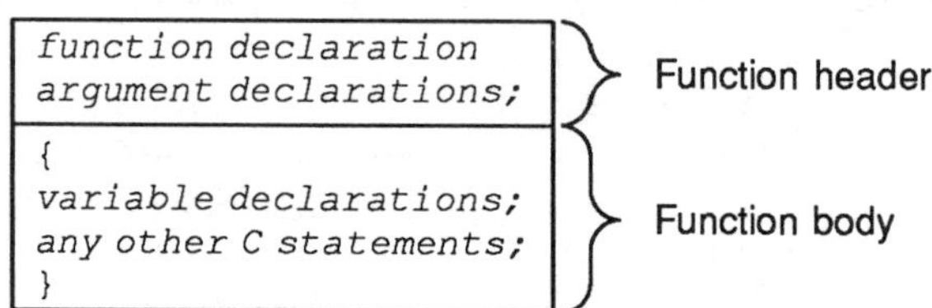

declaration must also declare the type of value that will be returned. Since `find_max()` will not return any value, its function declaration consists only of the function name `find_max()` and a list of arguments. For example, the following declaration can be used:

```
find_max(x,y)   <-------- no semicolon
```

The names of the arguments in the function declaration line, in this case `x` and `y`, are chosen by the programmer. Any two names selected according to the rules used to choose variable names can be used.

The argument names in the declaration line are also called *formal arguments* and are used to store the values passed to the function when it is called. Thus, the argument `x` will be used to store the first value passed to `find_max()` and the argument `y` will be used to store the second value passed at the time of the function call. The function itself does not know where the values come from when the call is made from `main()`. The first part of the call procedure executed by the computer involves going to the variables `firstnum` and `secnum` and retrieving the values stored. These values are then passed to `find_max()` and ultimately stored in the formal arguments `x` and `y` (see Figure 7-5).

As far as the function `find_max()` is concerned, the arguments `x` and `y` are treated like variables. They must be declared and then can be used anywhere within the `find_max()` function. The declaration of these two arguments is given by an argument declaration statement that is placed immediately after the function declaration line.

Argument declarations, as the name implies, declare the data type of the arguments expected by the function. Since `find_max()` receives two integer values that will be stored in the arguments `x` and `y`, any of the following argument declaration statements can be used:

```
int x,y;        int y,x;        int x;        int y;
                                int y;        int x;
```

FIGURE 7-5 Storing Values in Arguments

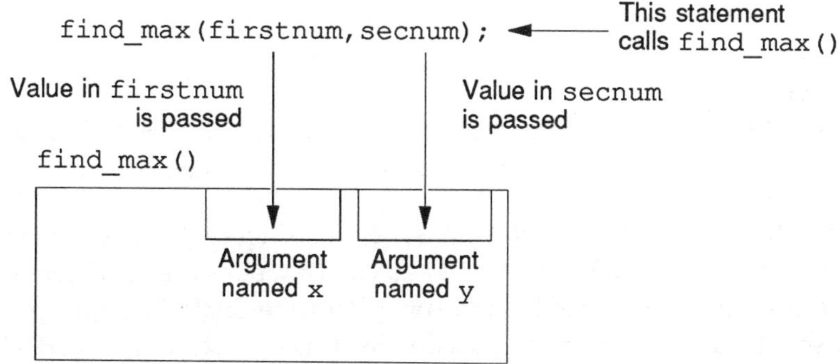

As illustrated in these declarations, the order of the arguments is not important. The only requirement is that each argument be declared. Notice that these argument declarations are identical to variable declarations. The only difference between argument declarations and variable declarations is their placement in the function. Argument declarations always begin on the second line of the function immediately after the function declaration, while variable declarations are placed within the function body. From a programming viewpoint, arguments can be considered as variables whose values are assigned outside the function and passed to the function when it is called. Variables are declared within a function body and have values assigned by statements within the function.

Putting all this together, a valid function header for the `find_max()` function is:

```
find_max(x,y)       /* this is the function declaration */
int x,y;            /* argument declarations            */
```

Now that we have written the function header, we can construct the body of the function `find_max()`. You have already written many function bodies. A function body begins with an opening brace, `{`, contains any necessary variable declarations followed by any valid C statements, and ends with a closing brace, `}`. This is illustrated in Figure 7-6. You should recognize it as the same structure you have been using in all the `main()` functions you have written. This should not be a surprise, since `main()` is itself a function and must adhere to the rules required for constructing all legitimate functions.

In the body of the function `find_max()`, we will declare one variable that will store the maximum of the two numbers passed to `find_max()`. We will then use an `if-else` statement to find the maximum of the two numbers. Finally, the `printf()` function will be called to display the maximum. The complete function code is:

```
find_max(x,y)           /* function declaration       */
int x,y;                /* argument declarations      */
{                       /* start of function body     */
  int max;              /* variable declaration       */

  if (x >= y)           /* find maximum number        */
    max = x;
  else
    max = y;
  printf("\nThe maximum of the two numbers is %d.", max);
}     /* end of function body and end of function     */
```

Notice that the argument declarations are made before the opening brace that starts the function body and that the variable declarations are made immediately after the opening brace. This is in keeping with the fact that argument values are passed to a function from outside the function, and that variables are

```
{
  variable declarations (if any)
  other C statements
}
```

FIGURE 7-6 Structure of a Function Body

declared and assigned values from within the function body.

Program 7-2 includes the `find_max()` function within the program code previously listed in Program 7-1.

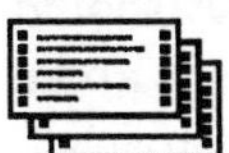

Program 7-2

```
main()
{
  int firstnum,secnum;

  printf("Enter a number: ");
  scanf("%d", &firstnum);
  printf("Great! Please enter a second number: ");
  scanf("%d", &secnum);

  find_max(firstnum, secnum);
}

/* following is the function find_max         */

find_max(x,y)       /* function declaration     */
int x,y;            /* argument declarations    */
{                   /* start of function body  */
  int max;          /* variable declaration     */

  if (x >= y)       /* find the maximum number */
    max = x;
  else
    max = y;

  printf("\nThe maximum of the two numbers is %d.", max);
}           /* end of function body and end of function  */
```

Program 7-2 can be used to select and print the maximum of any two integer numbers entered by the user. Following is a sample run with Program 7-2:

```
Enter a number: 25
Great! Please enter a second number: 5

The maximum of the two numbers is 25.
```

The placement of the `find_max()` function after the `main()` function in Program 7-2 is a matter of choice. Some programmers prefer to put all called functions at the top of a program and make `main()` the last function listed. As we will see in the next section, putting `main()` last has some advantages when the other functions return noninteger values.

We prefer to list `main()` first because it is the driver function that should give anyone reading the program an idea of what the complete program is about before encountering the details of each function. Either placement approach is acceptable and you will encounter both styles in your programming work. In no case, however, can `find_max()` be placed inside `main()`. This is true for all C functions, which must be defined by themselves outside any other function. Each C function is a separate and independent entity with its own arguments and variables; nesting of functions is never permitted.

7.2 Returning Values

As described in the last section, a function need not return any result back to the calling function. A function must, of course, process the data passed to it, or there would be no need for the function. In this section we see how the result produced can be returned directly to the calling function.

In keeping with our original definition of a function as a module that can accept data, operate on the data, and return a result, all C functions are restricted to returning at most one "legitimate" value (see Figure 7-7). As you might expect, given C's flexibility, there is a way of returning more than a single value, but that is the topic of Section 7.4. Here, we are concerned only with the return of a single value from a called function.

As with the initial calling of a function, returning a value requires that the interface between the called and calling functions be handled correctly. From its side of the return transaction, the called function must provide the following items:

- the data type of the returned value
- the actual value being returned.

A function returning a value must specify, in its declaration line, the data type of the value that will be returned. Recall that the function declaration line is the

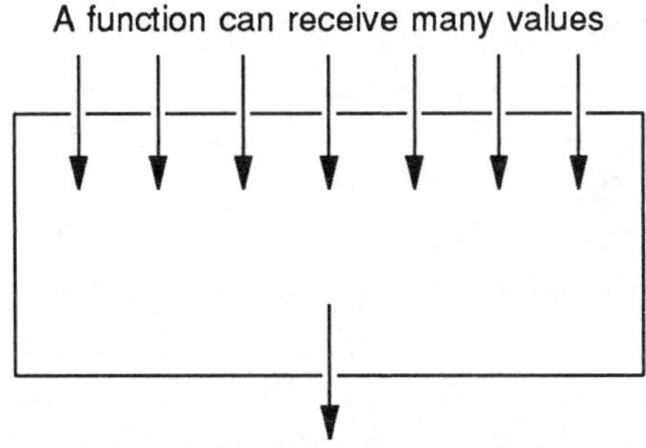
A function can receive many values
Only one value can be directly returned

FIGURE 7-7 A Function Returns at Most One Value

first line of the function, which includes both the function's name and a list of argument names. As an example, consider the `find_max()` function written in the last section. It determined the maximum value of two numbers passed to the function. For convenience, the original code of `find_max()` is listed below.

```
find_max(x,y)          /* function declaration      */
int x,y;               /* argument declarations     */
{                      /* start of function body    */
  int max;             /* variable declaration      */
  if (x >= y)          /* find the maximum number */
    max = x;
  else
    max = y;
  printf("\nThe maximum of the two numbers is %d.", max);
}
```

As written, the function's declaration is `find_max(x,y)`, where `x` and `y` are the names chosen for the function's formal arguments.

If `find_max()` is now to return a value, the function's declaration line must be amended to include the data type of the value being returned. For example, if an integer value is to be returned, the proper function declaration line is

```
int find_max(x,y)
```

Similarly, if the function is to return a floating point value, the correct function declaration line is

```
float find_max(x,y)
```

If the function is to return a double precision value, the declaration would be

```
double find_max(x,y)
```

Let us now modify the function `find_max()` to return the maximum value of the two numbers passed to it. To do this, we must first determine the data type of the value that is to be returned and include this data type in the function's declaration line.

Since the maximum value determined by `find_max()` is stored in the integer variable `max`, it is the value of this variable that the function will return. Returning an integer value from `find_max()` requires that the function declaration be `int find_max(x,y)`. Observe that this is the same as the original function declaration for `find_max()` with the addition of the reserved word `int` to declare the data type of the returned value.

Having declared the data type that `find_max()` will return, all that remains is to include a statement within the function to cause the return of the correct value. To return a value, a function must use a `return` statement, which has the form:

```
return(expression);
```

When the `return` statement is encountered, the expression inside the parentheses is evaluated first. The value of the expression is then automatically converted to the data type declared in the function header before being sent back to the calling function. After the value is returned, program control reverts to the calling function. Thus, to return the value stored in `max`, all we need do is add the statement `return(max);` before the closing brace of the `find_max()` function. The complete function code is:

These should be the same data type.

```
int find max (x,y)        /* function declaration    */
int x,y;                  /* argument declaration    */
{                         /* start of function body */
  int max;                /* variable declaration    */

  if (x >= y)
   max = x;
  else
   max = y;

  return (max);           /* return statement        */
}
```

In the new code for the function `find_max()`, note that the data type of the expression contained within the parentheses of the return statement correctly matches the data type in the function's declaration line. It is up to the programmer to ensure that this is so for every function returning a value. Failure to match the return value with the function's declared data type will not result in an error when your program is compiled, but it may lead to undesired results since the return value is always converted to the data type declared in the function declaration. Usually this is a problem only when the fractional part of a returned floating point or double precision number is truncated because the function was declared to return an integer value.

Having taken care of the sending side of the return transaction, we must now prepare the calling function to receive the value sent by the called function. On the calling (receiving) side, the calling function must:

- be alerted to the type of value to expect
- properly use the returned value.

We will consider these items in reverse order.

To prepare the calling function to use a returned value, we must either provide a variable to store the value or use the value directly in an expression. Storing the returned value in a variable is done by using a standard assignment statement. For example, the assignment statement

```
maxnum = find_max(firstnum,secnum);
```

can be used to store the value returned by `find_max()` in the variable named `maxnum`. This assignment statement does two things. First, the right-hand side of the assignment statement calls `find_max()`, and then the result returned by `find_max` is stored in the variable maxnum. Since the value returned by `find_max()` is an integer, the variable `maxnum` must also be declared as an integer variable within the calling function's variable declarations.

The value returned by a function need not be stored directly in a variable; it can be used in any valid expression. For example, the expression `2 * find_max(firstnum,secnum)` multiplies the value returned by `find_max()` by two, and the statement

```
printf("%d", find_max(firstnum,secnum));
```

displays the returned value.

Finally, we must ensure that the calling function knows the data type of the function being called before a value is actually returned. This can always be taken care of by declaring the called function in the same way that a variable is declared. For example, including the declaration statement

```
int find_max();
```

with `main()`'s variable declarations is sufficient to alert `main()` that `find_max()` is a function that will return an integer value.

Program 7-3 illustrates the inclusion of both declaration and assignment statements for `main()` to correctly declare, call, and store a returned value from `find_max()`. As before, and in keeping with our convention of placing the `main()` function first, we have placed the `find_max()` function after `main()`.

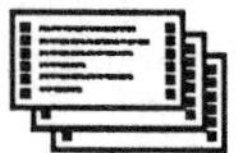

Program 7-3

```
main()
{
  int find_max();          /* function declaration statement */
  int firstnum, secnum, maxnum;    /* variable declarations */

  printf("Enter a number: ");
  scanf("%d", &firstnum);
  printf("Great! Please enter a second number: ");
  scanf("%d", &secnum);

  maxnum = find_max(firstnum,secnum);

  printf("\nThe maximum of the two numbers is %d.",maxnum);
}

int find_max(x,y)                    /* function declaration    */
int x,y;                             /* argument declarations   */
{
  int max;                           /* variable declarations   */

  if (x >= y)
    max = x;
  else
    max = y;

  return(max);                       /* return statement        */
}
```

In reviewing Program 7-3, it is important to note the four items we have introduced in this section. The first is the declaration of `find_max()` within `main()`. This statement, which ends with a semicolon, as all statements do, alerts `main()` to the data type that `find_max()` will be returning. The parentheses after the name `find_max` inform `main()` that `find_max` is a function rather than a variable. The second item to notice in `main()` is the use of an assignment statement to call `find_max()` and to store the returned value in the variable `maxnum`. We have also made sure to correctly declare `maxnum` as an integer within `main()`'s variable declarations so that it matches the data type of the returned value.

The last two items concern the coding of the `find_max()` function. The first line of `find_max()` declares that the function will return an integer value, and the expression in the return statement evaluates to a matching data type. Thus, `find_max()` is internally consistent in sending an integer value back to `main()`, and `main()` has been correctly alerted to receive and use the returned integer.

In writing your own functions, you must always keep these four items in mind. For another example, see if you can identify these four items in Program 7-4.

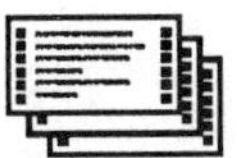

Program 7-4

```
main()
{
  int count;                         /* start of declarations */
  double fahren;

  double tempvert();

  for(count = 1; count <= 4; ++count)
  {
    printf("Enter a Fahrenheit temperature: ");
    scanf("%f", &fahren);
    printf("The Celsius equivalent is %6.2f\n\n", tempvert(fahren) );
  }
}

double tempvert(in_temp)            /* function declaration   */
double in_temp;                     /* argument declaration   */
{
  return( (5.0/9.0) * (in_temp - 32.0) );
}
```

In reviewing Program 7-4, let us first analyze the function `tempvert()`. The complete definition of the function begins with the function's declaration line and ends with the closing brace after the return statement. The function is declared as a double, which means the expression in the function's return statement must evaluate to a double precision number. Since a function declaration is not a statement but the start of the code defining the function, the function declaration line does not end with a semicolon.

Within `tempvert()`, `in_temp` is declared as a double precision argument. Since an expression with a double precision number yields a double precision value, the correct data type, a double precision number, is returned by the function.

On the receiving side, main() has a declaration statement for the function tempvert() that agrees with tempvert()'s function declaration. As with all declaration statements, multiple declarations of the same type may be made within the same statement. Thus, we could have used the same declaration statement to declare both the function tempvert() and the variable fahren as double precision data types. If we had done so, the single declaration statement

```
double fahren, tempvert();
```

could have been used to replace the two individual declarations for tempvert() and fahren. For clarity, however, we will always keep function declaration statements separate from variable declaration statements. No additional variable is declared in main() to store the returned value from tempvert() because the returned value is immediately passed to printf() for display.

One further point is worth mentioning here. One of the purposes of declarations, as we learned in Chapter 2, is to alert the computer to the amount of internal storage reserved for the data. The declaration statement within main() for find_max() performs this task and tells the computer how much storage area must be accessed by main() when the returned value is retrieved. Had we placed the find_max() function before main(), however, the function declaration line for find_max() would suffice to alert the computer to the amount of storage needed for the returned value. In this case, the function declaration statement for find_max(), within main(), could be eliminated. Since we have chosen always to list main() as the first function in a file, we must include function declaration statements for all functions called by main().

More on Returning Values (void Type)

From our discussion of returned data types, you might conclude that if no data type is listed in the function declaration line, no value is returned. Unfortunately, this conclusion is incorrect.

If a data type is omitted in a function declaration line, the function may return either an integer type or no type at all. That is, the default data type returned by a C function is an integer. Thus, the omission of a data type is no guarantee that the function will not return a value. It is a sign of poor programming practice to neglect to clearly identify a returned integer value. In this text we will omit the data type declaration only if the function truly does not return a value. If a value is returned, its type will be explicitly included in the function's declaration.

Newer versions of C have a data type called void. When the term void precedes the function's name in the function declaration line, both the computer and anyone reading the program are alerted to the fact that the function will not return any value to the calling function. If this data type is available on the version of C you are using, we recommend it for functions that do not return a value to the calling function.

Whether a function returns a value or not, it is good programming practice to include a return statement in the function. Although control is automatically returned to the calling program when the closing brace of a function is reached, this is considered "falling off the edge" of the called function. Using an explicit return statement is a better means of formally returning control to the calling function. If no value is to be returned, simply omit the parentheses and write the return statement as `return;`.

Finally, the fact that a function returns a value does not require that the calling function use the value. A function can be called without either using the returned value in an expression or assigning it to a variable. For example, the statement `tempvert(in_temp);` could be included in Program 7-4. This statement properly calls the function `tempvert()` without further using the returned value. Calling a function without using the returned value is almost always a sign of an error on the part of the programmer, but the error will not be identified or indicated during program compilation.

7.3 Standard Library Functions

All C programs have access to a standard, preprogrammed set of functions for handling input and output of data, computing mathematical quantities, and manipulating strings of characters. These preprogrammed functions are stored in a system library that contains the collection of standard and tested functions available on your system.

Before using the functions available in the system library, you must know:

the name of each available function
the arguments required by each function
the data type of the result (if any) returned by each function
a description of what each function does

The first three items are provided by the function header. For example, consider the function named `sqrt()`, which calculates the square root of its argument. The function header for this function is:

```
double sqrt(num)
double num;          /* argument declaration */
```

This header lists all of the information required to call the `sqrt()` function. `sqrt()` expects a double precision argument and returns a double precision value.

Many library functions require a standard set of common declarations and other information for proper operation. This information is always contained in a standard file named `stdio.h`. To include the information in this file in your program, one of the following statements must be included as the first statement of your program:

```
#include <stdio.h>      <----- no semicolon
#include "stdio.h"      <----- no semicolon
```

Which of the above statements you must use depends on your C compiler and is listed in the C reference manual for your system. If you intend to use a library function in your program, placing the appropriate `#include` statement at the top of the program ensures proper access to the library function.

Input/Output Library Functions

We have already made extensive use of two input/output (I/O) library functions, `printf()` and `scanf()`. In this section, we present two additional I/O library functions.

The `getchar()` function can be used for single character input. The function header for `getchar()` is:

```
char getchar()
```

This declaration is correct unless a noncharacter end-of-file sentinel must be detected. In this case, the declaration

```
int getchar();
```

is required (as described later in Section 12.5). The function `getchar()` expects no arguments to be passed to it and returns a character data type. The actual character returned by `getchar()` is the next single character entered at the terminal. For example, a statement such as

```
in_char = getchar();
```

causes the next character entered at the terminal to be stored in the variable `in_char`. This is equivalent to the longer statement

```
scanf("%c",&in_char);
```

The `getchar()` function is extremely useful when continuously inputting strings of characters, which is the topic of Chapter 10.

The output library function corresponding to `getchar()` is the `putchar()` function. The function header for `putchar()` is:

```
putchar(ch)
char ch;
```

Thus, `putchar()` expects a character argument and does not return any value. `putchar()` simply displays the character passed to it on the terminal. The statement `putchar('a')` is equivalent to the longer statement `printf("%c",'a')`.

Mathematical Library Functions

Table 7-1 lists the more commonly available system library mathematical functions. Before trying to use these functions, make sure they are available on your system.

TABLE 7-1 Commonly Available Mathematical Functions

Function Header	Description
`int abs(num)` `  int num;`	Returns the absolute value of an integer argument.
`int labs(num)` `  int num;`	Returns the absolute value of a long integer argument.
`double fabs(num)` `  double num;`	Returns the absolute value of a double precision argument.
`double pow(x,y)` `  double x,y;`	Returns *x* raised to the *y* power.
`int rand()`	Returns a pseudorandom number.
`double sin(angle)` `  double angle;`	Returns the sine of an angle. The angle must be in radians.
`double cosin(angle)` `  double angle;`	Returns the cosine of an angle. The angle must be in radians.
`double square(num)` `  double num;`	Returns the square of its argument.
`double sqrt(num)` `  double num;`	Returns the square root of its argument. Returns a zero for negative arguments.

As with user-written functions, the arguments passed to a mathematical library function do not have to be numbers. The argument of a library function can be an expression, provided the expression can be evaluated to yield an argument of the required data type. For example, the following arguments are valid for the given functions:

```
sqrt(4.0 + 7 * 3)                abs(-24 % 3 + 6)
sqrt(25.0 * 3 - 1.04)            abs(a * b - m * n)
sqrt(a * b - c/6.0)              pow(p*q,5.0)
square(-32.0/8.0 - 6.0)          pow(2.,n+3.)
```

The expressions in parentheses are evaluated first to yield a specific value. Thus, before the variables `a, b, c, m, n, p,` and `q` are used in the above expressions, actual values would have to be assigned to these variables. The value of the expression is then passed to the function. Table 7-2 lists the final value of selected expressions and the value returned by the listed function.

Like user-written functions, library functions can be included as part of a larger expression. The value returned by the function is computed before any other operation is performed. For example:

```
5 * square(2.0*7.0-4.0) - 200 = 5 * 100.0 - 200   = 300.0
3.0 * pow(2,10) / 5.0         = 3 * 1024.0 / 5.0 = 614.4
36 / sqrt(3.0*4.0-3.0)        = 36 / 3.0         = 12.0
```

TABLE 7-2 Selected Function Examples

Original Expression	Evaluated Expression	Returned Value
`sqrt(4.0+7.0*3.0)`	`sqrt(25.0)`	5.0
`sqrt(25.0*3.0-1.04)`	`sqrt(73.96)`	8.6
`square(-32.0/8.0-6.0)`	`square(-10.0)`	100
`abs(-24/3 + 6)`	`abs(-2)`	2

The expression `4 * sqrt(5.0*20.0-3.96)/7.0` is evaluated as:

1. Perform multiplication in argument: `4*sqrt(100.0-3.96)/70`
2. Complete argument computation: `4*sqrt(96.04)/7.0`
3. Call the function: `4*9.8/7.0`
4. Perform the multiplication: `29.2/7.0`
5. Perform the division: `5.6`

Program 7-5 illustrates the use of the `sqrt()` function to determine the time it will take a ball to hit the ground after it has been dropped from a building. The mathematical formula used to calculate the time in seconds that it takes to fall a given distance in feet is:

```
time = sqrt(2 * distance / g)
```

where g is the gravitational constant equal to 32.2 ft/sec^2.

Program 7-5

```
#include <stdio.h>
#define GRAV 32.2
main()
{
  double time, distance;
  double sqrt();          /* declare the sqrt() function */

  printf("Enter the distance (in feet): ");
  scanf("%lf", &distance);
  time = sqrt(2 * distance / GRAV);

  printf("\nIt will take %4.2lf seconds", time);
  printf("\nto fall %7.3lf feet.", distance);
}
```

Notice that Program 7-5 contains a `#include` statement and also a `#define` statement that equates the value of the gravitational constant 32.2 to the symbolic name `GRAV`. Additionally, just as all functions that `main()` uses must be declared (unless they are located in the same file before `main()`), we have included a declaration for `sqrt()` with `main()`'s declaration statements. Although the actual code for the `sqrt()` function is contained within the standard system library, the proper declaration must be provided by the programmer. Alternatively, all compilers have a standard file named `math.h` that contains appropriate declaration statements for the supplied mathematical functions. Including the line `#include <math.h>` or `#include "math.h"` (see your compiler reference manual for the correct form) before `main()` removes the necessity of explicitly typing declarations for the mathematical functions as was done in Program 7-5. Following is a sample run with Program 7-5:

```
Enter the distance (in feet): 600

It will take 6.10 seconds
to fall 600.000 feet.
```

String Library Functions

Almost all C compilers have an extensive set of library functions for the input, comparison, manipulation, and output of strings of characters. A list and description of these functions is given in Table 7-3. We will describe these functions in Chapter 10, where character strings are presented.

TABLE 7-3 String Library Functions

Name	Description
`strcat(string1,string2)`	Concatenate `string2` to `string1.`
`strchr(string,character)`	Locate the position of the character within the string.
`strcmp(string1,string2)`	Compare `string2` to `string1.`
`strcpy(string1,string2)`	Make `string1` equal to `string2.`
`strlen(string)`	Determine the length of the string.

Miscellaneous Routines

In addition to the input/output, mathematical, and string functions, all system libraries have an extensive collection of miscellaneous functions and other routines. Some of the more useful of these are listed in Table 7-4.

These routines are sometimes included in a standard file named `ctype.h.` To access and use them in a program may require one of the following statements before `main()`:

```
#include <ctype.h>   <------- no semicolon
#include "ctype.h"   <------- no semicolon
```

Check your compiler's reference manual for the appropriate form.

The routines listed in Table 7-4 are particularly useful for checking characters input by a user. For example, Program 7-6 repeatedly requests that a user enter a character and determines if the character is a letter or a digit. The program exits the `while` loop when an `f` is typed. So that the user won't have to decide whether a lowercase or uppercase `f` must be entered to stop the program, the program converts all input to lowercase and checks only for a lowercase `f.`

A few remarks are in order in reviewing Program 7-6. First, the condition being tested in the `if-else` statement makes use of the fact that a condition is considered true if it evaluates to a nonzero value. Thus, the condition `( isalpha(in_char) )` could have been written as `( isalpha(in_char) != 0 ),` and the condition `( isdigit(in_char) )` could have been written `(isdigit(in_char) != 0 ).` The second call to `getchar()` in the `do-while` loop is used to remove the ENTER key.

TABLE 7-4 Miscellaneous Routines

Name	Description
`isalpha(character)`	Returns a nonzero number if the character is a letter; otherwise it returns a zero.
`isupper(character)`	Returns a nonzero number if the character is uppercase; otherwise it returns a zero.
`islower(character)`	Returns a nonzero number if the character is lowercase; otherwise it returns a zero.
`isdigit(character)`	Returns a nonzero number if the character is a digit (0 through 9); otherwise it returns a zero.
`toupper(character)`	Returns the uppercase equivalent if the character is lowercase; otherwise it returns the character unchanged.
`tolower(character)`	Returns the lowercase equivalent if the character is uppercase; otherwise it returns the character unchanged.

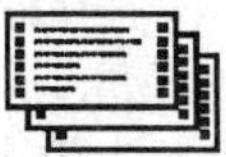

Program 7-6

```
#include <stdio.h>
main()
{
  char in_char;

  do
  {
    printf("\nPush any key (type an f to stop) ");
    in_char = getchar();       /* get the next character typed */
    in_char = tolower(in_char);       /* convert to lowercase  */
    getchar();                 /* get and ignore the enter key */
    if ( isalpha(in_char) )    /* a nonzero value is true in C */
      printf("\nThe character entered is a letter.");
    else if ( isdigit(in_char) )
      printf("\nThe character entered is a digit.");
  } while (in_char != 'f');

}
```

Since functions return values, a function may itself be an argument to a function (including itself). For example, the two statements in Program 7-6:

```
in_char = getchar();          /* get the next character typed */

in_char = tolower(in_char);         /* convert to lowercase   */
```

can be combined into the single statement:

```
in_char = tolower(getchar());
```

7.4 Variable Scope

Now that we have begun to write programs containing more than one function, we can look more closely at the variables declared within each function and their relationship to variables in other functions.

By their very nature, C functions are independent modules. As we have seen, values are passed to a function by using the function's argument list and a value is returned from a function by using a return statement. Seen in this light, a function can be thought of as a closed box, with slots at the top to receive values and a single slot at the bottom of the box to return a value (see Figure 7-8).

The metaphor of a closed box is useful because it emphasizes the fact that what goes on inside the function, including all variable declarations within the function's body, are hidden from the view of all other functions. Since the variables created inside a function are available only to the function itself, they are said to be local to the function, or *local variables.* This term refers to the *scope* of a variable, where scope is defined as the section of the program where the variable is valid, or "known". A variable can either have a local scope or a global scope. A variable with a *local scope* is simply one that has had storage locations set aside for it by a declaration statement made within a function body. Local variables are meaningful only when used in expressions or statements inside the function that declared them. This means that the same variable name can be declared and used in more than one function. For each function that declares the variable, a separate and distinct variable is created.

All the variables we have used until now have been local variables. This is a direct result of placing our declaration statements inside functions and using them as definition statements that cause the computer to reserve storage for the declared variable. As we shall see, declaration statements can be placed outside functions and need not act as definitions that cause new storage areas to be reserved for the declared variable.

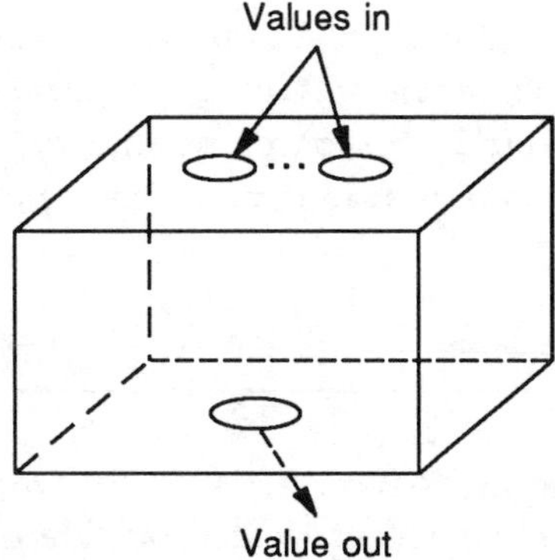

FIGURE 7-8 A Function Can Be Considered a Closed Box

A variable with *global scope,* more commonly termed a *global variable,* is one whose storage has been created for it by a declaration statement located outside any function. Global variables are also referred to as *external* variables. These variables can be used by all functions in a program that are placed after the global variable declaration. This is shown in Program 7-7, where we have purposely used the same variable name inside both functions contained in the program.

Program 7-7

```
int firstnum;        /* create a global variable named firstnum */
main()
{
  int secnum;        /* create a local variable named secnum      */

  firstnum = 10;     /* store a value into the global variable    */
  secnum = 20;       /* store a value into the local variable     */
  printf("\nFrom main(): firstnum = %d",firstnum);
  printf("\nFrom main(): secnum = %d\n",secnum);
  valfun();          /* call the function valfun */
  printf("\nFrom main() again: firstnum = %d",firstnum);
  printf("\nFrom main() again: secnum = %d",secnum);
}

valfun()          /* no values are passed to this function        */
{
  int secnum;     /* create second local variable named secnum    */
```

continued

```
    secnum = 30; /* this only affects this local variable's value */
    printf("\nFrom valfun(): firstnum = %d",firstnum);
    printf("\nFrom valfun(): secnum = %d\n",secnum);
    firstnum = 40;    /* this changes firstnum for both functions */
    return;
}
```

The variable `firstnum` in Program 7-7 is a global variable because its storage is created by a declaration statement located outside of a function. Since both functions, `main()` and `valfun()`, follow the declaration of `firstnum`, both of these functions can use this global variable with no further declaration needed.

Program 7-7 also contains two separate local variables, both named `secnum`. Storage for the `secnum` variable named in `main()` is created by the declaration statement located in `main()`. A different storage area for the `secnum` variable in `valfun()` is created by the declaration statement located in the `valfun()` function. Figure 7-9 illustrates the three distinct storage areas reserved by the three declaration statements found in Program 7-7.

Each of the variables named `secnum` are local to the function in which their storage is created, and each of these variables can be used only from within the appropriate function. Thus, when `secnum` is used in `main()`, the storage area reserved by `main()` for its `secnum` variable is accessed, and when `secnum` is used in `valfun()`, the storage area reserved by `valfun()` for its `secnum` variable is accessed. The following output is produced when Program 7-7 is run:

```
From main(): firstnum = 10
From main(): secnum = 20

From valfun(): firstnum = 10
From valfun(): secnum = 30

From main() again: firstnum = 40
From main() again: secnum = 20
```

FIGURE 7-9 The Three Storage Areas Created by Program 7-7

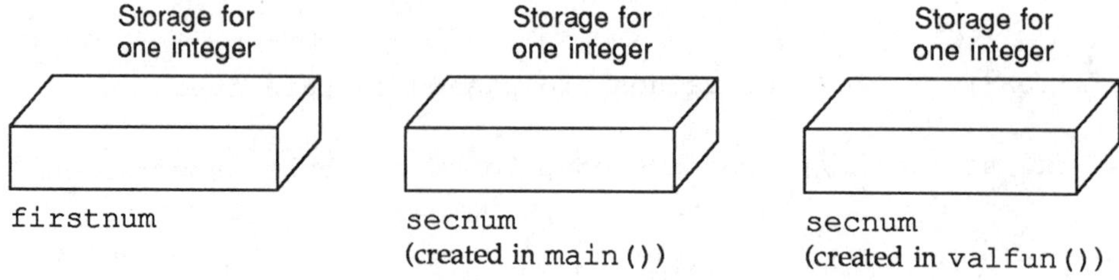

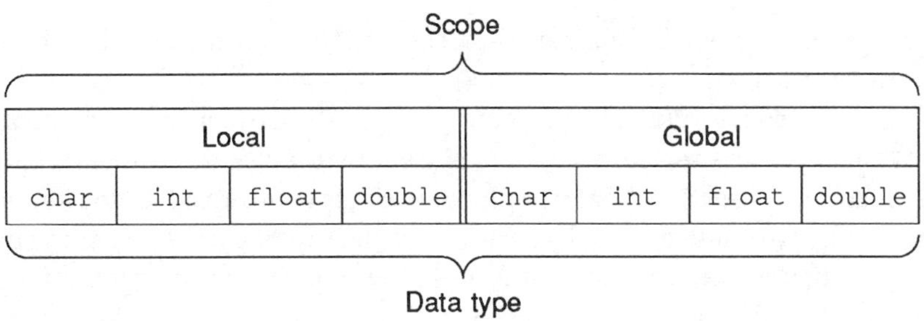

FIGURE 7-10 Relating the Scope and Type of a Variable

Let us analyze the output produced by Program 7-7. Since `firstnum` is a global variable, both the `main()` and `valfun()` functions can use and change its value. Initially, both functions print the value of `10` that `main()` stored in `firstnum`. Before returning it, `valfun()` changes the value of `firstnum` to `40`, which is the value displayed when the variable `firstnum` is next displayed from `main()`.

Since each function knows only its own local variables, `main()` can send only the value of its `secnum` to the `printf()` function, and `valfun()` can send only the value of its `secnum` to the `printf()` function. Thus, whenever `secnum` is obtained from `main()`, the value of `20` is displayed and, whenever `secnum` is obtained from `valfun()`, the value `30` is displayed.

C does not confuse the two `secnum` variables because only one function can execute at a given moment. Only the storage area for the variables created by the function currently being executed are accessed. If a variable that is not local to the function is used by the function, the program searches the global storage areas for the correct name.

The scope of a variable in no way influences or restricts the data type of the variable. Just as a local variable can be a character, integer, float, double, or any of the other data types (long/short) we have introduced, so can global variables be of these data types, as illustrated in Figure 7-10. The scope of a variable is determined solely by the placement of the declaration statement that reserves storage for it, while the data type of the variable is determined by the use of the appropriate reserved word (`char`, `int`, `float`, `double`, etc.) before the variable's name in a declaration statement.

Misuse of Globals

One caution should be mentioned here. Global variables allow the programmer to "jump around" the normal safeguards provided by functions. Rather than passing variables to a function, it is possible to make all variables global ones. *Do not do this.* By indiscriminately making all variables global you instantly destroy the safeguards C provides to make functions independent and insulated from each other, including the necessity of carefully designating the type of arguments needed by a function, the variables used in the function, and the value returned.

Using only global variables can be especially disastrous in larger programs that have many user-created functions. Since all variables in a function must be declared, creating functions that use global variables requires that you remember to write the appropriate global declarations at the top of each program using the function — they no longer come along with the function. More devastating than this, however, is the horror of trying to track down an error in a large program using global variables. Since a global variable can be accessed and changed by any function following the global declaration, it is a time-consuming and frustrating task to locate the origin of an erroneous value.

Global variables, however, are extremely useful in creating tables of data that must be shared between many functions. If many functions require access to a group of tables, global variables allow the functions to make efficient changes to the same table without the need for multiple table passing. We will see this when we explore arrays and data structures in the next three chapters.

7.5 Variable Storage Class

The scope of a variable defines the location within a program where that variable can be used. Given a program, you could take a pencil and draw a box around the section of the program where each variable is valid. The space inside the box would represent the scope of a variable. From this viewpoint, the scope of a variable can be thought of as the space within the program where the variable is valid.

In addition to the space dimension represented by its scope, variables also have a time dimension. The time dimension refers to the length of time that storage locations are reserved for a variable. For example, all variable storage locations are released to the computer when a program is finished running. However, while a program is still executing, interim variable storage areas are reserved and subsequently released to the computer. Where and how long a variable's storage locations are kept before they are released can be determined by the storage class of the variable.

The four available storage classes are *auto, static, extern,* and *register*. If one of these class names is used, it must be placed before the variable's data type in a declaration statement. Examples of declaration statements that include a storage class designation are:

```
auto int num;        /* auto storage class, int data type     */
static int miles;    /* static storage class, int data type   */
```

```
register int dist;   /* register storage class, int data type  */
extern int price;    /* extern storage class, int data type    */
auto float coupon;   /* auto storage class, float data type    */
static double yrs;   /* static storage class, double data type */
extern float yld;    /* extern storage class, float data type  */
auto char in_key;    /* auto storage class, char variable      */
```

To understand what the storage class of a variable means, we will first consider local variables (those variables created inside a function) and then global variables (those variables created outside a function).

Local Variable Storage Classes

Local variables can be members only of the auto, static, or register storage classes. If no class description is included in the declaration statement, the variable is automatically assigned to the auto class. Thus, auto is the default class used by C. All the local variables we have used, since the storage class designation was omitted, have been auto variables.

The term *auto* is short for *automatic.* Storage for automatic local variables is automatically reserved or created each time a function declaring automatic variables is called. As long as the function has not returned control to its calling function, all automatic variables local to the function are "alive" — that is, storage for the variables is available. When the function returns control to its calling function, its local automatic variables "die" — that is, the storage for the variables is released to the computer. This process repeats itself each time a function is called. For example, consider Program 7-8, where the function `testauto()` is called three times from `main()`.

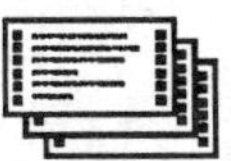

Program 7-8

```
main()
{
  int count;                /* create the auto variable count */

  for(count = 1; count <= 3; ++count)
    testauto();
}

testauto()
{
  int num = 0; /* create auto variable num, initialize to zero */
```

continued

```
    printf("\nValue of the automatic variable num is %d", num);
    ++num;
    return;
}
```

The output produced by Program 7-8 is:

```
Value of the automatic variable num is 0
Value of the automatic variable num is 0
Value of the automatic variable num is 0
```

Each time `testauto()` is called, the automatic variable `num` is created and initialized to zero. When the function returns control to `main()` the variable `num` is destroyed along with any value stored in `num`. Thus, the effect of incrementing `num` in `testauto()`, before the function's return statement, is lost when control is returned to `main()`.

For most applications, the use of automatic variables works just fine. There are cases, however, where we would like a function to remember values between function calls. This is the purpose of the *static* storage class. A local variable that is declared as `static` causes the program to keep the variable and its latest value even when the function that declared it is through executing. Examples of static variable declarations are:

```
static int rate;
static float taxes;
static double amount;
static char in_key;
static long years;
```

A local static variable is not created and destroyed each time the function declaring the static variable is called. Once created, local static variables remain in existence for the life of the program. This means that the last value stored in the variable when the function is finished executing is available to the function the next time it is called.

Since local static variables retain their values, they are not initialized within a declaration statement in the same way as automatic variables. To see why, consider the automatic declaration `int num = 0;`, which causes the automatic variable `num` to be created and set to zero each time the declaration is encountered. This is called a *run-time initialization* because initialization occurs each time the declaration statement is run. This type of initialization would be disastrous for a static variable, because resetting the variable's value to zero each time the function is called would destroy the very value we are trying to save.

The initialization of static variables (both local and global) is done only once, when the program is first compiled. At compilation time, the variable is created and any initialization value is placed in it. Thereafter, the value in the variable is kept without further initialization each time the function is called. To see how this works, consider Program 7-9.

Program 7-9

```
main()
{
  int count;              /* count is a local auto variable */

  for(count = 1; count <= 3; ++count)
    teststat();
}

teststat()
{
  static int num = 0;     /* num is a local static variable */

  printf("\nValue of the static variable num is now %d", num);
  ++num;
  return;
}
```

The output produced by Program 7-9 is:

```
Value of the static variable num is now 0
Value of the static variable num is now 1
Value of the static variable num is now 2
```

As illustrated by the output of Program 7-9, the static variable `num` is set to zero only once. The function `teststat()` then increments this variable just before returning control to `main()`. The value that `num` has when leaving the function `teststat()` is retained and displayed when the function is next called.

Unlike automatic variables that can be initialized by either constants or expressions using both constants and previously initialized variables, static variables can be initialized only by using constants or constant expressions, such as `3.2 + 8.0`. Also, unlike automatic variables, all static variables are set to zero when no explicit initialization is given. Thus, the specific initialization of `num` to zero in Program 7-9 is not required.

The remaining storage class available to local variables, the *register* class, is not used as extensively as either automatic or static variables. Examples of register variable declarations are:

```
register int time;
register double diffren;
register float coupon;
```

Register variables have the same time duration as automatic variables; that is, a local register variable is created when the function declaring it is entered, and is destroyed when the function completes execution. The only difference between register and automatic variables is where the storage for the variable is located.

Storage for all variables (local and global), except register variables, is reserved in the computer's memory area. Most computers have a few additional high-speed storage areas located directly in the computer's processing unit that can also be used for variable storage. These special high-speed storage areas are called *registers.* Since registers are actually located in the computer's processing unit, they can be accessed faster than the normal memory storage areas located in the computer's memory unit. Also, computer instructions that reference registers typically require less space than instructions that reference memory locations because there are fewer registers that can be accessed than there are memory locations.

For example, although the AT&T *WE*® 32100 Central Processing Unit has nine registers that can be used for local C program variables, it can be connected to memories that have more than four billion bytes. Most other computers have a similar set of user-accessible registers but millions of memory locations. When the compiler substitutes the location of a register for a variable during program compilation, less space in the instruction is needed than is required to address a memory having millions of locations.

Besides decreasing the size of a compiled C program, using register variables can also increase the execution speed of a C program, if the computer you are using supports this data type. Variables declared with the register storage class are automatically switched to the auto storage class if your computer does not support register variables or if the declared register variables exceed the computer's register capacity.

The only restriction in using the register storage class is that the address of a register variable, using the address operator `&`, cannot be taken. This is easily understood when you realize that registers do not have standard memory addresses.

Global Variable Storage Classes

Global variables, also referred to as external variables, are created by declaration statements external to a function. By their nature, these externally defined variables do not come and go with the calling of any function. Once an external (global) variable is created, it exists until the program in which it is declared is finished executing. Thus, external variables cannot be declared as either auto or register variables, which are created and destroyed as the program is executing. Global variables may, however, be further declared as members of the static or extern storage classes. Examples of declaration statements including these two class descriptions are:

```
extern int sum;
extern double price;
static double yield;
```

The static and extern classes affect only the scope, not the duration, of global variables. As with static local variables, all global variables are initialized to zero during compilation if no explicit initialization value is present.

The purpose of the extern storage class is to extend the scope of a global variable beyond its normal boundaries. To understand this, we must first note that each of the programs we have written so far have been contained in one file. Thus, when you have saved or retrieved programs you have needed only to give the computer a single name for your program. This is not required by C.

Larger programs typically consist of many functions that are stored in multiple files. An example of this is shown in Figure 7-11, where the three functions `main()`, `func1()`, and `func2()` are stored in one file and the two functions `func3()` and `func4()` are stored in a second file.

FIGURE 7-11 A Program May Extend Beyond One File

file1

```
int price;
float yield;
static double coupon;
main()
{
  func1();
  func2();
  func3();
  func4();
}
func1()
{
     •
     •
     •
}
func2()
{
     •
     •
     •
}
```

file2

```
double interest;
func3()
{
     •
     •
     •
}
func4()
{
     •
     •
     •
}
```

For the files illustrated on Figure 7-11, the global variables `price`, `yield`, and `coupon` declared in `file1` can used only by the functions `main()`, `func1()`, and `func2()` in this file. The single global variable, `interest`, declared in `file2` can be used only by the functions `func3()` and `func4()` in `file2`.

Although the variable `price` has been created in `file1`, we may want to use it in `file2`. Placing the declaration statement `extern int price;` in `file2`, as shown in Figure 7-12, allows us to do this. Putting this statement at the top of `file2` extends the scope of the variable `price` into `file2` so that it can be used by both `func3()` and `func4()`.

Similarly, placing the statement `extern float yield;` in `func4()` extends the scope of this global variable, created in `file1`, into `func4()`, and the scope of the global variable `interest`, created in `file2`, is extended into `func1()` and `func2()` by the declaration statement `extern double interest;` placed before `func1()`. Notice `interest` is not available to `main()`.

A declaration statement that specifically contains the word `extern` is different from every other declaration statement in that it does not cause the creation of a new variable by reserving new storage for the variable. An *extern* declaration statement simply informs the computer that the variable already exists and can now be used. The actual storage for the variable must be created somewhere else in the program by using one, and only one, global declaration

FIGURE 7-12 Extending the Scope of a Global Variable

file1

```
int price;
float yield;
static double coupon;
main()
{
  func1();
  func2();
  func3();
  func4();
}
extern double interest;
func1()
{
  .
  .
  .
}
func2()
{
  .
  .
  .
}
```

file2

```
double interest;
extern int price;
func3()
{
  .
  .
  .
}
func4()
{
  extern float yield;
  .
  .
  .
}
```

statement in which the word `extern` has not been used. Initialization of the global variable can, of course, be made with the original declaration of the global variable. Initialization within an `extern` declaration statement is not allowed and will cause a compilation error.

The existence of the `extern` storage class is the reason we have been so careful to distinguish between the creation and declaration of a variable. Declaration statements containing the word `extern` do not create new storage areas; they only extend the scope of existing global variables.

The last global class, *static* global variables, is used to prevent the extension of a global variable into a second file. Global static variables are declared in the same way as local static variables, except that the declaration statement is placed outside any function.

The scope of a global static variable cannot be extended beyond the file in which it is declared. This provides a degree of privacy for static global variables. Since they are known only and can be used only in the file in which they are declared, other files cannot access or change their values. Static global variables cannot be subsequently extended to a second file by using an `extern` declaration statement. Trying to do so will result in a compilation error.

7.6 Passing Addresses

In the normal course of operation, a called function receives values from its calling function, stores the passed values in its own local arguments, manipulates these arguments appropriately, and possibly returns a single value. This method of calling a function and passing values to it is referred to as a function *call by value.*

This call by value procedure is a distinct advantage of C. It allows functions to be written as independent entities that can use any variable name without concern that other functions may also be using the same name. In writing a function, arguments can conveniently be thought of as either initialized variables or variables that will be assigned values when the function is executed. At no time, however, does the called function have direct access to any local variable contained in the calling function.

There are times when it is convenient to give a function access to local variables of its calling function. This allows the called function to use and change the value in the variable without the knowledge of the calling function, where the local variable is declared. To do this requires that the address of the variable be passed to the called function. Once the called function has the variable's address, it "knows where the variable lives," so to speak, and can access the variable using the address and the indirection operator.

Passing addresses is referred to as a function *call by reference,* since the called function can reference, or access, the variable by using the passed address. In this section, we describe the techniques required to pass addresses to a function and illustrate the function accepting and using the passed addresses.

Passing, Storing, and Using Addresses

To pass, store, and use addresses requires the use of the address operator (&), pointers, and the indirection operator (*). Let us review these topics before applying them to writing a function.

The address operator is the ampersand symbol, &. Recall that the ampersand followed immediately by a variable means "the address of" the variable. Examples of this are:

```
&firstnum means "the address of firstnum"
&secnum means "the address of secnum"
```

Addresses themselves are values that can be stored in variables. The variables that store addresses are called *pointers.* Again, recall that pointers, like all variables, must be declared. In declaring pointers, the data type corresponding to the contents of the address being stored must be included in the declaration. Since all addresses appear the same, this additional information is needed by the computer to know how many storage locations to access when it uses the address stored in the pointer. Examples of pointer declarations are:

```
char *in_addr;
int *num_pt;
float *dst_addr:
double *nml_addr;
```

To understand pointer declarations, read them backwards, starting with the indirection operator, the asterisk, *. Again, recall that an asterisk followed immediately by a variable or argument can be translated as either "the variable (or argument) whose address is stored in" or "the variable (or argument) pointed to by." Thus, `*in_addr` can be read as either "the variable whose address is stored in `in_addr`" or "the variable pointed to by `in_addr`." Applying this to pointer declarations, the declaration `char *in_key;`, for example, can be read as either "the variable whose address is stored in `in_key` is a character" or "the variable pointed to by `in_key` is a character." Both of these statements are frequently shortened to the simpler statement that "`in_key` points to a character." As all three interpretations of the declaration statement are correct, select and use whichever description makes a pointer declaration meaningful to you.

We now put all this together to pass two addresses to a function named `sortnum()`. The function will be written to compare the values contained in the passed addresses and to swap the values, if necessary, so that the smaller value is stored in the first address.

Passing addresses to a function should be familiar to you, because we have been using addresses each time we have called the scanf() function. Consider Program 7-10.

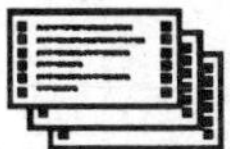

Program 7-10

```
main()
{
  double firstnum, secnum;

  printf("Enter two numbers: ");
  scanf("%lf %lf", &firstnum, &secnum);

  sortnum(&firstnum, &secnum);

  printf("The smaller number is %lf", firstnum);
  printf("\nThe larger number is %lf", secnum);
}
```

Observe in Program 7-10 (also see Figure 7-13) that addresses are passed to both scanf() and sortnum(). Had just the values of firstnum and secnum been passed to sortnum(), the function could not have swapped them in the variables because it would not have had access to firstnum and secnum.

One of the first requirements in writing sortnum() is to declare two arguments that can store the passed addresses. The following declarations can be used:

```
double *nm1_addr; /*nm1_addr points to a double precision variable*/
double *nm2_addr; /*nm2_addr points to a double precision variable*/
```

The choice of the argument names nm1_addr and nm2_addr is, as with all argument names, up to the programmer.

Putting what we have together, the function header for sortnum() is:

```
sortnum(nm1_addr,nm2_addr)        /* function declaration  */
double *nm1_addr, *nm2_addr;      /* argument declarations */
```

Notice that a single declaration is used to declare the two pointers, nm1_addr and nm2_addr.

Before writing the body of sortnum() to actually compare and swap values, let us first check that the values accessed by using the addresses in nm1_addr and nm2_addr are correct. This is done in Program 7-11.

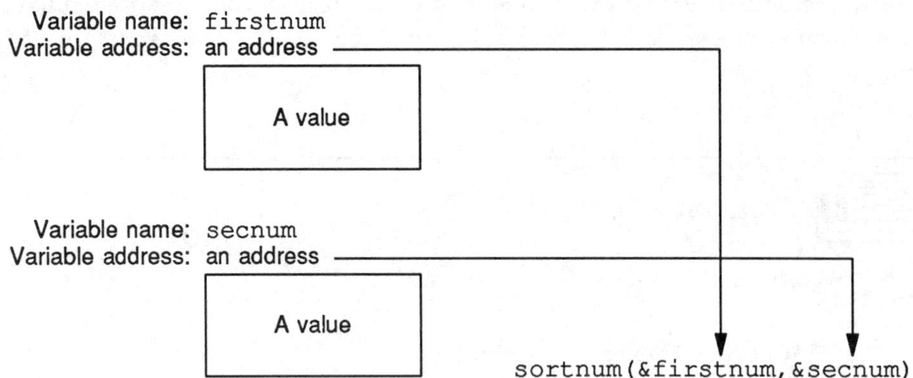

FIGURE 7-13 Passing Addresses to `sortnum()`

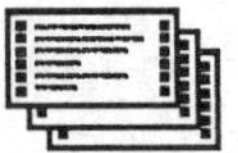

Program 7-11

```
main()
{
  double firstnum = 20.0, secnum = 5.0;

  sortnum(&firstnum, &secnum);
}

sortnum(nm1_addr,nm2_addr)
double  *nm1_addr,  *nm2_addr;
{
  printf("The number whose address is in nm1_addr is %lf",  *nm1_addr);
  printf("\nThe number whose address is in nm2_addr is %lf",  *nm2_addr);

}
```

The output displayed when Program 7-11 is run is:

```
The number whose address is in nm1_addr is 20.000000
The number whose address is in nm2_addr is  5.000000
```

In reviewing Program 7-11, note two things. First, `sortnum()` is not declared in `main()` because it returns no direct value to `main()`. Second, within `sortnum()`, the indirection operator is used to access the values stored in firstnum and secnum. sortnum() itself has no knowledge of these variable names, but it does have the address of firstnum stored in nm1_addr and the address of secnum stored in nm2_addr. The expression *nm1_addr used in the first printf() call means "the variable whose address is in nm1_addr." This is, of course, the variable firstnum. Similarly, the second printf() call obtains the value stored in secnum as "the variable whose address is in nm2_addr." Thus, we have successfully used pointers to allow sortnum() to access variables in main(). Figure 7-14 illustrates the storing of addresses in arguments.

Having verified that sortnum() can access main()'s local variables firstnum and secnum, we can now expand sortnum() to compare the values in these variables with an if statement to see if they are in the desired order. Using pointers, the if statement takes the form

```
if (*nm1_addr > *nm2_addr)
```

This statement should be read: "if the variable whose address is in nm1_addr is larger than the variable whose address is in nm2_addr." If the condition is true, the values in main()'s variables firstnum and secnum can be interchanged from within sortnum(), using the three-step interchange algorithm:

1. Store firstnum's value in a temporary location.
2. Store secnum's value in firstnum.
3. Store the temporary value in secnum.

Using pointers from within sortnum(), this takes the form:

1. Store the variable pointed to by nm1_addr in a temporary location. The statement temp = *nm1_addr; does this (see Figure 7-15).
2. Store the variable whose address is in nm2_addr in the variable whose address is in nm1_addr. The statement *nm1_addr = *nm2_addr; does this (see Figure 7-16).

FIGURE 7-14 Storing Addresses in Arguments

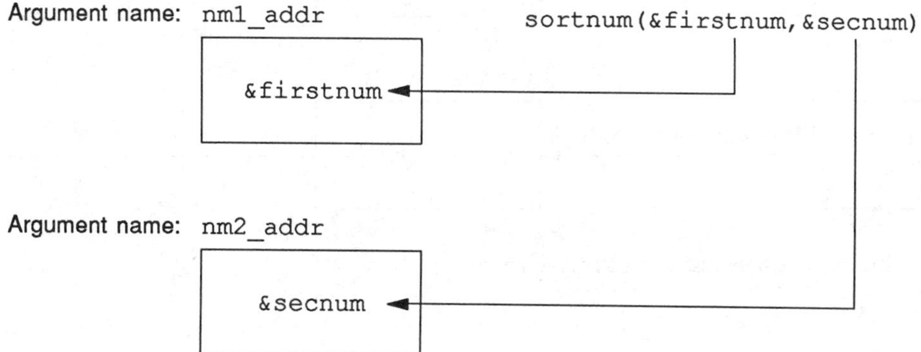

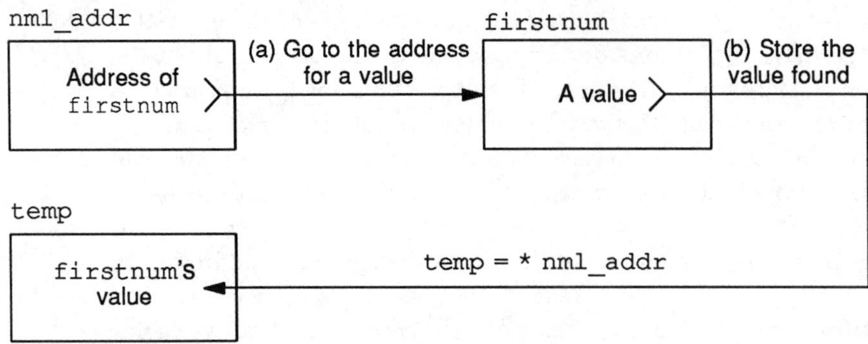

FIGURE 7-15 Indirectly Storing firstnum 's Value

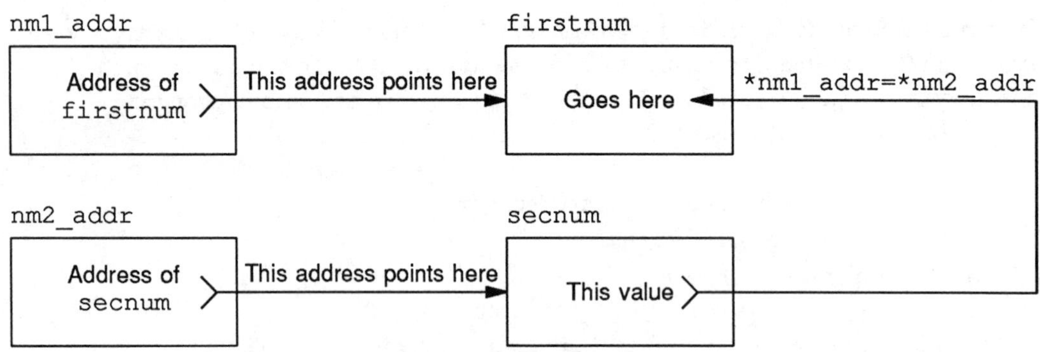

FIGURE 7-16 Indirectly Changing firstnum's Value

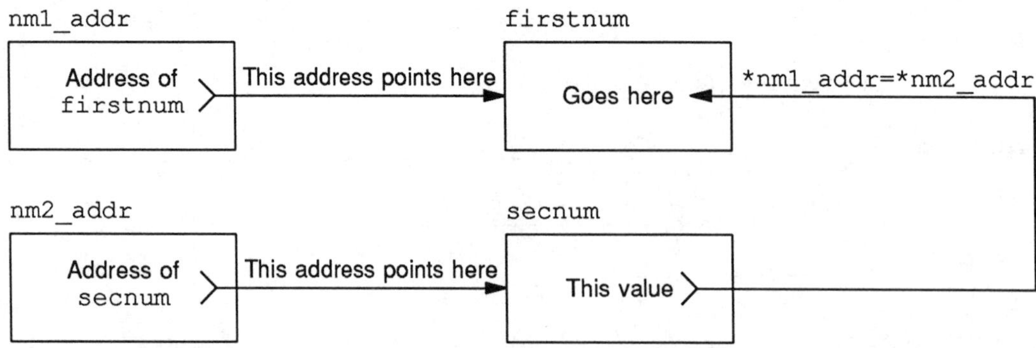

FIGURE 7-17 Indirectly Changing firstnum's Value

3. Move the value in the temporary location into the variable whose address is in nm2_addr. The statement *nm2_addr = temp; does this (see Figure 7-17).

Program 7-12 contains the final form of sortnum(), written according to our description.

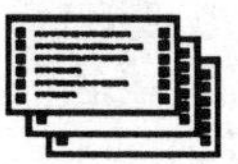

Program 7-12

```
main()
{
  double firstnum, secnum;

  printf("Enter two numbers: ");
  scanf("%lf %lf", &firstnum, &secnum);
  sortnum(&firstnum, &secnum);                    /* call sortnum() */
  printf("The smaller number is %6.2lf", firstnum);
  printf("\nThe larger number is %6.2lf", secnum);
}

sortnum(nm1_addr,nm2_addr)
double *nm1_addr, *nm2_addr;                /* declare two pointers */
{
  double temp;

  if (*nm1_addr > *nm2_addr)
  {
    temp = *nm1_addr;                      /* save firstnum's value */
    *nm1_addr = *nm2_addr;     /* move secnum's value in firstnum */
    *nm2_addr = temp;                     /* change secnum's value */
  }
  return;
}
```

The following sample run was obtained using Program 7-12:

```
Enter two numbers: 20.6 3.9
The smaller number is 3.90
The larger number is 20.60
```

In reviewing Program 7-12, note that the sole reason for using pointers is to allow us to swap firstnum's value if the values are not in the desired order.

7.7 Common Programming Errors

The most common programming error related to functions is passing values to a function that is not prepared to receive them. The values passed to a function must correspond to the data types of the arguments declared within the function. The simplest way to verify that correct values have been received is to display all passed values within a function's body before any calculations are made. Once this verification has taken place, the display can be dispensed with.

The next common error occurs when the same variable is declared locally within both the calling and called functions. Even though the variable name is the same, a change to one local variable does not alter the value in the other local variable.

Related to this is the error caused when a local variable has the same name as a global variable. Within the function declaring the local variable, the use of the variable name affects only the local contents. Thus, the value of the global variable can never be altered by the function.

The last common error is omitting the called function's declaration within the calling function. The called function must be alerted to the type of value that will be returned, and this information is provided by the function declaration. This declaration can be omitted only if the called function is placed in a program before its calling function or the called function returns an integer or void data type. The actual value returned by a function can be verified by displaying it both before and after it is returned.

7.8 Chapter Summary

1. A function is called by giving its name and passing any data to it in the parentheses following the name. If a variable is one of the arguments in a function call, the called function receives a copy of the variable's value.
2. The general form of a user-written function is:

```
function_type function_name(argument list)
argument declarations;
{
  variable declarations;

  other C statements;
  return(expression);
}
```

The first two lines of the function are referred to as the function's header. The opening and closing braces of the function and all statements in between these braces constitute the function's body.

3. A function's type is the data type of the value returned by the function. If no type is declared, the function is assumed to return an integer value. If the function does not return a value, it should be declared as a `void` type.
4. Argument declarations declare the data type of the values passed to the function. They are placed before the opening brace that defines the function's body.
5. Functions can formally return only one value to their calling functions. This value is the value of the expression in the return statement.
6. A function that returns a value must be declared in the calling function. This can be done either by placing the called function above the calling function in the program or by including a function declaration within the calling program.
7. A set of preprogrammed functions for input, output, mathematical procedures, and string handling are included in the standard library provided with each C compiler. To use one of these functions, you must obtain the name of the function, the arguments expected by the function, the data type of the returned value (if any), and a description of what the function does.
8. Every variable used in a program has a scope, which determines where in the program the variable can be used. The scope of a variable is either local or global and is determined by where the variable's definition statement is placed. A local variable is defined within a function and can be used only within its defining function. A global variable is defined outside a function and can be used in any function following the variable's definition. All global variables (which are formally called external variables) are initialized to zero and can be shared between files by using the keyword `extern`.
9. Every variable has a class. The class of a variable determines how long the value in the variable will be retained. Automatic (auto) variables are local variables that exist only while their defining function is executing. Register variables are similar to automatic variables but are stored in a computer's internal registers rather than in memory. Static variables can be either global or local and retain their values for the duration of a program's execution. Static variables are also set to zero when they are defined.
10. A function can also be passed the address of a variable. This address must be stored in a pointer of the proper type and can be used to directly alter the value stored at the passed address. By passing addresses, a function has the capability of effectively returning many values.

Sample Problem

A simple algorithm for rounding any floating point or double precision number to two decimal places is:

1. Multiply the number by 100.0.
2. Add 0.5 to the number.
3. Determine the integer part of the number.
4. Divide the integer part by 100.0.

The following program calls a user-written function called `round()` to perform these steps on any value passed to it.

```
main()
{
  double num, round();

  printf("Enter a number: ");
  scanf("%lf", &num);
  printf("The rounded number is %f\n", round(num));
}
double round(num)
double num;
{
  int whole;

  whole = num * 100.0 + 0.5;    /* retain the integer part */
  return(whole/100.0);
}
```

The key element of the `round()` function is the assignment statement `whole = num * 100.0 + 0.5`, which effectively performs steps 1, 2, and 3 of the rounding algorithm. Steps 1 and 2 are computed by the right-hand side of the assignment statement. The retention of the integer portion of this calculation, which corresponds to step 3 in the rounding algorithm, is performed by assigning this result to an integer variable.

For example, if the number passed to `round()` were `23.56789`, the expression `num * 100.0 + 0.5` would produce the value `2357.289`. Assigning this value to the integer variable `whole` would result in the value `2357` being stored in `whole`. Note that the statement `whole = (int) num * 100.0 + 0.5`, which uses a *cast* to explicitly coerce the value of the expression to an integer value, can also be used. Casts are described in Section 14.1 Finally, dividing the value in whole by 100.0 completes the algorithm. A sample run produced the following display:

```
Enter a number: 23.56789
The rounded number is 23.570000
```

Complex Data Types

Part Four

Arrays

Chapter Eight

The variables used so far have all had a common characteristic: each variable could only be used to store a single value at a time. For example, although the variables `in_key`, `counter`, and `price` declared in the statements

```
char in_key;
int counter;
float price;
```

are of different data types, each variable can store only one value of the declared data type. These types of variables are called *scalar variables.* A scalar variable is a single variable that cannot be further subdivided or separated into a legitimate data type.

Frequently we may have a set of values, all of the same data type, that form a logical group. For example, Figure 8-1 illustrates three groups of items. The first group is a list of five integer grades, the second group is a list of four character codes, and the last group is a list of six floating point prices.

A simple list consisting of individual items of the same scalar data type is called a *single-dimensional array.* In this chapter, we describe how single-dimensional arrays are declared, initialized, stored inside a computer, and used. We will then explore the use of single-dimensional arrays with example programs and present the procedures for declaring and using multidimensional arrays.

8.1 Single-Dimensional Arrays

A single-dimensional array, also called a *one-dimensional array,* is a list of values of the same data type. For example, consider the list of grades illustrated in Figure 8-2. All the grades in the list are integer numbers and must be declared as such. However, the individual items in the list do not have to be declared separately; they can be declared as a single unit and stored under a common variable name called the *array name.* For convenience, we chose `grades` as the name for the list shown in Figure 8-2. To declare that `grades` is to be used to store five individual integer values requires the declaration statement

FIGURE 8-1 Three Lists of Items

Grades	Codes	Prices
98	x	10.96
87	a	6.43
92	m	2.58
79	n	.86
85		12.27
		6.39

Grades
98
87
92
79
85

FIGURE 8-2 A List of Grades

`int grades[5];`. Notice that this declaration statement gives the array (or list) name, the data type of the items in the array, and the number of items in the array. Further examples of array declarations are:

```
char code[4];        /* array of four character codes          */
double prices[6];    /* Array of six double precision prices */
float amount[100];   /* array of 100 floating point amounts   */
```

Each array has sufficient memory reserved for it to hold the number of data items given in the declaration statement. Thus, the `grades` array has storage reserved for five integers, the `code` array has storage reserved for four characters, and the `prices` array has storage reserved for six double precision numbers for the individual prices. Figure 8-3 illustrates the storage reserved for the `code` and `grades` arrays. For illustrative purposes, we have assumed that each character is stored as one byte and that each integer requires two bytes of storage.

Each item in a list is officially called an *element*, or *component*, of the array. The individual elements stored in the arrays illustrated in Figure 8-3 are stored sequentially, with the first array element stored in the first reserved location, the second element stored in the second reserved location, and so on until the last element is stored in the last reserved location.

FIGURE 8-3 The `code` and `grades` Arrays in Memory

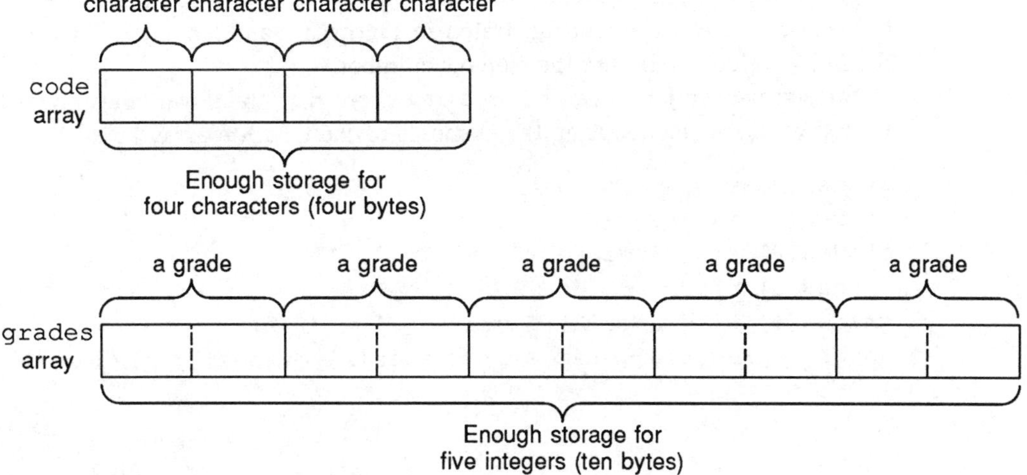

To access individual elements in a one-dimensional array requires some unique means of identifying each element. Fortunately, each item in the list is stored sequentially. Any single item can be accessed by giving the name of the array and the position of the item in the array. The element's position is called its *index,* or *subscript value.* The first element has an index of 0, the second element has an index of 1, and so on. The index gives the number of elements to move over, starting from the beginning of the array, to locate the desired element. In C, the array name and index are combined by listing the index in square brackets after the array name. For example:

```
grades[0] refers to first grade stored in grades array
grades[1] refers to second grade stored in grades array
grades[2] refers to third grade stored in grades array
grades[3] refers to fourth grade stored in grades array
grades[4] refers to fifth grade stored in grades array
```

Figure 8-4 illustrates the `grades` array in memory with the correct designation for each array element. Each individual element is called an *indexed variable,* or a *subscripted variable,* since both a variable name and an index or subscript value must be used to reference the element. Remember that the index, or subscript, value gives the position of the element in the array. When we read a subscripted variable, such as `grades[0]`, we read the variable as "grades sub zero." This is a shortened way of saying "the grades array subscripted by zero," and distinguishes the first element in an array from a scalar variable that could be declared as `grades0`. Similarly, `grades[1]` is read as "grades sub one" and `grades[4]` is read as "grades sub four."

Although it may seem unusual to reference the first element with an index of zero, doing so increases the computer's speed of accessing array elements. Internally, unseen by the programmer, the computer uses the index as an offset from the array's starting position. As illustrated in Figure 8-5, the index tells the computer how many elements to skip, starting from the beginning of the array, to get to the desired element. From a programmer's viewpoint, it is easier to think of the fourth element illustrated in Figure 8-5 as Element 3. This makes the index value agree with the element number.

Subscripted variables can be used anywhere that scalar variables are valid. Examples of statements using the elements of the `grades` array are:

```
grades[0] = 98;
grades[1] = grades[0] - 11;
grades[2] = 2 * (grades[0] - 6);
grades[3] = 79;
grades[4] = (grades[2] + grades[3] - 3)/2;
total = grades[0]+grades[1]+grades[2]+grades[3]+grades[4];
```

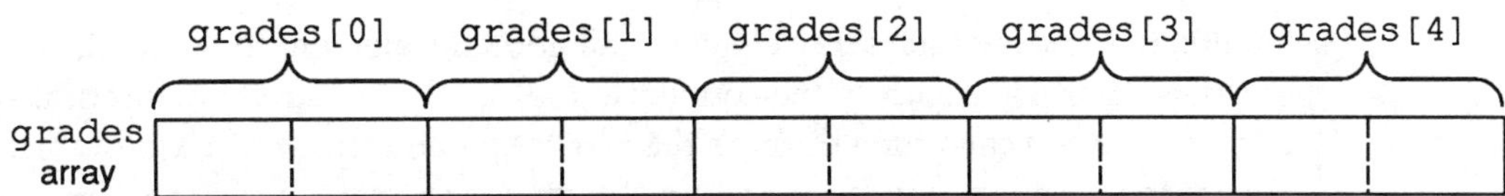

FIGURE 8-4 Identifying Individual Array Elements

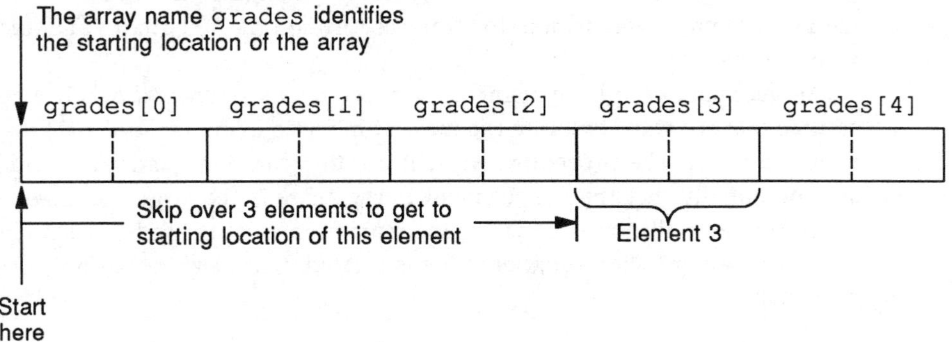

FIGURE 8-5 Accessing an Individual Element — Element 3

The index contained within square brackets need not be an integer. Any expression that evaluates to an integer may be used as an index. For example, assuming that `i` and `j` are integer values, the following subscripted variables are valid:

```
grades[i]
grades[2*i]
grades[j-i]
```

One extremely important advantage of using integer expressions as subscripts is that it allows sequencing through an array by using a `for` loop. This makes statements like

```
total = grades[1]+grades[2]+grades[3]+grades[4]+grades[5];
```

unnecessary. The index value in each of the subscripted variables in this statement can be replaced by the counter in a `for` loop to access each element in the array sequentially. For example, the code:

```
total = 0;                    /* initialize total to zero  */
for (i = 0; i <= 4; ++i)
total = total + grades[i];              /* add in a grade */
```

sequentially retrieves each array element and adds the element to the total. Here, the variable `i` is used both as the counter in the `for` loop and as a subscript. As `i` increases by one each time through the `for` loop, the next element in the array is referenced. The procedure for adding the array elements within the `for` loop is the same procedure we have used many times before.

The advantage of using a `for` loop to sequence through an array becomes apparent when you work with larger arrays. For example, if the `grades` array contains 100 values rather than just 5, simply changing the number 4 to 99 in the `for` statement is sufficient to sequence through the 100 grades and add each grade to the total.

As another example of using a `for` loop to sequence through an array, assume that we want to locate the maximum value in an array of 1000 elements named `price`. The procedure we will use to locate the maximum value is to assume initially that the first element in the array is the largest number. Then, as we sequence through the array, the maximum is compared to each element. When an element with a higher value is located, that element becomes the new maximum.

```
maximum = price[0];           /* set maximum to element zero      */
for(i = 1; i <= 999; ++i)     /* cycle through rest of array      */
  if (price[i] > maximum)     /* compare each element to maximum */
    maximum = price[i];       /* capture new high value          */
```

In this code, the `for` statement consists of one `if` statement. The search for a new maximum value starts with element 1 of the array and continues through the last element. In a thousand-element array, the last element is element 999.

Input and Output of Array Values

Individual array elements can be assigned values using individual assignment statements or, interactively, by using the `scanf()` function. Examples of individual data entry statements are:

```
price[5] = 10.69;
scanf("%d %lf", &grades[0], &price[2]);
scanf("%c", &code[0]);
scanf("%d %d %d", &grades[0], &grades[1], &grades[2]);
```

Alternatively, a `for` statement can be used to cycle through the array for interactive data input. For example, the code

```
for(i = 0; i <= 4; ++i)
{
  printf("Enter a grade: ");
  scanf("%d", &grades[i]);
}
```

prompts for five grades. The first grade input is stored in `grades[0]`, the second grade input in `grades[1]`, and so on until all five grades are entered.

One caution should be mentioned about storing data in an array. C does not check the value of the index being used (called a *bounds check*). If an array has been declared as consisting of 10 elements, for example, and you use an index of 12, which is outside of the bounds of the array, C will not notify you of the error when the program is compiled. The program will attempt to access element 12 by skipping over the appropriate number of bytes from the start of the array. Usually this results in a program crash, but not always. If the referenced location itself contains a value of the correct data type, the new value will simply overwrite the value in the referenced memory locations. This leads to more errors, which are particularly troublesome to locate when the variable legitimately assigned to the storage location is used at a different point in the program.

During output, individual array elements can be displayed by using the `printf()` function or complete sections of the array can be displayed by including a `printf()` function call within a `for` loop. For example:

```
printf("%lf," price[6]);
printf("The value of element %d is %d", i, grades[i]);
for( n = 5; n <= 20; ++n)
  printf("%d %lf", n, price[n]);
```

The first call to `printf()` displays the value of the double precision subscripted variable `price[6]`. The second call to `printf()` displays the value of `i` and the value of `grades[i]`. Before this statement can be executed, `i` would have to have an assigned value. Finally, the last example includes `printf()` within a `for` loop. Both the value of the index and the value of the elements from 5 to 20 are displayed.

8.2 Array Initialization

Arrays, like scalar variables, can be declared either inside or outside a function. Arrays declared inside a function are *local arrays* and arrays declared outside a function are *global arrays*. For example, consider the following section of code:

```
int gallons[20];              /* a global array         */
static double dist[25];       /* a static global array  */
main()
{
```

continued

```
  int i;

   for (i = 1; i <= 10; ++i)
    mpg(i);                   /* call mpg() ten times    */
       .
       .
       .
}
mpg(car_no)                   /* function declaration     */
int car_no;                   /* argument declaration     */
{
  int miles[15];              /* an automatic local array */
  static course[15];          /* a static local array     */
      .
      .
      .
  return;
}
```

As indicated in the code, both the `dist` and `gallons` arrays are globally declared arrays, `miles` is an automatic local array, and `course` is a static local array. As with scalar variables, all global arrays and local static arrays are created once, at compilation time, and retain their values until `main()` finishes executing. `auto` arrays are created and destroyed each time the function they are local to is called. Thus, the `dist, gallons,` and `course` arrays are created once, and the `miles` array is created and destroyed ten times.

Creating and destroying individual scalar variables does not typically affect the time it takes to run a program. This is also true for small automatic arrays. The creation and destruction of large arrays, however, can have a noticeable impact on system performance. If automatic arrays were initialized each time they are created, the effect on total program execution time could be significant. It is for this reason that the temporary automatic arrays cannot be initialized within the declaration statement creating them (they can, of course, be initialized by using a `for` loop, as can local static and globally declared arrays). The case is different for global arrays and local static arrays.

Global and local static arrays can be initialized from within their declaration statements by listing the desired values within braces and separating these by commas. Examples of this for static arrays (local and global) are:

```
static int grades[5] = {98, 87, 92, 79, 85};
static char codes[6] = {'s', 'a', 'm', 'p', 'l', 'e'};
static double prices[10] = {10.96, 6.43, 2.58, .86};
```

Examples of external global array declarations, including initializers, are:

```
int gallons[20] = {19, 16, 14, 19, 20, 18,   /* initializing values */
                   12, 10, 22, 15, 18, 17,   /* may extend across   */
                   16, 14, 23, 19, 15, 18,   /* multiple lines      */
                   21, 5};

double yield[6] = {9.05, 9.10, 9.15, 9.20, 9.25, 9.30};
```

If the number of initializers is less than the formally declared maximum number of elements listed in square brackets, the initializers are applied from the beginning of the array, that is, array element zero. Thus, in the initialization of the `static` `prices` array, only `prices[0]`, `prices[1]`, `prices[2]`, and `prices[3]` are initialized with the listed values.

If no specific initializers are given in the declaration statement, all local `static` and global (both `static` and `extern`) array elements are set to zero (this is also true for local `static` and global scalar variables). For example, the declaration `static int dist[100];` sets all elements of the `dist` array equal to zero at compilation time. Similarly, since `prices[4]` through `prices[9]` were not specifically initialized when the `prices` array was declared, these elements are also set to zero.

Unfortunately, there is no method of either indicating repetition of an initialization value or initializing later array elements without first specifying values for earlier elements.

A unique feature of initializers is that the size of an array may be omitted when initializing values are included in the declaration statement. For example, the declaration

```
static int gallons[] = {16, 12, 10, 14, 11};
```

reserves enough storage room for five elements. Similarly, the following two declarations are equivalent:

```
static char codes[6] = {'s', 'a', 'm', 'p', 'l', 'e'};
static char codes[ ] = {'s', 'a', 'm', 'p', 'l', 'e'};
```

Both of these declarations set aside six character locations for an array named `codes`.

An interesting and useful simplification can also be used when initializing character arrays. For example, the declaration

```
static char codes[] = "sample";    /* no braces or commas */
```

uses the string `"sample"` to initialize the `codes` array. Recall that a string is any sequence of characters enclosed in double quotation marks. This last declaration creates an array named `codes`, which has seven elements, and fills the array with the seven characters illustrated in Figure 8-6. The first six characters, as

codes[0]	codes[1]	codes[2]	codes[3]	codes[4]	codes[5]	codes[6]
s	a	m	p	l	e	\0

FIGURE 8-6 A String Is Terminated with a Special Sentinel

expected, consist of the letters `s`, `a`, `m`, `p`, `l`, and `e`. The last character, which is the escape sequence `\0`, is called the *null character.* The null character is automatically appended to all strings by the C compiler. This character has an internal storage code that is numerically equal to zero (the storage code for the zero character has a numerical value of 24, so the two cannot be confused by the computer), and is used as a marker, or sentinel, to indicate the end of a string. As we will in Chapter 10, this marker is invaluable when manipulating strings of characters.

8.3 Passing Arrays

Individual array elements are passed to a function by simply including them as subscripted variables in the function call argument list. For example, the function call `find_min(grades[2], grades[6]);` passes the values of the elements `grades[2]` and `grades[6]` to the function `find_min()`.

Passing a complete array to a function is in many respects an easier operation than passing individual elements. The called function receives access to the actual array, rather than a copy of the values in the array. For example, if `grades` is an array, the function call `find_max(grades);` makes the complete `grades` array available to the `find_max()` function. This is different from passing a single variable to a function.

When passing a single scalar or single array element, the called function always receives a copy of the value stored in the variable. Passing an array this way requires making a complete and separate copy of all array values. For large arrays, making duplicate copies of the array for each function call would be wasteful of computer storage, consume large amounts of execution time, and frustrate the effort to return multiple element changes made by the called program. To avoid these problems, the called function is given direct access to the original array. Thus, any changes made by the called function are made directly to the array itself. For the following specific examples of function calls, assume that the arrays `nums`, `keys`, `units`, and `prices` are declared as:

```
int nums[5];                      /* 1 array of 5 integers     */
char keys[256];                   /* 1 array of 256 characters */
double units[500], prices[500]; /* 2 arrays of 500 doubles */
```

For these arrays, the following function calls can be made:

```
find_max(nums);
find_ch(keys);
calc_tot(nums, units, prices);
```

In each case, the called function receives direct access to the named array.

On the receiving side, the called function must be alerted that an array is being made available. For example, suitable function declarations for the previous functions are:

```
find_max(vals)       find_ch(in_keys)         calc_tot(arr1,arr2,arr3)
int vals[5];         char in_keys[256];       int arr1[5];
                                              double arr2[500],arr3[500];
```

In each of these function declarations, the names in the argument list are chosen by the programmer and are local to the function. However, the internal local names used by the functions still refer to the original array created outside the function. This is made clear in Program 8-1.

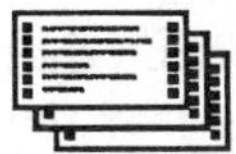

Program 8-1

```
main()
{
  static int nums[5] = {2, 18, 1, 27, 16};

  find_max(nums);
}

find_max(vals)              /* find the maximum value */
int vals[5];
{
  int max = vals[0];

  for (i = 1; i <= 4; ++i)
    if (max < vals[i]) max = vals[i];

  printf("The maximum value is %d", max);
}
```

Only one array is created in Program 8-1. In `main()`, this array is known as `nums` and, in `find_max()`, it is known as `vals`. As illustrated in Figure 8-7,

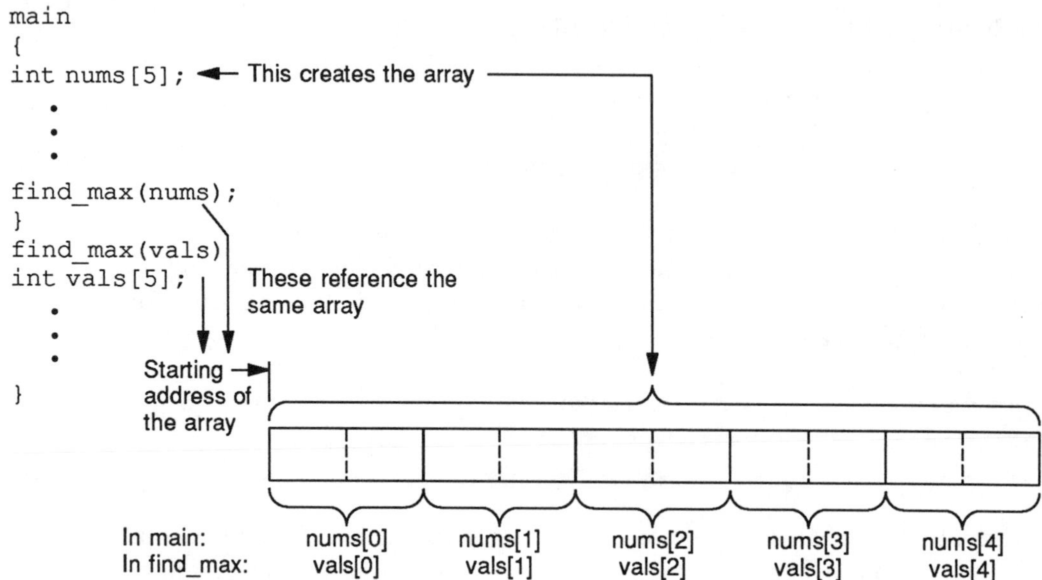

FIGURE 8-7 Only One Array Is Created

both names refer to the same array. Thus, in Figure 8-7, `vals[3]` is the same element as `nums[3]`.

The argument declaration in `find_max()` actually contains information that is not required by the function. All that `find_max()` must know is that the argument `vals` references an array of integers. Since the array has been created in `main()` and no additional storage space is needed in `find_max()`, the declaration for `vals` can omit the size of the array. Thus, an alternative function declaration is:

```
find_max(vals)
int vals[];
```

This form of the function declaration makes more sense when you realize that only one item is actually passed to `find_max` when the function is called. As you might have suspected, the item passed is the starting address of the `nums` array. This is illustrated in Figure 8-8.

Since only one item is passed to `find_max`, the number of elements in the array need not be included in the declaration for `vals`. In fact, it is generally

FIGURE 8-8 The Starting Address of the Array Is Passed

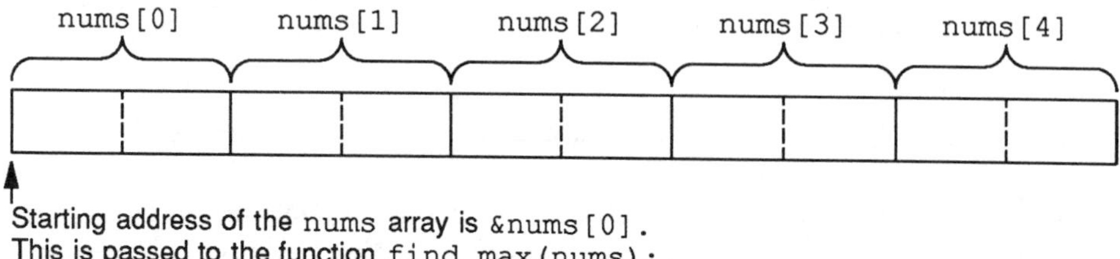

advisable to omit the size of the array in the argument declaration. For example, consider the more general form of `find_max()`, which can be used to find the maximum value of an integer array of arbitrary size.

```
int find_max(vals,num_els)    /* find maximum value */
int vals[], num_els;
{
  int i, max = vals[0];

  for (i = 1; i <= (num_els - 1); ++i)
   if (max < vals[i]) max = vals[i];

  return(max);
}
```

The more general form of `find_max()` declares that the function returns an integer value. The function expects the starting address of an integer array and the number of elements in the array as arguments. Then, using the number of elements as the boundary for its search, the function's `for` loop causes each array element to be examined in sequential order to locate the maximum value. Since the highest subscript allowed is always one less than the total number of elements in the array, the expression (`num_els - 1`) is used to terminate the loop. Program 8-2 illustrates the use of `find_max()` in a complete program.

Program 8-2

```
main()
{
  static int nums[5] = {2, 18, 1, 27, 16};
  int find_max();

  printf("The maximum value is %d", find_max(num,5));
}

int find_max(vals,num_els);
int vals[], num_els;
{
  int i, max = vals[0];
  for (i = 1; i <= (num_els - 1); ++i)
   if (max < vals[i]) max = vals[i];

  return(max);
}
```

The output displayed by Program 8-2 is:

```
The maximum value is 27
```

8.4 Two-Dimensional Arrays

A *two-dimensional array* consists of both rows and columns of elements. For example, the array of numbers

```
 8   16    9   52
 3   15   27    6
14   25    2   10
```

is called a two-dimensional array of integers. This array consists of three rows and four columns. To reserve storage for this array, both the number of rows and the number of columns must be included in the array's declaration. Calling the array `val`, the appropriate declaration for this two-dimensional array is

```
int val[3][4];
```

Similarly, the declarations

```
double prices[10][5];
char code[6][26];
```

declare that the array `prices` consists of 10 rows and 5 columns of double precision numbers and that the array `code` consists of 6 rows and 26 columns of characters.

In order to locate each element in a two-dimensional array, an element is identified by its position in the array. As illustrated in Figure 8-9, the term `val[1][3]` uniquely identifies the element in row 1, column 3. As with

FIGURE 8-9 Each Array Element Is Identified by Its Row and Column

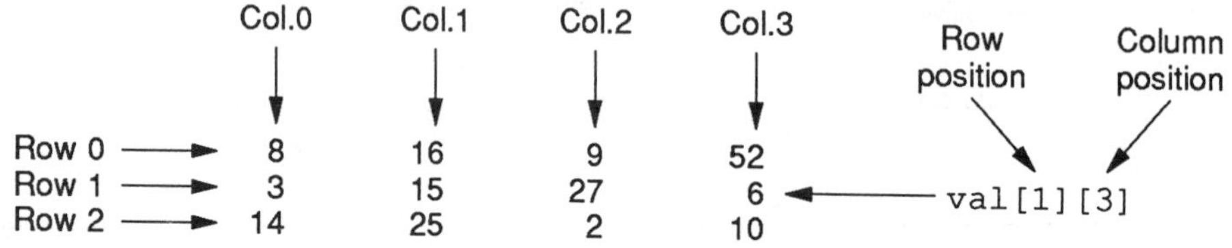

single-dimensional array variables, double-dimensional array variables can be used anywhere that scalar variables are valid. Examples using elements of the `val` array are:

```
num       = val[2][3];
val[0][0] = 62;
new_num   = 4 * (val[1][0] - 5);
sum_row0  = val[0][0] + val[0][1] + val[0][2] + val[0][3];
```

The last statement causes the values of the four elements in row 0 to be added and the sum stored in the scalar variable `sum_row0`.

As with single-dimensional arrays, two-dimensional arrays can be declared either inside or outside a function. Arrays declared inside a function are *local arrays*; arrays declared outside a function are *global arrays*. For example, consider the following section of code:

```
int bingo[2][3];
main()
{
  static double lotto[104][6];
  double pick_six[52][6];
              .
              .
              .
}
```

The `bingo` array is a globally declared two-dimensional array consisting of 2 rows and 3 columns; the `lotto` array is a local static two-dimensional array consisting of 104 rows and 6 columns; and the `pick_six` array is a local automatic array of 52 rows and 6 columns.

As with single-dimensional arrays, all global and local static two-dimensional arrays can be initialized from within their declaration statements. This is done by listing the initial values within braces and separating them by commas. Additionally, braces can be used to separate individual rows. For example, the declaration

```
static int val[3][4] = { {8,16,9,52},
                         {3,15,27,6},
                         {14,25,2,10} };
```

declares `val` to be an array of integers with three rows and four columns, with the initial values given in the declaration. The first set of internal braces contains the values for row 0 of the array, the second set of internal braces contains the values for row 1, and the third set of braces the values for row 2.

Although the commas in the initialization braces are always required, the inner braces can be omitted. Thus, the initialization for `val` can be written as

```
static int val[3][4] = {8,16,9,52,
                        3,15,27,6,
                        14,25,2,10};
```

The separation of initial values into rows in the declaration statement is not necessary since the compiler assigns values by beginning with the [0][0] element and proceeding row by row to fill in the remaining values. Thus, the initialization

```
static int val[3][4] = {8,16,9,52,3,15,27,6,14,25,2,10};
```

is equally valid but does not clearly illustrate to another programmer where one row ends and another begins.

Passing two-dimensional arrays into functions is a process identical to passing single-dimensional arrays. The called function receives access to the entire array. For example, the function call `display(val);` makes the complete `val` array available to the function named `display()`. Thus, any changes made by `display()` will be made directly to the `val` array. Assuming that the following two-dimensional arrays named `test`, `code`, and `stocks` are declared as:

```
int test[7][9];
char code[26][10];
float stocks[256][52];
```

the following function calls are valid:

```
find_max(test);
obtain(code);
price(stocks);
```

On the receiving side, the called function must be alerted that a two-dimensional array is being made available. For example, suitable function declarations for the previous functions are:

```
find_max(nums)     obtain(key)          price(names)
int nums[7][9];    char key[26][10];    float names[256][52];
```

In each of these function declarations, the argument names chosen are local to the function. However, the internal local names used by the function still refer to the original array created outside the function. If the array is a global one, there is no need to pass the array because the function can reference the array by its global name. Program 8-3 illustrates passing a local, two-dimensional array into a function that displays the array's values.

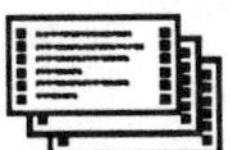

Program 8-3

```
main()
{
  static int val[3][4] = {8,16,9,52,
                          3,15,27,6,
                          14,25,2,10};

  display(val);
}

display(nums)
int nums[3][4];
{
  int row_num, col_num;

  for (row_num = 0; row_num < 3; ++row_num)
  {
    for(col_num = 0; col_num < 4; ++col_num)
      printf("%4d",nums[row_num][col_num]);
    printf("\n");
  }
}
```

Only one array is created in Program 8-3. This array is known as `val` in `main()` and as `nums` in `display()`. Thus, `val[0][2]` refers to the same element as `nums[0][2]`.

Notice the use of the nested `for` loop in Program 8-3. Nested `for` statements are especially useful when dealing with multidimensional arrays because they allow the programmer to cycle through each element. In Program 8-3, the variable `row_num` controls the outer loop and the variable `col_num` controls the inner loop. For each pass through the outer loop, which corresponds to a row, the inner loop makes one pass through the column elements. After a complete column is printed, the `\n` escape sequence causes a new line to be started for the next row. The effect is a display of the array in a row-by-row fashion:

```
   8  16   9  52
   3  15  27   6
  14  25   2  10
```

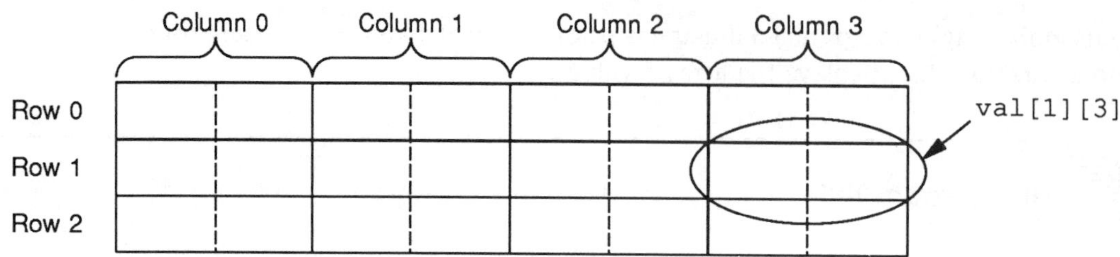

FIGURE 8-10 Storage of the `val` Array

The argument declaration for `nums` in `display()` contains information not required by the function. The declaration for `nums` can omit the row size of the array. Thus, an alternative function declaration is:

```
display(nums)
int nums[][4];
```

The reason the column size must be included while the row size is optional becomes obvious when you consider how the array elements are stored in memory. Starting with element `val[0][0]`, each succeeding element is stored consecutively, row by row, as `val[0][0]`, `val[0][1]`, `val[0][2]`, `val[0][3]`, `val[1][0]`, `val[1][1]`, etc., as illustrated in Figure 8-10.

As with all array accesses, an individual element of the `val` array is obtained by adding an offset to the starting location of the array. For example, the element `val[1][3]` is located at an offset of 14 bytes from the start of the array. Internally, the computer, using the row index, column index, and column size, determines this offset by making the calculation shown in Figure 8-11. The number of columns is necessary in the offset calculation so that the computer can determine the number of positions to skip in order to get to the desired row.

Larger-Dimensional Arrays

Although arrays with more than two dimensions are not commonly used, C does allow any size array to be declared. This is done by listing the maximum

FIGURE 8-11 Offset Calculation

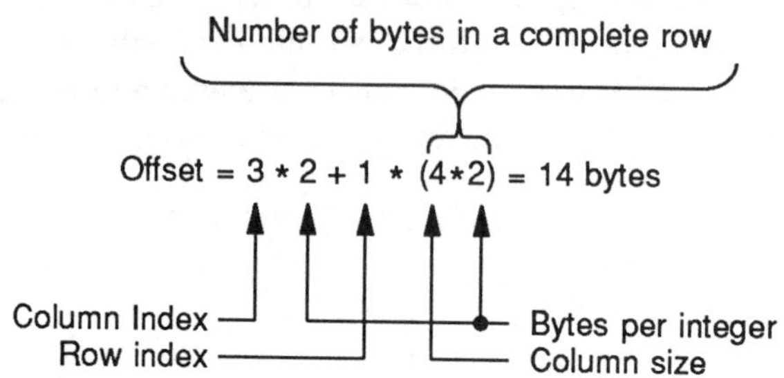

size of all indices for the array. For example, the declaration `int response[4][10][6];` declares a three-dimensional array. The first element in the array is designated as `response[0][0][0]` and the last element as `response[3][9][5]`. Similarly, arrays with four, five, six, or more dimensions can be declared. In declaring these higher-dimensional arrays as function arguments, all but the first index size must be included in the argument declaration.

8.5 Common Programming Errors

The most common programming error associated with arrays is the use of a subscript to reference a nonexistent array element. As the C compiler does no bounds checking on arrays, this error is not caught when the program is compiled. This is always a run-time error that results in either a program crash or a value that has no relation to the intended element being accessed from memory. In either case, it is usually an extremely troublesome error to locate. The only solution to this problem is to make sure, either by specific programming statements or by careful coding, that each subscript references a valid array element.

A second error occurs when an attempt is made to initialize a nonstatic local array (all global arrays can be initialized). This error, however, will be found by the compiler.

8.6 Chapter Summary

1. A single-dimensional array is a data structure that can be used to store a list of values of the same data type. Such arrays must be declared by giving the data type of the values that are stored in the array and the array size. For example, the declaration

   ```
   int num[100];
   ```

   creates an array of 100 integers.
2. Array elements are stored in contiguous locations in memory and referenced by using the array name and a subscript, for example, `num[22]`. Any nonnegative integer-value expression can be used as a subscript and the subscript `0` always refers to the first element in an array.

3. Arrays can be declared either as global or local arrays. Global array elements are automatically initialized to zero if no other explicit initialization is given. Global static arrays and local static arrays are also initialized to zero if no other explicit initialization is given. Automatic local arrays cannot be initialized when they are declared and contain unknown values when they are created.
4. Two-dimensional arrays are declared by specifying both a row and a column size. For example, the declaration

   ```
   float rates[12][20];
   ```

   reserves memory space for a table of 12 by 20 floating point values. Individual elements in a two-dimensional array are identified by providing both a row and a column index. The element in the first row and first column has row and column subscripts of 0.
5. Automatic two-dimensional arrays cannot be initialized and contain unknown values when they are created. All `static` arrays (local or global) and all global two-dimensional array elements are set to zero unless explicitly initialized.
6. Arrays are passed to a function by passing the name of the array as an argument. The value actually passed is the address of the first array storage location. Thus, the called function receives direct access to the original array and not a copy of the array elements. Within the called function, a formal argument must be declared to receive the passed array name. The declaration of the formal argument can omit the row size of the array.

Sample Problem

Write a program that declares three single-dimensional arrays named `current`, `resist`, and `volts`. Each array should be declared in `main()` and should be capable of holding five double precision numbers. The numbers to be stored in the `current` array are:

```
10.621, 48.913, 21.165, 5.186, 2.947
```

The numbers to be stored in the `resist` array, which correspond to resistance values, are:

```
4.85, 6.73, 5.91, 5.33, 5.42
```

The values in these arrays are to be passed to a function named `calcvolt()`, which calculates the elements in the `volts` array as the product of equivalent elements in the `current` and `resist` arrays. Thus,

```
volts[i] = current[i] * resist[i].
```

After calcvolt() has placed values into the volts array, the values in all three arrays should be displayed from within main().

The following program performs the required processing:

```
main()
{
  int i;
  static double current[5] = {10.621, 48.913, 21.165, 5.186, 2.947};
  static double resist[5] = {4.85, 6.73, 5.91, 5.33, 5.42};
  static double volts[5];
  calcvolt(current, resist, volts);
  printf("\n Current   Resistance    Volts");
  printf("\n -------   ----------   -------");
  for(i = 0; i <= 4; ++i)
    printf("\n%7.3f   %7.3f   %7.3f", current[i], resist[i], volts[i]);
}
calcvolt(cur,res,vlts)
double cur[], res[], vlts[];
{
  int i;
  for(i = 0; i <= 4; ++i)
    vlts[i] = cur[i] * res[i];
}
```

The following display is produced by this program:

```
Current   Resistance    Volts
-------   ----------   -------
 10.621      4.850      51.512
 48.913      6.730     329.184
 21.165      5.910     125.085
  5.186      5.330      27.641
  2.947      5.420      15.973
```

Arrays, Addresses, and Pointers

Chapter Nine

There is a direct and intimate relationship among arrays, addresses, and pointers. In fact, although generally unknown to programmers of such high-level languages as FORTRAN, BASIC, and COBOL, addresses run rampant throughout the executable versions of their programs. These addresses are used by the computer to keep track of where data and instructions are kept.

One of C's advantages is that it allows the programmer access to the addresses used by the program. Although we have already used addresses in calling the `scanf()` function and in function calls by reference, the real power of pointers is in dealing with arrays, strings, and other data structure elements. In this chapter, we explore the exceptionally strong interrelationship that exists among arrays, addresses, and pointers. The programming techniques learned in this chapter are then extended in the following chapters to strings and data structures.

9.1 Array Names as Pointers

Figure 9-1 illustrates the storage of a single-dimensional array named `grades`, which contains five integers. Assume that each integer requires two bytes of storage.

Using subscripts, the fourth element in the `grades` array is referred to as `grades[3]`. The use of a subscript, however, conceals the extensive use of addresses by the computer. Internally, the computer immediately uses the subscript to calculate the address of the desired element based on both the starting address of the array and the amount of storage used by each element. Calling the fourth element `grades[3]` forces the computer, internally, into the address computation

```
&grades[3] = &grades[0] + (3 * 2)
```

Since the address operator, &, means "the address of," this last statement is read "the address of `grades[3]` equals the address of `grades[0]` plus 6." Figure 9-2 illustrates the address computation used to locate `grades[3]`.

FIGURE 9-1 The `grades` Array in Storage

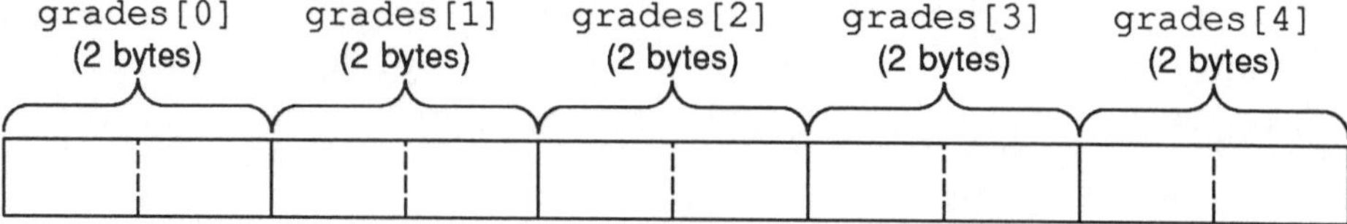

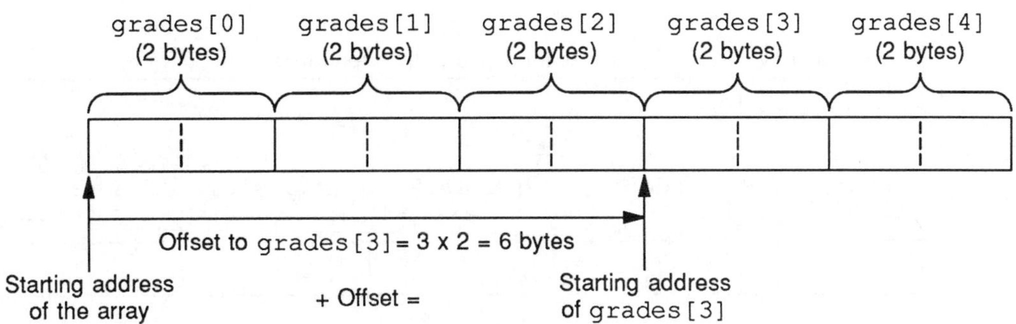

FIGURE 9-2 Using a Subscript to Obtain an Address

Recall that a pointer is a variable used to store addresses. If we create a pointer to store the address of the first element in the grades array, we can mimic the operation used by the computer to access the array elements. Before we do this, let us first consider Program 9-1.

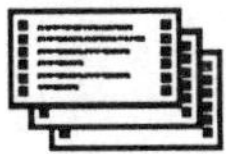

Program 9-1

```
main()
{
  int i;
  static int grades = {98, 87, 92, 79, 85};
  for (i = 0; i <= 4; ++i)
    printf("\nElement %d is %d", i, grades[i]);
}
```

When Program 9-1 is run, the following display is obtained:

```
Element 0 is 98
Element 1 is 87
Element 2 is 92
Element 3 is 79
Element 4 is 85
```

Program 9-1 displays the values of the static array `grades` using standard subscript notation. Now, let us store the address of array element 0 in a pointer. Then, using the indirection operator, `*`, we can use the address in the pointer to access each array element. For example, if we store the address of `grades[0]` in a pointer named `g_ptr` (using the assignment statement `g_ptr =`

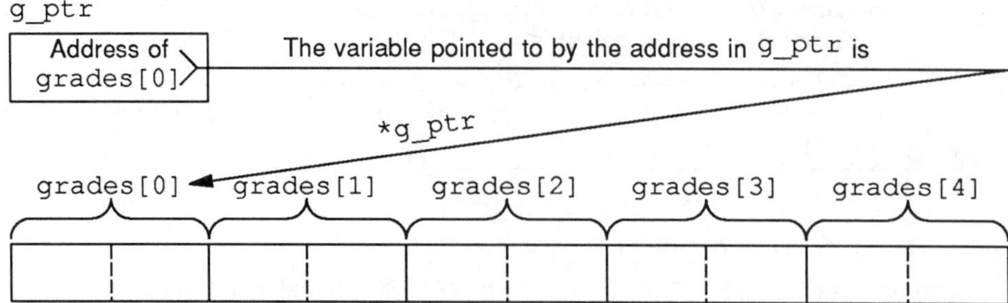

FIGURE 9-3 The Variable Pointed to by `*g_ptr` is `grades[0]`

`&grades[0];)`, and then, as illustrated in Figure 9-3, the expression `*g_ptr`, which means "the variable pointed to by `g_ptr`," references `grades[0]`.

One unique feature of pointers is that *offsets* can be included in expressions by using pointers. For example, the 1 in the expression `*(g_ptr + 1)` is an offset. The complete expression references the integer variable that is one beyond the variable pointed to by `g_ptr`. Similarly, as illustrated in Figure 9-4, the expression `*(g_ptr + 3)` references the variable that is three integers beyond the variable pointed to by `g_ptr`. This is the variable `grades[3]`.

Table 9-1 lists the complete correspondence between elements referenced by subscripts and by pointers and offsets. The relationships listed in Table 9-1 are illustrated in Figure 9-5.

TABLE 9-1 Array Elements May Be Referenced in Two Ways

Array Element	Subscript Notation	Pointer Notation
Element 0	`grades [0]`	`*g_ptr`
Element 1	`grades [1]`	`*(g_ptr + 1)`
Element 2	`grades [2]`	`*(g_ptr + 2)`
Element 3	`grades [3]`	`*(g_ptr + 3)`
Element 4	`grades [4]`	`*(g_ptr + 4)`

FIGURE 9-4 An Offset of 3 from the Address in `g_ptr`

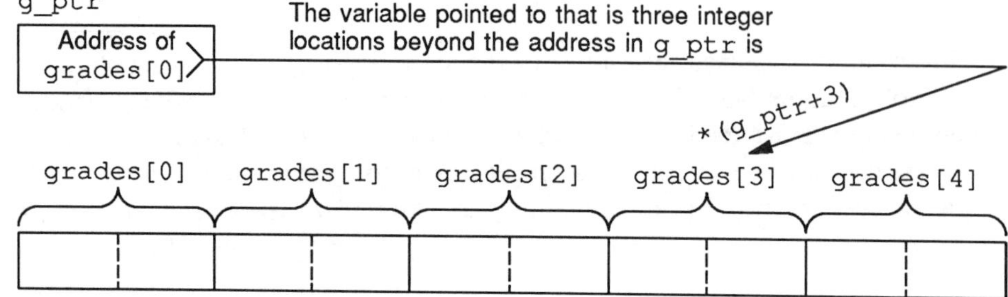

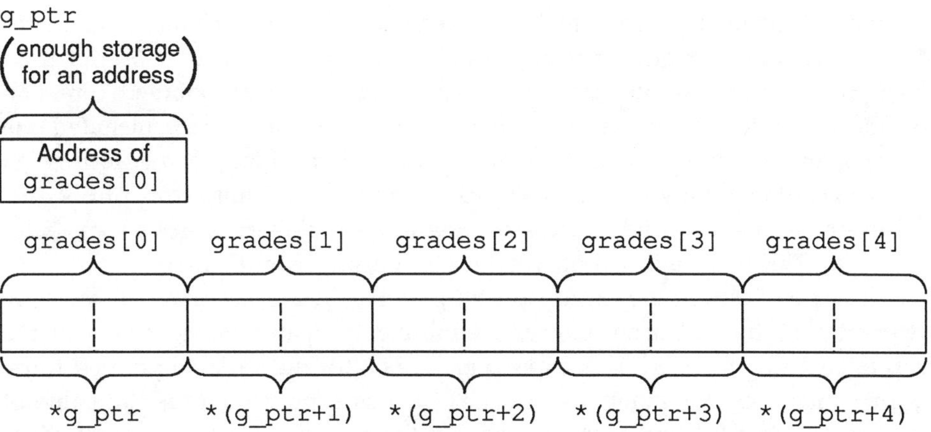

FIGURE 9-5 The Relationship Between Array Elements and Pointers

Using the correspondence between pointers and subscripts illustrated in Figure 9-5, the array elements previously accessed in Program 9-1 by using subscripts can now be accessed by using pointers. This is done in Program 9-2.

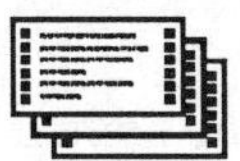

Program 9-2

```
main()
{
  int *g_ptr;              /* declare a pointer to an int      */
  int i;
  static int grades = {98, 87, 92, 79, 85};

  g_ptr = &grades[0];      /* store the starting array address */
  for (i = 0; i <= 4; ++i)
    printf("\nElement %d is %d", i, *(g_ptr + i) );
}
```

The following display is obtained when Program 9-2 is run:

```
Element 0 is 98
Element 1 is 87
Element 2 is 92
Element 3 is 79
Element 4 is 85
```

Notice that this is the same display produced by Program 9-1.

The method used in Program 9-2 to access *individual* array elements simulates how the computer internally references *all* array elements. Any subscript used by a programmer is automatically converted to an equivalent pointer expression by the computer. In our case, since the declaration of `g_ptr` included the information that integers are pointed to, any offset added to the address in `g_ptr` is automatically scaled by the size of an integer. Thus, `*(g_ptr + 3)`, for example, refers to the address of `grades[0]` plus an offset of six bytes `(3 * 2)`. This is the address of `grades[3]` illustrated in Figure 9-2.

The parentheses in the expression `*(g_ptr + 3)` are necessary to correctly reference the desired array element. Omitting the parentheses results in the expression `*g_ptr + 3`. This expression adds 3 to "the variable pointed to by `g_ptr`." Since `g_ptr` points to `grades[0]`, this expression adds the value of `grades[0]` and 3 together. Note also that the expression `*(g_ptr + 3)` does not change the address stored in `g_ptr`. Once the computer uses the offset from the starting address in `g_ptr` to locate the correct variable, the offset is discarded and the address in `g_ptr` remains unchanged.

Although the pointer `g_ptr` used in Program 9-2 was specifically created to store the starting address of the `grades` array, this was, in fact, unnecessary. When an array is created, the compiler automatically creates an internal pointer constant for it and stores the starting address of the array in this pointer. In almost all respects, a pointer constant is identical to a pointer variable created by a programmer; but, as we shall see, there are some differences.

For each array created, the name of the array becomes the name of the pointer constant created by the compiler for the array, and the starting address of the first location reserved for the array is stored in this pointer. Thus, declaring the `grades` array in both Program 9-1 and Program 9-2 actually reserved enough storage for five integers, created an internal pointer named `grades`, and stored the address of `grades[0]` in the pointer. This is illustrated in Figure 9-6.

FIGURE 9-6 Creating an Array Also Creates a Pointer

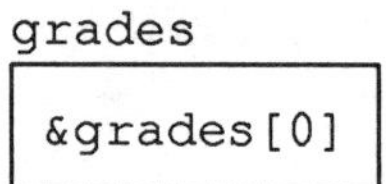

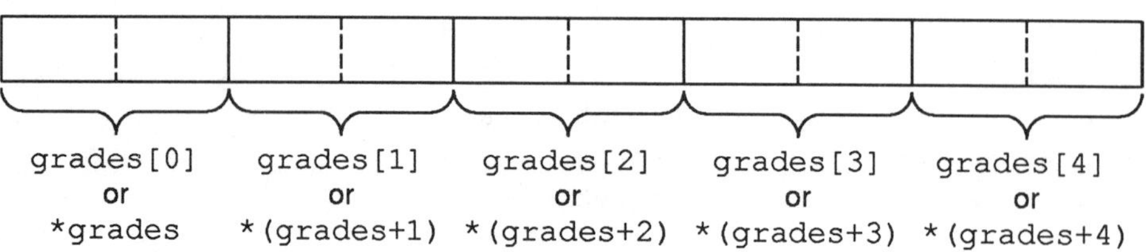

The implication is that every reference to grades using a subscript can be replaced by an equivalent reference using `grades` as a pointer. Thus, wherever the expression `grades[i]` is used, the expression `*(grades + i)` can also be used. This is illustrated in Program 9-3, where `grades` is used as a pointer to reference all of its elements.

Program 9-3

```
main()
{
  int i;
  static int grades = {98, 87, 92, 79, 85};
  for (i = 0; i <= 4; ++i)
    printf("\nElement %d is %d", i, *(grades + i) );
}
```

Executing Program 9-3 produces the same output previously produced by Program 9-1 and Program 9-2. However, using `grades` as a pointer made it unnecessary to declare and initialize the pointer `g_ptr` used in Program 9-2.

In most respects, an array name and pointer can be used interchangeably. A true pointer, however, is a variable and the address stored in it can be changed. An array name is a pointer constant and the address stored in the pointer cannot be changed by an assignment statement. Thus, a statement such as `grades = &grades[2];` is invalid. This should come as no surprise. Since the whole purpose of an array name is to correctly locate the beginning of the array, allowing a programmer to change the address stored in the array name would defeat this purpose and lead to havoc whenever array elements were referenced. Also, expressions taking the address of an array name are invalid because the pointer created by the compiler is internal to the computer, not stored in memory as are pointer variables. Thus, trying to store the address of `grades` using the expression `&grades` results in a compiler error.

An interesting sidelight to the observation that elements of an array can be referenced using pointers is that a pointer reference can always be replaced with a subscript reference. For example, if `num_ptr` is declared as a pointer variable, the expression `*(num_ptr + i)` can also be written as `num_ptr[i]`. This is true even though `num_ptr` is not created as an array. As before, when the compiler encounters the subscript notation, it replaces it internally with the pointer notation.

9.2 Pointer Arithmetic

Pointer variables, like all variables, contain values. The value stored in a pointer is, of course, an address. Thus, by adding and subtracting numbers to pointers we can obtain different addresses. Additionally, the addresses in pointers can be compared by using any of the relational operators (==, !=, < ,>, etc.) that are valid for comparing other variables. In performing arithmetic on pointers, we must be careful to produce addresses that point to something meaningful. In comparing pointers, we must also make comparisons that make sense. Consider the declarations:

```
int nums[100];
int *n_pt;
```

To set the address of nums[0] in n_pt, either of the following two assignment statements can be used:

```
n_pt = &nums[0];
n_pt = nums;
```

The two assignment statements produce the same result because nums is a pointer constant that itself contains the address of the first location in the array, that is, the address of nums[0]. Figure 9-7 illustrates the allocation of memory resulting from the previous declaration and assignment statements, assuming that each integer requires two bytes of memory and that the location of the beginning of the nums array is at address 18934.

Once n_pt contains a valid address, values can be added and subtracted from the address to produce new addresses. When adding or subtracting numbers to pointers, the computer automatically adjusts the number to ensure that the result still "points to" a value of the correct type. For example, the statement n_pt =

FIGURE 9-7 The nums Array in Memory

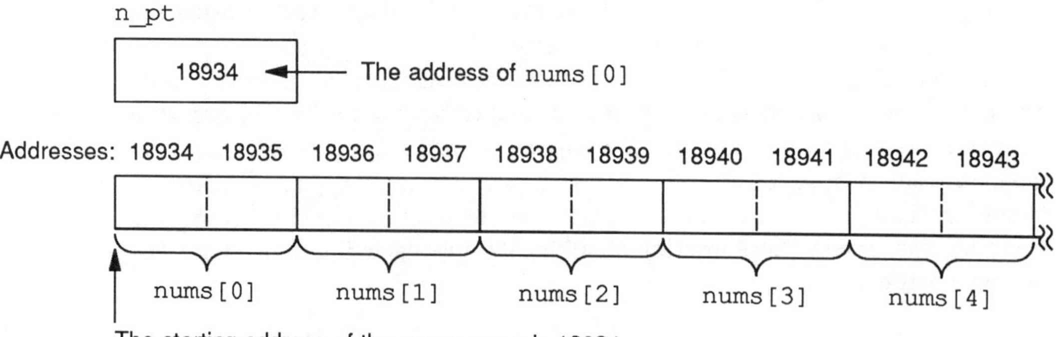

n_pt + 4; forces the computer to scale the 4 by the correct number to ensure that the resulting address is the address of an integer. Assuming that each integer requires two bytes of storage, as illustrated in Figure 9-7, the computer multiplies the 4 by two and adds eight to the address in n_pt. The resulting address is 18942, which is the correct address of nums[4].

This automatic scaling by the computer ensures that the expression n_pt + i, where i is any positive integer, correctly points to the *i*th element beyond the one currently being pointed to by n_pt. Thus, if n_pt initially contains the address of nums[0], n_pt + 4 is the address of nums[4], n_pt + 50 is the address of nums[50], and n_pt + i is the address of nums[i]. Although we have used actual addresses in Figure 9-7 to illustrate the scaling process, the programmer need never know or care about the actual addresses used by the computer. The manipulation of addresses by using pointers generally does not require knowledge of the actual address.

Addresses can also be incremented or decremented using both prefix and postfix increment and decrement operators. Adding 1 to a pointer causes the pointer to point to the next element of the type being pointed to. Decrementing a pointer causes the pointer to point to the previous element. For example, if the pointer variable p is a pointer to an integer, the expression p++ causes the address in the pointer to be incremented to point to the next integer. This is illustrated in Figure 9-8.

In reviewing Figure 9-8, notice that the increment added to the pointer is correctly scaled to account for the fact that the pointer is used to point to integers. It is, of course, up to the programmer to ensure that the correct type of data is stored in the new address contained in the pointer.

The increment and decrement operators can be applied as both prefix and postfix pointer operators. All of the following combinations using pointers are valid:

```
*pt_num++      /* use the pointer and then increment it */
*++pt_num      /* increment the pointer before using it */
*pt_num--      /* use the pointer and then decrement it */
*--pt_num      /* decrement the pointer before using it */
```

FIGURE 9-8 Increments Are Scaled When Used with Pointers

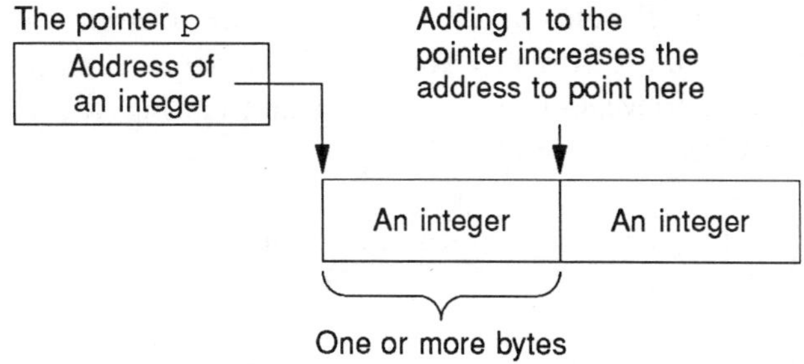

Of the four possible forms, the most commonly used is `*pt_num++`. This is because such an expression allows each element in an array to be accessed as the address is "marched along" from the starting address of the array to the address of the last array element. To see the use of the increment operator, consider Program 9-4. In this program each element in the `nums` array is retrieved by successively incrementing the address in `n_pt`.

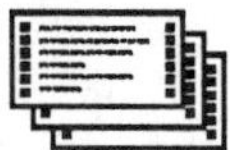

Program 9-4

```
main()
{
  static int nums[5] = {16, 54, 7, 43, -5};
  int total = 0, i, *n_pt;

  n_pt = nums;      /* store address of nums[0] in n_pt */
  for (i = 0; i <= 4; ++i)
    total = total + *n_pt++;

  printf("The total of the array elements is %d", total);
}
```

The output produced by Program 9-4 is:

```
The total of the array elements is 115
```

The expression `total = total + *n_pt++` used in Program 9-4 is a standard accumulating expression. Within this expression, the term `*n_pt++` first causes the computer to retrieve the integer pointed to by `n_pt`. This is done by the `*n_pt` part of the term. The postfix increment, `++`, then adds 1 to the address in `n_pt` so that `n_pt` now contains the address of the next array element. The increment is scaled by the computer so that the actual address in `n_pt` is the correct address of the next element.

Pointers can also be compared. This is particularly useful when dealing with pointers that point to elements in the same array. For example, rather than using a counter in a `for` loop to correctly access each element in an array, the address in a pointer can be compared to the starting and ending address of the array itself. The expression

```
n_pt <= &nums[4]
```

is true (nonzero) as long as the address in n_pt is less than or equal to the address of nums[4]. Since nums is a pointer constant that contains the address of nums[0], the term &nums[4] can be replaced by the equivalent term nums + 4. Using either of these forms, Program 9-4 can be rewritten as Program 9-5 to continue adding array elements while the address in n_pt is less than or equal to the address of the last array element.

Program 9-5

```
main()
{
  static int nums[5] = {16, 54, 7, 43, -5};
  int total = 0, *n_pt;

  n_pt = nums;     /* store address of nums[0] in n_pt  */

  while (n_pt <= nums + 4)
    total += *n_pt++;

  printf("The total of the array elements is %d", total);
}
```

Notice that in Program 9-5 the compact form of the accumulating expression, total += *n_pt++, was used in place of the longer form, total = total + *n_pt++. Also, the expression nums + 4 does not change the address in nums. Since nums is an array name and not a pointer variable, its value cannot be changed. The expression nums + 4 first retrieves the address in nums, adds 4 to this address (appropriately scaled), and then uses the result for comparison purposes. Expressions, such as *nums++, that attempt to change the address, are invalid. Expressions, such as *nums or *(nums + i), that use the address without attempting to alter it are valid.

Pointer Initialization

Like all variables, pointers can be initialized when they are declared. When initializing pointers, however, you must be careful to set an address in the pointer. For example, an initialization such as

```
int *pt_num = &miles;
```

is valid only if miles itself were declared as an integer variable prior to pt_num. Here we are creating a pointer to an integer and setting the address in the pointer to the address of an integer variable. Notice that, if the variable `miles` is declared subsequent to `pt_num`, as follows,

```
int *pt_num = &miles;
int miles;
```

an error occurs. This is because the address of `miles` is used before `miles` has even been defined. Since the storage area reserved for `miles` has not been allocated when `pt_num` is declared, the address of `miles` does not yet exist.

Pointers to arrays can be initialized within their declaration statements. For example, if `prices` has been declared to be array of floating point numbers, either of the following two declarations can be used to initialize the pointer named `zing` to the address of the first element in `prices`:

```
float *zing = &prices[0];
float *zing = prices;
```

The last initialization is correct because `prices` is itself a pointer constant containing an address of the proper type. The variable name `zing` was selected in this example to reinforce the idea that any variable name can be selected for a pointer.

9.3 Passing and Using Array Addresses

When an array is passed to a function, its address is the only item actually passed. By this we mean the address of the first location used to store the array, as illustrated in Figure 9-9. Since the first location reserved for an array corresponds to element 0 of the array, the address of the array is also the address of element 0.

For a specific example in which an array is passed to a function, let us consider Program 9-6. In this program, the `nums` array is passed to the `find_max()` function by using conventional array notation.

FIGURE 9-9 The Address of an Array Is the Address of the First Location Reserved for the Array

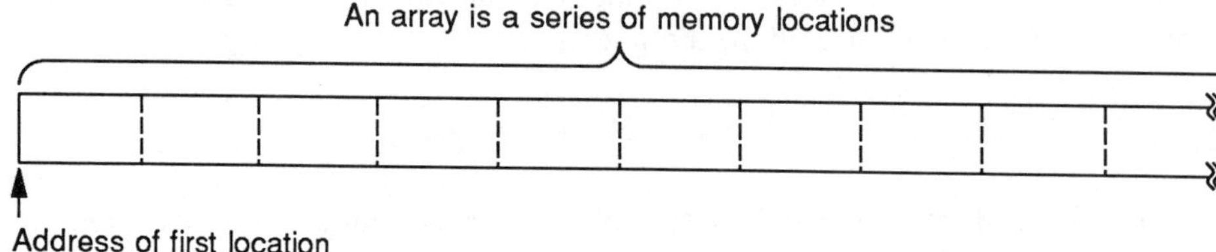
An array is a series of memory locations
Address of first location

Program 9-6

```
main()
{
  static int nums[5] = {2, 18, 1, 27, 16};
  int find_max();

  printf("The maximum value is %d", find_max(nums,5));
}

int find_max(vals,num_els)        /* find the maximum value */
int vals[], num_els;
{
  int i, max = vals[0];

  for (i = 1; i <= (num_els - 1); ++i)
   if (max < vals[i]) max = vals[i];

  return(max);
}
```

The output displayed when Program 9-6 is executed is:

```
The maximum value is 27
```

The argument named `vals` in the declaration line for `find_max()` actually receives the address of the array `nums`. As such, `vals` is really a pointer, since pointers are variables (or arguments) used to store addresses. Since the address passed into `find_max()` is the address of an integer, another suitable declaration for `find_max()` is:

```
find_max(vals,num_els)
int *vals;  /* vals declared as a pointer to an integer */
int num_els;
```

The declaration `int *vals;` declares that `vals` is used to store an address of an integer. The address stored is, of course, the location of the beginning of an array. Following is a rewritten version of the `find_max()` function that uses the new pointer declaration for `vals` but retains the use of subscripts to refer to individual array elements:

```
int find_max(vals,num_els)        /* find the maximum value */
int *vals;     /* vals declared as a pointer to an integer */
int num_els;
{
  int i, max = vals[0];

  for (i = 1; i <= (num_els - 1); ++i)
   if (max < vals[i]) max = vals[i];

  return(max);
}
```

One further observation needs to be made. Regardless of how `vals` is declared in the function header or how it is used within the function body, it is truly a pointer variable. As such, the address in `vals` can be modified. This is not true for the name `nums`. Since `nums` is the name of the originally created array, it is a pointer constant. As described in Section 9.1, this means that the address in `nums` cannot be changed and that the expression `&nums` is invalid. No such restrictions, however, apply to the pointer variable named `vals`. All the address arithmetic we learned in the previous section can be legitimately applied to `vals`.

We will write two additional versions of `find_max()`, both using pointers instead of subscripts. In the first version, we simply substitute pointer notation for subscript notation. In the second version, we use address arithmetic to change the address in the pointer.

As previously stated, a reference to an array element using the subscript notation `array_name[i]` can always be replaced by the pointer notation `*(array_name + i)`. In our first modification to `find_max()`, we make use of this correspondence by simply replacing all references to `vals[i]` with the equivalent expression `*(vals + i)`.

```
int find_max(vals,num_els)        /* find the maximum value */
int *vals;     /* vals declared as a pointer to an integer */
int num_els;
{
  int i, max = *vals;

  for (i = 1; i <= (num_els - 1); ++i)
   if (max < *(vals + i) )  max = *(vals + i);

  return(max);
}
```

Our last version of `find_max()` makes use of the fact that the address stored in `vals` can be changed. After each array element is retrieved using the address in `vals`, the address itself is incremented by one in the altering list of the `for` statement. The expression `*vals++` used to initially set `max` to the value of `vals[0]` also adjusts the address in `vals` to point to the second element in the array. The element obtained from this expression is the array element pointed to by `vals` before `vals` is incremented. The postfix increment, `++`, does not change the address in `vals` until after the address has been used to retrieve the array element.

```
int find_max(vals,num_els)       /* find the maximum value     */
int *vals;                      /* vals declared as a pointer  */
int num_els;
{
  int i, max = *vals++; /* get first element and increment */

  for (i = 1; i <= (num_els - 1); ++i, ++vals)
  {
    if (max < *vals) max = *vals;
  }
  return(max);
}
```

Let us review this version of `find_max()`. Initially, the maximum value is set to "the thing pointed to by `vals`." Since `vals` initially contains the address of the first element in the array passed to `find_max()`, the value of this first element is stored in `max`. The address in `vals` is then incremented by 1. The 1 added to `vals` is automatically scaled by the number of bytes used to store integers. Thus, after the increment, the address stored in `vals` is the address of the next array element. This is illustrated in Figure 9-10. The value of this next element is compared to the maximum and the address is again incremented, this time from within the altering list of the `for` statement. This process continues until all the array elements have been examined.

The version of `find_max()` that appeals to you is a matter of personal style and taste. Generally, beginning programmers are more comfortable using subscripts than using pointers. Also, if the program uses an array as the natural storage structure for the application and data at hand, an array reference using subscripts is more appropriate to clearly indicate the intent of the program. However, as we learn about strings and data structures, the use of pointers becomes an increasingly useful and powerful tool in its own right. In these instances, there is no simple or easy equivalence using subscripts.

One further trick can be gleaned from our discussion. Since passing an array to a function really involves passing an address, we can just as well pass any valid address. For example, the function call

```
find_max(&nums[2],3)
```

passes the address of `nums[2]` to `find_max()`. Within `find_max()`, the pointer `vals` stores the address and the function starts the search for a maximum

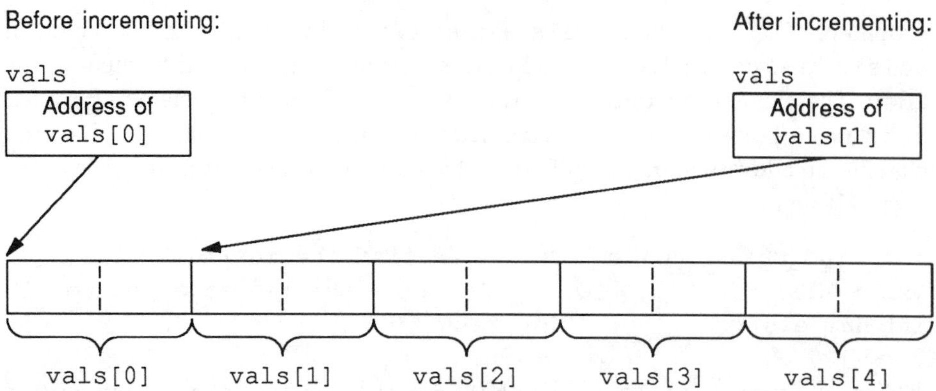

FIGURE 9-10 Pointing to Different Elements

at the element corresponding to this address. Thus, from `find_max()`'s perspective, it has received an address and proceeds appropriately.

Advanced Pointer Notation

Access to multidimensional arrays can also be made by using pointer notation, although the notation becomes more and more cryptic as the array dimensions increase. An extremely useful application of this notation occurs with two-dimensional character arrays, one of the topics of the next chapter. Here we consider pointer notation for two-dimensional numeric arrays. For example, consider the declaration

```
static int nums[2][3] = { {16,18,20},
                          {25,26,27} };
```

This declaration creates an array of elements and a set of pointer constants named `nums`, `nums[0]`, and `nums[1]`. The relationship between these pointer constants and the elements of the `nums` array are illustrated in Figure 9-11.

The availability of the pointer constants associated with a two-dimensional array allows us to reference array elements in a variety of ways. One way is to consider the two-dimensional array as an array of rows, where each row

FIGURE 9-11 Storage of the nums Array and Associated Pointer Constants

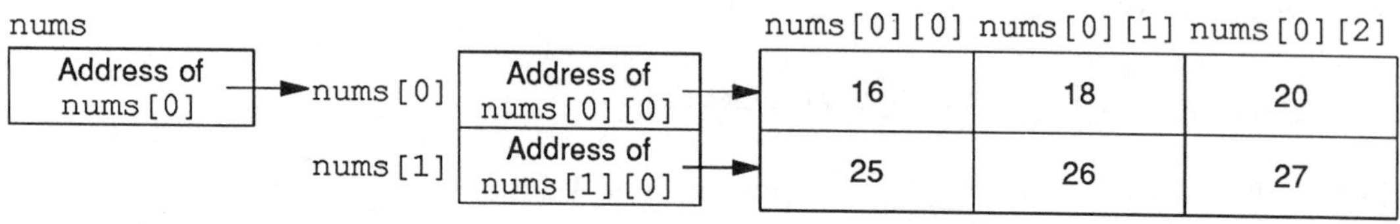

is itself an array of three elements. Considered in this light, the address of the first element in the first row is provided by `nums[0]` and the address of the first element in the second row is provided by `nums[1]`. Thus, the variable pointed to by `nums[0]` is `num[0][0]` and the variable pointed to by `nums[1]` is `num[1][0]`. Once the nature of these constants is understood, each element in the array can be accessed by applying the appropriate offset to the appropriate pointer. Thus, the following notations are equivalent:

Pointer Notation	**Subscript Notation**	**Value**
`*nums[0]`	`nums[0][0]`	16
`*(nums[0] + 1)`	`nums[0][1]`	18
`*(nums[0] + 2)`	`nums[0][2]`	20
`*nums[1]`	`nums[1][0]`	25
`*(nums[1] + 1)`	`nums[1][1]`	26
`*(nums[1] + 2)`	`nums[1][2]`	27

We can now go even further and replace `nums[0]` and `nums[1]` with their respective pointer notations, using the address of `nums` itself. As illustrated in Figure 9-11, the variable pointed to by `nums` is `nums[0]`. That is, `*nums` is `nums[0]`. Similarly, `*(nums + 1)` is `nums[1]`. Using these relationships leads to the following equivalences:

Pointer Notation	**Subscript Notation**	**Value**
`*(*nums)`	`nums[0][0]`	16
`*(*nums + 1)`	`nums[0][1]`	18
`*(*nums + 2)`	`nums[0][2]`	20
`*(*(nums + 1))`	`nums[1][0]`	25
`*(*(nums + 1) + 1)`	`nums[1][1]`	26
`*(*(nums + 1) + 2)`	`nums[1][2]`	27

The same notation applies when a two-dimensional array is passed to a function. For example, assume that the two-dimensional array `nums` is passed to the function `calc()` the using the call `calc(nums);`. Here, as with all array passes, an address is passed. A suitable function header for the function `calc()` is:

```
calc(pt)
int pt[2][3];
```

As we have already seen, the argument declaration for `pt` can also be

```
int pt[][3];
```

Using pointer notation, another suitable declaration is

```
int (*pt)[3];
```

In this last declaration, the parentheses are required to create a single pointer to objects of three integers. Each object is, of course, equivalent to a single row of the nums array. By suitably offsetting the pointer, each element in the array can be accessed. Notice that, without the parentheses, the declaration becomes

```
int *pt[3];
```

which inappropriately creates an array of three pointers, each one pointing to a single integer.

Once the correct declaration for pt is made (any of the appropriate declarations), the following notations within the function calc() are all equivalent:

Pointer Notation	Subscript Notation	Value
*(*pt)	pt [0] [0]	16
*(*pt + 1)	pt [0] [1]	18
*(*pt + 2)	pt [0] [2]	20
((pt + 1))	pt [1] [0]	25
((pt + 1) + 1)	pt [1] [1]	26
((pt + 1) + 2)	pt [1] [2]	27

The last two notations using pointers are encountered in more advanced C programs. The first of these occurs because functions can return any valid C scalar data type, including pointers to any of these data types. If a function returns a pointer, the data type being pointed to must be declared in the function's declaration. For example, the declaration

```
int *calc()
```

declares that calc() returns a pointer to an integer value. This means that *an address* of an integer variable is returned. Similarly, the declaration

```
float *taxes()
```

declares that taxes() returns a pointer to a floating point value. This means that *an address* of a floating point variable is returned.

In addition to declaring pointers to integers, floating point numbers, and C's other data types, pointers can also be declared that point to (contain the address of) a function. Pointers to functions are possible because function names, like array names, are themselves pointer constants. For example, the declaration

```
int (*calc)()
```

declares `calc` to be a pointer to a function that returns an integer. This means that `calc` will contain the address of a function, and the function whose address is in the variable `calc` returns an integer value. If, for example, the function `sum()` returns an integer, the assignment `calc = sum;` is valid.

9.4 Common Programming Errors

A common programming error occurs when pointers are used to reference nonexistent array elements. For example, if `nums` is an array of ten integers, the expression `*(nums + 15)` points six integer locations beyond the last element of the array. As C does not do any bounds checking on array references, this type of error is not caught by the compiler. This is the same error as using a subscript to reference an out-of-bounds array element disguised in its pointer notation form.

The remaining errors are not specific to pointers used for array references, but are common whenever pointer notation is used. These errors result from incorrect use of the address and indirection operators. For example, if `pt` is a pointer variable, the expressions

```
pt = &45
pt = &(miles + 10)
```

are both invalid because they attempt to take the address of a value. Notice that the expression `pt = &miles + 10`, however, is valid. Here, `10` is added to the address of `miles`. Again, it is the programmer's responsibility to ensure that the final address "points to" a valid data element.

Addresses cannot be taken of any register variable. Thus, for the declarations

```
register int total;
int *pt_tot;
```

the assignment

```
pt_tot = &total;
```

is invalid. The reason for this is that register variables are stored in a computer's internal registers, and these storage areas do not have standard memory addresses.

Addresses of pointer constants also cannot be taken. For example, given the declarations

```
int nums[25];
int *pt;
```

the assignment

```
pt = &nums;
```

is invalid. `nums` is a pointer constant that is itself equivalent to an address. The correct assignment is `pt = nums`.

Another common mistake made by beginner programmers is to initialize pointer variables incorrectly. For example, the initialization

```
int *pt = 5;
```

is invalid. Since `pt` is a pointer to an integer, it must be initialized with a valid address.

A more confusing error results from using the same name as both a pointer and a nonpointer variable. For example, assume that `minutes` is declared to be an integer variable in `main()` and that `main()` passes the address of `minutes` to the function `time()` by using the function call `time(&minutes);`. Due to the scope of local variables, the same names used in `main()` can also be used in `time()` without causing the computer any confusion. Thus, a valid function header for `time()` could be

```
time(minutes)
int *minutes;
```

With these declarations, the value stored in `minutes` within `main()` is accessed using the variable's name, while the same value is accessed in `time()` by using the notation `*minutes`. This can be very confusing to a programmer. To avoid this, most programmers usually develop their own systems for naming pointer arguments and variables. For example, prefixing pointer names by `pt_` or suffixing them with the characters `_addr` helps to indicate clearly that the arguments or variables are pointers.

The final error that occurs is one common to pointer usage in general. The situation always arises when the beginning C programmer becomes confused about whether a variable *contains* an address or *is* an address. Pointer variables and pointer arguments contain addresses. Although a pointer constant is synonymous with an address, it is useful to treat pointer constants as pointer variables with two restrictions:

1. The address of a pointer constant cannot be taken.
2. The address "contained in" the pointer constant cannot be altered.

Except for these two restrictions, pointer constants and variables can be used almost interchangeably. Therefore, when an address is required any of the following can be used:

- a pointer variable name
- a pointer argument name
- a pointer constant name
- a nonpointer variable name preceded by the address operator (e.g. &variable)
- a nonpointer argument name preceded by the address operator (e.g. &argument)

Some of the confusion surrounding pointers is caused by the cavalier use of the word *pointer.* For example, the phrase "a function requires a pointer argument" is more clearly understood when it is realized that the phrase really means "a function requires an address as an argument." Similarly, the phrase "a function returns a pointer" really means "a function returns an address." Since an address is returned, a suitably declared pointer must be available to store the returned address.

If you are ever in doubt as to what is really contained in a variable, or how it should be treated, use the `printf()` function to display either the contents of the variable, the thing pointed to, or the address of the variable. Seeing what is displayed frequently helps sort out what is really in the variable.

9.5 Chapter Summary

1. An array name is a pointer constant. The value of the pointer constant is the address of the first element in the array. Thus, if `val` is the name of an array, `val` and `&val[0]` can be used interchangeably.
2. Any reference to an array element by subscript notation can always be replaced by pointer notation. That is, the notation `a[i]` can always be replaced by the notation `*(a + i)`. This is true whether `a` was initially declared explicitly as an array or as a pointer.
3. Arrays are passed to functions by reference. The called function always receives direct access to the originally declared array elements.

4. When a single-dimensional array is passed to a function, the argument declaration for the function can be either an array declaration or a pointer declaration. Thus, the following argument declarations are equivalent:

```
float a[];
float *a;
```

5. Pointers can be incremented, decremented, and compared. Numbers added to or subtracted from a pointer are automatically scaled. The scale factor used is the number of bytes required to store the data type originally pointed to.

Sample Problem

Two sample problems are present for this chapter. The first problem involves the simple passing of a string to a function for subsequent display by the function. The second problem uses pointer notation to replace the array notation used in the sample problem for Chapter Eight.

Problem 1. Write a `main()` function that stores the string "Meet me in St. Louie, Louie" into a static array named `message`. Then pass this message to a function named `display()`, which uses pointer notation to display the individual characters in the string.

```
main()
{
  static char message[] = "Meet me in St. Louie, Louie";
  display(message);
}
display(strng)
char *strng;
{
  int i = 0;
  while( *(strng+i) != '\0')
  {
    printf("%c",*(strng+i));
    ++i;
  }
  return;
}
```

The output produced by this program is:

```
Meet me in St. Louie, Louie
```

Problem 2. Rewrite the problem presented in the Chapter Summary for Chapter Eight using pointer notation rather than array notation. The program should accept and process three arrays passed to a function named `calcvolt()`.

The following program performs the required processing:

```
main()
{
  int i;
  static double current[5] = {10.621, 48.913,
                              21.165, 5.186, 2.947};
  static double resist[5] = {4.85, 6.73, 5.91, 5.33, 5.42};
  static double volts[5];
  calcvolt(current, resist, volts);
  printf("\n Current   Resistance   Volts");
  printf("\n -------   ----------   -------");
  for(i = 0; i <= 4; ++i)
    printf("\n%7.3f     %7.3f      %7.3f",
           current[i], resist[i], volts[i]);
}
calcvolt(cur,res,vlts)
double *cur, *res, *vlts;
{
  int i;
  for (i = 0; i <= 4; ++i )
    *vlts++ = (*cur++) * (*res++);
}
```

Notice that within the `calcvolt()` function the variables `vlts`, `cur`, and `res` are true pointer variables. An expression such as `vlts++` is valid and increments the address located in `vlts`. This is not true for the pointer constants `current`, `resist`, and `volts` created in `main()`. Within `main()` an expression such as `*(volts + i)` would have to be used, which would offset the `volts` address without attempting to change this pointer constant. The variable `i` would have to be incremented by the expression `++i` to access the next element in the array.

The output produced by this program is:

```
 Current   Resistance    Volts
 -------   ----------   -------
  10.621      4.850       51.512
  48.913      6.730      329.184
  21.165      5.910      125.085
   5.186      5.330       27.641
   2.947      5.420       15.973
```

Character Strings

Chapter Ten

On a fundamental level, strings are simply arrays of characters that can be manipulated by standard element-by-element array-processing techniques. On a higher level, string library functions are available for treating strings as complete entities. This chapter explores the input, manipulation, and output of strings, using both approaches. We will also examine the particularly close connection between string-handling functions and pointers.

10.1 String Fundamentals

A *string constant,* informally referred to as a *string,* is any sequence of characters enclosed in double quotes. For example, "This is a string", "Hello World!", and "xyz 123 *!#@&" are all strings.

A string is stored as an array of characters terminated by a special end-of-string marker called the *null character*. The null character, represented by the escape sequence `\0`, is the sentinel marking the end of the string. For example, Figure 10-1 illustrates how the string "Good Morning!" is stored in memory. The string uses fourteen storage locations, with the last character in the string being the end-of-string marker `\0`. The double quotes are not stored as part of the string.

Since a string is stored as an array of characters, the individual characters in the array can be input, manipulated, or output by using standard array-handling techniques utilizing either subscript or pointer notations. The end-of-string null character is useful for detecting the end of the string when handling strings in this fashion.

String Input and Output

Although the programmer has the choice of using either a library or a user-written function for processing a string already in memory, inputting a string from a keyboard or displaying a string always requires some reliance on standard library functions. Table 10-1 lists the commonly available library functions for both character-by-character and complete string input/output.

The `gets()` and `puts()` functions deal with strings as complete units. Both are written using the more elemental functions `getchar()` and `putchar()`.

FIGURE 10-1 Storing a String in Memory

G	o	o	d		M	o	r	n	i	n	g	!	\0

TABLE 10-1 Standard String and Character Library Function

Input	Output
`gets()`	`puts()`
`scanf()`	`printf()`
`getchar()`	`putchar()`

The `getchar()` and `putchar()` functions provide for the input and output of individual characters. Programs that access any of these four functions must contain an `include` instruction of the form `#include <stdio.h>`. The `stdio.h` file contains definitions required by the accessed library functions.

Program 10-1 illustrates the use of `gets()` and `puts()` to input and output a string entered at the user's terminal.

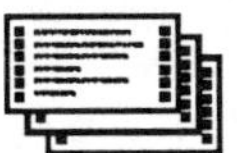

Program 10-1

```
#include <stdio.h>
main()
{
  char message[81];   /* enough storage for a complete line */

  printf("Enter a string:\n");
  gets(message);
  printf("\nThe string just entered is:\n");
  puts(message);
}
```

The following is a sample run of Program 10-1:

```
Enter a string:
This is a test input of a string of characters.

The string just entered is:
This is a test input of a string of characters.
```

The `gets()` function used in Program 10-1 continuously accepts and stores the characters typed at the terminal into the character array named `message`. Pressing the ENTER key at the terminal generates a newline character, `\n`, which is interpreted by `gets()` as the end-of-character entry. All the characters

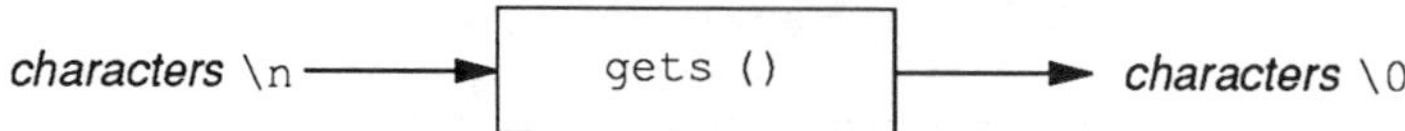

FIGURE 10-2a `gets()` substitutes `\0` for the entered `\n`

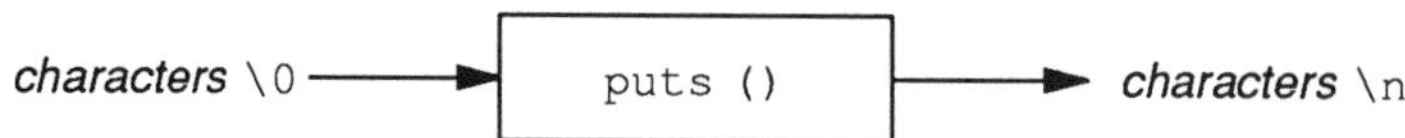

FIGURE 10-2b `puts()` substitutes `\n` when `\0` is encountered

encountered by `gets()`, except for the newline character, are stored in the `message` array. Before returning, the `gets()` function appends the null character to the stored set of characters, as illustrated in Figure 10-2a. The `puts()` function is then used to display the string. As illustrated in Figure 10-2b, the `puts()` function automatically sends a newline escape sequence to the display terminal after the string has been printed.

In general, a `printf()` function call can always be used in place of a `puts()` function call. For example, the statement `printf("%s\n",message);` is a direct replacement for the statement `puts(message);` used in Program 10-1. The newline escape sequence in the `printf()` function call is substituted for the automatic newline generated by `puts()` after the string is displayed.

The one-to-one correspondence between the output functions `printf()` and `puts()` is not duplicated by the input functions `scanf()` and `gets()`. For example, `scanf("%s",message)` and `gets(message)` are not equivalent. The `scanf()` function reads a set of characters up to either a blank space or a newline character, whereas `gets()` stops accepting characters only when a newline is detected. Trying to enter the characters `This is a string` by using the statement `scanf("%s",message);` results in the word `This` being assigned to the `message` array. Entering the complete line by using a `scanf()` function call would require a statement such as

```
scanf("%s %s %s %s", message1, message2, message3, message4);
```

Here, the word `This` would be assigned to the string `message1`, the word `is` assigned to the string `message2`, and so on. The fact that a blank is used as a delimiter by `scanf()` makes this function not that useful for entering string data.

Note that, if the `scanf()` function is used for inputting string data, the `&` is not used before the array name. Since an array name is a pointer constant equivalent to the address of the first storage location reserved for the array, `message` is the same as `&message[0]`. Thus, the function call `scanf("%s",&message[0])` can be replaced by `scanf("%s",message)`.

String Processing

Strings can be manipulated by using either standard library functions or standard array-processing techniques. The library functions typically available for use are presented in the next section. For now, we will concentrate on processing a string in a character-by-character fashion. This will allow us to understand how the standard library functions are constructed and to create our own library functions. For a specific example, consider the function `strcopy()` that copies the contents of `string1` to `string2`.

```
strcopy(string1, string2)          /* copy string1 to string2 */
char string1[], string2[];         /* two arrays are passed   */
{
  int i = 0;                       /* i is used as subscript  */

  while (string1[i] != '\0')       /* Check for end-of-string */
  {
    string2[i] = string1[i];       /* copy element to string2 */
    ++i;
  }
  string2[i] = '\0';               /* terminate second string */
  return;
}
```

Although this string copy function can be shortened considerably and written more compactly, the function illustrates the main features of string manipulation. The two strings are passed to `strcopy()` as arrays. Each element of `string1` is then assigned to the equivalent element of `string2` until the end-of-string marker is encountered. The detection of the null character forces the termination of the `while` loop which controls the copying of elements. Since the null character is not copied from `string1` to `string2`, the last statement in `strcopy()` appends an end-of-string character to `string2`. Prior to calling `strcopy()`, the programmer must ensure that sufficient space has been allocated for the `string2` array to be able to store the elements of the `string1` array.

Program 10-2 includes the `strcopy()` function in a complete program.

Program 10-2

```
#include <stdio.h>
main()
{
  char message[81];    /* enough storage for a complete line    */
  char new_mess[81];   /* enough storage for a copy of message  */
```

continued

```
  printf("Enter a sentence:");
  gets(message);
  strcopy(message,new_mess);  /* pass two array addresses       */
  puts(new_mess);

}

strcopy(string1, String2)      /* copy string1 to string2        */
char string1[], string2[];     /* two arrays are passed          */
{
  int i = 0;                   /* i will be used as a subscript */

  while ( string1[i] != '\0') /* check for the end-of-string   */
  {
    string2[i] = string1[i];  /* copy the element to string2   */
    ++i;
  }
  string2[i] = '\0';           /* terminate the second string   */
  return;
}
```

The following is a sample run of Program 10-2:

```
Enter a sentence: How much wood could a woodchuck chuck.
How much wood could a woodchuck chuck.
```

Character-by-Character Input

Just as strings can be processed with character-by-character techniques, they can also be entered and displayed in this manner. For example, consider Program 10-3, which uses the character-input function `getchar()` to enter a string one character at a time. The boxed portion of Program 10-3 essentially replaces the `gets()` function previously used in Program 10-1.

Program 10-3

```
#include <stdio.h>
main()
{
  char message[81],c;   /* enough storage for a complete line */
  int i;
```

continued

```
    printf("Enter a string:\n");

    i = 0;
    while( i < 81 && (c = getchar()) != '/n')
    {
      message[i] = c;      /* store the character entered */
      ++i;
    }
    message[i] = '\0';     /* terminate the string */

    printf("The string just entered is:\n");
    puts(message);
}
```

The following is a sample run of Program 10-3:

```
Enter a string:
This is a test input of a string of characters.
The string just entered is:
This is a test input of a string of characters.
```

The `while` statement in Program 10-3 causes characters to be read, providing that the number of characters entered is less than 81 and the character returned by `getchar()` is not the newline character. The parentheses around the expression `c = getchar()` are necessary to assign the character returned by `getchar()` to the variable `c` prior to comparing it to the newline escape sequence. Otherwise, the comparison operator, !=, which takes precedence over the assignment operator, causes the entire expression to be equivalent to

```
c = (getchar() != '\n')
```

This has the effect of first comparing the character returned by `getchar` to '\n'. The value of the relational expression `getchar() != '\n'` is either 0 or 1, depending on whether or not `getchar()` received the newline character. The value assigned to `c` then would also be either 0 or 1, as determined by the comparison.

Program 10-3 also illustrates a very useful technique for developing functions. The boxed statements constitute a self-contained unit for entering a complete line of characters from a terminal. As such, these statements can be removed from `main()` and placed together in a new function. Program 10-4 illustrates placing these statements in a new function called `getline()`.

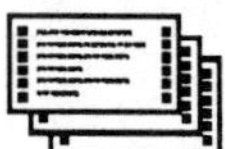

Program 10-4

```
#include <stdio.h>
main()
{
  char message[81];    /* enough storage for a complete line */
  int;

  printf("Enter a string:\n");
  getline(message);
  printf("The string just entered is:");
  puts(message);
}

getline(strng)
char strng[];
{
  int i = 0;
  char c;
  while( i < 81 && (c = getchar()) != '/n')
  {
    strng[i] = c;          /* store the character entered     */
    ++i;
  }
  strng[i] = '\0';         /* terminate the string            */
  return;
}
```

Since the `getline()` function does not formally return a value to `main()`, it does not have to be declared in `main()`. However, if your C compiler supports the `void` data type, `getline()` should be declared in `main()` as `void getline();`. We can further refine `getline()` and write it more compactly by having the character returned by `getchar()` assigned directly to the `strng` array. This eliminates the need for the local variable `c` and results in the following version:

```
getline(strng)
char strng[]
{
  int i = 0;
  while( i < 81 && (strng[i++] = getchar()) != '/n')
    ;
  strng[i] = '\0';         /* terminate the string     */
  return;
}
```

Notice that, in addition to assigning the returned character from getchar() directly to the strng array, the assignment statement

strng[i++] = getchar()

increments the subscript i by using the postfix operator, ++. The null statement, ;, then fulfills the requirement that a while loop contain at least one statement. Both versions of getline() are suitable replacements for gets(), and show the interchangeability between user-written and library functions.

C's enormous flexibility is shown by its ability to replace a library function with a user-written version and its ability to have functions written in various ways. Neither version of getline() is "more correct" from a programming standpoint. Each version presented (and more versions can be created) has its advantages and disadvantages. While the second version is more compact, the first version is clearer to beginning programmers. In creating your own C programs, select a style that is comfortable and remain with it until your growing programming expertise dictates modifications to your style.

10.2 Pointers and Library Functions

Pointers are exceptionally useful in constructing string-handling functions. When pointer notation is used in place of subscripts to access individual characters in a string, the resulting statements are both more compact and more efficient. In this section, we describe the equivalence between subscripts and pointers when accessing individual characters in a string.

Consider the strcopy() function introduced in the previous section. This function was used to copy the characters of one string to a second string. For convenience, this function is repeated here.

```
strcopy(string1,string2)       /* copy string1 to string2      */
char string1[], string2[];
{
  int i = 0;

  while ( string1[i] != '\0') /* check for the end-of-string */
  {
    string2[i] = string1[i];  /* copy the element to string2 */
    ++i;
  }
  string2[i] = '\0';           /* terminate the second string */
  return;
}
```

The function `strcopy()` is used to copy the characters from one array to another array, one character at a time. As currently written, the subscript `i` in the function is used successively to reference each character in the array named `string1` by moving along the string one character at a time. Before we write a pointer version of `strcopy()`, we will make two modifications to the function to make it more efficient.

The `while` statement in `strcopy()` tests each character to ensure that the end of the string has not been reached. As with all relational expressions, the tested expression, `string[i] != '\0'`, is either true or false. Using the string `this is a string` illustrated in Figure 10-3 as an example, as long as `string[i]` does not reference the end-of-string character the value of the expression is nonzero and is considered to be true. The expression is false only when the value of the expression is zero. This occurs when the last element in the string is accessed.

Recall that C defines false as zero and true as anything else. Thus, the expression `string[i] != '\0'` becomes zero, or false, when the end of the string is reached. It is nonzero, or true, everywhere else. Since the null character has an internal value of zero by itself, the comparison to '\0' is not necessary. When `string[i]` references the end-of-string character, the value of `string[i]` is zero. When `string[i]` references any other character, the value of `string[i]` is the value of the code used to store the character and is nonzero. Figure 10-4 lists the ASCII codes for the string `this is a string`. As seen in the figure, each element has a nonzero value except for the null character.

Since the expression `string[i]` is zero only at the end of a string and nonzero for every other character, the expression `while (strng[i] != '\0')` can be replaced by the simpler expression `while (strng[i])`. Although this may appear confusing at first, the revised test expression is certainly more compact than the longer version. Since end-of-string tests are frequently written by advanced C programmers in this shorter form, it is worthwhile being familiar with this expression. Including this expression in `strcopy1()` results in the following version of `strcopy()`:

```
strcopy(string1,string2)      /* copy string1 to string2     */
char string1[], string2[];
{
  int i = 0;

  while (string1[i])
  {
    string2[i] = string1[i]; /* copy the element to string2 */
    ++i;
  }
  string2[i] = '\0';          /* terminate the second string */
  return;
}
```

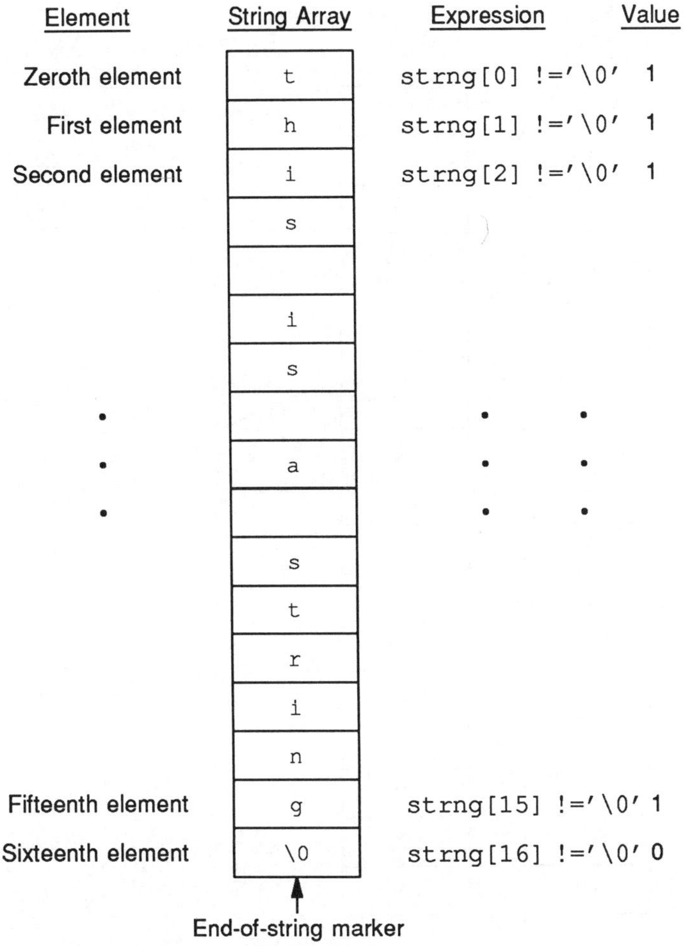

Element	String Array	Expression	Value
Zeroth element	t	strng[0] !='\0'	1
First element	h	strng[1] !='\0'	1
Second element	i	strng[2] !='\0'	1
	s		
	i		
	s		
•		•	•
•	a	•	•
•		•	•
	s		
	t		
	r		
	i		
	n		
Fifteenth element	g	strng[15] !='\0'	1
Sixteenth element	\0	strng[16] !='\0'	0

End-of-string marker

FIGURE 10-3 The `while` Test Becomes False at the End of the String

The second modification that can be made to this string copy function is to include the assignment inside the test portion of the `while` statement. Our new version of the string copy function is:

```
strcopy(string1,string2)     /* copy string1 to string2 */
char string1[], string2[];
{
  int i = 0;

  while (string2[i] = string1[i])
    ++i;
  return;
}
```

String Array	Stored Codes	Expression	Value
t	116	strng[0]	116
h	104	strng[1]	104
i	105	strng[2]	105
s	115		
	32		
i	105		
s	115		
	32	.	.
a	97	.	.
	32	.	.
s	115		
t	116		
r	114		
i	105		
n	110		
g	103	strng[15]	113
\0	0	strng[16]	0

FIGURE 10-4 The ASCII Codes Used to Store `this is a string`

Notice that including the assignment statement within the test part of the `while` statement eliminates the necessity of separately terminating the second string with the null character. The assignment within the parentheses ensures that the null character is copied from the first string to the second string. The value of the assignment expression only becomes zero after the null character is assigned to `string2`, at which point the `while` loop is terminated.

The conversion of `strcopy()` from subscript notation to pointer notation is now straightforward. Although each subscript version of `strcopy` can be rewritten using pointer notation, the following is the equivalent of our last subscript version:

```
strcopy(string1,string2)    /* copy string1 to string2 */
char *string1, *string2;
{
```

```
  while (*string2 = *string1)
  {
    string1++;
    string2++;
  }
  return;
}
```

In both subscript and pointer versions of `strcopy()`, the function receives the name of the array being passed. Recall that passing an array name to a function actually passes the address of the first location of the array. In our pointer version of `strcopy()`, the two passed addresses are stored in the pointer arguments `string1` and `string2`, respectively.

The declarations `char *string1;` and `char *string2;` used in the pointer version of `strcopy()` indicate that `string1` and `string2` are both pointers containing the address of a character, and stress the treatment of the passed addresses as pointer values rather than array names. These declarations are equivalent to the declarations `char string1[]` and `char string2[]`, respectively.

Internal to `strcopy()`, the pointer expression `*string1`, which refers to "the element whose address is in `string1`," replaces the equivalent subscript expression `string1[i]`. Similarly, the pointer expression `*string2` replaces the equivalent subscript expression `string2[i]`. The expression `*string2 = *string1` causes the element pointed to by `string1` to be assigned to the element pointed to by `string2`. Since the starting addresses of both strings are passed to `strcopy()` and stored in `string1` and `string2`, respectively, the expression `*string1` initially refers to `string1[0]` and the expression `*string2` initially refers to `string2[0]`.

Consecutively incrementing both pointers in `strcopy()` with the expressions `string1++` and `string2++` simply causes each pointer to point to the next consecutive character in the respective string. As with the subscript version, the pointer version of `strcopy` moves along, copying element by element, until the end of the string is copied.

One final change to the string copy function can be made by including the pointer increments as postfix operators within the test part of the `while` statement. The final form of the string copy function is:

```
strcopy(string1,string2)   /* copy string1 to string2 */
char *string1, *string2;
{
  while ( *string2++ = *string1++ )
    ;
  return;
}
```

There is no ambiguity in the expression `*string2++ = *string1++` even though the indirection operator, `*`, and the increment operator, `++`, have the same precedence. The associativity of these operators is from left to right, so the character pointed to is accessed before the pointer is incremented. Only after completion of the assignment `*string2 = *string1` are the pointers incremented to correctly point to the next characters in the respective strings.

Most C compilers include a string copy function in their standard library. This library function is typically written exactly like our pointer version of `strcopy()`.

Library Functions

Extensive collections of string and character handling functions and routines are included with most C compilers. These were previously listed in Section 7.3, and for convenience are repeated in Table 10-2.

Library functions and routines are called in the same manner that all C functions are called. This means that, if a library function returns a value the function must be declared within your program before it is called. For example, if a library function named `strngfoo()` returns a pointer to a character, the calling function must be alerted that an address is being returned. Thus, the statement `char *strngfoo();`, which declares that `strngfoo()` returns the address of a character (pointer to `char`), must be placed either as an external declaration or directly within the calling function's variable declarations.

Before attempting to use any standard library function, check that it is included in the C compiler available on your computer system. Be careful to check the type of arguments expected by the function, the data type of any returned value, and if any standard header files, such as `ctype.h`, must be included in your program to access these routines.

10.3 String Definitions and Pointer Arrays

The definition of a string automatically involves a pointer. For example, the definition `static char message1[81];` both reserves storage for 81 characters and automatically creates a pointer constant, `message1`, which contains the address of `message1[0]`. As a pointer constant, the address associated with the pointer cannot be changed — it must always "point to" the beginning of the created array.

Instead of initially creating a string as an array, however, it is also possible to create a string by using a pointer. This is similar in concept to declaring a

TABLE 10-2 String and Character Library Functions and Routines

Name	Description
`strcat (string1,string2)`	Concatenates `string2` to `string1`.
`strchr (string,character)`	Locates the position of the character within the string. Returns the address of the character.
`strcmp (string1,string2)`	Compares `string2` to `string1`. Returns the address of the first nonmatching character.
`strcpy (string1,string2)`	Copies `string2` to `string1`.
`strlen (string)`	Returns the length of the string.
`isalpha (character)`	Returns a nonzero number if the character is a letter; otherwise, it returns a zero.
`isupper (character)`	Returns a nonzero number if the character is uppercase; otherwise, it returns a zero.
`islower (character)`	Returns a nonzero number if the character is lowercase; otherwise, it returns a zero.
`isdigit (character)`	Returns a nonzero number if the character is a digit (0 through 9); otherwise, it returns a zero.
`toupper (character)`	Returns the uppercase equivalent if the character is lowercase; otherwise, it returns the character unchanged.
`tolower (character)`	Returns the lowercase equivalent if the character is uppercase; otherwise, it returns the character unchanged.

passed array as either an array or a pointer argument internal to the receiving function. For example, the definition `char *message2;` creates a pointer to a character. In this case, `message2` is a true pointer variable. Once a pointer to a character is defined, assignment statements, such as `message2 = "this is a string";`, can be made. In this assignment, `message2` receives the address of the first location used by the computer to store the string.

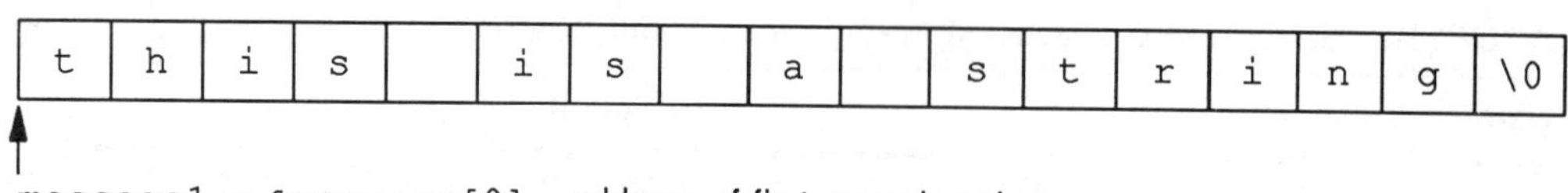

a. Storage allocation for a string defined as an array

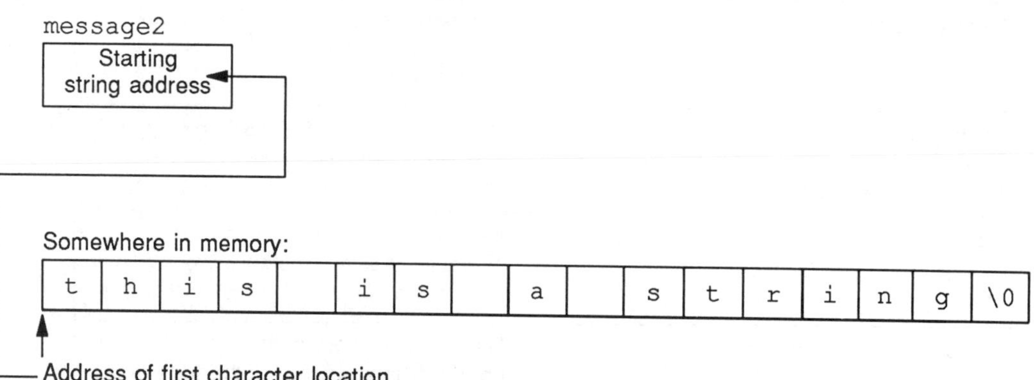

b. Storage of a string using a pointer

FIGURE 10-5 String Storage Allocation

The main difference in the definitions of `message1` as an array and `message2` as a pointer is the way the pointer is created. Defining `message1` using the declaration `static char message1[81]` explicitly calls for a fixed amount of storage for the array. This causes the compiler to create a pointer constant. Defining `message2` by using the declaration `char *message2` explicitly creates a pointer variable first. This pointer is then used to hold the address of a string when the string is actually specified. The difference between the two ways of defining a string has both storage and programming consequences.

From a programming perspective, defining `message2` as a pointer to a character allows string assignments, such as `message2 = "this is a string";`, to be made. Similar assignments are not allowed for strings defined as arrays. Thus, the statement `message1 = "this is a string";` is not valid. Both definitions, however, allow initializations to be made by using a string assignment. For example, both of the following initializations are valid:

```
static char message1[81] = "this is a string";
char *message2 = "this is a string";
```

As with all array initializations, the `static` designation is required for initializing local arrays; it is not required for initializing global arrays. The same is not true for `message2`. The initialization of `message2` consists of setting an initial address into a pointer variable. As such, the `static` designation required for local array initialization is not necessary.

From a storage perspective, the allocation of space for `message1` and `message2` is different, as illustrated in Figure 10-5. As shown in this figure, both initializations cause the computer to store the same string internally. In the case of `message1`, a specific set of 81 storage locations is reserved and the first 17 locations are initialized. For `message1`, different strings can be stored, but each string will overwrite the previously stored characters. The same is not true for `message2`.

The definition of `message2` reserves enough storage for one pointer. The initialization then causes the string to be stored and the starting storage address of the string to be loaded into the pointer. If a later assignment is made to `message2`, the initial string remains in memory and new storage locations are allocated to the new string. Program 10-5 uses the `message2` character pointer to successively point to two different strings.

Program 10-5

```
main()
{
  char *message2 = "this is a string";

  printf("\nThe string is: %s", message2);
  printf("\n The first address of this string is %u", message2);

  message2 = "A new message";
  printf("\nThe string is now: %s", message2);
  printf("\n The first address of this string is %u", message2);
}
```

A sample output for Program 10-5 is:

```
The string is: this is a string
 The first address of this string is 1048672
The string is now: A new message
 The first address of this string is 1048727
```

In Program 10-5, the variable message2 is initially created as a pointer variable and loaded with the starting storage address of the first string. The printf() function is then used to display this string. When the %s conversion character is encountered by printf(), it alerts the function that a string is being referenced. The printf() function then expects either a string constant or a pointer containing the address of the first character in the string. This pointer can be either an array name or a pointer variable. The printf() function uses the address provided to correctly locate the string, and then continues accessing and displaying characters until it encounters a null character. As illustrated by the output, the address of the first character in the string is 1048672.

After the first string and its starting address are displayed, the next assignment statement in Program 10-5 causes the computer to store a second string and change the address in message2 to point to the starting location of this new string. The printf() function then displays this string and its starting storage address.

It is important to realize that the second string assigned to message2 does not overwrite the first string, but simply changes the address in message2 to point to the new string. As illustrated in Figure 10-6, both strings are stored inside the computer. Any additional string assignment to message2 would result in the additional storage of the new string and a corresponding change in the address stored in message2.

FIGURE 10-6 Storage Allocation for Program 10-5

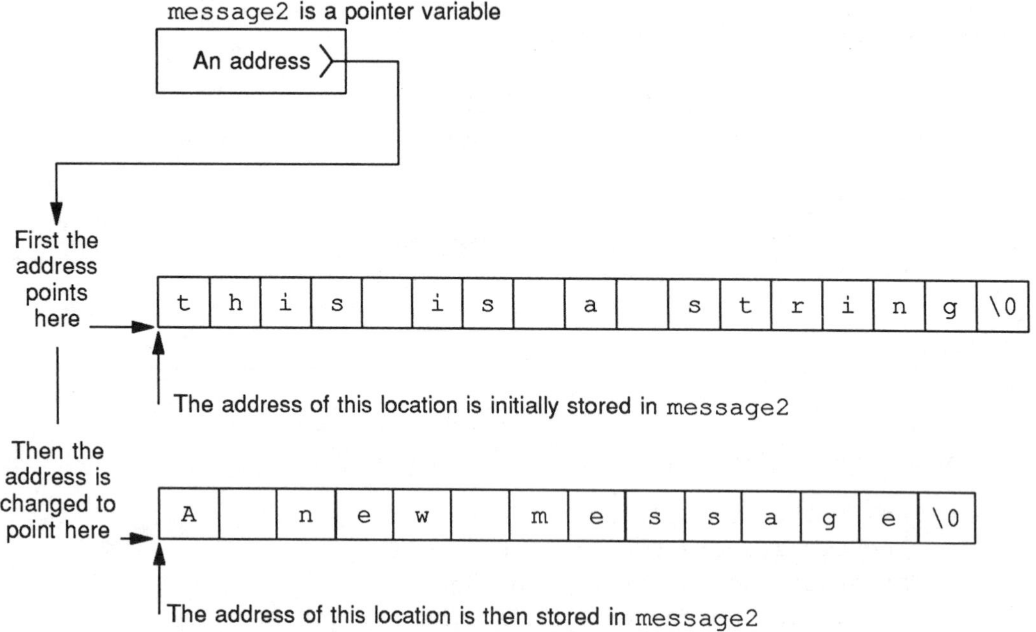

Pointer Arrays

The declaration of an array of character pointers is an extremely useful extension of single string pointer declarations. For example, the declaration

```
static char *seasons[4];
```

creates an array of four elements, where each element is a pointer to a character. As individual pointers, each pointer can be assigned to point to a string by using string assignment statements. Thus, the statements

```
seasons[0] = "winter";
seasons[1] = "spring";
seasons[2] = "summer";
seasons[3] = "fall";
```

set appropriate addresses in the respective pointers. Figure 10-7 illustrates the addresses loaded into the pointers for these assignments.

As illustrated in Figure 10-7, the `seasons` array does not contain the actual strings assigned to the pointers. These strings are stored elsewhere in the computer, in the normal data area allocated to the program. The array of pointers contains only the addresses of the starting location for each string.

The initializations of the `seasons` array can also be incorporated directly in the definition of the array, as follows:

```
static char *seasons[4] = { "winter",
                            "spring",
                            "summer",
                             "fall"};
```

This declaration both creates an array of pointers and initializes the pointers with appropriate addresses. Once addresses have been assigned to the pointers, each pointer can be used to access its corresponding string. Program 10-6 uses the `seasons` array to display each season by using a `for` loop.

FIGURE 10-7 The Addresses Contained in the `seasons[]` Pointers

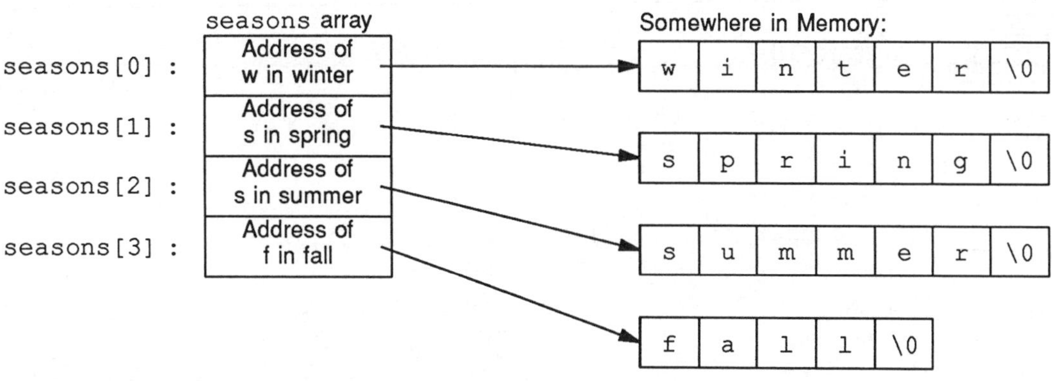

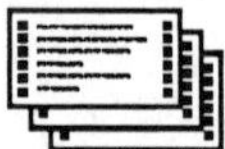

Program 10-6

```
main()
{
  int n;
  static char *seasons[] = { "winter",
                             "spring",
                             "summer",
                             "fall"};


  for( n = 0; n < 4; ++n)
    printf("\nThe season is %s.",seasons[n]);
}
```

The output obtained for Program 10-6 is:

```
The season is winter.
The season is spring.
The season is summer.
The season is fall.
```

The advantage of using a list of pointers is that logical groups of data headings can be collected together and accessed with one array name. For example, the months in a year can be collectively grouped in one array called `months`, and the days in a week collectively grouped together in an array called `days`. The grouping of like headings allows the programmer to access and print an appropriate heading by simply specifying the correct position of the heading in the array. Program 10-7 uses the `seasons` array to correctly identify and display the season corresponding to a user-input month.

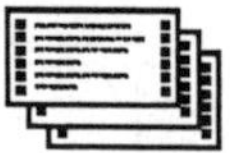

Program 10-7

```
main()
{
  int n;
  static char *seasons[] = { "winter",
                             "spring",
                             "summer",
                             "fall"};
```

continued

```
    printf("\nEnter a month (use 1 for Jan., 2 for Feb., etc.): ");
    scanf("%d", &n);
    n = (n % 12) / 3;    /* create the correct subscript */
    printf("\nThe month entered is a %s month.",season[n]);
}
```

Except for the expression `n = (n % 12) / 3`, Program 10-7 is straightforward. The program requests the user to input a month, and accepts the number corresponding to the month by using a `scanf()` function call.

The expression `n = (n % 12) / 3` uses a common program "trick" to scale a set of numbers into a more useful set. Using subscripts, the four elements of the seasons array must be accessed by using a subscript from 0 through 3. Thus, the months of the year, which correspond to the numbers 1 through 12, must be adjusted to correspond to the correct season subscript. This is done by using the expression `n = (n % 12) / 3`. The expression `n % 12` adjusts the month entered to be within the range 0 through 11, with 0 corresponding to December, 1 to January, etc. Dividing by 3 then causes the resulting number to range between 0 and 3, corresponding to the possible `seasons` elements. The result of the division by 3 is assigned to the integer variable `n`. The months 0, 1, and 2, when divided by 3, are set to 0; the months 3, 4, and 5 are set to 1; the months 6, 7, and 8 are set to 2; and the months 9, 10, and 11 are set to 3. This is equivalent to the following assignments:

Months	**Season**
December, January, February	winter
March, April, May	spring
June, July, August	summer
September, October, November	fall

The following is a sample output of Program 10-7:

```
Enter a month (use 1 for Jan., 2 for Feb., etc.): 12
The month entered is a winter month.
```

10.4 Formatting Strings

Besides the special string-handling functions in the standard library provided with your C compiler, both the `printf()` and `scanf()` functions have string-formatting capabilities. Additionally, two related functions, `sprintf()` and sscanf(), provide further string-processing features. In this section, we present the features that these functions provide when used with strings.

Field width specifiers can be included in a printf() control sequence to control the spacing of integers and decimal numbers. These specifiers can also be used with the %s control sequence to control the display of a string. For example, the statement

```
printf("|%25s|","Have a Happy Day");
```

displays the message Have a Happy Day, right justified, in a field of 25 characters, as follows:

```
|        Have a Happy Day|
```

We have placed a bar (|) at the beginning and end of the string field to delineate clearly the field being printed. Placing a minus sign (-) in front of the field width specifier forces the string to be left justified in the field. For example, the statement

```
printf("|%-25s|","Have a Happy Day");
```

causes the display:

```
|Have a Happy Day         |
```

If the field width specifier is too small for the string, the specifier is ignored and the string is displayed, using sufficient space to accommodate the complete string.

The precision specifier used for determining the number of digits displayed to the right of a decimal number can also be used as a string specifier. When used with strings, the precision specifier determines the maximum number of characters that will be displayed. For example, the statement

```
printf("|%25.12s|","Have a Happy Day");
```

cause the first twelve characters in the string to be displayed, right justified, in a field of 25 characters. This produces the display:

```
|             Have a Happy|
```

Similarly, the statement

```
printf("|%-25.12s|","Have a Happy Day");
```

causes twelve characters to be left justified in a field of 25 characters. This produces the display:

```
|Have a Happy             |
```

When a precision specifier is used with no field width specifier, the indicated number of characters is displayed in a field sufficiently large to hold the designated number of characters. Thus, the statement

```
printf("|%.12s|","Have a Happy Day");
```

causes the first twelve characters in the string to be displayed in a field of 12 characters. If the string has less than the number of characters designated by the precision specifier, the display is terminated when the end-of-string is encountered.

In-Memory String Conversions

While `printf()` displays data to the standard device used by your computer for output and `scanf()` scans the standard device used for input, the `sprintf()` and `sscanf()` functions provide similar capabilities for writing and scanning strings to and from memory variables. For example, the statement

```
sprintf(dis_strn,"%d %d", num1, num2);
```

writes the numerical values of `num1` and `num2` into `dis_strn` rather than displaying the values on the standard output terminal. Here, `dis_strn` is a programmer-selected variable name that must be declared as either an array of characters, sufficiently large to hold the resulting string, or as a pointer to a string.

Typically, the `sprintf()` function is used to assemble a string from smaller pieces until a complete line of characters is ready to be written, either to the standard output device or to a file (writing data to a file is described in Chapter 12). For example, another string could be concatenated to `dis_strn`, using the `strcat()` function, and the complete string displayed, using the `printf()` function.

In contrast to `sprintf()`, the string scan function `sscanf()` may be used to "disassemble" a string into smaller pieces. For example, if the string `"$23.45 10"` were stored in a character array named `data`, the statement

```
sscanf(data,"%c%lf %d",&dol,&price,&units);
```

would scan the string stored in the data array and strip off three data items. The dollar sign would be stored in the variable named `dol`, the `23.45` would be converted to a double precision number and stored in the variable named `price`, and the `10` would be converted to an integer value and stored in the variable named `units`. For a useful result, the variables `dol`, `price`, and `units` would have to be declared as the appropriate data types. In this way `sscanf()` provides a useful means of converting parts of a string into other data types. Typically, the string being scanned by `sscanf()` is used as a working storage area, or buffer, for storing a complete line from either a file or the standard input. Once the string has been filled, `sscanf()` disassembles the string into component parts and suitably converts each data item into the designated data type. For programmers familiar with COBOL, this is equivalent to first reading data into a working storage area before moving the data into smaller fields.

Format Strings

When you use any of the four functions, `printf()`, `scanf()`, `sprintf()`, or `sscanf()`, the control string containing the control sequences need not be explicitly contained within the function. For example, the control string `"$%5.2 %d"`, contained within the function call

```
printf("$%5.2d %d",num1,num2);
```

can itself be stored as a string and the address of the string can be used in the call to `printf()`. If either of the following declarations for `fmat` are made:

```
char *fmat = "$%5.2 %d";
```

or

```
char fmat[] = "$%5.2d %d";
```

the function call, `printf(fmat,num1,num2);` can be made in place of the previous call to `printf()`. Here, `fmat` is a pointer that contains the address of the control string used to determine the output display.

The technique of storing and using control strings in this manner is very useful for clearly listing format strings with other variable declarations at the beginning of a function. If a change to a format must be made, it is easy to find the desired control string without searching through the complete function to locate the appropriate `printf()` or `scanf()` function call. Restricting the definition of a control string to one place is also advantageous when the same format control is used in multiple function calls.

10.5 Common Programming Errors

Four errors are frequently made when pointers to strings are used. The most common is using the pointer to point to a nonexisting data element. This error is, of course, the same error we have already seen in using subscripts. Since C compilers do not perform bounds checking on arrays, it is the programmer's responsibility to ensure that the address in the pointer is the address of a valid data element.

The second common error occurs when an attempt is made to initialize a local array of characters. Even though a local character pointer can be initialized without being declared as a `static` variable, only `static` local arrays can be initialized.

The third common error lies in not providing sufficient space for the end-of-string null character when a string is defined as an array of characters, and not including the null (`\0`) character when the array is initialized.

Finally, the last error relates to a misunderstanding of terminology. For example, if `text` is defined as

```
char *text;
```

the variable `text` is sometimes referred to as a string. Thus, the terminology "store the characters `Hooray for the Hoosiers` into the `text` string" may be encountered. Strictly speaking, calling `text` a string or a string variable is incorrect. The variable `text` is a pointer that contains the address of the first character in the string. Nevertheless, referring to a character pointer as a string occurs frequently enough that you should be aware of it.

10.6 Chapter Summary

1. A string is an array of characters that is terminated by the null character.
2. Strings can always be processed with standard array-processing techniques. The input and display of a string, however, always requires reliance on a standard library function.
3. The `gets()`, `scanf()`, and `getchar()` library functions can be used to input a string. The `scanf()` function tends to be of limited usefulness for string input because it terminates input when a blank is encountered.
4. The `puts()`, `printf()`, and `putchar()` functions can be used to display strings.
5. In place of subscripts, pointer notation and pointer arithmetic are especially useful for manipulating string elements.
6. Many standard library functions exist for processing a string as a complete unit. Internally, these functions manipulate strings in a character-by-character manner, usually by using pointers.
7. String storage can be created by declaring an array of characters or a pointer to a character. A pointer to a character can be assigned a string directly. String assignment to an array of characters is invalid except when in a declaration statement.
8. As with all arrays, only `static` and external character arrays can be initialized. These arrays can be initialized by using a string assignment of the form

```
char *arr_name[] = "text";
```

This initialization is equivalent to

```
char *arr_name[] = {'t','e','x','t','\0'};
```

Sample Problem

This sample C program displays the month of the year corresponding to a user-entered integer between 1 and 12. The names of the months are stored using an array of pointers. The following program performs the required processing:

```
main()
{
  int num;

  printf("Enter a number from 1 to 12: ");
  scanf("%d", &num);
  which_month(num);
}

which_month(choice)
int choice;
{
  char *month[] = {"January", "February", "March", "April", "May",
                   "June", "July", "August", "September", "October",
                   "November", "December" };

  --choice;          /* January now corresponds to 0 */
  printf("\nMonth %d of the year is %s.", choice + 1, month[choice]);
}
```

The following sample output was obtained with this program:

```
Enter a number from 1 to 12: 9

Month 9 of the year is September.
```

Structures

Chapter Eleven

In the broadest sense, *structure* refers to the way individual elements of a group are arranged or organized. For example, a corporation's structure refers to the organization of the people and departments in the company and a government's structure refers to its form or arrangement. In programming, a structure refers to the way individual data items are arranged to form a cohesive and related unit. For example, consider the data items typically used in preparing mailing labels, as illustrated in Figure 11-1.

Each of the individual data items listed in the figure is an entity by itself. Taken together, all the data items form a single unit, representing a natural organization of the data for a mailing label. This larger grouping of related individual items is commonly called a *record.* In C, a record is referred to as a structure.

Although there could be thousands of names and addresses in a complete mailing list, the form of each mailing label, or its structure, is identical. In dealing with structures it is important to distinguish between the form of the structure and the data content of the structure.

The *form* of a structure consists of the symbolic names, data types, and arrangement of individual data items in the structure. The *content* of a structure refers to the actual data stored in the symbolic names. Figure 11-2 shows acceptable contents for the structure illustrated in Figure 11-1.

In this chapter, we describe the C statements required to create, fill, use, and pass structures between functions.

11.1 Single Structures

Using structures requires the same two steps needed for using any C variable. First the structure must be declared. Then specific values can be assigned to the

FIGURE 11-1 Typical Mailing List Components

Name:
Street Address:
City:
State:
Zip Code:

FIGURE 11-2 The Contents of a Structure

Rhona Bronson-Karp
614 Freeman Street
Orange
NJ
07052

individual structure elements. Declaring a structure requires listing the data types, data names, and arrangement of data items. For example, the definition

```
struct
{
  int month;
  int day;
  int year;
}  birth;
```

gives the form of a structure called `birth` and reserves storage for the individual data items listed in the structure. The `birth` structure consists of three data items, which are called *members of the structure.*

Assigning actual data values to the data items of a structure is called *populating the structure,* and is a relatively straightforward procedure. Each member of a structure is accessed by giving both the structure name and individual data item name, separated by a period. Thus, `birth.month` refers to the first member of the `birth` structure, `birth.day` refers to the second member of the structure, and `birth.year` refers to the third member. Program 11-1 illustrates assigning values to the individual members of the `birth` array (observe that the `printf()` statement call has been continued across two lines).

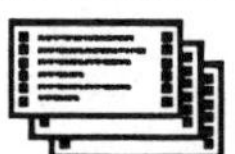

Program 11-1

```
main()
{
  struct
  {
  int month;
    int day;
    int year;
  }  birth;

  birth.month = 12;
  birth.day = 28;
  birth.year = 52;

  printf("My birth date is %d/%d/%d",
          birth.month, birth.day,birth.year);
}
```

The output produced by Program 11-1 is:

```
My birth date is 12/28/52
```

As in most C statements, the spacing of a structure definition is not rigid. For example, the `birth` structure could just as well have been defined

```
struct {int month; int day; int year;} birth;
```

Also, as with all C definition statements, multiple variables can be defined in the same statement. For example, the definition statement

```
struct {int month; int day; int year;} birth, current;
```

creates two structures having the same form. The members of the first structure are referenced by the individual names `birth.month`, `birth.day`, and `birth.year`, while the members of the second structure are referenced by the names `current.month`, `current.day`, and `current.year`. Notice that the form of this particular structure definition statement is identical to the form used in defining any program variable: the data type is followed by a list of variable names.

A useful modification to defining structures is to list the form of the structure without a variable name. In this case, however, the list of structure members must be preceded by a *tag name.* For example, in the declaration

```
struct date
{
  int month;
  int day;
  int year;
};
```

the term `date` is a tag name. The declaration for the `date` structure provides a *template* for the structure without actually reserving any storage locations. As such it is not a definition statement. The template presents the form of a structure called `date` by describing how individual data items are arranged within the structure. Actual storage for the members of the structure is reserved only when specific variable names are assigned. For example, the definition statement

```
struct date birth, current;
```

reserves storage for two structures named `birth` and `current`, respectively. Each of these individual structures has the form previously declared for the `date` structure. In effect, the declaration for `date` creates a *structure type* named `date`. The variables `birth` and `current` are then defined to be of this structure type.

Like all variable declarations, a structure can be declared globally or locally. Program 11-2 illustrates the global declaration of a `date` structure. Internal to `main()`, the variable `birth` is defined by using this global template.

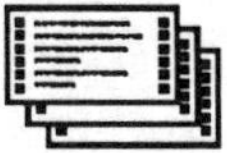

Program 11-2

```
struct date
  {
    int month;
    int day;
    int year;
  };
main()
{
  struct date   birth;
  birth.month = 12;
  birth.day = 28;
  birth.year = 52;
  printf("My birth date is %d/%d/%d", birth.month,
          birth.day,birth.year);
}
```

The output produced by Program 11-2 is identical to the output produced by Program 11-1.

The initialization of structures follows the same rules as that for the initialization of arrays: external and `static` structures can be initialized by following the definition with a list of initializers. For example, the definition statement

```
static struct date birth = {12, 28, 52};
```

can be used to replace the first four statements internal to `main()` in Program 11-2. Notice that the initializers are separated by commas, not semicolons.

The individual members of a structure are not restricted to integer data types, as illustrated by the `birth` structure. Any valid C data type can be used. For example, consider an employee record consisting of the following data items:

```
Name:
Identification Number:
Regular Pay Rate:
Overtime Pay Rate:
```

A suitable declaration for these data items is:

```
struct pay_rec
{
  char name[20];
  int id_num;
  float reg_rate;
  float ot_rate;
};
```

Once the template for pay_rec is declared, a specific structure using the pay_rec template can be defined and initialized. For example, the definition

```
struct pay_rec employee = {"H. Price",12387,15.89,25.50};
```

creates a structure named employee by using the pay_rec template. The individual members of employee are initialized with the respective data listed between braces in the definition statement.

Notice that a single structure is simply a convenient method for combining and storing related items under a common name. Although a single structure is useful in explicitly identifying the relationship among its members, the individual members could be defined as separate variables. The real advantage to using structures is realized only when the same template is used in a list many times over. Creating lists with the same structure template is the topic of the next section.

Before leaving single structures, it is worth noting that the individual members of a structure can be any valid C data type, including both arrays and structures. An array of characters was used as a member of the employee structure defined previously. Accessing an element of a member array requires giving the structure's name, followed by a period, followed by the array designation. For example, employee.name[4] refers to the fifth character in the name array.

Including a structure within a structure follows the same rules as those for including any data type in a structure. For example, assume that a structure is to consist of a name and a date of birth, where a date structure has been declared as:

```
struct date
{
  int month;
  int date;
  int year;
};
```

A suitable definition of a structure that includes a name and a date structure is:

```
struct
{
  char name[20];
  struct date birth;
} person;
```

Notice that, in declaring the date structure, the term `date` is a structure tag name. A tag name always appears before the braces in the declaration statement and identifies a structure template. In defining the `person` structure, `person` is the name of a specific structure, not a structure tag name. The same is true of the variable named `birth`. This is the name of a specific structure having the form of `date`. Individual members in the `person` structure are accessed by preceding the desired member with the structure name followed by a period. For example, `person.birth.month` refers to the `month` variable in the `birth` structure contained in the `person` structure.

11.2 Arrays of Structures

The real power of structures is realized when the same structure is used for lists of data. For example, assume that the data shown in Figure 11-3 must be processed.

Clearly, the employee numbers can be stored together in an array of long integers, the names in an array of pointers, and the pay rates in an array of either floating point or double precision numbers. In organizing the data in this fashion, each column in Figure 11-1 is considered as a separate list, which is

FIGURE 11-3 A List of Employee Data

Employee Number	Employee Name	Employee Pay Rate
32479	Abrams, B.	6.72
33623	Bohm, P.	7.54
34145	Donaldson, S.	5.56
35987	Ernst, T.	5.43
36203	Gwodz, K.	8.72
36417	Hanson, H.	7.64
37634	Monroe, G.	5.29
38321	Price, S.	9.67
39435	Robbins, L.	8.50
39567	Williams, B.	7.20

	Employee Number	Employee Name	Employee Pay Rate
1st record →	32479	Abrams, B.	6.72
2nd record →	33623	Bohm, P.	7.54
3rd record →	34145	Donaldson, S.	5.56
4th record →	35987	Ernst, T.	5.43
5th record →	36203	Gwodz, K.	8.72
6th record →	36417	Hanson, H.	7.64
7th record →	37634	Monroe, G.	5.29
8th record →	38321	Price, S.	9.67
9th record →	39435	Robbins, L.	8.50
10th record →	39567	Williams, B.	7.20

FIGURE 11-4 A List of Records

stored in its own array. Using arrays, the correspondence between items for each individual employee is maintained by storing an employee's data in the same array position in each array.

The separation of the complete list into three individual arrays is unfortunate, since all of the items relating to a single employee constitute a natural organization of data into records, as illustrated in Figure 11-4.

Using a structure, the integrity of the data organization as a record can be maintained and reflected by the program. Under this approach, the list illustrated in Figure 11-4 can be processed as a single array of ten structures.

Declaring an array of structures is the same as declaring an array of any other variable type. For example, if the template `pay_rec` is declared as

```
struct pay_rec {long idnum; char name[20]; float rate;};
```

an array of ten such structures can be defined as

```
struct pay_rec employee[10];
```

This definition statement constructs an array of ten elements, each of which is a structure of the type `pay_rec`. Notice that the creation of an array of ten structures has the same form as the creation of any other array. For example, creating an array of ten integers named `employee` requires the declaration

```
int employee[10];
```

In this declaration the data type is integer, while in the former declaration for `employee` the data type is a structure using the `pay_rec` template.

Once an array of structures is declared, a particular data item is referenced by giving the position of the desired structure in the array followed by a period and the appropriate structure member. For example, the variable `employee[0].rate` references the `rate` member of the first `employee` structure in the `employee` array. Including structures as elements of an array permits a list of records to be processed with standard array programming techniques. Program 11-3 displays the first five employee records illustrated in Figure 11-4.

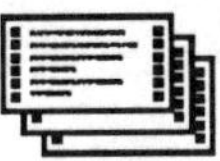

Program 11-3

```
struct pay_rec
{
  long id;
  char name[20];
  float rate;
};                /* construct a global template */
main()
{
  int i;
  static struct pay_rec employee[5] =
                  {
                   { 32479, "Abrams, B.", 6.72 },
                   { 33623, "Bohm, P.", 7.54},
                   { 34145, "Donaldson, S.", 5.56},
                   { 35987, "Ernst, T.", 5.43 },
                   { 36203, "Gwodz, K.", 8.72 }
                  };

for ( i = 0; i < 5; ++i)
  printf("%ld %-20s, %f",employee[i].id,employee[i].name,
                          employee[i].rate);
}
```

The output displayed by Program 11-3 is:

```
32479 Abrams, B.          6.72
33623 Bohm, P.            7.54
34145 Donaldson, S.       5.56
35987 Ernst, T.           5.43
36203 Gwodz, K.           8.72
```

In reviewing Program 11-3, notice the initialization of the array of structures. As with all array initializers, the array must be either global or `static` to be initialized. Although the initializers for each structure have been enclosed in inner braces, these are not strictly necessary because all members have been initialized. As with all external and `static` variables, in the absence of explicit initializers, the numeric elements of both `static` and external arrays or structures are initialized to zero and their character elements are initialized to nulls. The `%-20s` format included in the `printf()` function call forces each name to be displayed left justified in a field of 20 spaces.

11.3 Passing and Returning Structures

Individual structure members can be passed to a function in the same manner as any scalar variable. For example, given the structure definition

```
struct
{
  int id_num;
  double pay_rate;
  double hours;
} emp;
```

The statement

```
display(emp.id_num);
```

passes a copy of the structure member `emp.id_num` to a function named `display()`. Similarly, the statement

```
calc_pay(emp.pay_rate,emp.hours);
```

passes copies of the values stored in structure members `emp.pay_rate` and `emp.hours` to the function `calc_pay()`. Both functions, `display()` and `calc_pay()`, must declare the correct data types of their respective arguments.

On most compilers, complete copies of all members of a structure can also be passed to a function by including the name of the structure as an argument to the called function. For example, the function call

```
calc_net(emp);
```

passes a copy of the complete `emp` structure to `calc_net()`. Internal to `calc_net()`, an appropriate declaration must be made to receive the structure. Program 11-4 declares a global template for an employee record. This template is then used by both the main() and calc_net() functions to define specific structures with the names emp and temp, respectively.

Program 11-4

```
struct employee                      /* declare a global template */
{
  int id_num;
  double pay_rate;
  double hours;
};
main()
{
  static struct employee emp = {6782, 8.93, 40.5};
  double net_pay, calc_net();

  net_pay = calc_net(emp); /* pass copies of the values in emp */
  printf("The net pay for employee %d is $%6.2f",emp.id_num,net_pay);
}

double calc_net(temp);
struct employee temp;   /* temp is of data type struct employee */
{
  return(temp.pay_rate * temp.hours);
}
```

The output produced by Program 11-4 is:

```
The net pay for employee 6782 is $361.66
```

In reviewing Program 11-4, observe that both main() and calc_net() use the same global template to define their individual structures. The structure defined in main() and the structure defined in calc_net() are two completely different structures. Any changes made to the local temp structure in calc_net() are not reflected in the emp structure of main(). In fact, since both structures are local to their respective functions, the same structure name could have been used in both functions with no ambiguity.

When calc_net() is called by main(), copies of emp's structure values are passed to the temp structure. calc_net() then uses two of the passed member values to calculate a number, which is returned to main(). Since calc_net()

returns a noninteger number, the data type of the value returned must be included in all declarations for calc_net().

Although the structures in both main() and calc_net() use the same globally defined template, this is not strictly necessary. For example, the structure in main() could have been defined directly as:

```
static struct
{
  int id_num;
  double pay_rate;
  double hours;
}  emp = {6782, 8.93, 40.5};
```

Similarly, the structure in calc_net() could have been defined as:

```
struct
{
  int id_num;
  double pay_rate;
  double hours;
} temp;
```

However, the global declaration of the employee template provided in Program 11-4 is highly preferable to these latter two individual structure specifications because the global template centralizes the declaration of the structure's organization. Any change that must subsequently be made to the structure need be made only once, to the global template. Making changes to individual structure definitions requires that all occurrences of the structure definition be located, in every function defining the structure. For larger programs, this usually results in an error when a change to one of the structure definitions is inadvertently omitted.

An alternative to passing a copy of a structure is to pass the address of the structure. This, of course, allows the called function to make changes directly to the original structure. For example, referring to Program 11-4, the call to calc_net() can be modified to

```
calc_net(&emp);
```

In this call, an address is passed. To correctly store this address calc_net() must declare the argument as a pointer. A suitable function definition for calc_net() is

```
calc_net(pt)
struct employee *pt;
```

Here, the declaration for pt declares this argument as a pointer to a structure of type employee. The pointer variable, pt, receives the starting address of a structure whenever calc_net() is called. Within calc_net(), this pointer is used to directly reference any member in the structure. For example, (*pt).id_num refers to the id_num member of the structure, (*pt).pay_rate refers to the pay_rate member of the structure, and (*pt).hours refers to the hours member of the structure. These relationships are illustrated in Figure 11-5.

The parentheses around the expression *pt in Figure 11-5 are necessary to initially access "the structure whose address is in pt." This is followed by a reference to access the desired member within the structure. In the absence of the parentheses, the structure member operator . takes precedence over the indirection operator. Thus, the expression *pt.hours is another way of writing *(pt.hours), which would refer to "the variable whose address is in the pt.hours variable." This last expression clearly makes no sense because there is no structure named pt and hours does not contain an address.

As illustrated in Figure 11-5, the starting address of the emp structure is also the address of the first member of the structure. Thus, the expressions *pt and (*pt).id_num both refer to the id_num member of the emp structure.

The use of pointers is so common with structures that a special notation exists for them. The general expression (*pointer).member can always be replaced with the notation pointer->member, where the -> operator is constructed using a minus sign followed by a right-facing arrow (greater-than symbol). Either expression can be used to locate the desired member. For example, the following expressions are equivalent:

```
(*pt).id_num      can be replaced by   pt->id_num
(*pt).pay_rate    can be replaced by   pt->pay_rate
(*pt).hours       can be replaced by   pt->hours
```

Program 11-5 illustrates passing a structure's address and using a pointer with the new notation to directly reference the structure.

FIGURE 11-5 A Pointer Can Be Used to Access Structure Members

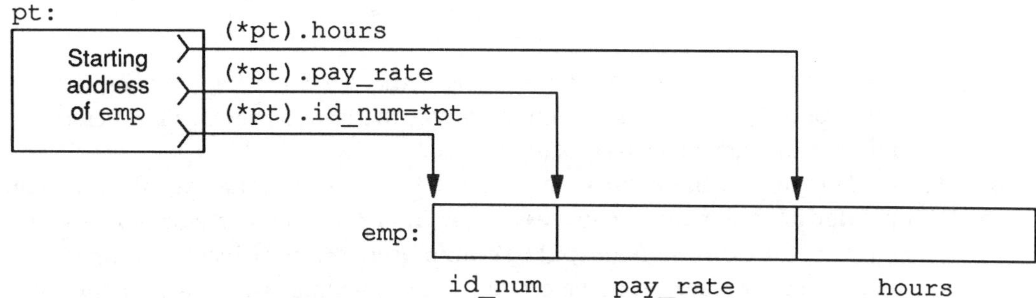

The name of the pointer argument declared in Program 11-5 is, of course, selected by the programmer. When `calc_net()` is called, emp's starting address is passed to the function. Using this address as a reference point, individual members of the structure are accessed by including their names with the pointer.

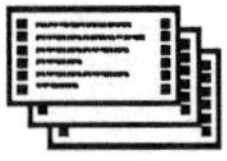

Program 11-5

```
struct employee        /* declare a global template */
{
  int id_num;
  double pay_rate;
  double hours;
};
main()
{
  static struct employee emp = {6782, 8.93, 40.5};
  double net_pay, calc_net();

  net_pay = calc_net(&emp);         /* pass an address */
  printf("The net pay for employee %d is $%6.2f",emp.id_num,net_pay);
}

double calc_net(pt)
struct employee *pt;  /* pt is a pointer to a structure of employee type */
{
  return(pt->pay_rate * pt->hours);
}
```

As with all C expressions that reference a variable, the increment and decrement operators can also be applied to structure references. For example, the expression

```
++pt->hours
```

adds 1 to the `hours` member of the emp structure. Since the `->` operator has a higher priority than the increment operator, the `hours` member is accessed first and then the increment is applied.

Alternatively, the expression `(pt++)->hours` uses the postfix increment operator to increment the address in `pt` after the `hours` member is accessed. Similarly, the expression `(++pt)->hours` uses the prefix increment operator to increment the address in `pt` before the `hours` member is accessed. In both cases,

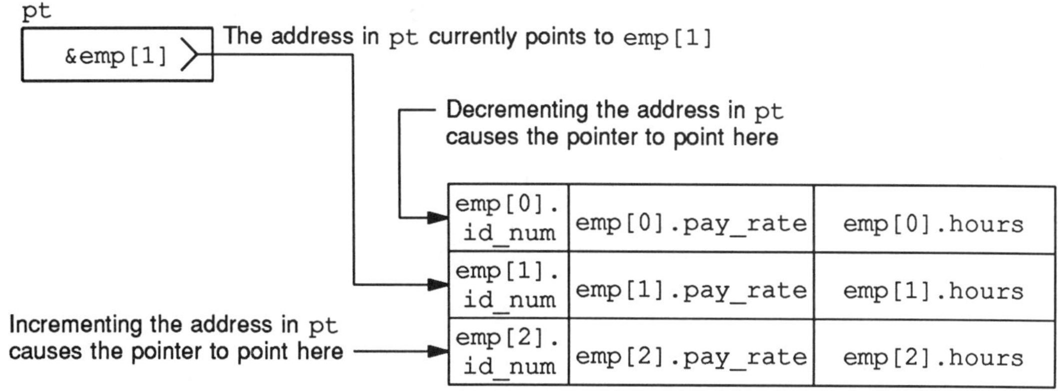

FIGURE 11-6 Changing Pointer Addresses

however, there must be sufficient numbers of defined structures to ensure that the incremented pointers actually point to legitimate structures.

As an example, Figure 11-6 illustrates an array of three structures of type `employee`. Assuming that the address of `emp[1]` is stored in the pointer variable `pt`, the expression `++pt` changes the address in `pt` to the starting address of `emp[2]`, while the expression `--pt` changes the address to point to `emp[0]`.

Returning Structures

In practice, most structure-handling functions receive direct access to a structure by passing the address of the structure to the function. Then, the function can use pointer references to make changes directly. If you want to have a function return a separate structure, however, and your compiler supports this option, you must follow the same procedures for returning complete structures as for returning scalar values. These include both declaring the function appropriately and alerting any calling function to the type of structure being returned. For example, the function `get_vals()` in Program 11-6 returns a complete structure to `main()`.

Program 11-6

```
struct employee          /* declare a global template */
{
  int id_num;
  double pay_rate;
  double hours;
};
```

continued

```
main()
{
  struct employee emp;
  struct employee get_vals();
  emp = get_vals();
  printf("\nThe employee id number is %d", emp.id_num);
  printf("\nThe employee pay rate is $%5.2f", emp.pay_rate);
  printf("\nThe employee hours are %5.2f", emp.hours);
}

struct employee get_vals()
{
  struct employee new;

  new.id_num = 6789;
  new.pay_rate = 16.25;
  new.hours = 38.0;
  return(new);
}
```

The following output is displayed when Program 11-6 is run:

```
The employee id number is 6789
The employee pay rate is $16.25
The employee hours are 38.00
```

Since the `get_vals()` function returns a structure, the function header for `get_vals()` must contain the type of structure being returned. As `get_vals()` does not receive any arguments, the function header has no argument declarations and consists of the single line

```
struct employee get_vals()
```

Within `get_vals()`, the variable `new` is defined as a structure of the type to be returned. After values have been assigned to the new structure, the structure values are returned by including the structure name within the parentheses of the return statement.

On the receiving side, `main()` must be alerted that the function `get_vals()` will be returning a structure. This is handled by including a function declaration for `get_vals()` in `main()`. Notice that these steps for returning a structure from a function are identical to the normal procedures for returning scalar data types previously described in Chapter 7. Before attempting to pass or return a structure, however, be sure to check that the compiler you are using supports these options. Whether or not these options are available, structures can always be passed and directly altered by using pointers.

11.4 Linked Lists

A classic data-handling problem is making additions or deletions to existing records that are maintained in a specific order. This is best illustrated by considering the alphabetical telephone list shown in Figure 11-7. Starting with this initial set of names and telephone numbers, we desire to add new records to the list in the proper alphabetical sequence and to delete existing records in such a way that the storage for deleted records is eliminated.

Although the insertion or deletion of ordered records can be accomplished by using an array of structures, these arrays are not efficient representations for adding or deleting records internal to the array. Arrays are fixed and prespecified in size. Deleting a record from an array creates an empty slot that requires either special marking or the shifting up of all elements below the deleted record to close the empty slot. Similarly, adding a record to the body of an array of structures requires that all elements below the addition be shifted down to make room for the new entry; or, the new element can be added to the bottom of the existing array and the array then resorted to restore the proper order of the records. Thus, either adding or deleting records to such a list generally requires restructuring and rewriting the list — a cumbersome, time consuming, and inefficient practice.

A *linked list* provides a convenient method of maintaining a constantly changing list, without the need to continually reorder and restructure the complete list. A linked list is simply a set of structures in which each structure contains at least one member whose value is the address of the next logically

FIGURE 11-7 A Telephone List in Alphabetical Order

Acme, Sam
(201)898-2392

Dolan, Edith
(213)682-3104

Lanfrank, John
(415)718-4581

Mening, Stephen
(914)382-7070

Zemann, Harold
(718)219-9912

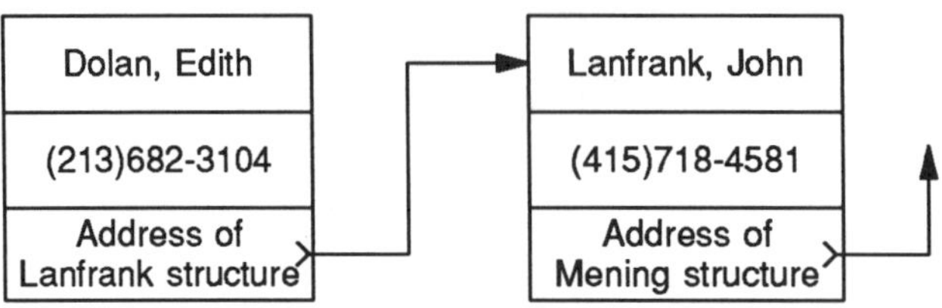

FIGURE 11-8 Using Pointers to Link Structures

ordered structure in the list. Rather than requiring each record to be physically stored in the proper order, each new record is physically added either to the end of the existing list or wherever the computer has free space in its storage area. The records are "linked" together by including the address of the next record in the record logically preceding it. From a programming standpoint, the current record being processed contains the address of the next record, no matter where the next record is actually stored.

The concept of a linked list is illustrated in Figure 11-8. Although the actual data for the Lanfrank structure illustrated in the figure may be physically stored anywhere in the computer, the additional member included at the end of the Dolan structure maintains the proper alphabetical order. This member provides the starting address of the location where the Lanfrank record is stored. As you might expect, this member is a pointer.

To see the usefulness of the pointer in the Dolan record, let us add a telephone number for June Hagar to the alphabetical list shown in Figure 11-7. The data for June Hagar is stored in a data structure that uses the same template as that used for the existing records. To ensure that the telephone number for Hagar is correctly displayed after the Dolan telephone number, the address in the Dolan record must be altered to point to the Hagar record and the address in the Hagar record must be set to point to the Lanfrank record. This is illustrated in Figure

FIGURE 11-9 Adjusting Addresses to Point to Appropriate Records

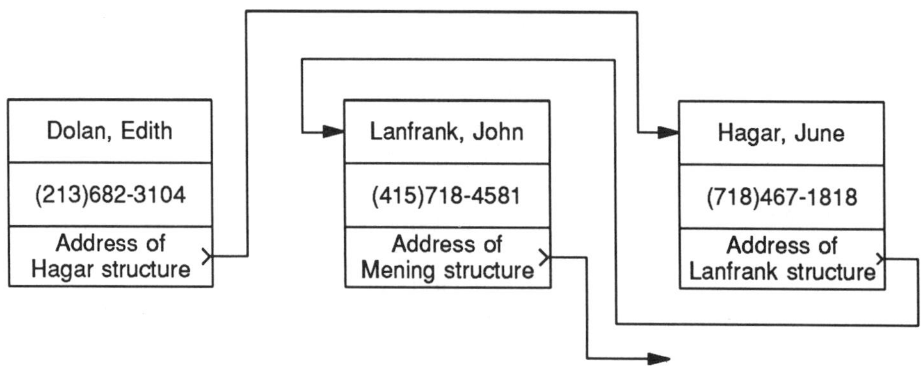

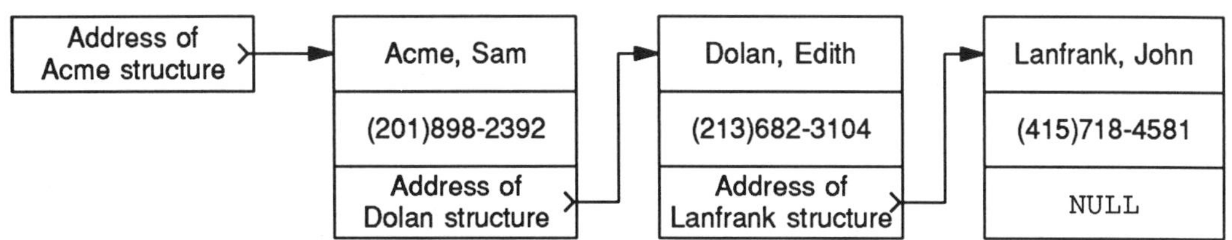

FIGURE 11-10 Use of the Initial and Final Pointer Values

11-9. Notice that the pointer in each structure simply points to the location of the next ordered structure, even if that structure is not physically located in the correct order.

Removal of a structure from the ordered list is the reverse process of adding a record. The actual record is logically removed from the list by simply changing the address in the structure preceding it to point to the structure immediately following the deleted record.

Each structure in a linked list has the same format; however, it is clear that the last record cannot have a valid pointer value that points to another record, since there is none. C provides a special pointer value called `NULL` that acts as a sentinel or flag to indicate when the last record has been processed. The `NULL` pointer value, like its end-of-string counterpart, has a numerical value of zero.

Besides an end-of-list sentinel value, a special pointer must also be provided for storing the address of the first structure in the list. Figure 11-10 illustrates the complete set of pointers and structures for a list consisting of three names.

The inclusion of a pointer in a structure should not seem surprising. As we discovered in Section 11.1, a structure can contain any C data type. For example, the structure declaration

```
struct test
{
  int id_num;
  double *pt_pay
};
```

declares a structure template consisting of two members. The first member is an integer variable named `id_num`, and the second variable is a pointer named `pt_pay`, which is a pointer to a double precision number. Program 11-7 illustrates that the pointer member of a structure is used in the same way as any other pointer variable.

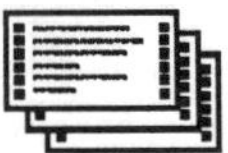

Program 11-7

```
struct test
{
  int id_num;
  double *pt_pay;
};
main()
{
  struct test emp;
  double pay = 456.20;

  emp.id_num = 12345;
  emp.pt_pay = &pay;

  printf("Employee number %d was paid $%6.2f",
             emp.id_num, *emp.pt_pay);
}
```

The output produced by executing Program 11-7 is:

```
Employee number 12345 was paid $456.20
```

Figure 11-11 illustrates the relationship between the members of the `emp` structure defined in Program 11-7 and the variable named `pay`. The value assigned to `emp.id_num` is the number 12345 and the value assigned to `pay` is 456.20. The address of the `pay` variable is assigned to the structure member `emp.pt_pay`. Since this member has been defined as a pointer to a double precision number, placing the address of the double precision variable `pay` in it is a correct use of this member. Finally, since the member operator, ., has a higher precedence than the indirection operator, *, the expression used in the `printf()` call in Program 11-7 is correct. The expression `*emp.pt_pay` is equivalent to

FIGURE 11-11 Storing an Address in a Structure Member

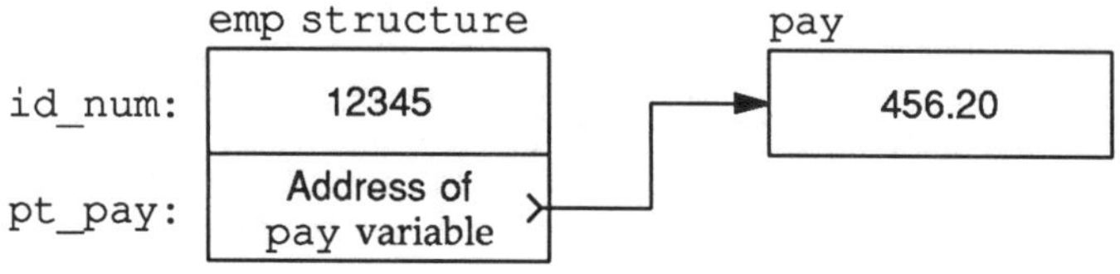

the expression `*(emp.pt_pay)`, which is translated as "the variable whose address is contained in the member `emp.pt_pay`."

Although the pointer defined in Program 11-7 has been used in a rather trivial fashion, the program does illustrate the concept of including a pointer in a structure. This concept can be easily extended to creating a linked list of structures suitable for storing the names and telephone numbers previously listed in Figure 11-7. The following declaration creates a template for such a structure:

```
struct tele_typ
{
  char name[30];
  char phone_no[15];
  struct tele_typ *nextaddr;
};
```

The `tele_type` template consists of three members. The first member is an array of 30 characters, suitable for storing names with a maximum of 29 letters and an end-of-string marker. The next member is an array of 15 characters, suitable for storing telephone numbers with their respective area codes. The last member is a pointer suitable for storing the address of a structure of the `tele_typ` type.

Program 11-8 illustrates the use of the `tele_typ` template by specifically defining three structures having this form. The three structures are named `t1`, `t2`, and `t3`, respectively, and the name and telephone number members of each of these structures are initialized when the structures are defined, using the data previously listed in Figure 11-7.

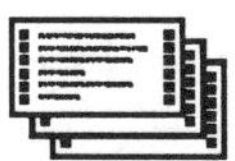

Program 11-8

```
#include <stdio.h>
struct tele_typ
{
  char name[30];
  char phone_no[15];
  struct tele_typ *nextaddr;
};
main()
{
  static struct tele_typ t1 = {"Acme, Sam","(201) 898-2392"};
  static struct tele_typ t2 = {"Dolan, Edith","(213) 682-3104"};
```

continued

```
    static struct tele_typ t3 = {"Lanfrank, John","(415) 718-4581"};
    struct tele_typ *first;     /* create a pointer to a structure    */

    first = &t1;                /* store t1's address in first        */
    t1.nextaddr = &t2;          /* store t2's address in t1.nextaddr  */
    t2.nextaddr = &t3;          /* store t3's address in t2.nextaddr  */
    t3.nextaddr = NULL;         /* store NULL address in t3.nextaddr  */

    printf("\n%s\n%s\n%s",first->name,t1.nextaddr->name,
            t2.nextaddr->name);
}
```

The output produced by executing Program 11-8 is:

```
Acme, Sam
Dolan, Edith
Lanfrank, John
```

Program 11-8 demonstrates the use of pointers to access successive structure members. As illustrated in Figure 11-12, each structure contains the address of the next structure in the list.

The initialization of the names and telephone numbers for each of the structures defined in Program 11-8 is straightforward. Although each structure consists of three members, only the first two members of each structure are initialized. As both of these members are arrays of characters, they can be initialized with strings. The remaining member of each structure is a pointer. To create a linked list, each structure pointer must be assigned the address of the next structure in the list.

The four assignment statements in Program 11-8 perform the correct assignments. The expression `first = &t1` stores the address of the first structure in the list in the pointer variable named `first`. The expression `t1.nextaddr = &t2` stores the starting address of the `t2` structure in the pointer member of the `t1` structure. Similarly, the expression `t2.nextaddr = &t3` stores the starting address of the `t3` structure in the pointer member of the `t2` structure. To end the list, the value of the `NULL` pointer, which is zero, is stored in the pointer member of the `t3` structure.

Once values have been assigned to each structure member and correct addresses have been stored in the appropriate pointers, the addresses in the pointers are used to access each structure's name member. For example, the expression `t1.nextaddr->name` refers to the `name` member of the structure whose address is in the `nextaddr` member of the `t1` structure. The precedence of the member operator, ., and the structure pointer operator, `->`, are equal and are evaluated from left to right. Thus, the expression `t1.nextaddr->name` is evaluated as `(t1.nextaddr)->name`. Since `t1.nextaddr` contains the address of the `t2` structure, the proper name is accessed.

The expression `t1.nextaddr->name` can, of course, be replaced by the equivalent expression `(*t1.nextaddr).name`, which uses the more conventional indirection operator. This expression also refers to "the name member of the variable whose address is in `t1.nextaddr`."

The addresses in a linked list of structures can be used to loop through the complete list. As each structure is accessed it can be either examined to select a specific value or used to print out a complete list. For example, the `display()` function in Program 11-9 illustrates the use of a `while` loop, which uses the address in each structure's pointer member to cycle through the list and successively display data stored in each structure.

FIGURE 11-12 The Relationship Between Structures in Program 11-8

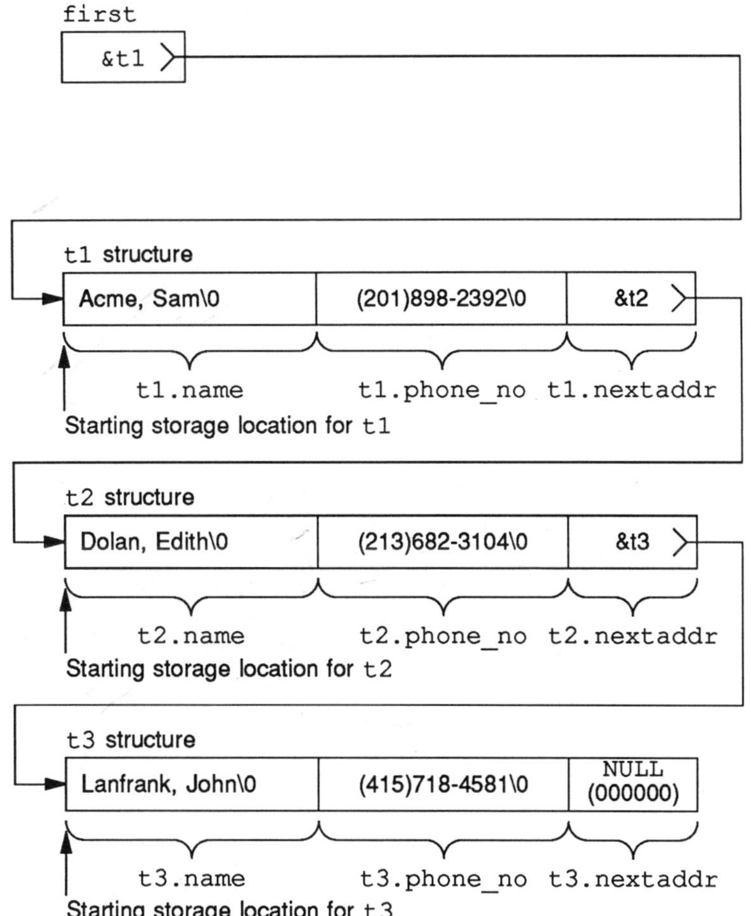

Program 11-9

```
#include <stdio.h>
struct tele_typ
{
  char name[30];
  char phone_no[15];
  struct tele_typ *nextaddr;
};
main()
{

  static struct tele_typ t1 = {"Acme, Sam","(201) 898-2392"};
  static struct tele_typ t2 = {"Dolan, Edith","(213) 682-3104"};
  static struct tele_typ t3 = {"Lanfrank, John","(415) 718-4581"};
  struct tele_typ *first;        /* create a pointer to a structure    */

  first = &t1;               /* store t1's address in first              */
  t1.nextaddr = &t2;         /* store t2's address in t1.nextaddr        */
  t2.nextaddr = &t3;         /* store t3's address in t2.nextaddr        */
  t3.nextaddr = NULL;        /* store the NULL address in t3.nextaddr    */

  display(first);            /* send the address of the first structure */
}

display(contents)                /* display till end of linked list    */
struct tele_type  *contents;     /* a pointer to a structure           */
{                                /* of type tele_typ                   */
  while (contents != NULL)
  {
    printf("\n%30s %20s",contents->name, contents->phone_no);
    contents = contents->nextaddr;      /* get next address            */
  }
  return;
}
```

The output produced by Program 11-9 is:

```
Acme, Sam                        (201) 898-2392
Dolan, Edith                     (213) 682-3104
Lanfrank, John                   (415) 718-4581
```

The important concept illustrated by Program 11-9 is the use of the address in one structure to access members of the next structure in the list. When the `display()` function is called, it is passed the value stored in the variable named `first`. Since `first` is a pointer variable, the actual value passed is an address (the address of the `t1` structure). The `display()` function accepts the passed value in the argument named `contents`. To store the passed address correctly, `contents` is declared as a pointer to a structure of the `tele_typ` type. Within `display()`, a `while` loop is used to cycle through the linked structures, starting with the structure whose address is in `contents`. The condition tested in the `while` statement compares the value in `contents`, which is an address, to the `NULL` value. For each valid address, the name and phone number members of the addressed structure are displayed. The address in `contents` is then updated with the address in the pointer member of the current structure. The address in `contents` is then retested, and the process continues as long as the address in `contents` is not equal to the `NULL` value. `display()` "knows" nothing about the names of the structures declared in `main()` or even how many structures exist. It simply cycles through the linked list, structure by structure, until it encounters the end-of-list `NULL` address. Since the value of `NULL` is zero, the tested condition can be replaced by the equivalent expression `!contents`.

A disadvantage of Program 11-9 is that exactly three structures are defined in `main()` by name and storage for them is reserved during compilation. Should a fourth structure be required, it would have to be declared and the program recompiled. In the next section, we show how to have the computer dynamically allocate and release storage for structures when the program is run, as storage is required. Only when a new structure is to be added to the list, and while the program is running, is storage for the new structure created. Similarly, when a structure is no longer needed and can be deleted from the list, the storage for the deleted record is relinquished and returned to the computer.

11.5 Dynamic Storage Allocation

As each variable is defined in a program, sufficient storage for it is assigned from a pool of computer memory locations made available to the compiler. Once specific memory locations have been reserved for a variable, these locations are fixed, whether they are used or not. For example, if a function requests storage for an array of 500 integers, the storage for the array is allocated and fixed while the program is running. If the application requires less than 500 integers, the unused allocated storage is not released to the system until the program ends execution. If, on the other hand, the application requires more than 500 integers, the size of the integer array must be increased and the function defining the array recompiled.

An alternative to this fixed, or static, allocation of memory storage locations is the *dynamic allocation* of memory. Under a dynamic allocation scheme, storage is allocated to a program and released back to the computer while the program is running, rather than being fixed when the program is compiled.

The dynamic allocation of memory is extremely useful when dealing with lists of structures because it allows the list to expand as new records are added and contract as records are deleted. For example, in constructing a list of names and phone numbers, the exact number of structures ultimately needed may not be known. Rather than creating a fixed array of structures, it is extremely useful to have a mechanism whereby the list can be enlarged and shrunk as needed. Most standard C libraries provide functions that have this dynamic allocation capability. Two of these functions, called `malloc()` and `free()`, are described in Table 11-1.

TABLE 11-1 Function Having Dynamic Allocation Capability

Function Name	Description
`malloc()`	Reserves the number of bytes requested by the argument passed to the function. Returns the address of the first reserved location or `NULL` if sufficient memory is not available.
`free()`	Releases a block of bytes previously reserved. The address of the first reserved location is passed as an argument to the function.

In requesting additional storage space, the user must provide the `malloc()` function with an indication of the amount of storage needed. This may be done by requesting a specific number of bytes or, more usually, by requesting enough space for a particular type of data. For example, the function call `malloc(10)` requests 10 bytes of storage, while the function call `malloc(sizeof(int))` requests enough storage to store an integer number. A request for enough storage for a data structure typically takes the second form. For example, using the structure declaration

```
struct tel_typ
{
  char name[25];
  char phone_no[15];
};
```

the function call `malloc( sizeof(struct tel_typ) );` reserves enough storage for one structure of the `tel_typ` type.

In allocating storage dynamically, we have no advance indication as to where the computer system will physically reserve the requested number of bytes, and we have no explicit name to access the newly created storage locations. To provide access to these locations, `malloc()` returns the address of the first location that has been reserved. This address must, of course, be assigned to a pointer. The return of a pointer by `malloc()` is especially useful for creating a linked list of data structures. As each new structure is created, the pointer returned by `malloc()` to the structure can be assigned to a member of the previous structure in the list. Before illustrating the actual dynamic allocation of such a structure in a program, we will consider one logistical problem created by `malloc()`.

The `malloc()` function always returns a pointer to the first byte of storage reserved and considers this first byte as a character. As such, the function declaration of `malloc()` is `char *malloc()`. Any function that calls `malloc()` must include this declaration in order to be alerted that a pointer to a character will be returned. This presents a slight problem when using `malloc()` to reserve enough storage for a structure. Although `malloc()` will reserve the necessary number of bytes for a structure and return the correct address of the first reserved byte, this address will be interpreted as the address of a character. To use this address to reference subsequent structure members, it must be reinterpreted as pointing to a structure.

The mechanism for converting one data type into another is called a *cast*. In this case, then, we need to cast (or force) a pointer to a character into a pointer to a structure. The cast expression `(struct template_name *)` can be used to do this. For example, if the variable `lis_point` is a pointer to a character, the expression `(struct emp *)lis_point` redefines the address in the pointer to be an address of a structure of type `emp`. The address is not changed physically, but any subsequent reference to the address will now cause the correct number of bytes to be accessed for the appropriate structure. Casts are more fully described in Chapter 14. For now, however, we will simply use cast expressions to convert the address returned by `malloc()` into the correct pointer type for referencing a structure.

Program 11-10 illustrates the use of `malloc()` to create a structure dynamically in response to a user-input request.

Program 11-10

```
#include <stdio.h>
struct tel_typ
{
  name[30];
  phone_no[15];
};
```

continued

```
main()
{
  char key;
  char *malloc();
  struct tel_typ *rec_point;    /* rec_point is a pointer to a */
                                /* structure of type tel_typ   */

  printf("Do you wish to create a new record (respond with y or n): ");
  key = getchar();
  if (key == 'y')
  {
    rec_point = (struct tel_typ *)malloc(sizeof(struct tel_typ));
    populate(rec_point);
    disp_one(rec_point);
  }
  else
    printf("\nNo record has been created.");
}

populate(record)             /* get a name and phone number             */
struct tel_typ *record;      /* a pointer to a structure of type tel_typ */
{
  printf("Enter a name: ");
  gets(record->name);
  printf("Enter the phone number: ");
  gets(record->phone_no);
  return;
}

disp_one(contents)           /* display the contents of one record      */
struct tel_typ *contents;    /* a pointer to a structure of type tel_typ */
{
  printf("\The contents of the record just created is:");
  printf("\nName: %s",contents->name);
  printf("\nPhone Number: %s", contents->phone_no);
  return;
}
```

A sample session produced by Program 11-10 is:

```
Do you Wish to create a new record (respond with y or n): y
Enter a name: Monroe, James
Enter the phone number: (617) 555-1817
```

```
The contents of the record just created is:
Name: Monroe, James
Phone Number: (617) 555-1817
```

In reviewing Program 11-10, notice that only three declarations are made in `main()`. The variable `key` is declared as a character variable, the `malloc()` function is declared as providing a pointer to a character, and the variable `rec_point` is declared as being a pointer to a structure of the `tel_typ` type. Since the declaration for the template `tel_typ` is global, `tel_typ` can be used within `main()` to define `rec_point` as a pointer to a structure of the `tel_typ` type.

If `y` is the response to the first prompt in `main()`, a call to `malloc()` is made. The argument passed to `malloc()` is the size of the required structure. Although `malloc()` returns the address of the first reserved location, this address is considered to be pointing to a character. To store the address in `rec_point`, which has been declared as a pointer to a structure, the address returned by `malloc()` is coerced into the proper type by use of the expression `(struct tel_typ *)`.

Once `rec_point` has been loaded with the proper address, this address can be used to access the newly created structure. The function `populate()` is used to prompt the user for data needed in filling the structure and to store the user-entered data in the correct members of the structure. The argument passed to `populate()` is the pointer `rec_point`. Like all passed arguments, the value contained in `rec_point` is passed to the function. Since the value in `rec_point` is an address, `populate()` actually receives the address of the newly created structure.

Within `populate()`, the value received is stored in the argument named `record`. Since the value to be stored in `record` is the address of a structure, `record` must be declared as a pointer to a structure. This declaration is provided by the statement `struct tel_typ *record;`. The statements within `populate()` use the address in `record` to locate the respective members of the structure.

The `disp_one()` function in Program 11-10 is used to display the contents of the newly created and populated structure. The address passed to `disp_one()` is the same address passed to `populate()`. Since this passed value is the address of a structure, the argument name used to store the address is declared as a pointer to the correct structure type.

One further comment is in order. Since both `populate()` and `disp_one()` return no values to `main()`, they are not declared in `main()`. This is done in Program 11-10 to ensure that the program can be run on the computer you are using. If your compiler supports the `void` data type, however, the declaration

```
void populate(), disp_one();
```

should be included with main()'s other declarations.

Once you understand the mechanism of calling malloc(), you can use this function to construct a linked list of structures. As described in the previous section, the structures used in a linked list must contain one pointer member. The address in the pointer member is the starting address of the next structure in the list. Additionally, a pointer must be reserved for the address of the first structure, and the pointer member of the last structure in the list is given a NULL address to indicate that no more members are being pointed to. Program 11-11 illustrates the use of malloc() to construct a linked list of names and phone numbers. The populate() function used in Program 11-11 is the same function previously used in Program 11-10, while the display() function is the same function used in Program 11-9.

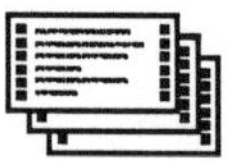

Program 11-11

```
#include <stdio.h>
struct tel_typ
{
  char name[25];
  char phone_no[15];
  struct tel_typ *nextaddr;
};
main()
{
  int i;
  struct tel_typ *list, *current; /* two pointers to structures of */
                                  /* type tel_typ                  */
  char *malloc();          /* malloc() returns a pointer to a char  */

  /* get a pointer to the first structure in the list              */
  list = (struct tel_typ *) malloc(sizeof(struct tel_typ));
  current = list;

  /* populate the current structure and create two more structures */
  for(i = 0; i < 2; ++i)
  {
    populate(current);
    current->nextaddr = (struct tel_typ *) malloc(sizeof(struct tel_typ));
    current = current->nextaddr;
  }
```

continued

```
  populate(current);            /* populate the last structure        */
  current->nextaddr = NULL;     /* set the last address               */
  printf("\nThe list consists of the following records:\n");
  display(list);                /* display the structures             */
}

populate(record)              /* get a name and phone number         */
struct tel_typ *record;       /* pointer to structure of type tel_typ */
{
  printf("Enter a name: ");
  gets(record->name);
  printf("Enter the phone number: ");
  gets(record->phone_no);
  return;
}
display(contents)             /* display till end of linked list     */
struct tel_typ *contents;     /* pointer to structure of type tel_typ */
{
  while (contents != NULL)
  {
    printf("\n%-30s %-20s",contents->name, contents->phone_no);
    contents = contents->nextaddr;
  }
  return;
}
```

The first time `malloc()` is called in Program 11-11, it is used to create the first structure in the linked list. As such, the address returned by `malloc()` is stored in the pointer variable named `list`. The address in `list` is then assigned to the pointer named `current`. This pointer variable is always used by the program to point to the current structure. Since the `current` structure is the first structure created, the address in the pointer named `list` is assigned to the pointer named `current`.

Within `main()`'s `for` loop, the name and phone number members of the newly created structure are populated by calling `populate()` and passing the address of the `current` structure to the function. Upon return from `populate()`, the pointer member of the `current` structure is assigned an address. This address is the address of the next structure in the list, which is obtained from `malloc()`. The call to `malloc()` creates the next structure and returns its address into the pointer member of the `current` structure. This completes the population of the `current` member. The final statement in the `for` loop resets the address in the `current` pointer to the address of the next structure in the list.

After the last structure has been created, the final statements in `main()` populate this structure, assign a `NULL` address to the pointer member, and call `display()` to display all the structures in the list. A sample run of Program 11-11 is provided below:

```
Enter a name: Acme, Sam
Enter the phone number: (201) 898-2392
Enter a name: Dolan, Edith
Enter the phone number: (213) 682-3104
Enter a name: Lanfrank, John
Enter the phone number: (415) 718-4581

The list consists of the following records:

Acme, Sam                (201) 898-2392
Dolan, Edith             (213) 682-3104
Lanfrank, John           (415) 718-4581
```

Just as `malloc()` dynamically creates storage while a program is executing, the `free()` function restores a block of storage to the computer while the programming is executing. The only argument required by `free()` is the starting address of a block of storage that was dynamically allocated. Thus, any address returned by `malloc()` can subsequently be passed to `free()` to restore the reserved memory to the computer. `free()` does not alter the address passed to it, but simply removes the storage that the address references.

11.6 Unions

A *union* is a data type that reserves the same area in memory for two or more variables, each of which can be a different data type. A variable declared as a union data type can be used to hold a character variable, an integer variable, a double precision variable, or any other valid C data type. Each of these types, but only one at a time, can actually be assigned to the union variable.

The declaration for a union is identical in form to a structure declaration, with the reserved word `union` used in place of the reserved word `structure`. For example, the declaration

```
union
{
  char key;
  int num;
```

```
        double price;
    } val;
```

creates a union variable named `val`. If `val` were a structure, it would consist of three individual members. As a union, however, `val` contains a single member that can be a character variable named `key`, an integer variable named `num`, or a double precision variable named `price`. In effect, a union reserves sufficient memory locations to accommodate its largest member's data type. This same set of locations is then referenced by different variable names, depending on the data type of value currently residing in the reserved locations. Each value stored overwrites the previous value, using as many bytes of the reserved memory area as necessary.

Individual union members are referenced with the same notation as structure members. For example, if the `val` union is currently being used to store a character, the correct variable name to access the stored character is `val.key`. Similarly, if the union is used to store an integer, the value is accessed by the name `val.num`, and if the union is used to store a double precision number, its value is accessed by the name `val.price`. In using union members, it is the programmer's responsibility to ensure that the correct member name is used for the data type currently residing in the union.

Typically, a second variable is used to keep track of the current data type stored in the union. For example, the following code could be used to select the appropriate member of `val` for display. Here the value in the variable `u_type` determines the currently stored data type in the `val` union.

```
switch(u_type)
{
  case 'c': printf("%c", val.key);
            break;
  case 'i': printf("%d", val.num);
            break;
  case 'd': printf(%f", val.price);
            break;
  default : printf("Invalid type in u_type : %c", u_type);
}
```

As was done for structures, tag names can be associated with a union to create templates. For example, the declaration

```
union date_time
{
   long int days;
   double time;
};
```

provides a template for a union without actually reserving any storage locations. The template can then be used to define any number of variables of the union type date_time. For example, the definition

```
union date_time first, second, *pt;
```

creates a union variable named first, a union variable named second, and a pointer that can be used to store the address of any union having the form of date_time. Once a pointer to a union has been declared, the same notation used to access structure members can be used to access union members. For example, if the assignment pt = &first; is made, pt->date references the date member of the union named first.

Unions can themselves be members of structures and arrays, or structures, arrays, and pointers can be members of unions. In each case, the notation used to access a member must be consistent with the nesting employed. For example, in the structure defined by

```
struct
{
  int u_type;
  union
  {
    char *text;
    float rate;
  } u_tax;
}  flag;
```

the variable rate is referenced as

```
flag.u_tax.rate
```

Similarly, the first character of the string whose address is stored in the pointer text is referenced as

```
*flag.u_tax.text
```

11.7 Common Programming Errors

Three common errors are often made when using structures or unions. The first error occurs because structures and unions, as complete entities, cannot be used in relational expressions. For example, even if tel_typ and phon_type are two structures of the same type, the expression tel_typ == phon_typ is invalid. Individual members of a structure or union can, of course, be compared by using any of C's relational operators.

The second common error is really an extension of a pointer error as it relates to structures and unions. Whenever a pointer is used to point to either of these data types, or whenever a pointer is itself a member of a structure or a union, care must be taken to use the address in the pointer to access the appropriate data type. Should you be confused about just what is being pointed to, remember, "if in doubt, print it out."

The final error relates specifically to unions. Since a union can store only one of its members at a time, you must be careful to keep track of the currently stored variable. Storing one data type in a union and accessing it by the wrong variable name can result in an error that is particularly troublesome to locate.

11.8 Chapter Summary

1. A structure allows individual variables to be grouped under a common variable name. Each variable in a structure is referenced by its structure name, followed by a period, followed by its individual variable name. Another term for a structure is a *record*. The general form for declaring a structure is:

```
struct
{

  individual member declarations;

} structure_name;
```

2. A tag name can be used to create a generalized structure template describing the form and arrangement of elements in a structure. This tag name can then be used to define specific structure variables.
3. Structures are particularly useful as elements of arrays. Used in this manner, each structure becomes one record in a list of records.
4. Individual members of a structure are passed to a function in the manner appropriate to the data type of the member being passed. Some C compilers also allow complete structures to be passed, in which case the called function receives a copy of each element in the structure. The address of a structure can also be passed, which provides the called function with direct access to the structure.
5. Structure members can be any valid C data type, including structures, unions, arrays, and pointers. When a pointer is included as a structure member a linked list can be created. Such a list uses the pointer in one structure to point to (contain the address of) the next logical structure in the list.

6. Unions are declared in the same manner as structures. The definition of a union creates a memory overlay area, with each union member using the same memory storage locations. Thus, only one member of a union can be active at a time.

Sample Problem

Declare a single structure template suitable for the following part number record:

```
Part Number   Description   Unit Cost   Quantity in Stock
-----------   -----------   ---------   -----------------
1011          bulbs           2.60           10
1020          screwdriver     4.55           15
1024          wrenches        6.92           20
1036          bolts            .25          100
```

Using the declared structure template, write a C program to interactively accept the data into an array of four structures. After the data has been entered, create an inventory report that lists the part number, description, and dollar value of the inventory.

The following program performs the required processing:

```
struct part_rec
{
  int part_num;
  char descrip[15];
  float cost;
  int quantity;
}
main()
{
  struct part_rec parts[4];
  int i;
  for(i = 0; i <= 3; ++i)
  {
    printf("\nEnter part number: ");
    scanf("%d", &parts[i].part_num);
    printf("Enter part description: ");
    scanf("%s", parts[i].descrip);
    printf("Enter cost of part: ");
    scanf("%f",&parts[i].cost);
    printf("Enter quantity in stock: ");
    scanf("%d", &parts[i].quantity);
  }
```

```
  printf("\n\nPart No.  Description   Value of Inventory\n");
  for( i = 0; i <= 3; ++i)
    printf("%6d     %-15s     $%8.2f\n", parts[i].part_num,
            parts[i].descrip, parts[i].cost*parts[i].quantity);
}
```

The following sample run was obtained using this program:

```
Enter part number: 1011
Enter part description: bulbs
Enter cost of part: 2.60
Enter quantity in stock: 10

Enter part number: 1020
Enter part description: screwdriver
Enter cost of the part: 4.55
Enter quantity in stock: 15

Enter part number: 1024
Enter part description: wrenches
Enter cost of the part: 6.92
Enter quantity in stock: 20

Enter part number: 1036
Enter part description: bolts
Enter cost of the part: .25
Enter quantity in stock: 100


Part No.     Description        Value of Inventory

  1011       bulbs                $   26.00
  1020       screwdrivers         $   68.25
  1024       wrenches             $  138.40
  1036       bolts                $   25.00
```

Additional Topics

Part Five

Data Files

Chapter Twelve

The data for the programs we have seen so far has either been defined within the programs or entered interactively during program execution. This type of data creation and retention precludes sharing data between programs and is a disadvantage in larger systems consisting of many interconnecting programs. For these larger systems, the data used by one program typically must be made available to other programs, without being recreated or redefined.

Sharing data between programs requires that the data be saved independently and separately from any single program. For example, consider the following data:

Code	Description	Price	Amount in Stock
QA134	Battery	35.89	10
QA136	Bulbs	3.22	123
CM104	Fuses	1.03	98
CM212	Degreaser	4.74	62
HT435	Cleaner	3.98	50

This data might be needed by both an inventory control program and a billing program. Therefore, the data would be stored by itself on a floppy diskette, hard disk, or magnetic tape in a data file.

A *data file* is any collection of data that is stored together under a common name on a storage medium other than the computer's main memory. This chapter describes the C statements needed to create data files and to read and write data to them.

12.1 Declaring, Opening, and Closing Files

Each data file in a computer is physically stored by using a unique file name. Typically, most computers require that a *file name* consist of no more than eight characters followed by an optional period and an extension of up to three characters. Using this convention, the following are all valid computer data file names:

```
balances.dat      records        info.dat
report.bnd        prices.bnd     math.mem
```

Computer file names should be chosen to indicate both the type of data in the file and the application for which it is used. Frequently, the first eight characters are used to describe the data itself and the three characters after the decimal point are used to describe the application. For example, the file name `prices.bnd` is useful for describing a file of prices used in a bond application.

Within a C program, a file is always referenced by a variable name that must be declared within the program. For files, the variable is actually a pointer to a special file structure and, as such, must be declared as a pointer to a file. Examples of such variable declarations are:

```
FILE *in_file;
FILE *prices;
FILE *fp;
```

In each of these declarations, the pointer name is selected by the programmer. It is the name of the data file as it will be referenced by the program. This name need not be the same as the external name used by the computer to store the file.

The term `FILE` in each declaration is the tag name of a special data structure used by C for storing information about the file, including whether the file is available for reading or writing, the next available character in the file, and where this character is stored. The actual declaration of a file structure and the equivalence of the structure to the symbolic name `FILE` is contained in the `stdio.h` standard header file, which must be included at the top of each program that uses a data file.

Opening a File

Opening a file is a "cookbook" procedure that accomplishes two purposes, only one of which is directly pertinent to the programmer. First, opening a file establishes a physical communication link between the program and the data file. Since the specific details of this link are handled by the computer's operating system and are transparent to the program, the programmer normally need not consider them.

From a programming perspective, the second purpose of opening a file is relevant. Besides establishing the actual physical connection between a program and a data file, the open statement also equates the file's external computer name to the pointer name used internally by the program.

Appropriately enough, the file open function is called `fopen()` and is available in the standard C library supplied with each C compiler. One of the arguments passed to `fopen()` is the file's external name. `fopen()` returns the starting address of a `FILE` structure that is needed for reading data from the file and writing data to it. Since `fopen()` returns an address to a `FILE`, the declaration

```
FILE *fopen();
```

must be included in any program that calls `fopen()`. Thus, both the `fopen()` function that returns an address and the variable used to store this address must be declared as pointers to `FILE`. For example, if a data file is to be opened in main() and the pointer name out_file is used to store the address returned by fopen(), the following section of code is necessary:

```
#include <stdio.h>
main()
{
  FILE *fopen(), *out_file;          /* FILE declarations */
  any other variable declarations;
}
```

Here, the FILE declarations for fopen() and out_file have been combined in one declaration statement. out_file, of course, is a programmer-selected name for the file, as the file will be "known" internal to main(). If the file were to be opened in some other function, these FILE declarations would have to be included with the declarations for that function.

It now remains to actually call fopen() to connect the file's external name to its internal name. In using fopen(), two arguments are required. The first argument is the computer's name for the file; the second argument is the mode in which the file is to be used. Permissible modes are "r", "w", or "a", which represent reading, writing, or appending to a file.

A file opened for writing creates a new file and makes the file available for output by the function opening the file. If a file exists with the same name as a file opened for writing, the old file is erased. For example, the statement

```
out_file = fopen("prices.bnd","w");
```

opens a file named prices.bnd that can now be written to. Once this file has been opened, the program accesses the file by using the pointer name out_file, while the computer saves the file under the name prices.bnd.

A file opened for appending makes an existing file available for data to be added to the end of the file. If the file opened for appending does not exist, a new file with the designated name is created and made available to receive output from the program. For example, the statement

```
out_file = fopen("prices.bnd","a");
```

opens a file named prices.bnd and makes it available for data to be appended to the end of the file.

The only difference between a file opened in write mode and one opened in append mode is where the data is physically placed in the file. In write mode, the data is written starting at the beginning of the file, while in append mode the data is written starting at the end of the file. For a new file, the two modes are identical.

For files opened in either write or append mode, the functions needed to write data to it are similar to the printf(), puts(), and putchar() functions used for displaying data on a terminal. These functions are described in the next section.

A file opened in read mode retrieves an existing file and makes its data available as input to the program. For example, the open statement

```
in_file = fopen("prices.bnd","r");
```

opens the file named `prices.bnd` and makes the data in the file available for input. Within the function opening the file, the file is read by using the pointer name `in_file`. The functions used to read data from a file are similar to the `scanf()`, `gets()`, and `getchar()` functions used for inputting data from the keyboard. These functions are also described in the next section.

If a file opened for reading does not exist, the `fopen()` function returns the `NULL` address value. This is the same `NULL` address previously described in Section 11.4. It can be used to test that an existing file has, in fact, been opened.

Notice that, in all of the open statements, both the external file name and the mode arguments passed to `fopen()` are strings contained between double quotes. If the external file name is first stored in either an array of characters or as a string, the array or string name, without quotes, can be used as the first argument to `fopen()`.

Program 12-1 illustrates the statements required to open a file in read mode and the use of the returned value from `fopen()` to check for a successful opening of the file. The program prompts the user for the external file name and stores the name in the array `f_name[13]`.

Program 12-1

```
include <stdio.h>
main()
{
  FILE *in_file, *fopen;
  char f_name[13];

  printf("\nEnter a file name: ");
  gets(f_name);

  in_file = fopen(f_name,"r");         /* open the file */

  if (in_file == NULL)
  {
    printf("\nThe file cannot be opened.");
```

continued

```
    printf("\nPlease check that the file currently exists.");
  }
  else
    printf("\nThe file has been successfully opened for reading");

}
```

Program 12-1 requests that an external data file name be entered by the user. The entered name is stored in the character array `f_name` and the array name is then passed to the `fopen()` function. A sample run using Program 12-1 produced the output:

```
Enter a file name: prices.bnd
The file has been successfully opened for reading
```

Although Program 12-1 can be used to open an existing file in read mode, it clearly lacks statements to read the data in the file and then close the file. These topics are discussed next. Before leaving Program 12-1, however, note that the opening of the file and assignment of the returned address can be included directly within the program's `if` statement. The single expression

```
if ( (in_file = fopen(name,"r")) == NULL )
```

can be used to replace the two lines

```
in_file = fopen(name,"r");
if (in_file == NULL)
```

Closing a File

A file is closed by using the `fclose()` function. This function breaks the link between the file's external and internal names, releasing the internal file pointer name, which can then be used for another file. For example, the statement

```
fclose(in_file);
```

closes the `in_file` file. The argument used with `fclose()` is always the pointer name used when the file was opened. `fclose()` does not return a value.

Since all computers have a limit on the maximum number of files that can be open at one time, closing files that are no longer needed makes good sense. Any open files existing at the end of normal program execution are also automatically closed by the operating system.

12.2 Reading and Writing Files

Reading or writing to an open file involves almost the identical standard library functions for reading input from a terminal and writing data to a display screen. For writing to a file, these functions are:

Function	Description
`putc (c,filename)`	Write a single character to the file.
`fputs (string, filename)`	Write a string to the file.
`fprintf (filename,"format",args)`	Write the values of the arguments to the file according to the format.

In each of these functions, the file name is the internal pointer name specified when the file was opened. For example, if `out_file` is the internal pointer name of a file opened in either the write or append modes, the following output statements are valid.

```
putc('a',out_file);             /* write an a to file   */
fputs("Hello world!",out_file);/* write string to file */
fprintf(out_file,"%s %n",descrip,price);
```

Notice that the `putc()`, `fputs()`, and `fprintf()` file functions are used in the same manner as the equivalent `putchar()`, `puts()`, and `printf()` functions, with the addition of a file name as an argument. The file name simply directs the output to a specific file instead of to the standard display device. Program 12-2 illustrates the use of the file write function `fprintf()` to write a list of descriptions and prices to a file.

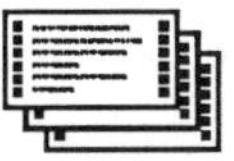

Program 12-2

```
#include <stdio.h>
main()
{
  int i;
  FILE *fopen(), *out_file;                  /* FILE declarations */
  static float price[] = {39.95,3.22,1.03}; /* a list of prices  */
```

continued

```
  static char *descrip[] = { "Batteries",     /*   a list of       */
                             "Bulbs",         /*  descriptions     */
                             "Fuses"};

  out_file = fopen("prices.bnd","w");         /*  open the file    */

  for(i = 0; i < 3; ++ i)
    fprintf(out_file,"%-9s %5.2f\n",descrip[i],price[i]);

  fclose(out_file);
}
```

When Program 12-2 is executed, a file named `prices.bnd` is created and saved by the computer. The file is a sequential file consisting of the following three lines:

```
Batteries 39.95
Bulbs      3.22
Fuses      1.02
```

The prices in the file line up one after another because the control sequence %-9s in the `printf()` function call forced the descriptions to be left justified in a field of nine character positions. Similarly, the prices are right justified in a field of five characters, beginning one space from the end of the description field.

The actual storage of characters in the file depends on the character codes used by the computer. Although only 45 characters appear to be stored in the file, corresponding to the descriptions, blanks, and prices written to the file, the file actually contains 49 characters. The extra characters consist of the newline escape sequences at the end of each line and a special end-of-file marker placed as the last item in the file when the file is closed.

Assuming that characters are stored by using the ASCII code, the `prices.bnd` file is physically stored as illustrated in Figure 12-1. For convenience, the character corresponding to each hexadecimal code is listed below the code. A code of 20 represents the blank character. For systems that

FIGURE 12-1 The `prices.bnd` File as Stored by the Computer

```
42 61 74 74 65 72 69 65 73 20 33 39 2e 39 35 0a 42 75 6c 62 73
 B  a  t  t  e  r  i  e  s     3  9  .  9  5 \n  B  u  l  b  s

20 20 20 20 20 20 33 2e 32 32 0a 46 75 73 65 73 20 20 20 20 20
                   3  .  2  2 \n  F  u  s  e  s

20 31 2e 30 32 0a 26
    1  .  0  2 \n ^z
```

generate a separate line feed and carriage return for each newline character, the file contains 52 characters. Although the actual code used for the end-of-file marker depends on the system you are using, the hexadecimal code 26, corresponding to Control-Z, is common.

Reading data from a file is almost identical to reading data from a standard keyboard, with the exception that you must include the file name to indicate where the data is coming from. The file functions available for reading from a file are:

Function	Description
`getc (filename)`	Read a character from the file.
`fgets (stringname,n,filename)`	Read n–1 characters from the file and store the characters in the given string name.
`fscanf (filename,"format",&args)`	Read values for the listed arguments from the file, according to the format.

For example, if `in_file` is the internal pointer name of a file opened in read mode, the following statements could be used to read data from the file:

```
getc(in_file);                 /* Read next character in file  */

fgets(message,10,in_file);     /* Read next 9 characters from  */
                               /* file into message            */

fscanf(in_file,"%f",&price); /* Read a floating point number */
```

All the input functions correctly detect the end-of-file marker. The functions `getc()` and `fscanf()`, however, return the named constant `EOF` when the marker is detected. The function `fgets()` returns a `NULL (\0)` when it detects the end of a file. Both of these named constants, `EOF` and `NULL`, are useful sentinels for detecting the end of a file being read.

Reading data from a file requires that the programmer knows how the data appears in the file. This is necessary for correct stripping of the data from the file into appropriate variables for storage. All files are read sequentially, so that once an item is read the next item in the file becomes available for reading.

Program 12-3 illustrates reading the `prices.bnd` file created in Program 12-2. The program also illustrates using the `EOF` marker, which is returned by `fscanf()` when the end of the file is encountered.

Program 12-3

```
#include <stdio.h>
main()
{
  char descrip[10];
  float price;
  FILE *fopen(), *in_file;

  in_file = fopen("prices.bnd","r");

  while (fscanf(in_file,"%s %f",descrip,&price) != EOF)
    printf("%-9s %5.2f\n",descrip,price);

  fclose(in_file);
}
```

Program 12-3 continues to read the file until the `EOF` marker has been detected. Each time the file is read, a string and a floating point number are input to the program. The display produced by Program 12-3 is:

```
Batteries 39.95
Bulbs      3.22
Fuses      1.02
```

In place of the `fscanf()` function used in Program 12-3, an `fgets()` function call can also be used. `fgets()` requires three arguments: an address where the first character read will be stored, the maximum number of characters to be read, and the name of the input file. For example, the function call

```
fgets(line,81,in_file);
```

causes a maximum of 80 characters (one less than the specified number) to be read from the file named `in_file` and stored, starting at the address contained in the pointer named `line`. `fgets()` continues reading characters until 80 characters have been read or a newline character has been encountered. If a newline character is encountered, it is included with the other entered characters before the string is terminated with the end-of-string marker, `\0`. `fgets()` also detects the end-of-file marker, but returns the `NULL` character when the end of the file is encountered. Program 12-4 illustrates the use of `fgets` in a working program.

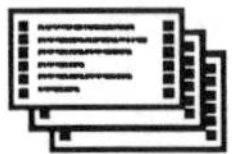

Program 12-4

```
#include <stdio.h>
main()
{
  char line[81],descrip[10];
  float price;
  FILE *fopen(), *in_file;

  in_file = fopen("prices.bnd","r");

  while (fgets(line,81,in_file) != NULL)
    printf("%s",line);

  fclose(in_file);
}
```

Program 12-4 is really a line-by-line text-copying program, reading a line of text from the file and then displaying it on the terminal. Thus, the output of Program 12-4 is identical to the output of Program 12-3. If it were necessary to obtain the description and price as individual variables, either Program 12-3 should be used or the string returned by `fgets()` in Program 12-4 must be processed further using the string scan function, `sscanf()`. For example, the statement

```
sscanf(line,"%s %f",descrip,&price)
```

could be used to extract the description and price from the string stored in the line character array (see Section 10.4 for a description of in-memory string formatting).

Standard Device Files

The data file pointers we have used have all been logical file pointers. A *logical file pointer* is one that references a file of logically related data that has been saved under a common name; that is, it points to a data file. In addition to logical file pointers, C also supports physical file pointers. A *physical file pointer* points to a hardware device, such as a keyboard, screen, or printer.

The actual physical device assigned to your program for data entry is formally called the *standard input file.* Usually this is a keyboard. When a `scanf()` function call is encountered in a C program, the computer automatically goes to this standard input file for the expected input. Similarly, when a `printf()` function call is encountered, the output is automatically displayed or written to a device that has been assigned as the *standard output file.* For most systems, this is a CRT screen, although it can be a printer.

When a program is run, the keyboard used for entering data is automatically opened and assigned to the internal file pointer named `stdin`. Similarly, the output device used for display is assigned to the file pointer named `stdout`. These file pointers are always available for programmer use.

The similarities between `printf()` and `fprintf()` and between `scanf()` and `fscanf()` are not accidental. `printf()` is a special case of `fprintf()` that defaults to the standard output file, and `scanf()` is a special case of `fscanf()` that defaults to the standard input file. Thus,

```
fprintf(stdout,"Hello World!");
```

causes the same display as the statement

```
printf("Hello World!");
```

and

```
fscanf(stdin,"%d",&num);
```

is equivalent to the statement

```
scanf("%d",&num);
```

In addition to the `stdin` and `stdout` file pointers, a third pointer named `stderr` is assigned to the output device used for system error messages. Although `stderr` and `stdout` frequently refer to the same device, the use of `stderr` provides a means of redirecting any error messages away from the file being used for normal program output, as described in Appendix C.

Just as `scanf()` and `printf()` are special cases of `fscanf()` and `fprintf()`, respectively, the functions `getchar()`, `gets()`, `putchar()`, and `puts()` are also special cases of the more general file functions listed in Table 12-1.

TABLE 12-1 Correspondence Between Selected I/O Functions

Function	General Form
putchar(character)	putc(character,stdout)
puts(string)	fputs(string,stdout)
getchar()	getc(stdin)
gets(stringname)	fgets(stringname,n,stdin)

The character function pairs listed in Table 12-1 can be used as direct replacements for each other. This is not true for the string-handling functions. The differences between the string-handling functions are described below.

At input, as previously noted, the `fgets()` function reads data from a file until a newline escape sequence or a specified number of characters has been read. If `fgets()` encounters a newline escape sequence, as we saw in Program 12-4, it is stored with the other characters entered. The `gets()` function, however, does not store the newline escape sequence in the final string. Both functions terminate the entered characters with an end-of-string `NULL` character.

At output, both `puts()` and `fputs()` write all the characters in the string except the terminating end-of-string `NULL;` however, `puts()` automatically adds a newline escape sequence at the end of the transmitted characters while `fputs()` does not.

Other Devices

The keyboard, display, and error-reporting devices are automatically opened and assigned the internal file names `stdin`, `stdout`, and `stderr`, respectively, whenever a C program begins execution. Additionally, other devices can be used for input or output if the name assigned by the system is known. For example, most IBM or IBM-compatible personal computers assign the name `prn` to the printer connected to the computer. For these computers, the statement `fprintf("prn","Hello World!");` causes the string `Hello World!` to be printed directly at the printer. As with `stdin`, `stdout`, and `stderr`, `"prn"` is the name of a physical device. Unlike `stdin`, `stdout`, and `stderr`, `prn` is not a pointer constant but the actual name of the device; as such, it must be enclosed in double quotes.

12.3 Random File Access

File organization refers to the way data is stored in a file. All the files we have used have *sequential organization.* This means that the characters in the file are stored in a sequential manner, one after another. Additionally, we have read the file in a sequential manner. The way data is retrieved from the file is called *file access.* That the characters in the file are stored sequentially, however, does not force us to access the file sequentially.

The standard library functions `rewind()`, `fseek()`, and `ftell()` can be used to provide random access to a file. In random access, any character in the file can be read immediately, without first having to read all the characters stored ahead of it.

The `rewind()` function resets the current position to the start of the file. `rewind()` requires the pointer name used for the file as its only argument. For example, the statement

```
rewind(in_file);
```

resets the file so that the next character accessed is the first character in the file. A `rewind()` is done automatically when a file is opened in read mode.

The `fseek()` function allows the programmer to move to any position in the file. In order to understand this function, you must first clearly understand how data is referenced in the file.

Each character in a data file is located by its position in the file. The first character in the file is located at position 0, the next character at position 1, and so on. A character's position is also referred to as its offset from the start of the file. Thus, the first character has a 0 offset, the second character has an offset of 1, and so on for each character in the file.

The `fseek()` function requires three arguments: the pointer name of the file; the offset, as a long integer, into the file; and where the offset is to be calculated from. The general form of `fseek()` is

```
fseek(file_name, offset, origin)
```

The values of the origin argument can be either 0, 1, or 2. An origin of 0 means the offset is the true offset from the start of the file; an origin of 1 means that the offset is relative to the current position in the file; and an origin of 2 means the offset is relative to the end of the file. A positive offset means to move forward in the file and a negative offset means to move backward. Examples of `fseek()` are:

```
fseek(in_file,4L,0);      /* go to 5th character in file */
fseek(in_file,4L,1);      /* move ahead 5 characters     */
fseek(in_file,-4L,1);     /* move back 5 characters      */
fseek(in_file,0L,0);      /* go to start of file         */
                          /*   - same as rewind          */
fseek(in_file,0L,2);      /* go to end of file           */
fseek(in-file,-10L,2);    /* go to 10 characters before  */
                          /*   file's end                */
```

In these examples, `in_file` is the name of the file pointer used when the data file was opened. Notice that the offset passed to `fseek()` must be a long integer.

The last function, `ftell()`, simply returns the offset value of the next character to be read or written. For example, if 10 characters have already been read from a file named `in_file`, the function call

```
ftell(in_file);
```

returns the long integer 10. This means that the next character to be read is offset 10 byte positions from the start of the file and is the eleventh character in the file.

Program 12-5 illustrates the use of `fseek()` and `ftell()` to read a file in reverse order, from last character to first. As each character is read, it is also displayed.

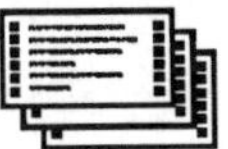

Program 12-5

```
#include <stdio.h>
main()
{
int ch, n;
long int offset, last, ftell();
FILE *fopen(), *in_file;

in_file = fopen("test.dat","r");
fseek(in_file,0,2);              /* move to the end of the file    */
last = ftell(in_file);           /* save offset of last character */
for(offset = 0; offset <= last; ++offset)
{
  fseek(in_file, -offset, 2);  /* move back to next character    */
  ch = getc(in_file);           /* get the character              */
  switch(ch)
  {
    case '\n : printf("LF : ");
               break;
    case EOF : printf("EOF: ");
               break;
    default  : printf("%c : ",ch);
               break;
  }
}
fclose(in_file);
}
```

Assuming the file `test.dat` contains the following data,

```
Bulbs   3.12
```

The output of Program 12-5 is:

```
EOF : 2 : 1 : . : 3 :  :  :  : s : b : l : u : B :
```

Program 12-5 initially goes to the last character in the file. The offset of this character, which is the end-of-file character, is saved in the variable `last`. Since `ftell()` returns a long integer, both `ftell()` and `last` have been declared as long integers.

Starting from the end of the file, `fseek()` positions the next character to be read, referencing it from the back of the file. As each character is read, it is displayed and the offset adjusted in order to access the next character.

12.4 Passing and Returning File Names

Internal file names are passed to a function by using the same procedures as those used for passing function arguments. For passing a file name, the passed argument must be declared as a pointer to a `FILE`. For example, in Program 12-6 a file named `out_file` is opened in `main()` and the file name passed to the function `in_out()`, which is then used to write five lines of user-entered text to the file.

Within `main()`, the file is known as `out_file`. The value in `out_file`, which is an address, is passed to the `in_out()` function. The function `in_out()` stores the address in the argument named `fname` and correctly declares `fname` to be a pointer to a `FILE`.

Returning a file name from a function also requires following the same rules as those that apply to returning any value from a function. These are including the data type of the returned value in the function header, making sure the correct variable type is actually returned from the function, and alerting the calling function to the returned data type. For example, assume that the function `get_open()` is to prompt a user for a file name, open the file for output, and return the file name to the calling function. Since `get_open()` returns a file name that is actually a pointer to a `FILE`, the correct function declaration for `get_open()` is:

```
FILE *get_open()
```

This declaration specifically declares that the function `get_open()` will return a pointer to a `FILE`. It is consistent with the pointer declarations that have been made previously.

Once a function has been declared to return a pointer to a `FILE`, there must be at least one variable or argument in the function consistent with this

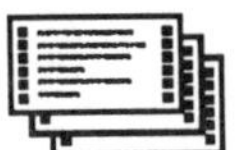

Program 12-6

```
#include <stdio.h>
main()
{
  FILE *fopen(), *out_file;

  out_file = fopen("prices.dat","w");
  in_out(out_file);
  fclose(out_file);
}

in_out(fname)
FILE *fname;       /* fname is a pointer to a FILE */
{
  int count;
  char line[81]; /* enough storage for one line of text */

  printf("Please enter five lines of text:\n");
  for (count = 0; count < 5; ++count)
  {
    gets(line);
    fprintf(fname,"%s\n",line);
  }
  return;
}
```

declaration that can be used for the actual returned value. Consider Program 12-7. In this program, `get_open()` returns a file name to `main()`.

Program 12-7 is simply a modified version of Program 12-6 that now allows the user to enter a file name from the standard input device. Although the function `get_open()` is in "bare bones" form, it illustrates the correct function declaration for returning a file name. The `get_open()` function declaration defines the function as returning a pointer to a `FILE`. Within `get_open()`, the returned variable, `fname`, is the correct data type. Finally, since `get_open()` is defined in the program after `main()`, `main()` is alerted to the returned value by the inclusion of a declaration statement for the `get_open()` function.

`get_open()` does no checking on the file being opened for output. If the name of an existing data file is entered, the file will be destroyed when it is opened in write mode. One way to prevent this type of mishap is to open the

Program 12-7

```
#include <stdio.h>
main()
{
  FILE *get_open(), *out_file;

  out_file = get_open();
  in_out(out_file);
  fclose(out_file);
}

FILE *get_open()    /* get_open() returns a pointer to a FILE */
{
  FILE *fopen, *fname;
  char name[13];

  printf("\nEnter a file name: ");
  gets(name)
  fname = fopen(name,"w");
  return(fname);
}

in_out(fname)
FILE *fname;         /* fname is a pointer to a FILE           */
{
  int count;
  char line[81];    /* enough storage for one line of text    */

  printf("Please enter five lines of text:\n");
  for (count = 0; count < 5; ++count)
  {
    gets(line);
    fprintf(fname,"%s\n",line);
}
```

entered file name in read mode. Then, if the file exists, the `fopen()` function returns a nonzero pointer to indicate that the file is available for input. This can be used to alert the user that a file with the entered name currently exists in the system and to request confirmation that the data in the file can be destroyed and the file name used for the new output file. Before the file can be reopened in write mode, of course, it would have to be closed.

12.5 Common Programming Errors

Four programming errors are common when using files. The most common error is to use the file's external name in place of the internal file pointer variable when accessing the file. The only standard library function that uses the data file's external name is the `fopen()` function. All the other standard functions presented in this chapter require the pointer variable assigned to the file when it was initially opened.

The next error is to omit the file pointer name altogether. Programmers used to functions that access the standard input and output devices, where a specific file pointer is not required, sometimes forget to include a file pointer when accessing data files.

A third error occurs when using the `EOF` marker to detect the end of a file. Any variable used to accept the `EOF` must be declared as an integer variable, not a character variable. For example, if `ch` has been declared as a character variable the expression

```
while ( (ch = getc(in_file)) != EOF)
```

produces an infinite loop. This occurs because a character variable can never take on an `EOF` code. `EOF` is an integer value (usually -1) that has no character representation. This ensures that the `EOF` code can never be confused with any legitimate character encountered as normal data in the file. To terminate the above expression, the variable `ch` must be declared as an integer variable.

The last error concerns the offset argument sent to the function `fseek()`. This offset must be a long integer constant or variable. Any other value passed to `fseek()` can produce unpredictable results.

12.6 Chapter Summary

1. A data file is any collection of data stored together in an external storage medium under a common name.
2. A data file is opened using the `fopen()` standard library function. This function connects a file's external name with an internal pointer name. After the file is opened, all subsequent accesses to the file require the internal pointer name.
3. A file can be opened for reading, writing, or appending. A file opened for writing creates a new file and erases any existing file having the same name as the opened file. A file opened for appending makes an existing file available

for data to be added to the end of the file. If the file does not exist, it is created. A file opened for reading makes an existing file's data available for input.

4. The `fopen()` function and any internal file name must be declared as a pointer to a `FILE`. This means that a declaration similar to

```
FILE *fopen(), *f_name;
```

must be included with the declarations in which the file is opened. `f_name` can be replaced with any user-selected file name.

5. In addition to any files opened within a function, the standard files `stdin`, `stdout`, and `stderr` are automatically opened when a program is run. `stdin` is the pointer name of the physical file used for data entry by `scanf()`, `stdout` is the pointer name of the physical file device used for data display by `printf()`, and `stderr` is the pointer name of the physical file device used for displaying system error messages.
6. Data files can be accessed randomly, using the `rewind()`, `fseek()`, and `ftell()` functions.
7. Table 12-2 lists the standard file library functions.

TABLE 12-2 Standard File Library Functions

Function Name	Purpose
`fopen()`	Open or create a file
`fclose()`	Close a file
`getc()`	Character input
`getchar()`	Character input from `stdin`
`fgets()`	String input
`gets()`	String input from `stdin`
`fscanf()`	Formatted input
`scanf()`	Formatted input from `stdin`
`putc()`	Character output
`putchar()`	Character output to `stdout`
`fputs()`	String output
`puts()`	String output to `stdout`
`fprintf()`	Formatted output
`printf()`	Formatted output to `stdout`
`fseek()`	File positioning
`rewind()`	File positioning
`ftell()`	Position reporting

Sample Problem

Write a C program to create a data file named employ.dat that contains the following data:

```
Employee Name     Date Hired     Number of Dependents
-------------     ----------     --------------------
George Adams       10/18/88                5
Nancy Folger        6/1/85                 2
Bill Hornsby       10/1/89                 3
Harriet Smith       3/1/87                 3
```

The data may be entered and written in a variety of ways. One approach is to enter the data line by line and to write each line to a file. A second approach is to enter the data as individual items and write them as individual items. A third approach is to enter the data as individual items, assemble the items into a complete string using in-memory string conversion, and then write the string to the file. The following program uses the third approach:

```
#include <stdio.h>
main()
{
  FILE *out, *fopen();
  char name[30], date[10], strng[81];
  int i, depend;

  out = fopen("employ.dat", "w");
  for (i = 0; i <= 3; ++i)
                /* get and write four records */
  {
    printf("\nEnter the name: ");
    gets(name);
    printf("Enter the date (ex. 12/6/65): ");
    scanf("%s",date);
    printf("Enter the number of dependents: ");
    scanf("%d",&depend);
          /* now assemble the line to be written */
    sprintf(strng, "%-30s %-10s %2d", name,
            date, depend);
    fputs(strng,out);  /* write the string out */
      putc('\n',out);
                /* append a newline character */
    getchar();    /* clear out the input buffer */
}
  fclose(out);
    printf("\nEnd of data input.");
    printf("\nThe file has been written.");
}
```

The following is a sample run made using this program:

```
Enter the name: George Adams
Enter the date (ex. 12/6/65): 10/18/88
Enter the number of dependents: 5

Enter the name: Nancy Folger
Enter the date (ex. 12/6/65): 6/1/85
Enter the number of dependents: 2

Enter the name: Bill Hornsby
Enter the date (ex. 12/6/65): 10/1/89
Enter the number of dependents: 3

Enter the name: Harriet Smith
Enter the date (ex. 12/6/65): 3/1/87
Enter the number of dependents: 3

End of data input.
The file has been written.
```

The following file was produced by this run:

```
George Adams                    10/18/88      5
Nancy Folger                    6/1/85        2
Bill Hornsby                    10/1/89       3
Harriet Smith                   3/1/87        3
```

12.7 Chapter Supplement: Control Codes

In addition to responding to the codes for letters, digits, and special punctuation symbols, which are collectively referred to as *printable characters,* such physical device files as printers and CRT screens can respond to a small set of *control codes.* These codes, which convey control information to the physical device, have no equivalent characters that can be displayed, and are called *nonprintable characters.*

Two of these codes, which are extremely useful in applications, are the *clear* and *bell control codes.* When the clear control code is sent to a printer, the printer ejects a page of paper and begins printing on the next sheet of paper. If you take care to align the printer to the top of a new page when printing begins, the clear control character can be used as an equivalent "top-of-page" command. When the equivalent clear code is sent to a CRT display, the screen is cleared of all text and the cursor is positioned at the lefthand corner of the screen.

Sending control codes to an output device is done in a manner similar to sending a printable character to a file. Recall that sending a printable character to a file requires two pieces of information: the file name and the character being written to the file. For example, the statement `putc('a',out_file);` causes the letter *a* to be written to the file named `out_file`. Instead of including the actual letter as an argument to `putc()`, we can substitute the numerical storage code for the letter. For computers that use the ASCII code, this amounts to substituting the equivalent ASCII numerical value for the appropriate letter. Referring to Appendix B, we see that in the ASCII code the value for a is 97 as a decimal number, 61 as a hexadecimal number, and 141 as an octal number. Any one of these numerical values can be used in place of the letter a in the previous `putc()` function call. Thus, the following four statements are all equivalent:

```
putc('a',out_file);
putc(97, out_file);
putc(0x61 out_file);
putc('\142',out_file);
```

Note that in each of these statements we have adhered to the notation used by C in identifying decimal, hexadecimal, and octal numbers. A number with no leading zero is considered a decimal number and a number with a leading `0x` is considered a hexadecimal value. Octal character codes must, however, be preceded by a backslash and enclosed in single quotation marks. Since the backslash identifies the number as an octal value, the normal leading zero required of octal values can be omitted. Since most control codes, by convention, are listed as octal values with the traditional leading zero, we will retain this convention in all further examples.

The importance of substituting the numerical code for the letter is realized only when a control code rather than a character code must be sent. Since no equivalent character exists for control codes, the actual code for the command must be used. Although each computer can have its own code for clearing the CRT screen, the bell code and the code for clearing a printer are fairly universal. To activate the bell, the octal code 07 is used. The octal clear code for most printers is 014. Thus, if the file `out_file` has been opened as "the printer in write mode," the statement

```
putc('\014',out_file);
```

causes the printer to eject the current page. Similarly, if `scrn` has been opened as "the CRT screen in write mode," the statement

```
putc('\07',scrn);
```

causes the bell to be activated for a short "beep."

For personal computers, the clear code for the CRT screen is a coded value. For your computer, check the manual for the CRT screen to obtain the proper clear-screen control code. You must also check the name by which your computer "knows" the printer and CRT screen. For IBM personal computers, the printer has the name `prn` and the CRT screen the name `con` (short for console). Program 12-8 illustrates the use of control codes to eject a page of paper from the printer and to alert the user with a "beep" if the printer is not turned on. Using `#define` commands, the appropriate codes have been equated to more readable symbolic names.

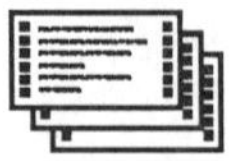

Program 12-8

```
#include <stdio.h>
#define BELL '\07'
#define TOP-OF-PAGE '\014'        /* page eject code              */
main()
{
  FILE *printer, *fopen;

  printer = fopen("prn:", "w");
  check(printer);
}

check(printer)  /* make sure printer is ready and eject a page */
FILE *printer;
{

  if(printer == 0)      /* check that the file has been opened  */
  {
    putc(BELL,stdout);
    printf("The printer cannot be opened for output.");
    printf("\nPlease check the printer is on and ready for use.");
  }
  else
    putc(TOP-OF-PAGE,printer);
  return;
}
```

The statements in the function `check()` are used to ensure that the printer has been opened and is ready for output. The symbolic constants `BELL` and `TOP-OF-PAGE` can be used freely within the `check()` function because they have been defined globally at the top of the program. Each of these constants is sent by using a `putc()` function call. Since the CRT screen is the standard output device for the computer used to run Program 12-8, the CRT did not have to be opened as a new file. Instead, the file name `stdout` was used to send the `BELL` constant to the screen.

In addition to the `BELL` code, all CRT screens have control codes to position the cursor directly at different screen locations. This enables the programmer to place messages anywhere on the screen. Since these codes differ for various CRT models, you should check the manual for your computer to determine the proper codes. Additionally, many C compilers for personal computers include standard library functions that provide the same cursor-positioning capabilities.

Bit Operations

Chapter Thirteen

C operates with complete data entities that are stored as one or more bytes, such as character, integer, and double precision constants and variables. In addition, C provides for the manipulation of individual bits of character and integer constants and variables. Generally, these bit manipulations are used in engineering and computer science programs and are not required in commercial applications.

The operators used to perform bit manipulations are called *bit operators*. They are listed in Table 13-1.

TABLE 13-1 Bit Operators

Operator	Description
&	Bitwise AND
|	Bitwise Inclusive OR
^	Bitwise Exclusive OR
~	Bitwise one's complement
<<	Left shift
>>	Right shift

All the operators listed in Table 13-1 are *binary operators,* requiring two operands. In using the bit operators, each operand is treated as a binary number consisting of a series of individual 1s and 0s. The respective bits in each operand are then compared on a bit-by-bit basis and the result is determined on the basis of the selected operation.

13.1 The AND Operator

The AND operator, &, causes a bit-by-bit AND comparison between its two operands. The result of each bit-by-bit comparison is a 1 only when both bits being compared are 1s, otherwise the result of the AND operation is a 0.

To perform an AND operation, each bit in one operand is compared to the bit occupying the same position in the other operand. Figure 13-1 illustrates the correspondence between bits for two operands. As shown in the figure, when both bits being compared are 1s, the result is a 1, otherwise the result is a 0. The result of each comparison is, of course, independent of any other bit comparison.

Program 13-1 illustrates the use of an AND operation. In this program, the variable `op1` is initialized to the octal value 325, which is the octal equivalent of the binary number `1 1 0 1 0 1 0 1`, and the variable `op2` is initialized to the

```
    1 0 1 1 0 0 1 1
  & 1 1 0 1 0 1 0 1
  -----------------
    1 0 0 1 0 0 0 1
```

FIGURE 13-1 A Sample AND Operation

octal value 263, which is the octal representation of the binary number `1 0 1 1 0 0 1 1`. These are the same two binary numbers illustrated in Figure 13-1.

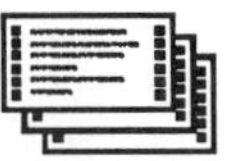

Program 13-1

```
main()
{
  int op1 = 0325, op2 = 0263;

  printf("%o ANDed with %o is %o", op1, op2, op1 & op2);
}
```

Program 13-1 produces the following output:

```
325 ANDed with 263 is 221
```

The result of ANDing the octal numbers 325 and 263 is the octal number 221. The binary equivalent of 221 is the binary number `1 0 0 1 0 0 0 1`, which is the result of the AND operation illustrated in Figure 13-1.

AND operations are extremely useful in masking, or eliminating, selected bits from an operand. This is a direct result of the fact that ANDing any bit (1 or 0) with a 0 forces the resulting bit to be a 0, while ANDing any bit (1 or 0) with a 1 leaves the original bit unchanged. For example, assume that the variable `op1` has the arbitrary bit pattern `x x x x x x x x`, where each `x` can be either a 1 or 0, independent of any other `x` in the number. The result of ANDing this binary number with the binary number `0 0 0 0 1 1 1 1` is:

```
   op1 =  x  x  x  x  x  x  x  x
   op2 =  0  0  0  0  1  1  1  1
--------------------------------
Result =  0  0  0  0  x  x  x  x
```

As can be seen from this example, the 0s in `op2` effectively mask, or eliminate, the respective bits in `op1`, while the 1s in `op2` filter, or pass through, the respective bits in op1 with no change in their values. In this example, the variable op2 is called a *mask*. By choosing the mask appropriately, any individual bit in an operand can be selected, or filtered, from an operand for inspection. For example, ANDing the variable op1 with the mask 0 0 0 0 0 1 0 0 forces all the bits of the result to be 0, except for the third bit. The third bit of the result will be a copy of the third bit of op1. Thus, if the result of the AND is 0, the third bit of op1 must have been 0, and if the result of the AND is a nonzero number, the third bit must have been a 1.

13.2 The Inclusive OR Operator

The inclusive OR operator, |, performs a bit-by-bit comparison of its two operands in a similar fashion to the bit-by-bit AND. The result of the OR comparison, however, is determined by the following rule:

The result of the comparison is 1, if either bit being compared is a 1; otherwise, the result is a 0.

Figure 13-2 illustrates an OR operation. As shown in the figure, when either of the two bits being compared is a 1, the result is a 1, otherwise the result is a 0. As with all bit operations, the result of each comparison is, of course, independent of any other comparison.

Program 13-2 illustrates an OR operation, using the octal values of the operands illustrated in Figure 13-2.

Program 13-2

```
main()
{
  int op1 = 0325, op2 = 0263;

  printf("%o ORed  with  %o is  %o",  op1, op2, op1 | op2);
}
```

Program 13-2 produces the following output:

```
325 ORed with 263 is 367
```

```
    1  0  1  1  0  0  1  1
|   1  1  0  1  0  1  0  1
  ------------------------
    1  1  1  1  0  1  1  1
```

FIGURE 13-2 A Sample OR Operation

The result of ORing the octal numbers 325 and 263 is the octal number 367. The binary equivalent of 367 is `1 1 1 1 0 1 1 1`, which is the result of the OR operation illustrated in Figure 13-2.

Inclusive OR operations are extremely useful in forcing selected bits to take on a value of 1 or for passing other bit values unchanged. This is a direct result of the fact that ORing any bit (1 or 0) with a 1 forces the resulting bit to be a 1, while ORing any bit (1 or 0) with a 0 leaves the original bit unchanged. For example, assume that the variable `op1` has the arbitrary bit pattern `x x x x x x x x`, where each `x` can be either 1 or 0, independent of any other `x` in the number. The result of ORing this binary number with the binary number `1 1 1 1 0 0 0 0` is:

```
   op1 =  x  x  x  x  x  x  x  x
   op2 =  1  1  1  1  0  0  0  0
--------------------------------
Result =  1  1  1  1  x  x  x  x
```

As can be seen from this example, the 1s in `op2` force the resulting bits to 1, while 0s in `op2` filter, or pass, the respective bits in `op1` with no change in their values. Thus, using an OR operation a similar masking operation can be produced as with an AND operation, except that the masked bits are set to 1s rather than cleared to 0s. Another way of looking at this is to say that ORing with a 0 has the same effect as ANDing with a 1.

13.3 The Exclusive OR Operator

The exclusive OR operator, `^`, performs a bit-by-bit comparison of its two operands. The result of the comparison determined by the following rule:

The result of the comparison is 1 if one and only one of the bits being compared is a 1; otherwise, the result is 0.

Figure 13-3 illustrates an exclusive OR operation. As shown in the figure, when both bits being compared are the same value (both 1 or both 0), the result

```
    1  0  1  1  0  0  1  1
 ^  1  1  0  1  0  1  0  1
   ----------------------
    0  1  1  0  0  1  1  0
```

FIGURE 13-3 A Sample Exclusive OR Operation

is a 0. Only when both bits have different values (one bit a 1 and the other a 0) is the result a 1. Again, the comparison of each bit pair is independent of any other bit pair comparison.

An exclusive OR operation can be used to create the opposite value, or complement, of any individual bit in a variable. This is a direct result of the fact that exclusive ORing any bit (1 or 0) with a 1 forces the resulting bit to be of the opposite value of its original state, while exclusive ORing any bit (1 or 0) with a 0 leaves the original bit unchanged. For example, assume that the variable `op1` has the arbitrary bit pattern `x x x x x x x x`, where each `x` can be either 1 or 0, independent of any other `x` in the number. Using the notation that $\overline{x}$ is the complement (opposite) value of `x`, the result of exclusive ORing this binary number with the binary number `0 1 0 1 0 1 0 1` is:

$$
\begin{array}{rcccccccc}
\texttt{op1} = & x & x & x & x & x & x & x & x \\
\texttt{op2} = & 0 & 1 & 0 & 1 & 0 & 1 & 0 & 1 \\
\hline
\texttt{Result} = & x & \overline{x} & x & \overline{x} & x & \overline{x} & x & \overline{x}
\end{array}
$$

As can be seen from this example, the 1s in `op2` force the resulting bits to be the complement of their original bit values, while the 0s in `op2` filter, or pass, the respective bits in `op1` with no change in their values.

13.4 The Complement Operator

The complement operator, `~`, is a unary operator that changes each 1 bit in its operand to 0 and each 0 bit to 1. For example, if the variable `op1` contains the binary number `11001010`, `~op1` replaces this binary number with the number `00110101`. The complement operator in conjunction with the AND operator can be used to force any bit in an operand to 0, independent of the actual number of bits used to store the number. For example, the statement

```
op1 = op1 &  07;
```

or its shorter form,

```
op1 &=  07;
```

both set the last three bits of `op1` to 0, regardless of how `op1` is stored within the computer. Either of these two statements can, of course, be replaced by ANDing the last three bits of `op1` with 0, if the number of bits used to store `op1` is known. In a computer that uses 16 bits to store integers, the appropriate AND operation is

```
op1 = op1 & 0177770;
```

For a computer that uses 32 bits to store integers, the above AND sets the leftmost or higher order 16 bits to 0 also, which is an unintended result. The correct statement for 32 bits is:

```
op1 = op1 & 027777777770;
```

Using the complement operator in this situation frees the programmer from having to determine the storage size of the operand and, more importantly, makes the program portable between machines using different integer storage sizes.

13.5 Different-Size Data Items

When the bit operators `&`, `|`, and `^` are used with operands of different sizes, the shorter operand is always increased in bit size to match the size of the larger operand. Figure 13-4 illustrates the extension of a 16-bit unsigned integer into a 32-bit number.

FIGURE 13-4 Extending 16-Bit Unsigned Data to 32 Bits

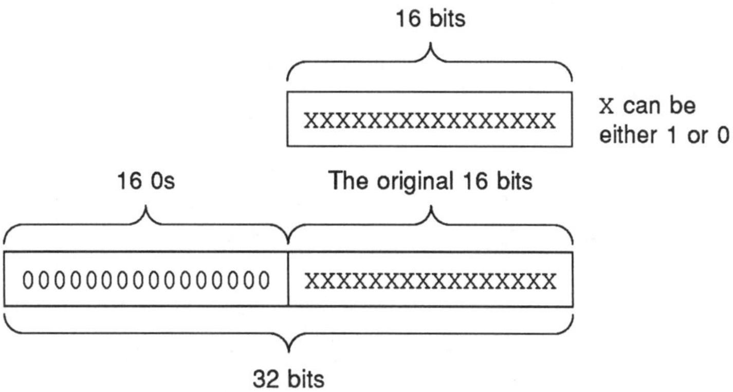

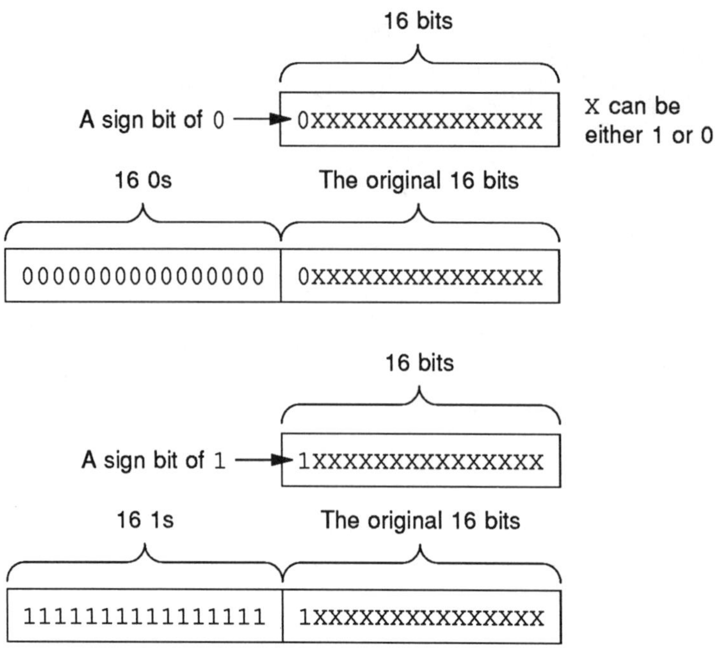

FIGURE 13-5 Extending 16-Bit Signed Data to 32 Bits

As the figure shows, the additional bits are added to the left of the original number and filled with 0s. This is the equivalent of adding leading 0s to the number, which has no effect on the number's value.

When extending signed numbers, the original leftmost bit is reproduced in the additional bits that are added to the number. As illustrated in Figure 13-5, if the original leftmost bit is 0, which corresponds to a positive number, 0 is placed in each of the additional bit positions. If the leftmost bit is 1, which corresponds to a negative number, 1 is placed in the additional bit positions. In either case, the resulting binary number has the same sign and magnitude as the original number.

13.6 The Shift Operators

The left shift operator, `<<`, causes the bits in an operand to be shifted to the left by a given amount. For example, the statement

```
op1 = op1 << 4;
```

cause the bits in `op1` to be shifted four bits to the left, filling any vacated bits with a 0. Figure 13-6 illustrates the effect of shifting the binary number `1111100010101011` to the left by four bit positions.

For unsigned integers, each left shift corresponds to multiplication by two. This is also true for signed numbers using two's complement representation, as long as the leftmost bit does not switch values. Since a change in the leftmost bit of a two's complement number represents a change in both the sign and magnitude represented by the bit, such a shift does not represent a simple multiplication by two.

The right shift operator, >>, causes the bits in an operand to be shifted to the right by a given amount. For example, the statement

```
op1 = op1 >> 3;
```

cause the bits in `op1` to be shifted to the right by three bit positions. Figure 13-7a illustrates the right shift of the unsigned binary number `1111100010101011` by three bit positions. As illustrated, the three rightmost bits are shifted "off the end" and are lost.

For unsigned numbers, the leftmost bit is not used as a sign bit. For this type of number, the vacated leftmost bits are always filled with 0s. This is illustrated in Figure 13-7a.

For signed numbers, what is filled in the vacated bits depends on the computer. Most computers reproduce the original sign bit of the number. Figure 13-7b illustrates the right shift of a negative binary number by four bit positions, with the sign bit reproduced in the vacated bits. Figure 13-7c illustrates the equivalent right shift of a positive signed binary number.

The type of fill illustrated in Figures 13-7b and c, in which the sign bit is reproduced in vacated bit positions, is called an *arithmetic right shift*. In an arithmetic right shift, each single shift to the right corresponds to a division by two.

Instead of reproducing the sign bit in right-shifted signed numbers, some computers automatically fill the vacated bits with 0s. This type of shift is called a *logical shift*. For positive signed numbers, where the leftmost bit is zero, both

FIGURE 13-6 An Example of a Left Shift

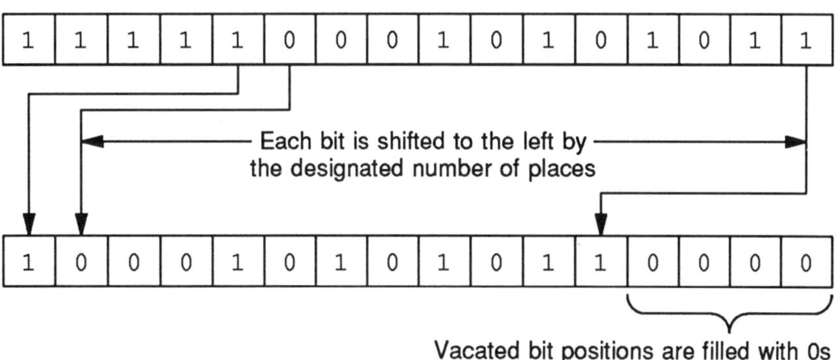

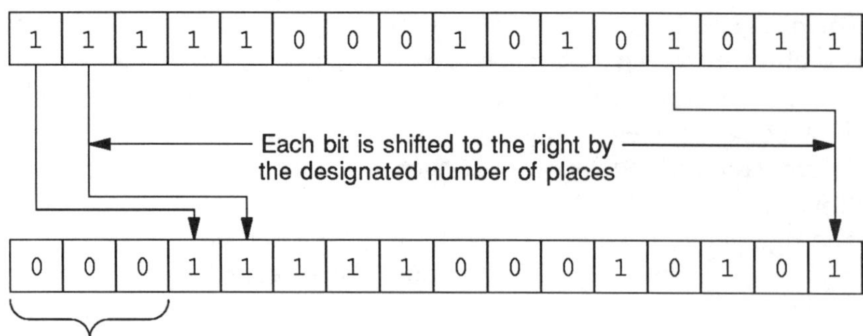

FIGURE 13-7a An Unsigned Arithmetic Right Shift

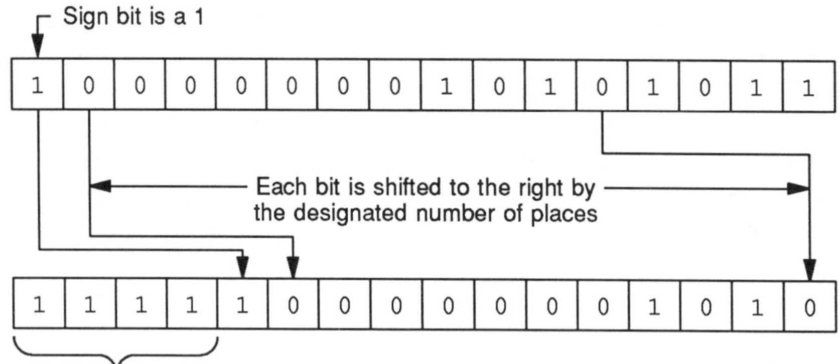

FIGURE 13-7b The Right Shift of a Negative Binary Number

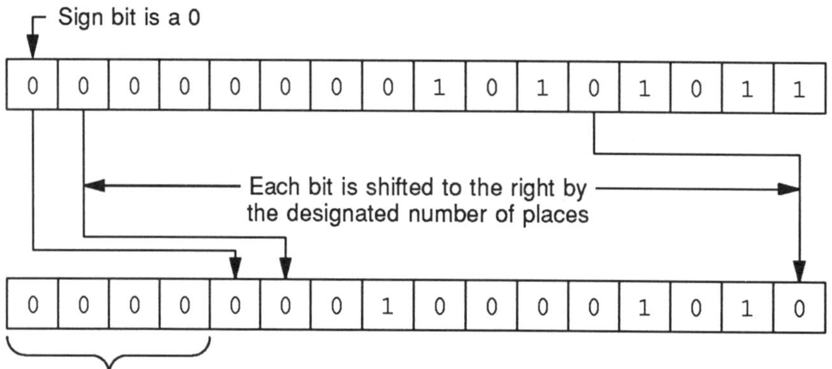

FIGURE 13-7c The Right Shift of a Positive Binary Number

arithmetic and logical right shifts produces the same result. The results of these two shifts are only different when negative numbers are involved.

13.7 Chapter Summary

1. Individual bits of character and integer variables and constants can be manipulated with C's bit operators. These are the AND, inclusive OR, exclusive OR, one's complement, left shift, and right shift operators.
2. The AND and inclusive OR operators are useful in creating masks. These masks can be used to pass or eliminate individual bits from the selected operand. The exclusive OR operator is useful in complementing an operand's bits.
3. When the AND and OR operators are used with operands of different sizes, the shorter operand is always increased in bit size to match the size of the larger operand.
4. The shift operators produce different results, depending on whether the operand is a signed or an unsigned value.

Sample Problem

The following algorithm reverses the bits in the integer variable `number` and places the results in the integer variable `reverse`:

1. Clear (set the bits to 0) all of the bits in `reverse`.
2. For all of the bits in `number`:
   a. Isolate the least significant bit using a mask
   b. Shift the bits in `reverse` one position to the left
   c. Add the masked least significant bit to `reverse`
   d. Shift the bits in `number` one position to the right

For example, if the bit pattern 11100101, which corresponds to the octal number 345, were assigned to `number`, the bit pattern 10100111, which corresponds to the octal number 247, would be produced in `reverse`. The C program on the next page uses the algorithm to perform bit reversal on the specified number.

```
main()
{
   int i, temp, number, reverse = 0;
   int mask = 001;            /* bit mask to isolate least */
                              /*   significant bit  (LSB)  */

  printf("Enter an octal number: ");
  scanf("%o",&number);
  for (i = 1; i <=8; ++i)
  {
    temp = number & mask;                /* strip off LSB */
    reverse = reverse << 1; /* shift left one position   */
    reverse += temp;        /* add least significant bit */
    number = number >> 1;   /* shift next bit into LSB   */
  }
    printf("\nReversed pattern, in octal, is %o", reverse);
}
```

A sample run for the program produced:

```
Enter an octal number: 345

Reversed pattern, in octal, is 247
```

Additional Capabilities

Chapter Fourteen

Previous chapters have presented C's basic capabilities and structure. Variations on these capabilities, which are almost endless, are a source of delight to many programmers who constantly find new possibilities for using the variations of the basic language building blocks. This chapter presents some of these additional capabilities.

14.1 Expressions Revisited

One of the most common pitfalls in C results from misunderstanding the full implications of an expression. Recall that an expression is any combination of operands and operators that yields a result. This definition is extremely broad and more encompassing than is initially apparent. For example, all of the following are valid C expressions:

```
a + 5
a = b
a == b
a = b = c = 6
flag = a == b
```

Assuming that the variables are suitably declared, each of the above expressions yields a result. Program 14-1 uses the `printf()` function to display the value of the first three expressions for specific initial values of the variables a and b.

Program 14-1

```
main()
{
  int a = 7, b = 10;

  printf("\nThe value of the first expression is %d", a + 5);
  printf("\nThe value of the second expression is %d", a = b);
  printf("\nThe value of the third expression is %d", a == b );
```

The display produced by Program 14-1 is:

```
The value of the first expression is 12
The value of the second expression is 10
The value of the third expression is 0
```

As the output of Program 14-1 illustrates, each expression, by itself, has a value associated with it. The value of the first expression is the sum of the variable a plus 5, which is 12. The value of the second expression is 10, which is also assigned to the variable a. The value of the third expression is 0, since a is not equal to b, and a false condition is represented in C with a value of 0. If the values in a and b had been the same, the relational expression a == b would be true and would have a value of 1.

In this section we will review the rules for evaluating expressions with multiple operators and "mixed" operands of different data types. We will also introduce a new expression type and C operator.

Expressions containing multiple operators are always evaluated by the priority, or precedence, of each operator. Table A-1 in Appendix A lists the relative priority of each C operator and its associativity.

Even when the order of evaluation is known, expressions with multiple operators can still produce unusual and undesired results, remaining a potential trap for the unwary. For example, consider the statement

```
flag = a == b;
```

Consulting Table A-1 we see that the == operator has a higher precedence than the = operator. Therefore, a is first compared to b. If a is equal to b, the result of the expression a == b is 1; otherwise, it is 0. The value of this expression is then assigned to flag. Thus, the variable flag will have either a value of 1 or a value of 0 after the statement is executed. A problem arises if the expression is inadvertently typed as flag = a = b. Here, the value of b is first assigned to a, which is then assigned to flag. Because of the mistake of typing an equal operator instead of the comparison operator, flag is assigned the value of b, rather than the 1 or 0 that was intended.

The real problem with the statement flag = a == b; is that it has been used in place of the more obvious and complete statement

```
if (a == b)
  flag = 1;
else
  flag = 0;
```

Although the same error can be made in substituting an equal operator for the comparison operator in this statement, the error can be detected more easily than in the more obscure expression flag = a == b.

Because of the generality of C expressions and the fact that most sequences of operands connected by operators can be evaluated to produce a result (including an unintended one), it is extremely important to be careful in creating expressions. To avoid undesired results and to make program checking, testing, and debugging easier, keep expressions as simple and as uncomplicated as possible. Generally, expressions using arithmetic operators (+, -, *, /, %, etc.)

should not be mixed with expressions using relational and logical operators (==, <, >, &&, ||, etc.), which, in turn, should not be mixed with expressions using bit operators (&, |, etc.).

One further point must be mentioned. Although Table A-1 appears to be all-inclusive, it is not. In particular, the order of evaluations for operands is not specified, as it is not specified in most computer languages. For example, in the expression `a + b`, it is not known which operand is accessed first. Generally, this is not a problem because the order of operand access does not affect the result of the expression. However, in expressions such as

```
(val[i]) + (i++)
```

the order of access is important. Here, the subscript may be either the old or the new value of `i`, depending on which operand is accessed first.

Similarly, the order of evaluation of function arguments is not specified in C. Thus, the function call

```
printf("%d %d", i, i++);
```

may result in the same number being printed twice if the second argument is evaluated before the first argument.

Expressions that depend on the order of operand access should always be avoided, because they can produce different results on different computers. Such expressions can always be replaced with temporary variables that explicitly define the desired evaluation order. For example, the statements

```
n = i++;
printf("%d %d", i, n);
```

clearly indicate the values to be passed to the `printf()` function.

Casts

We have already seen the forced conversion of an operand's data type in mixed binary arithmetic expressions. Such expressions consist of a binary arithmetic operator (+, -, *, /, %, etc.) connecting two operands of different data types. For example, if `val` is a double precision variable and `num` is an integer variable, `num`'s value is converted to double precision in the expression `val + num`.

The general rules for converting operands in mixed arithmetic expressions were presented in Chapter 2. A more complete set of conversion rules for arithmetic operators is listed in Table 14- 1.

TABLE 14-1 Conversion Rules for Arithmetic Operators*

Rule 1. All character and short integer operands are always converted to integer values. All floating point operands are converted to double precision values.
Rule 2. If one operand is a double precision value, then the other operand is converted to a double precision value and the result of the expression is a double precision value.
Rule 3. If one operand is a long integer value, then the other operand is converted to a long integer value and the resulting value of the expression is a long integer value.
Rule 4. If one operand is an unsigned integer value, then the other operand is converted to an unsigned integer value and the resulting value of the expression is an unsigned value.
Rule 5. If both operands are of type `int`, no conversions occur and the resulting value of the expression is an integer value.
*These rules are applied in sequence.

Forced conversions also take place across assignment operators. Here, the value of the expression on the right side of the equal sign is converted to the data type of the variable on the left side of the equal sign, which also becomes the value of the complete expression. For example, consider the evaluation of the expression

```
a = b * d - e % f
```

where `a` and `d` are integer variables, `e` is a short integer variable, `f` is a long integer variable, and `b` is a floating point variable. According to the order of operator precedence, the `*` and `%` operators will be evaluated first, followed by the subtraction and assignment operators. Thus, the priority of evaluation is

```
a = ( (b * d) - (e % f) )
```

Internally, the expression `b * d` consists of a floating point and integer operand. Referring to Rule 1 in Table 14-1, the value of `b` is converted to a double precision number. Since one of the operands is a double precision variable, Rule 2 provides that the second operand's value is converted to a double precision number and the resulting value of the expression `b * d` is a double precision number.

In the expression `e % f`, since `f` is a long integer variable, the value of `e` is converted to a long integer (Rule 3) and the value of the expression is itself a long integer value.

The subtraction of `(e % f)` from `(b * d)` forces the conversion of `(e % f)` to a double precision number. This occurs because the operand `(b * d)` is a double precision value. Since the left side of the assignment operator is an integer value, the double precision value of the expression `(b * d) - (e % f)` is forced to become an integer value.

In addition to the forced conversions made automatically to operands in mixed arithmetic expressions, C also provides for user-specified type conversions. The operator used to force the conversion of a value to another type is the *cast operator*. This is a unary operator having the symbol (`data type`), where `data type` is the desired data type of the operand following the cast. For example, the expression

```
(int) (a * b)
```

ensures that the value of the expression `a * b` is converted to an integer value. The parentheses around the expression `(a * b)` are required because the cast operator has a higher precedence than the multiplication operator.

As a last example, consider the expression `(int) a * b`, where both `a` and `b` are double precision variables. Here, only `a`'s value is cast into an integer before multiplication by `b`. The cast into an integer value causes the fractional part of `a`'s value to be truncated. Since `b` is a double precision operand, the value of the operand `(int) a` is converted back to a double precision number (Rule 2 in Table 14-1). The forced conversion back to a double precision number, however, does not restore the fractional part of `a`.

Conditional Expressions

In addition to expressions formed with the arithmetic, relational, logical, and bit operators, C provides a *conditional expression*. A conditional expression uses the conditional operator, `?:`, and provides an alternate way of expressing a simple `if-else` statement.

The general form of a conditional expression is:

```
expression1 ? expression2 : expression3
```

If the value of `expression1` is nonzero (true), `expression2` is evaluated; otherwise `expression3` is evaluated. The value for the complete conditional expression is the value of either `expression2` or expression3, depending on which expression was evaluated. As always, the value of the expression may be assigned to a variable.

Conditional expressions are most useful in replacing simple `if-else` statements. For example, the `if- else` statement

```
if ( hours > 40)
  rate = .045;
else
  rate = .02;
```

can be replaced with the one-line statement

```
rate = (hours > 40) ? .045 : .02;
```

Here, the complete conditional expression

```
(hours > 40) ? .045 : .02
```

is evaluated before any assignment is made to `rate`, because the conditional operator, `?:`, has a higher precedence than the assignment operator. Within the conditional expression, the expression `hours > 40` is evaluated first. If this expression has a nonzero value, which is equivalent to a logical true value, the value of the complete conditional expression is set to .045; otherwise the conditional expression has a value of .02. Finally, the value of the conditional expression, either .045 or .02, is assigned to the variable `rate`.

The conditional operator, `?:`, is unique in C in that it is a *ternary operator.* This means that the operator connects three operands. The first operand is always evaluated first. It is usually a conditional expression that uses the logical operators.

The next two operands are any other valid expressions, which can be single constants, variables, or more general expressions. The complete conditional expression consists of all three operands connected by the conditional operator symbols, ? and :.

Conditional expressions are useful only in replacing `if-else` statements when the expressions in the equivalent `if-else` statement are not long or complicated. For example, the statement

```
max_val = a > b ? a : b;
```

is a one-line statement that assigns the maximum value of the variables `a` and `b` to `max_val`. A longer, equivalent form of this statement is:

```
if (a > b)
  max_val = a;
else
  max_val = b;
```

Because of the length of the expressions involved, a conditional expression would not be useful in replacing the following `if-else` statement:

```
if (amount > 20000)
  taxes = .025(amount - 20000) + 400;
else
  taxes = .02 * amount;
```

14.2 User-Specified Data Types

In this section, we present two user-specified data types. The first permits a user to create new data types. Since the creation of a data type requires the programmer to specifically list or enumerate the values appropriate to the data type, these data types are referred to as enumerated data types. The second capability allows the programmer to create new names for existing data types.

Enumerated Data Types

An *enumerated data type* is a user-created data type in which the values appropriate to the data type are specified in a user-defined list. Such data types are identified by the reserved word `enum` followed by an optional, user-selected name for the data type and a listing of acceptable values for the data type. Consider the following user-specified data types:

```
enum flag {true, false};
enum time {am, pm};
enum day {mon, tue, wed, thr, fri, sat, sun};
enum color {red, green, yellow};
```

The first user-specified data type is `flag`. Any variable subsequently declared to be of this type can take on a value of true or false only. The second statement creates a data type named `time`. Any variable subsequently declared to be of type `time` can take on a value of am or pm only. Similarly, the third and fourth statements create the data types `day` and `color`, respectively, and list the valid values for variables of these two types. For example, the statement

```
enum color a,b,c;
```

declares the variables `a`, `b`, and `c` to be of type `color`, and is consistent with the declaration of variables that use such standard C data types as `char`, `int`, `float`, or `double`. Once variables have been declared as enumerated types, they can be assigned values or compared to variables or values appropriate to their type. This, again, is consistent with standard variable operations. For the variables `a`, `b`, and `c` declared above, the following statements are valid:

```
a = red;
b = a;
if (c == yellow) printf("\nThe color is yellow");
```

Internally, the acceptable values for each enumerated data type are ordered and assigned sequential integer values, beginning with 0. For example, for the values of the user-defined type `color`, the correspondences created by the C compiler are that `red` is equivalent to 0, `green` is equivalent to 1, and `yellow` is equivalent to 2. The equivalent numbers are required when inputting values with `scanf()` or printing values with `printf()`.

Program 14-2 illustrates a user-defined data type.

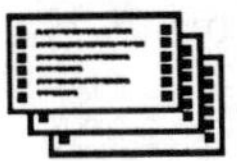

Program 14-2

```
main()
{
  enum color {red,green,yellow};
  enum color crayon = red;     /* crayon is declared as type    */
                               /*  color and initialized as red */
  printf("\nThe color is %d", crayon);
  printf("\nEnter in a value: ");
  scanf("%d", &crayon);
  if (crayon == red)
    printf("\nThe crayon is red.");
  else if (crayon == green)
    printf("\nThe crayon is green.");
  else if (crayon == yellow)
    printf("\nThe crayon is yellow.");
  else
    printf("\nThe color is not defined.");
}
```

A sample run of Program 14-2 produced the following output:

```
The color is 0
Enter a value: 2
The crayon is yellow.
```

As illustrated in Program 14-2, expressions containing variables declared as user-defined data types must be consistent with the values specifically listed for the type. Although a `switch` statement would be more appropriate in Program 14-2, the expressions in the `if-else` statement better highlight the use of enumerated values. Program 14-2 also shows that the initialization of a user-specified data type variable is identical to the initialization of standard data type variables. For input and output purposes, however, the equivalent integer value assigned by the C compiler to each enumerated value must be used in place of the actual data type value. This is also seen in the program.

In order to assign equivalent integers to each user-specified value, the C compiler retains the order of the values in the enumeration. A side effect of this ordering is that expressions can be constructed by using relational and logical operators. For example, for the data type `color` created in Program 14-2, expressions such as `crayon < yellow` and `red < green` are both valid.

The numerical value assigned by the compiler to enumerated values can be altered by direct assignment when a data type is created. For example, the definition

```
enum color (red,green = 7, yellow);
```

causes the compiler to associate the value `red` with the integer 0 and the value `green` with the integer 7. Altering the integer associated with the value `green` causes all subsequent integer assignments to be altered too; thus, the value `yellow` is associated with the integer 8. If any other values were listed after `yellow`, they would be associated with the integers 9, 10, 11, etc., unless another alteration was made.

Naming a user-defined data type is similar to naming a template for structures. Just as a template name can be omitted when defining a structure by declaring the structure directly, the same can be done with user-defined data types. For example, the declaration `enum {red,green,yellow} crayon;` defines `crayon` to be a variable of an unnamed data type with the valid values of `red`, `green`, and `yellow`.

Scope rules applicable to the standard C data types also apply to enumerated data types. For example, placing the statement `enum color {red, green, yellow};` before the `main()` function in Program 14-2 would make the data type named `color` global and available for any other function in the file.

Finally, since their is a one-to-one correspondence between integers and user-defined data types, the cast operator can either coerce integers into a user-specified data value or coerce a user-specified value into its equivalent integer. Assuming that `val` is an integer variable with a value of `1` and `color` has been declared as in Program 14-2, the expression `(enum color) val` has a value of `green` and the expression `(int) yellow` has a value of `2`. The compiler will not warn you, however, if a cast to a nonexistent value is attempted.

The `typedef` Statement

In addition to creating new data types, C allows both standard and user-defined data types to be renamed by using `typedef` statements. The statement

```
typedef float REAL;
```

makes the name REAL a synonym for float. The name REAL can now be used in place of the term float anywhere in the program after the synonym has been declared. For example, the definition

```
REAL val;
```

is equivalent to the definition

```
float val;
```

The typedef statement does not create a new data type; it creates a new name for an existing data type. Using uppercase names in typedef statements is not mandatory. It is done simply to alert the programmer to a user-specified name, similar to uppercase names in #define statements. In fact, the equivalence produced by a typedef statement can frequently be produced equally well by a #define statement. The difference between the two, is that typedef statements are processed directly by the compiler, while #define statements are processed by the preprocessor. Compiler processing of typedef statements allows for text replacements that are not possible with the preprocessor. For example, the statement

```
typedef float REAL;
```

actually specifies that REAL is a placeholder that will be replaced with another variable name. A subsequent declaration such as

```
REAL val;
```

has the effect of substituting the variable named val for the placeholder named REAL in the terms following the word typedef. Substituting val for REAL in the typedef statement and retaining all terms after the reserved word typedef results in the equivalent declaration float val;.

Once the mechanics of the replacement are understood, more useful equivalences can be constructed. Consider the statement

```
typedef int ARRAY[100];
```

Here the name ARRAY is actually a placeholder for any subsequently defined variables. Thus, a statement such as ARRAY first, second; is equivalent to the two definitions

```
int first[100];
int second[100];
```

Each of these definitions is obtained by replacing the name ARRAY with the variable names first and second in the terms following the reserved word typedef.

As another example, consider the following statement:

```
typedef struct
        {
          char name[20];
          int id_num;
        } EMP_REC;
```

Here EMP_REC is a convenient placeholder for any subsequent variable. For example, the declaration EMP_REC employee[75]; is equivalent to the declaration

```
struct
{
     char name[20];
     int id_num;
} employee[75];
```

This last declaration is obtained by directly substituting the term employee[75] in place of the word EMP_REC in the terms following the word typedef in the original typedef statement.

14.3 Defining Macros

In its simplest form, the #define preprocessor command is used to equate constants and operators to symbolic names. For example, the statement

```
#define SALESTAX .05
```

equates the symbolic name SALESTAX to the number .05. When SALESTAX is used in any subsequent statement or expression, the equivalent value of .05 is substituted for the symbolic name. The substitutions are made by the C preprocessor just prior to program compilation.

C places no restrictions on the equivalences that can be established with the #define statement. The symbolic name following the #define designation can be equated to any text and can even include arguments. For example:

```
#define  PI       3.1416
#define  TIMES    *
#define  EQUALS   =
#define  FORMAT   "Answer is %f"
```

The use of these equivalence statements is illustrated in Program 14-3.

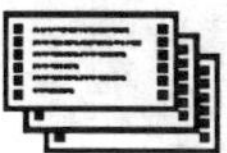

Program 14-3

```
#define  PI       3.1416
#define  TIMES    *
#define  EQUALS   =
#define  FORMAT   "Answer is %f"
main()
{
  float circum, radius = 6.3;

  circum EQUALS 2.0 TIMES PI TIMES radius;
  printf(FORMAT,circum);
}
```

Before Program 14-3 is compiled, the preprocessor directly substitutes the equivalent operator, constant, variable, or text in place of each subsequent occurrence of the symbolic name.

In addition to using `#define` preprocessor commands for simple equivalences, as in Program 14-3, these statements can also be used to equate symbolic names to either partial or complete expressions. When the equivalent text consists of more than a single value, operator, or variable, the symbolic name is referred to as a *macro*, and the substitution of the text in place of the symbolic name is called a *macro expansion* or *macro substitution*. The word macro refers to the direct, in-line expansion of one word into many words. For example,the equivalence established by the statement

```
#define CONVERT   2.0 * 3.1416
```

enables us to write the statement

```
circum = CONVERT * radius;
```

When this statement is encountered by the preprocessor, the symbolic name `CONVERT` is replaced by the equivalent text `2.0 * 3.1416`. The compiler always receives the expanded version after the text has been inserted in place of the symbolic name by the preprocessor. This direct substitution of the text for CONVERT occurs in every place that CONVERT is encountered after it has been defined. This allows a previously defined symbolic name to be used in subsequent symbolic definitions. For example, the definition for CONVERT could have been established with the following set of #define commands:

```
#define PI          3.1416

#define CONVERT     2.0 * PI
```

Since PI is equivalent to the constant 3.1416 in the first #define command, it can be used legitimately in any following #define command.

In addition to using #define commands for straight text substitutions, these commands can also be used to define equivalences that use arguments. For example, in the preprocessor command

```
#define SQUARE(x)     x * x
```

x is an argument. Here, SQUARE(x) is a true macro that is expanded into the expression x * x, where x is itself replaced by the variable or constant used when the macro is utilized. For example, the statement

```
y = SQUARE(num);
```

is expanded into the statement

```
y = num * num;
```

The advantage of using a macro, such as SQUARE(x), is that since the data type of the argument is not specified, the macro can be used with any data type argument. If num, for example, is an integer variable, the expression num * num produces an integer value. Similarly, if num is a double precision variable, the SQUARE(x) macro produces a double precision value. This is a direct result of the text substitution procedure used in expanding the macro.

Care must be taken when defining macros with arguments. For example, in the definition of SQUARE(x), there must be no space between the symbolic name SQUARE and the left parentheses used to enclose the argument. There can, however, be spaces within the parentheses if more than one argument is used.

Additionally, since the expansion of a macro involves direct text substitution, unintended results may occur if you do not use macros carefully. For example, the assignment statement

```
val = SQUARE(num1 + num2);
```

does not assign the value of (num1 + num2)^2 to val. Rather, the expansion of SQUARE(num1 + num2) results in the equivalent statement

```
val =  num1 + num2  *  num1 + num2;
```

This statement results from the direct text substitution of the term num1 + num2 for the argument x in the expression x * x produced by the preprocessor.

To avoid unintended results, always place parentheses around all macro arguments wherever they appear in the macro. For example, the macro

```
#define SQUARE(x)   (x) * (x)
```

ensures that a correct result is produced whenever the macro is invoked. Now the statement

```
val = SQUARE(num1 + num2);
```

is expanded to produce the desired assignment

```
val = (num1 + num2) * (num1 + num2);
```

Macros are extremely useful when the calculations or expressions they contain are relatively simple and can be kept to one or, at most, two lines. Larger macro definitions tend to become cumbersome and confusing and are better written as functions. If necessary, a macro definition can be continued on a new line by typing a backslash character, \, before the RETURN or ENTER key is pressed. The backslash acts as an escape character that causes the preprocessor to treat the RETURN literally and not include it in any subsequent text substitutions.

The advantage of using a macro instead of a function is increased execution speed. Since the macro is directly expanded and included in every expression or statement using it, there is no execution time loss due to the call and return procedures required by a function. The disadvantage is the increase in required program memory space when a macro is used repeatedly. Each time a macro is used the complete macro text is reproduced and stored as an integral part of the program. Thus, if the same macro is used in ten places, the final code includes ten copies of the expanded text version of the macro. A function, however, is stored in memory only once. No matter how many times the function is called, the same code is used. The memory space required for one copy of a function used extensively throughout a program can be considerably less than the memory required for storing multiple copies of the same code defined as a macro.

14.4 Command Line Arguments

Arguments can be passed to any function in a program, including the `main()` function. In this section we describe the procedures for passing arguments to `main()` when a program is initially invoked and having `main()` correctly receive and store the arguments passed to it. Both the sending and receiving sides of the transaction must be considered. Fortunately, the interface for transmitting arguments to a `main()` function have been standardized in C, so both sending and receiving arguments can be done almost mechanically.

All the programs that have been run so far have been invoked by typing the name of the executable version of the program after the operating system prompt is displayed. The command line for these programs consists of a single word, which is the name of the program. For computers that use the UNIX Operating System the prompt is usually a doller sign, `$`, and the executable name of the program is `a.out`. For these systems, the simple command line `$ a.out` begins program execution of the last compiled source program currently residing in `a.out`.

If you are using a C compiler on an IBM PC, the equivalent operating system prompt is either `A>` or `C>`, and the name of the executable program is typically the same name as the source program, with an `.exe` extension rather than a `.c` extension. Assuming that you are using an IBM PC with the `A>` operating system prompt, the complete command line for running an executable program named `showad.exe` is `A> showad`. As illustrated in Figure 14-1, this command line causes the `showad` program to begin execution with its `main()` function, but no arguments are passed to `main()`.

Now, assume that we want to pass the three separate string arguments, `three`, `blind`, and `mice` directly into `showad`'s main function. Sending arguments into a `main()` function is extremely easy: Simply include the arguments on the command line used to begin program execution. Because the arguments are typed on the command line, they are, naturally, called *command line arguments.* To pass the arguments `three`, `blind`, and `mice` directly into

FIGURE 14-1 Invoking the `showad` Program

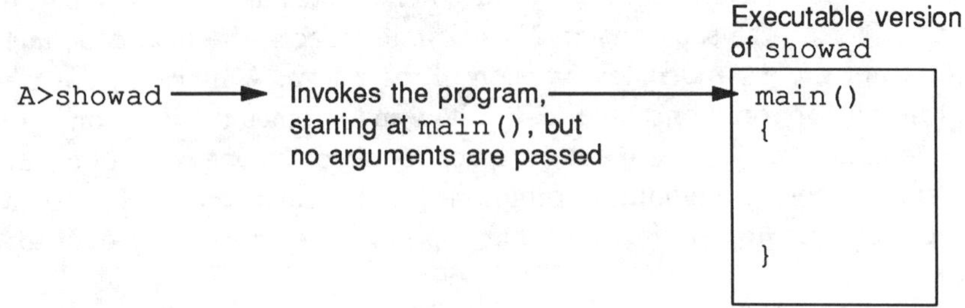

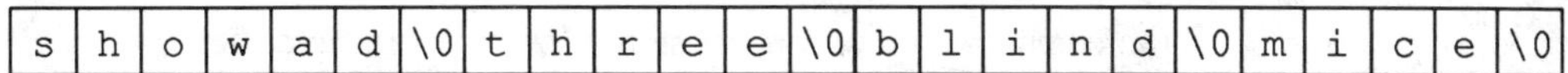

FIGURE 14-2 The Command Line Stored in Memory

the `main()` function of the `showad` program, we need to add only the desired words after the program name on the command line:

```
A> showad three blind mice
```

Upon encountering the command line `showad three blind mice`, the operating system stores it as a sequence of four strings. Figure 14-2 illustrates the storage of this command line, assuming that each character uses one byte of storage. As shown in the figure, each string terminates with the standard C null character, `\0`.

Sending command line arguments to `main()` is always this simple. The arguments are typed on the command line and the operating system stores them as a sequence of separate strings. We must now handle the receiving side of the transaction and let `main()` know that arguments are being passed to it.

Arguments passed to `main()`, like all function arguments, must be declared as part of the function's definition. To standardize argument passing to a `main()` function, only two items are allowed: a number and an array. The number is an integer variable, which must be named `argc` (short for argument counter), and the array is a one-dimensional list, which must be named `argv` (short for argument values). Figure 14-3 illustrates these two arguments.

The integer passed to `main()` is the total number of items on the command line. In our example, the value of `argc` passed to `main()` is 4, which includes the name of the program plus the three command line arguments. The one-dimensional list passed to `main()` is a list of pointers containing the starting storage address of each string typed on the command line, as illustrated in Figure 14-4.

We can now write the complete function definition for `main()` to receive arguments. Since an integer and an array are passed to `main()` and C requires

FIGURE 14-3 An Integer and an Array Are Passed to `main()`

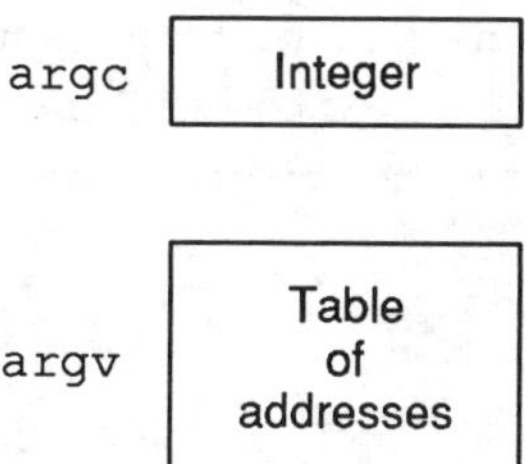

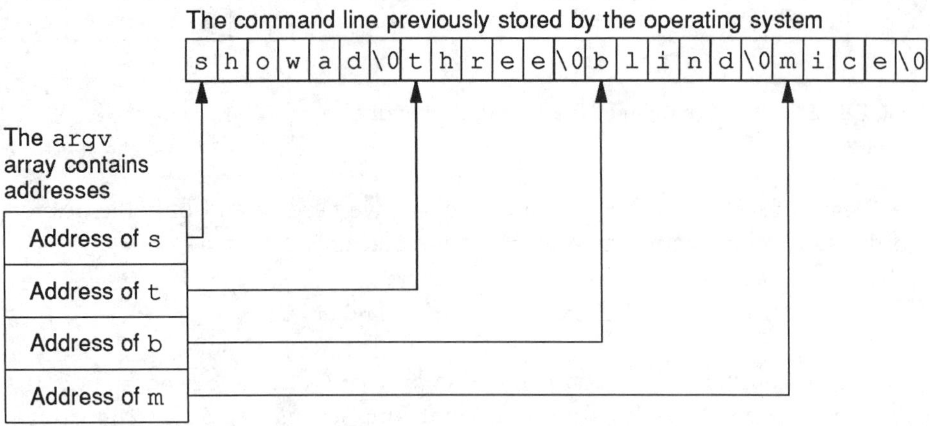

FIGURE 14-4 Addresses Are Stored in the `argv` Array

that these two items be named `argc` and `argv`, respectively, the first line in `main()`'s definition must be `main(argc,argv)`.

To complete `main()`'s definition, we must declare the data types of these two arguments. Because `argc` is an integer, its declaration is `int argc;`. Because `argv` is the name of an array whose elements are addresses that point to where the actual command line arguments are stored, its proper declaration is `char *argv[];`. This is nothing more than the declaration of an array of pointers. It is read "`argv` is an array whose elements are pointers to characters." Putting all this together, the full function header for a `main()` function that will receive command line arguments is:

```
main(argc,argv)       /* standard main() function */
int argc;             /* header for receiving     */
char *argv[];         /*  command line arguments  */
```

No matter how many arguments are typed on the command line, `main()` needs only the two standard pieces of information provided by `argc` and `argv`: the number of items on the command line and the list of starting addresses indicating where each argument is actually stored.

Program 14-4 verifies our description by printing the data actually passed to `main()`. The variable `argv[i]` used in Program 14-4 contains an address. The notation `*argv[i]` refers to "the character pointed to" by the address in `argv[i]`.

Program 14-4

```
#include <stdio.h>
main(argc,argv)
int argc;       /* number of items on the command line */
char *argv[];   /* an array of addresses               */
{
  int i;

  printf("\nThe number of items on the command line is %d\n\n",argc);
  for (i = 0; i < argc; ++i)
  {
    printf("Address stored in argv[%d] is %u\n", i, argv[i]);
    printf("Character pointed to is %c\n\n", *argv[i]);
  }
}
```

Assuming that the executable version of Program 14-4 is named `showad.exe`, a sample output for the command line `showad three blind mice` is:

```
Number of items on the command line is 4

Address stored in argv[0] is 786435
Character pointed to is s

Address stored in argv[1] is 786442
Character pointed to is t

Address stored in argv[2] is 786448
Character pointed to is b

Address stored in argv[3] is 786454
Character pointed to is m
```

The addresses displayed by Program 14-4 clearly depend on the machine used to run the program. Figure 14-5 illustrates the storage of the command line as displayed by the sample output. As anticipated, the addresses in the `argv` array point to the starting characters of each string typed on the command line.

Once command line arguments are passed to a C program, they can be used like any other C strings. Program 14-5 causes its command line arguments to be displayed from within `main()`.

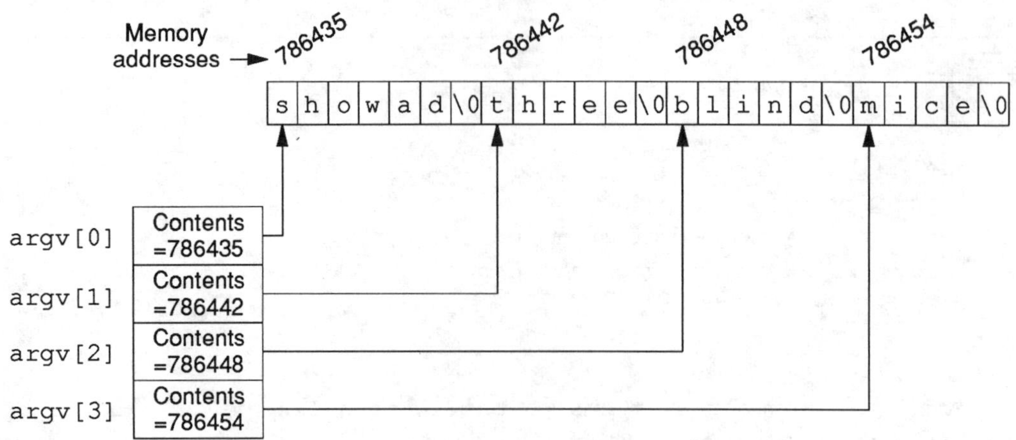

FIGURE 14-5 The Command Line Stored in Memory

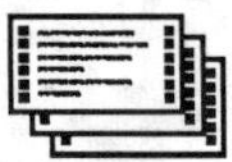

Program 14-5

```
/* A program that displays command line arguments */
#include <stdio.h>
main(argc,argv)
int argc;        /* standard argument declarations         */
char *argv[];    /*  for receiving command line arguments */
{
  int i;

  printf("\nThe following arguments were passed to main(): ");
  for (i = 1; i < argc; ++i)
    printf("%s ", argv[i]);
}
```

Assuming that the name of the executable version of Program 14-5 is `a.out`, the output of this program for the command line `a.out three blind mice` is:

```
The following arguments were passed to main(): three blind mice
```

Notice that, when the addresses in `argv[]` are passed to the `printf()` function in Program 14-5, the strings pointed to by these addresses are displayed. When these same addresses are passed to the `printf()` function in Program 14-4, the actual values of the addresses are printed. The difference in displays is caused by the `printf()` function. When a `%s` control sequence is used in `printf()`, as it is in Program 14-5, it alerts the function that a string will be accessed. `printf()` then expects the address of the first character in the string; this is exactly what each element in `argv[]` supplies. Once `printf()` receives the address, the function performs the required indirection to locate the actual string that is displayed. The `%u` control sequence used in Program 14-4 treats its argument as an unsigned integer and thus displays the value in `argv[i]`. As we have noted before, the use of the `%u` control sequence to display addresses is actually incorrect. Pointers are not unsigned integers — they are a unique data type that may or may not require the same amount of storage as an integer. The use of the `%u` control sequence simply provides us with a convenient way of displaying an address, since no specific control sequence exists for the output of addresses. Converting a pointer with the `%u` control sequence may actually display a meaningless number. The display, however, has no impact on how addresses are used within the program; it simply provides us with a useful output representation.

One final comment about command line arguments is in order. Any argument typed on a command line is considered to be a string. If you want numerical data passed to `main()`, it is up to you to convert the passed string into its numerical counterpart. This is seldom an issue, however, since most command line arguments are used as flags to pass appropriate processing control signals to an invoked program.

14.5 The goto Statement

The `goto` statement provides an unconditional transfer of control to some other statement in a program. The general form of a `goto` statement is

```
goto label;
```

where `label` is any unique name, chosen according to the rules for creating variable names. The label name must appear, followed by a colon, in front of any other statement in the function that contains the `goto` statement. For example, the following section of code transfers control to the label named `err` if division by 0 is attempted:

```
    if (denom == 0.0)
      goto err;
    else
      result = num /denom;
              .
              .
              .

err: printf("Error - Attempted Division by Zero");
```

The astute reader will realize that in this case goto provides a cumbersome solution to the problem. It would require a second goto above the printf() statement to stop this statement from always being executed. Generally, it is much easier either to call an error routine for unusual conditions or to use a break statement if this is necessary.

Theoretically, a goto statement is never required because C's normal structures provide sufficient flexibility to handle all possible flow control requirements. Also, a goto tends to complicate a program, especially if more than one is required. For example, consider the following code:

```
        if (a == 100)
          goto first;
        else
          x = 20;
        goto sec;
 first: x = 50;
   sec: y = 10;
```

Written without a goto this code is:

```
if (a == 100)
  x = 50;
else
  x = 20;
y = 10;
```

Both sections of code produce the same result; however, the second version is clearly easier to read. It is worthwhile to convince yourself that the two sections of code do, in fact, produce the same result by running the code on your computer. This will let you experience the sense of frustration when working with goto-invaded code.

In C, the goto statement should be used in a limited manner, if at all. The presence of goto statements can rapidly make a program extremely difficult to understand and almost impossible to modify.

14.6 Chapter Summary

1. A cast can be used to explicitly change the data type of a value. The general form of a cast is

```
(desired data type) expression
```

The cast changes the value of the expression to the indicated data type. For example, `(int) 2.6789` converts 2.6789 to the integer value of 2. When casts are used with variables, the data type of the variable and the variable's contents are not changed — only the value of the variable in the expression using the cast is altered.

2. A conditional expression provides an alternate way of expressing a simple `if-else` statement. The general form of a conditional expression is:

```
expression1 ? expression2 : expression3
```

The equivalent `if-else` statement for this is:

```
if (expression1)
  expression2;
else
  expression3;
```

3. An enumerated data type is a user-defined scalar data type. The user must select a name and list the acceptable values for the data type. For example, the enumeration

```
enum color {red, green, yellow};
```

creates a `color` data type. Any variable can be subsequently declared with this data type and can store one of the acceptable values listed.

4. A `typedef` statement creates synonyms for both standard and enumerated data types. For example, the statement

```
typedef int WHOLE_NUM;
```

makes `WHOLE_NUM` a synonym for `int`.

5. Using the `#define` command, complete expressions can be equated to symbolic names. These expressions can include arguments.
6. Arguments passed to `main()` are called command line arguments. C provides a standard argument-passing procedure in which `main()` can accept any number of arguments passed to it. Each argument passed to `main()` is considered a string and is stored by using a pointer array named `argv`. The total number of arguments on the command line is stored in an integer variable named `argc`.
7. C also provides a `goto` statement. In theory, this statement need never be used. In practice, it produces confusing and unstructured code, and should be used only in a very limited and controlled manner, if at all.

Sample Problem

Write a program that accepts the name of a file as a command line argument, opens the file, and displays its contents on the computer's standard output device.

The following program, named SHOW, performs the required processing by reading and displaying each character in the file on a character-by-character basis:

```
#include <stdio.h>
main(argc, argv)
int argc;            /* standard argc argument declaration */
char *argv[];        /* standard argv argument declaration */

{
  FILE *fopen(), *in_file;
  char ch;

  in_file = fopen(argv[1],"r");
  while( (ch = getc(in_file)) != EOF)
    putchar(ch);
  fclose(in_file);
}
```

A sample run of the above program, using the employ.dat file created in the sample program at the end of Chapter Twelve, produced the following output:

```
show employ.dat

George Adams                    10/18/88     5
Nancy Folger                    6/1/85       2
Bill Hornsby                    10/1/89      3
Harriet Smith                   3/1/87       3
```

Instead of reading characters until an end-of-file is reached, the fgets() function can be used to read one line at a time. Since fgets() returns a NULL when an end-of-file sentinel is read, the while statement in the program should be replaced with:

```
while (fgets(line, 81, in_file) != NULL)
```

with the variable line declared as

```
char line[81];
```

In a similar fashion, the puts() or fputs() functions can be used to output one line at a time. The puts() function adds a newline escape sequence at the end of each line, the fputs() function does not.

Appendices

A. Operator Precedence
B. ASCII Character Codes
C. Input, Output, and Standard Error Redirections
D. Quick C Reference
E. Function and Macro Reference

Appendix A. Operator Precedence

Table A-1 presents the symbols, precedence, description, and associativity of C's operators. Operators toward the top of sthe table have a higher precedence than those toward the bottom. Operators within each box have the same precedence and associativity.

TABLE A-1 Summary of C Operators

<table>
<tr><th>Operator</th><th>Description</th><th>Associativity</th></tr>
<tr><td>()
[]
->
.</td><td>Function call
Array element
Structure member pointer reference
Structure member reference</td><td>Left to right</td></tr>
<tr><td>++
--
-
!
~
(type)
sizeof
&
*</td><td>Increment
Decrement
Unary minus
Logical negation
One's complement
Type conversion (cast)
Storage size
Address of
Indirection</td><td>Right to left</td></tr>
<tr><td>*
/
%</td><td>Multiplication
Division
Modulus (remainder)</td><td>Left to right</td></tr>
<tr><td>+
-</td><td>Addition
Subtraction</td><td>Left to right</td></tr>
<tr><td><<
>></td><td>Left shift
Right shift</td><td>Left to right</td></tr>
<tr><td><
<=
>
>=</td><td>Less than
Less than or equal to
Greater than
Greater than or equal to</td><td>Left to right</td></tr>
<tr><td>==
!=</td><td>Equal to
Not equal to</td><td>Left to right</td></tr>
<tr><td>&</td><td>Bitwise AND</td><td>Left to right</td></tr>
<tr><td>^</td><td>Bitwise exclusive OR</td><td>Left to right</td></tr>
<tr><td>|</td><td>Bitwise inclusive OR</td><td>Left to right</td></tr>
<tr><td>&&</td><td>Logical AND</td><td>Left to right</td></tr>
<tr><td>||</td><td>Logical OR</td><td>Left to right</td></tr>
<tr><td>?:</td><td>Conditional expression</td><td>Left to right</td></tr>
<tr><td>=
+= -= *=
/= %= &=
^= |=
<<= >>=</td><td>Assignment
Assignment
Assignment
Assignment
Assignment</td><td>Left to right</td></tr>
<tr><td>,</td><td>Comma</td><td>Left to right</td></tr>
</table>

Appendix B. ASCII Character Codes

Key(s)	Dec	Oct	Hex	Key	Dec	Oct	Hex	Key	Dec	Oct	Hex
Ctrl 1	0	0	0	+	43	53	2B	V	86	126	56
Ctrl A	1	1	1	,	44	54	2C	W	87	127	57
Ctrl B	2	2	2	-	45	55	2D	X	88	130	58
Ctrl C	3	3	3	.	46	56	2E	Y	89	131	59
Ctrl D	4	4	4	/	47	57	2F	Z	90	132	5A
Ctrl E	5	5	5	0	48	60	30	[	91	133	5B
Ctrl F	6	6	6	1	49	61	31	\	92	134	5C
Ctrl G	7	7	7	2	50	62	32	]	93	135	5D
Ctrl H	8	10	8	3	51	63	33	^	94	136	5E
Ctrl I	9	11	9	4	52	64	34	_	95	137	5F
\n	10	12	A	5	53	65	35	`	96	140	60
Ctrl K	11	13	B	6	54	66	36	a	97	141	61
Ctrl L	12	14	C	7	55	67	37	b	98	142	62
RETURN	13	15	D	8	56	70	38	c	99	143	63
Ctrl N	14	16	E	9	57	71	39	d	100	144	64
Ctrl O	15	17	F	:	58	72	3A	e	101	145	65
Ctrl P	16	20	10	;	59	73	3B	f	102	146	66
Ctrl Q	17	21	11	<	60	74	3C	g	103	147	67
Ctrl R	18	22	12	=	61	75	3D	h	104	150	68
Ctrl S	19	23	13	>	62	76	3E	i	105	151	69
Ctrl T	20	24	14	?	63	77	3F	j	106	152	6A
Ctrl U	21	25	15	@	64	100	40	k	107	153	6B
Ctrl V	22	26	16	A	65	101	41	l	108	154	6C
Ctrl W	23	27	17	B	66	102	42	m	109	155	6D
Ctrl X	24	30	18	C	67	103	43	n	110	156	6E
Ctrl Y	25	31	19	D	68	104	44	o	111	157	6F
Ctrl Z	26	32	1A	E	69	105	45	p	112	160	70
Esc	27	33	1B	F	70	106	46	q	113	161	71
Ctrl <	28	34	1C	G	71	107	47	r	114	162	72
Ctrl /	29	35	1D	H	72	110	48	s	115	163	73
Ctrl =	30	36	1E	I	73	111	49	t	116	164	74
Ctrl -	31	37	1F	J	74	112	4A	u	117	165	75
Space	32	40	20	K	75	113	4B	v	118	166	76
!	33	41	21	L	76	114	4C	w	119	167	77
"	34	42	22	M	77	115	4D	x	120	170	78
#	35	43	23	N	78	116	4E	y	121	171	79
$	36	44	24	O	79	117	4F	z	122	172	7A
%	37	45	25	P	80	120	50	{	123	173	7B
&	38	46	26	Q	81	121	51	|	124	174	7C
'	39	47	27	R	82	122	52	}	125	175	7D
(	40	50	28	S	83	123	53	~	126	176	7E
)	41	51	29	T	84	124	54	del	127	177	7F
*	42	52	2A	U	85	125	55				

Appendix C. Input, Output, and Standard Error Redirection

The display produced by the `printf()` function is normally sent to the terminal where you are working. This terminal is called the standard output device because it is where the display is automatically directed, in a standard fashion, by the interface between your C program and your computer's operating system.

On most systems it is possible to redirect the output produced by `printf()` to some other device, or to a file, using the output redirection symbol > t the time the program is invoked. In addition to the symbol, you must specify where you want the displayed results to be sent.

For purposes of illustration, assume that the command to execute a compiled program named `salestax`, without redirection, is

```
salestax
```

This command is entered after your computer's system prompt is displayed on your terminal. When the `salestax` program is run, any `printf()` function calls within it automatically cause the appropriate display to be sent to your terminal. Suppose we would like to have the display produced by the program sent to a file named `results`. To do this requires the command

```
salestax > results
```

The redirection symbol > tells the operating system to send any display produced by `printf()` directly to a file named `results` rather than to the standard output device used by the system. The display sent to `results` can then be examined by using either an editor program or issuing another operating system command. For example, under the UNIX Operating System the command

```
cat results
```

causes the contents of the file `results` to be displayed on your terminal. The equivalent command under the IBM PC disk operating system (DOS) is

```
type results
```

In redirecting an output display to a file, the following rules apply:

1. If the file does not exist, it will be created.
2. If the file exists, it will be overwritten with the new display.

In addition to the output redirection symbol, the output append symbol >> can also be used. The append symbol is used in the same manner as the redirection symbol, but causes any new output to be added to the end of a file. For example, the command

```
salestax >> results
```

causes any output produced by `salestax` to be added to the end of the `results` file. If the `results` file does not exist, it will be created.

Besides having the display produced by `printf()` redirected to a file, using either the > or >> symbols, the display can also be sent to a physical device connected to your computer, such as a printer. You must, however, know the name used by your computer for accessing the desired device. For example, on an IBM PC or compatible computer, the name of the printer connected to the terminal is designated as `prn`. Thus, if you are working on an IBM or compatible machine, the command

```
salestax > prn:
```

causes the display produced in the salestax program to be sent directly to the printer connected to the terminal. In addition to `printf()`, output redirection also affects the placement of displays produced by the `puts()` and `putchar()` functions, and any other function that uses the standard output device for display.

Corresponding to output redirection, it is also possible to redesignate the standard input device for an individual program run using the input redirection symbol, <. Again, the new source for input must be specified immediately after the input redirection symbol.

Input redirection works in a similar fashion as output redirection but affects the source of input for the `scanf()`, `gets()`, and `getchar()` functions. For example, the command

```
salestax < dat_in
```

causes any input functions within `salestax` that normally receive their input from the keyboard to receive it from the `dat_in` file instead. This input redirection, like its output counterpart, is only in effect for the current execution of the program. As you might expect, the same run can have both an input and output redirection. For example, the command

```
salestax < dat_in > results
```

causes an input redirection from the file `dat_in` and an output redirection to the file `results`.

In addition to standard input and output redirection, the device to which all error messages are sent can also be redirected. On many systems this file is given an operating system designation as device file 2. Thus, the redirection

```
2> err
```

causes any error messages that would normally be displayed on the standard error device, which is usually your terminal, to be redirected to a file named `err`. As with standard input and output redirection, standard error redirection can be included on the same command line used to invoke a program. For example, the command

```
salestax < dat_in > show 2> err
```

causes the compiled program named `salestax` to receive its standard input from a file named `dat_in`, write its results to a file named `show`, and send any error messages to a file named `err`.

As the redirection of input, output, and error messages is generally a feature of the operating system used by your computer and not typically part of your C compiler, you must check the manuals for your particular operating system to ensure these features are available.

Appendix D. Quick C Reference

Reserved Words

auto	do	for	return	typedef
break	double	goto	short	union
case	else	if	sizeof	unsigned
char	enum	int	static	void
continue	extern	long	struct	while
default	float	register	switch	

Operators

Type	Symbols	Associativity
Primary	() [] . ->	left to right
Unary	++ -- & * - ! ~ sizeof	right to left
Arithmetic	* / %	left to right
Arithmetic	+ -	left to right
Shift	<< >>	left to right
Relational	< <= > >=	left to right
Relational	== !=	left to right
Bitwise	&(AND)	left to right
Bitwise	^(XOR)	left to right
Bitwise	|(OR)	left to right
Logical	&&(AND)	left to right
Logical	||(OR)	left to right
Conditional	?:	right to left
Assignment	= += -= /= %= etc.	right to left
Comma	,	left to right

Scalar Data Types

Type		Sample Declaration
char		char key;
int		int num;
short	(or short int)	short count;
long	(or long int)	long int date;
unsigned	(or unsigned int)	unsigned val;
float		float rate;
double	(or long float)	double taxes;

Arrays

An *array* is a list of elements of the same data type. The first element in an array is referred to as the zeroth element.

Examples:
```
int prices[5];
char name[20];
float rates[4][15];
```

Structures

A *structure* (or record) is a data type whose elements need not be of the same data type.

Example:
```
struct tel_rec      /* tel_rec is a tag name */
{
  char name[20];
  int id;
  double rate;
} phone;            /* phone is a structure variable */
```

Comments

Comments are enclosed within a /* and */.

```
/* this is a sample of a comment */
```

Statements

A *Null* statement consists of a semicolon only.

```
;    /* the Null statement */
```

A *Simple* statement is either a Null, declaration, expression, or function statement.

```
double a;                  /* declaration statement */
taxes = rate * income;     /* an expression statement */
printf("Hello World!");    /* function statement */
```

A *Compound* statement consists of one or more statements enclosed within braces.

Example:
```
{                          /* start of compound statement */
   taxes = rate * income;
   + + count;
}                          /* end of compound statement */
```

Flow control statements are structured statements consisting of a keyword (if, while, for, do, switch) followed by an expression within parentheses and a simple or compound statement.

Statement	Example

if (expression)
  statement;
	if (age = = 13)
	  printf("Welcome Teenager!");

if (expression)
  statement1;
else
  statement2;
	if (num = = 5)
	  printf("Bingo!");
	else
	  printf("You Lose!");

if (expression)
  statement1;
else if (expression)
  statement2;
    •
    •
else
  statement3;
	if (grade >= 90)
	  printf("You got an A");
	else if (grade >= 80)
	  printf("You got a B");
	else if (grade >= 70)
	  printf("You got a C");
	else
	  printf("You got a D");

switch (expression)
{
  case value_1: statement1;
  case value_2: statement2;
    •
  default: statementn;
}
	switch (marcode)
	{
	  case 1: printf("Good Morning");
	  case 2: printf("Good Afternoon");
	  case 3: printf("Good Night");
	  default: printf("Good Grief");
	}

for (init; expression; alter)
  statement;
	for (i = 0; i < 10; + + i)
	  printf("%d %d", i, i*i);

while (expression)
  statement;
	while (num < 10)
	{
	  printf("number is %d",num);
	  ++ num;
	}

do
  statement;
while (expression);
	do
	{
	  printf("Hello");
	  ++ count;
	}
	while (count < 10);

Appendix E. Function and Macro Reference

Formatted Output Functions

```
printf(control string, args)              /* print to standard output */
fprintf(filename, control string, args)   /* print to a file */
sprintf(address, control string, args)    /* print to memory */
```

The control string is contained within double quotes. There must be one *control sequence* within each control string for each argument.

Control Sequence	Meaning
%d	Print as signed decimal integer
%u	Print as unsigned decimal integer
%f	Print as floating point number
%e	Print in scientific notation
%g	Print using %e or %f, whichever is shorter
%c	Print as a character
%s	Print as a string
%o	Print as unsigned octal number
%x	Print as unsigned hexadecimal number
%l	Print a long integer or long floating point number (must be followed by either d, o, x, f, or u)

Format modifiers are placed after the % symbol and before the conversion character.

%–	Left justify the output
%+	Print the output with an appropriate sign
%(blank)	Prepend positive numbers with a space
%#	Prepend a 0 to octal numbers, 0x to hexadecimal numbers and append a decimal point to all floating point numbers

Field width specifiers are placed after format modifiers to specify field width and precision.

Examples:

%6d	Print an integer in a field 6 spaces wide
%–6d	Print a left justified integer in a field 6 spaces wide
%6.2f	Print a floating point number in a field 6 spaces wide with two digits after the decimal place

Formatted Input Functions

```
scanf(control string, args)              /* scan from standard input device */
fscanf(filename, control string, args)   /* scan from a file */
sscanf(address, control string, args)    /* scan from memory */
```

scanf() functions operate similar to their printf() counterparts, with the following exceptions:

Arguments following the control string must be addresses.
There is no %g control sequence.
%e and %f control sequences can be used interchangeably.
%lf must be used to input double precision numbers.
%h control sequence can be used to input short integers.
%ld must be used to input long integers.

Function and Macro Reference *(continued)*

Additional I/O Functions and Macros

fopen(filename, mode)	Open a file
fclose(filename)	Close a file
getc(filename)	Input a character from a file
fgets(string, n, filename)	Input a string from a file
putc(character, filename)	Print a character to a file
fputs(string, filename)	Print a string to a file
getchar()	Input a character from the standard input device
gets()	Input a string from the standard input device
putchar(character)	Print a character to the standard output device
puts(string)	Print a string to the standard output device

Conversion Macros

atof(string)	Convert ASCII string to floating point
atoi(string)	Convert ASCII string to an integer
ftoa(num, string, i, f)	Convert floating point to ASCII string
itoa(num, string)	Convert integer to ASCII string
itoh(num, string)	Convert integer to hexadecimal
toupper(character)	Convert character to uppercase
tolower(character)	Convert character to lowercase

Character Macros

These macros return a 1 if the test is true or a 0 if the test fails.

isalpha(character)	Is the character an alphanumeric
isascii(character)	Is the character an ASCII character
islower(character)	Is the character lowercase
isupper(character)	Is the character uppercase
isdigit(character)	Is the character a digit
isspace(character)	Is the character a whitespace
isprint(character)	Is this a printable character
ispunct(character)	Is this a punctuation character
iscntrl(character)	Is this a control character

String Functions

strcat(string1, string2)	Concatenate two strings
strcpy(tostring, fromstring)	Copy a string
strlen(string)	Determine the length of a string
strchr(string, character)	Find a character in a string
strcmp(string1, string2)	Compare two strings

Index

A

B

C

D

E

F

T

U

V

W